History of Crises Under the National Banking System

61st Congress, 2d Session | SENATE | Document No. 538

NATIONAL MONETARY COMMISSION

History of Crises under the National Banking System

BY

O. M. W. SPRAGUE
Assistant Professor of Banking and Finance in Harvard University

Washington : Government Printing Office : 1910

61st Congress, 2d Session — SENATE — Document No. 538

NATIONAL MONETARY COMMISSION

History of Crises under the National Banking System

BY

O. M. W. SPRAGUE

Assistant Professor of Banking and Finance in Harvard University

Washington : Government Printing Office : 1910

NATIONAL MONETARY COMMISSION

CONTENTS.

Contents

HISTORY OF CRISES UNDER THE NATIONAL BANKING SYSTEM.

CHAPTER I

THE CRISIS OF 1873

The crisis of 1873 was preceded by four years of general economic activity, which was by no means confined to the United States In agriculture, manufactures, and transportation much real progress was made, but, as subsequent events proved, the pace was more rapid than was consistent with healthy development. Facilities for the production of many commodities were provided beyond the limits of profitable demand, and many enterprises which were enlarged upon a quite insufficient foundation of working capital went to the wall when subjected to the strain of crisis and depression.[a] As in 1857, the most serious weakness was disclosed in connection with railroad building. Bonds often sold at a heavy discount had provided the means for building many roads which were in advance of any considerable population, and whose traffic proved insufficient to meet fixed charges. The situation of other roads was even more unsatisfactory. Before the crisis, construction had had to wait upon the slow sale of bonds

[a] For the general economic situation both before and after the crisis see "The Financial Crisis in America," by Horace White, in Fortnightly Review, 1876, pp 810–829

or the venturesome advances of bankers, and after the crisis construction had to be discontinued altogether, leaving a large mileage connecting nothing in particular.[a] A long period of depression and recuperation was inevitable, and its advent could not have been long postponed But, as always happens, the exact moment of collapse was determined by particular occurrences and might have come a little earlier or at a somewhat later date

BANK LOANS, 1869-1873

The extent to which the banks may be held responsible for the unsound conditions which had developed before the crisis of 1873 can not be determined exactly. In matters of this kind it is impossible to make a complete distinction between causes and effects The average quality of the loans of the banks must suffer if the general business situation becomes unsatisfactory On the other hand, this condition may be in part a consequence of the failure of the banks to exercise sufficient caution in granting accommodation to borrowers. As will be seen later, few banks failed during the crisis or during the subsequent months and years of depression. And of the failures which did occur hardly any involved serious loss to creditors.[b] There was, indeed, at the beginning of the crisis evidence of momentary loss of confidence in the banks, but this was primarily due to the disasters which had taken place in other branches of business, particularly among the railroads and the private bankers and brokers

---

[a] The Commercial and Financial Chronicle, January 10, 1874, contains a list of the railroads in default for nonpayment of interest on their bonds

[b] See p 81.

who dealt in their securities. There is, however, one method of estimating roughly the measure of responsibility which rests upon banks for the creation of crisis conditions. If the expansion of loans has been unusually rapid in the years just before a crisis, it must have contributed to the creation of the unhealthy situation Moreover, the expansion of credit liabilities, which is created by the increase of bank loans, may not be accompanied by a parallel increase in the cash reserves in the banks In that case the banks may be so weakened that, though able to withstand the shock of a crisis, they may not be able to extend that aid to the business community which may be reasonably expected from them These are matters which can be analyzed statistically, and, so far as the national banks are concerned, the periodical returns to the Comptroller of the Currency, together with the weekly returns of the clearing-house banks in the large cities, provide a mass of data which is far more complete than that in any other country Moreover, for the particular period under review the national-bank returns include a larger proportion of the banking operations of the country than is the case in later crises, because of the comparatively small number of state banks and trust companies at that time. In the tables which follow comparisons will be based upon the returns of the banks in June of each of the four years before 1873 The returns for that season of the year happen to have been made at almost the same date in successive years. They show the condition of the banks at a time when they were least influenced by special temporary circumstances, and when, it may be added, the ratio of reserves to demand liabilities was most satisfactory.

In a country with a growing population there are normally increasing requirements for banking accommodation, and these requirements become particularly large during years of active business Unless, therefore, the expansion of bank loans assumes large proportions, or unless there is direct evidence of reckless banking methods, the creation of unsound business conditions can not be laid at the doors of the banks simply because of an increase in bank loans In the particular case before us the banks can not be said to have been particularly at fault. The following table shows for June of each year from 1869 to 1873 the number, capital, surplus and undivided profits, and the loans of the banks:

[In millions]

June—	National banks	Capital	Surplus	Loans
1869	1,619	$422	$126	$686
1870	1,612	427	134	715
1871	1,723	450	144	789
1872	1,853	470	155	871
1873	1,968	490	172	926

During the four years loans were expanded at a fairly uniform rate, the total increase of $240,000,000 being almost exactly 35 per cent But in the meantime there had been an addition of $114,000,000 to the investment of the shareholders in the business In the second place it is to be noted that there were 349 more banks in the national system at the close of the interval, 313 of which were established in the South and West, which were insufficiently supplied with banks in 1869. For this reason the relatively large increase in loans in those parts of the country from $130,000,000 to $238,000,000 does not necessarily imply reckless or even unhealthfully rapid expansion of credit. Both relatively and absolutely the movement of loans in the North Atlantic States was confined within moderate limits In the case of the country banks of those States the increase was from $235,000,000 to $300,000,000, while by the city banks it was from $321,000,000 to $388,000,000 Finally, it should be noted, that in New York, where the railroads were largely financed and where the failures occurred which precipitated the crisis, there was strikingly little loan increase, only $21,000,000—from $174,000,000 to $195,000,000 The conclusion seems clear that the national banks can not be held very largely responsible for creating unhealthy conditions by an unwise policy of rapid loan expansion during the years immediately preceding the crisis of 1873

NATIONAL BANK RESERVES, 1869–1873

Even a moderate increase in loans may, however, weaken the banks if the greater liabilities thus created do not rest upon increasing cash reserves During the period in question the operations of the banks were carried on under highly exceptional circumstances as regards the influences to which the reserves were subject, and a somewhat lengthy digression is necessary to explain the exact situation. The money supply of the country was not susceptible to any influences which might bring about an appreciable change in its amount. The business of the country was being carried on upon a fixed amount of inconvertible paper money. This currency was redundant, as was clearly indicated by the premium on gold, but it was at a fixed point of redundancy, aside from variations in requirements for the use of money. There were almost exactly $700,000,000 of paper money in the country throughout the four years, of which $356,000,000 consisted of legal-tender United States notes, and of the remainder there were in 1869 nearly $300,000,000 of bank notes and $46,000,000 of 3 per cent certificates. These certificates did not circulate as money, but were available for bank reserves. The act of July 12, 1870, authorized an addition of $52,000,000 of new circulation, but provided at the same time for the withdrawal of the certificates. The change was made gradually, so that at no time did it involve any appreciable change in the available supply of paper money.[a]

Had the country been upon a specie basis the banks might have increased their reserves by securing some portion of current gold production The banks and also the Treasury did hold considerable amounts of specie throughout this period, and the specie could be included in the reserves required by law to be held by the banks, but it could not be used to meet the ordinary requirements of depositors. It was constantly at a premium of between 10 and 15 per cent. Like any other liquid asset of a bank, it could be disposed of, but its sale could not add to the money in circulation The Pacific coast was an exception, but the banks of that region were few

[a] The substitution of bank notes for certificates seems to have involved some slight contraction, since the banks were required at that time to hold a reserve against their circulating notes

in number, and their transactions may be disregarded when considering the situation of the banks as a whole. The banks had no inducement to increase their specie holdings, and in the country at large outside of New York, they held but an insignificant portion of their reserves in this form, seldom more than $6,000,000.[a] In New York the case was quite different. In that city was largely concentrated that portion of the business of the country which continued to be carried on upon a gold basis, such as the payment of import duties and foreign exchange dealings. There were at all times large deposits in the banks payable in gold, and there were regular gold as well as currency clearings at the clearing house The gold holdings of the New York banks fluctuated widely, but always formed a considerable portion of their total reserves, varying in amount from one-third to one-half that of their holdings of legal-tender notes. This gold would have been a valuable resource had specie payments been resumed, but in the existing conditions it was far less a real source of strength than would have been an equivalent amount of legal tenders. The specie held was required for the handling of the particular business transacted upon a gold basis, and although the greater part of it was in the nature of a special deposit earmarked and not available to meet the requirements of depositors generally, it was all included in the statement of the reserves. On September 12, 1873, the deposits payable in gold were $12,101,000, and the banks held in coin $14,586,000 [b] Practically the legal tenders

[a] See table in Comptroller's Report for 1873, p XLIV.
[b] Ibid, p XXIX

were the only reserve against the remaining $189,000,000 of deposit liabilities In analyzing the reserves of the New York banks, therefore, it will be necessary to distinguish carefully between the reserve which met the legal requirements and the available reserve in actual fact

As regards the legal-tender notes, it was impossible for the banks to enlarge their holdings for several reasons Prices and wages were at a high level on account of the redundancy of the currency, and consequently the requirements for money for everyday hand-to-hand use were large and tended to increase with the growth of population and business dealings. Moreover, a given volume of transactions in commodities at the high level of prices required correspondingly large credit accommodation expressed in terms of the depreciated paper The uses for the curency were, therefore, enlarged both as to reserves and outside the banks and to an extent which roughly corresponded with the high level of prices In these circumstances the increasing number and capital of the banks did not tend to provide them with more money for their operations As the number of banks increased the reserves became more widely scattered, and consequently somewhat less available, and larger capital and surplus would serve only to offset a part of the increase in demand liabilities created by the expansion of loans The conclusion is clear that it was practically impossible for the banks to strengthen themselves during a period of active business. On the other hand, during a period of inactive business it would be certain that a larger proportion of the money supply of the country would accumulate in the banks because of the diminished requirements for its use for everyday purposes outside the banks. This was the situation early in 1869, at the beginning of the period which we have taken for analysis.

Finally, it should be remembered that no distinction was made between deposit and note liability in the national banking law until 1874 Banks were required to hold the same kind of reserve for both kinds of liabilities, but even during the worst moments of the crisis of 1873 the liability for notes was not one which caused any depletion of reserves For this reason, and because it simplifies comparison with the condition of the banks before later crises, the relation between reserves and deposit liabilities will be specially emphasized in analyzing the situation of banks In the following table, however, the liabilities of the banks for both notes and deposits are presented, together with their specie and legal-tender reserves, from June, 1869, to June, 1873.

[In millions]

June—	Circulation	Deposits	Specie	Legals
1869	$292	$528	$18	$131
1870	291	575	31	138
1871	315	638	20	152
1872	333	656	24	135
1873	338	678	28	129

From this table it will be seen that in 1869 the banks were exceedingly strong in cash reserves, holding nearly 28 per cent in proportion to their deposits. Notwithstanding the considerable increase in deposit liabilities and the slight reduction in cash holdings, the proportion of reserve was reduced to only 23 per cent in 1873 Even if the liability for notes is included, the banks held 18 per cent in 1869 and 16½ per cent in 1873, proportions which, compared with the cash held in recent years by the banks against deposits alone, were exceptionally large. The percentage of reserve in June, 1873, was almost exactly that of the banks in July, 1908, when, on account of generally inactive business, the banks held far larger reserves than is now customary It would seem, therefore, that the cash foundation of the credit structure had not been seriously weakened. But the amount of cash required to insure the smooth working of the banking machinery of a country can not be determined by purely arithmetical calculations. Much depends upon the requirements which are likely to be made for money, and also upon the amount of cash which bankers have been accustomed to regard as a minimum, in order to avoid reducing which they would resort to drastic loan contraction and even to suspension

In this connection the increase in the number of banks—from 1,619 in 1869 to 1,968 in 1873—may be mentioned as a factor which tended to weaken somewhat the effectiveness of the aggregate reserve Each separate unit of reserve was, on the average, somewhat smaller, and was, therefore, less effective both for use and as a basis for public confidence Moreover, with the greater number of banks, the difficulty was enhanced of securing that cooperation which is required if the credit machinery is to work smoothly in emergencies.

We must now enter upon a more detailed analysis of the reserves of the banks, including not only the cash held, but also the deposits with reserve agents, which make up so large a part of the reserves of most of the banks in the national system. The country banks then, as now, were required to hold in their own vaults cash equal to at least 6 per cent of their deposit liabilities, and also, until 1874, 6 per cent of their liabilities in the form of bank notes. The remaining 9 per cent might be held by approved agents in the "redemption cities," as they were then called, a term which indicates the original purpose of the arrangement—to provide facilities for the regular redemption of circulation at the money centers. The following table shows the situation of the country banks in June of each year from 1869 to 1873:

[In millions.]

	1869	1870	1871	1872	1873
Net deposits	$209	$217	$231	$260	$292
Circulation	186	189	212	230	232
Total	395	406	443	490	524
Reserve	82	92	101	102	108
Cash	39	43	42	45	47
Due from reserve agents	43	49	59	57	61
Ratio to demand liabilities	20.8	22.6	22.8	20.6	27
Ratio to deposits	39.2	42.4	43.8	39.2	37

The reserves of the country banks were well above the requirements of the law. They held at all times in cash alone more than 15 per cent of their deposit liabilities, the ratio falling from 19 per cent in 1869 to 16 per cent in 1873. If deposits with agents are included, the country banks held a reserve of much more than one-third of their deposit liabilities, even at the close of the period. The country banks, therefore, would clearly seem to have been well supplied with funds to meet emergencies. It should, however, be noted that, although cash holdings had been increased by $8,000,000, deposits with reserve agents had increased $18,000,000 This indicated a greater power to withdraw money from the city banks and also a slightly greater probability that it would be exercised in case of unusual demands upon the country banks.

There were at this time, as at present, two classes of reserve or redemption cities Fifteen cities were designated in the national banking law the banks of which might become the agents of country banks The banks of these cities were required to hold a reserve of 25 per cent, one-half of which might be deposited in the banks of New York, which until 1887 was the only city of central reserve rank Taking first the banks of the fifteen reserve cities, the following table shows their condition during the four years before the crisis of 1873:

[In millions]

	1869	1870	1871	1872	1873.
Net deposits	$151	$168	$189	$199	$200
Circulation	71	69	72	75	78
Total	222	237	261	274	278
Reserve	64	75	82	79	79
Cash	45	50	49	46	46
Due from reserve agents	19	25	33	33	33
Ratio to demand liabilities	28 9	31 8	31 6	28 9	28 2
Ratio to deposits	42 6	44 6	43 4	39 6	39 5

The banks of the reserve cities, like the country banks, held a reserve considerably above legal requirements throughout this period. Taking liabilities for deposits alone, the proportion of cash fell off somewhat from 29 per cent to 23 per cent, while the deposits with agents, which increased rapidly until 1871, were thereafter practically stationary at $33,000,000. All of this amount was, of course, held by the banks of New York, the banks of which also held the deposited reserves of many of the country banks. The position of the New York banks was even more important as reserve agents than it has been in recent years. They held in bankers' balances quite 60 per cent more than the amount held by all the banks of the reserve cities. Although the country banks and those in reserve cities were well supplied with cash, many of the former and all of the latter possessed the right to withdraw large sums from New York, and, therefore, the condition of the New York banks is the most important single factor to be considered in estimating the strength of the system as a whole. For this reason it is advisable to make a somewhat detailed examination of the operations of the New York banks, and the following table therefore includes a number of items which were not included in the tables which had reference to the other banks:

Abstract of the returns of the New York national banks, 1869–1873

[In millions.]

	1869	1870	1871	1872	1873
Net deposits	$168	$190	$217	$197	$186
Circulation	35	33	31	28	27
Total	203	223	248	225	214
Reserve held	61	72	76	65	64
Specie	14	18	11	15	23
Legal-tender notes	47	54	65	50	41
Due to national banks	43	53	66	63	59
Due to other banks	14	16	20	18	17
Ratio to demand liabilities	30.7	32.4	30.9	29.1	30
Ratio of legal tender notes to deposits less specie held by the banks	30.5	31.4	31.5	27.3	25.2

In certain respects it will be noticed that the showing of the New York banks was quite as satisfactory as that of the other banks of the country Demand liabilities had increased only moderately, and since 1871 had actually declined The percentage of reserve to demand liabilities throughout the period was well above legal requirements But the composition of the reserve was somewhat less satisfactory, showing a distinct decline in the proportion of legal tenders. The specie holdings of the banks, it will be remembered, were not at that time available for ordinary purposes, and were largely held to secure special deposits. The most significant indication of the strength of the banks, therefore, is gained by taking the proportion of legal-tender notes to the deposit liabilities less the amount of specie holdings. Measured in this way it will be seen that there was a serious change for the worse in the condition of the banks. Against a deposit liability of $206,000,000 in 1871 the banks held $65,000,000 in legal-tender notes, while in 1873 they held but $41,000,000 against $163,000,000 of deposit liabilities One further test, and a most important one, of the condition of the banks is still to be made. Bankers' deposits show a rapid increase between 1869 and 1871 from $57,000,000 to $86,000,000. From that point there was a moderate decline to $81,000,000 in 1872, and to $76,000,000 in 1873, but in 1871 the banks held $65,000,000 in legal-tender notes, while in 1873 they held but $41,000,000. The other banks of the country had largely increased their credits with New York banks, which at the same time were much less well supplied with means to meet the heavy responsibility thus created. The efficient working of the credit system was evidently more and more dependent upon the ability of the New York banks to meet all the demands of their banking depositors, and this ability was diminishing.

THE CONCENTRATION OF BANKERS' DEPOSITS.

It is necessary to carry one step further this analysis of the reserves of the national banks Responsibility for bankers' deposits did not rest upon the New York banks as a whole. There were during this period some 50 national banks in the city, but the majority of them were not reserve agents, and their statements show only such small amounts due to banks as would naturally arise in the course of the ordinary business of any bank. The business of such banks was of a purely local character, having no more general significance than that of banks with an equal volume of business in Maine or Kentucky [a]

During the period before the crisis of 1873 some 15 of the 50 New York banks held practically all of the bankers' deposits acquired by the banks of the city, and 7 of them held between 70 and 80 per cent of these deposits.[b] These 7 banks were directly responsible for the satisfactory working of the credit machinery of the country, and their condition prior to the crisis must be carefully examined.

[a] The statement in the text may be qualified by the further observation that the failure of a purely local New York bank might cause loss of confidence in the New York banks generally, including those which were of national importance.

[b] The 7 banks were the First, Third, Fourth, Ninth, Central, Importers and Traders', and Park National banks

It has been too exclusively the practice to analyze the condition of the banks as a whole or by localities, a method which tends to obscure any real understanding of the working of our system It is of the utmost importance to locate the particular point at which the strain of a crisis will be most directly and severely felt, and to form an exact notion of the provision to meet it when it does come The returns of the condition of the individual banks have been included in the annual reports of the Comptroller of the Currency for only one date in each year—the return for the early autumn For a purely local bank such information is ample, but it is much to be desired that more complete information were provided for those of the banks which are reserve agents. Such data would be of value in following the changes which take place in the banking situation as a whole, and would also concentrate the attention of the public upon the peculiar responsibilities of banks which hold bankers' deposits. In the case of the New York banks further information, though of a less comprehensive nature, is to be had from the weekly clearing-house statements, but as these statements for the individual banks were discontinued during the crisis of 1873 it is necessary to take some other year in order to analyze the exact effects of demands upon New York from the outside banks. For this purpose the year 1872 has been selected. In any case attention should be given to that year, since it enables us to form an opinion of the power of the credit structure to withstand financial strain of moderate severity. Obviously, if moderate strain which can be foreseen can not be met easily, a banking system is in no position to meet the severe strain of a crisis.

The following table shows the condition on October 3, 1872, of the New York banks as a whole, that of the 7 banks which held the bulk of the bankers' deposits, and the condition of the other 43 banks

[In millions]

	50 banks	7 banks	43 banks
Capital	$71 3	$14 5	$56 8
Surplus and net profits	31 9	5 4	26 5
Circulation	28 0	7 4	20 6
Individual deposits	188 5	34 1	154 4
Due national banks	60 6	44 9	15 7
Due other banks	14 8	6 8	8 0
Total liabilities	395 1	113 1	282 0
Loans	183 4	58 2	125 2
Bonds	44 0	10 0	34 0
Due from other banks	16 5	6 7	9 8
Clearing-house exchanges and cash items	93 0	17 9	75 1
Bills of other national banks	2 7	6	2 1
Specie	6 4	1 1	5 3
Legal-tender notes	39 0	15 5	23 5

The situation disclosed by a survey of this table was certainly extraordinary Of the total bankers' deposits of $75,400,000 the seven banks held $51,700,000, 72 per cent; and if the more proper basis of net bankers' deposits is taken, they held $45,000,000 out of a total of $58,900,000, or nearly 76 per cent But the accumulation of bankers' deposits in a few banks is by no means the most striking feature of the table. The capital and surplus of the seven banks made up only 20 per cent that of all of the banks, and their individual deposits were but 18 per cent of total deposits. The bankers' deposits of the seven banks were $11,000,000 greater than their individual deposits, and if clearing-house exchanges are deducted from their individual deposits, liabilities to bankers were some three times those to individuals On the other side of the account it will be noticed that against net deposits (gross deposits less clearing-house exchanges, bills of and amounts due from other banks) of $60,600,000 and a note issue of $7,400,000 the seven banks with their reserve of $16,600,000 were six-tenths of 1 per cent below the 25 per cent legal requirement, while the other banks, with net deposits of $91,100,000 and circulation of $20,600,000, held a reserve of 25 8 per cent It is obvious that the seven banks were in no position to meet considerable demands from their depositors without a drastic contraction of their loans Furthermore, the total of their loans, $58,000,000, was exceedingly small when one considers the nature of their deposit liability A demand for money spread pretty evenly among the banks, and leading to a given amount of loan contraction, would cause far less disturbance than the same amount of contraction confined to the restricted circle of the borrowers of the seven banks The conclusion seems clear that these banks and the particular borrowers served by them were carrying on their operations almost wholly upon the unstable basis provided by the deposits of the out-of-town banks.

It is clear, then, that with this situation in New York an emergency would cause serious disturbance if it should lead to the withdrawal of any considerable amount of money by the outside banks, and there could not be the slightest doubt that this would be done or at least attempted Every year furnished ample evidence that the outside banks had a strong preference for reducing their balances with agents rather than their own cash reserves whenever their depositors resorted to them for even very moderate supplies of money The result is disclosed in the following table, which shows the cash reserves and the deposits with agents of the country national banks at the time of each of the five returns to the Comptroller of the Currency in 1871 and in 1872

[In millions]

	Cash	Deposits with agents		Cash	Deposits with agents
1871			1872		
Mar 18	$45	$55	Feb 27	$44	$58
Apr 29	43	55	Apr 19	46	52
June 10	42	59	June 10	44	57
Oct 2	43	55	Oct 3	45	52
Dec 16	42	49	Dec 27	46	51

From this table it will be seen that the cash reserves of the country banks remained almost stationary, even showing a slight tendency to increase at those times of the year when the demand was large from depositors Such demands were met entirely by withdrawals of money from reserve city agents With this table comparison should be made with the table which follows, showing the fluctuations in the net amount owed by the New York banks to other national banks at the same dates

[In millions]

1871		1872	
March	$64 0	February	$61 4
April	61 6	April	64 7
June	66 2	June	62 9
October	61 4	October	47 6
December	51 5	December	50 6

From this table it will be seen that bankers' deposits were regularly large at the beginning of each year The early spring months witnessed a moderate decline which was more than regained in the early summer, to be as regularly followed by a more considerable decline in the autumn Then, as now, the cause which made possible this alternate movement of funds was the seasonal differences in requirements for money for use outside the banks. Since there was a fixed amount of currency in the country, the amount of money in the possession of the banks varied with the seasons, but this circumstance did not necessarily involve the accumulation of bankers' deposits for short periods in New York The money might have remained diffused among the banks throughout the country. That it did not do so was primarily owing to the interest which could be secured upon such deposits from some of the city banks

The practice of paying interest upon deposits and in particular upon bankers' deposits was contrary to the best banking opinion of the time, and was adopted by only twelve of the sixty banks in the New York Clearing House Unavailing efforts, especially after the crisis of 1857, had been made to secure a unanimous agreement among the banks to discontinue the practice [a] It follows, therefore, that the seven banks, all of which paid interest upon deposits and which had secured the bulk of the bankers' deposits, were directly responsible for any disturbance in the New York money market, which was due

[a] For the strong case against the practice presented by a special clearing-house committee, see Bankers' Magazine, April, 1858, pp 822–831

to the use of these funds, and also for any failure to meet demands for their return to banks in the rest of the country

The payment of interest upon deposits had two undesirable consequences. Its most obvious result was to cause money to be sent to New York in larger quantities than would otherwise have been the case, though how much more was sent on this account can not be determined. Had no interest been offered by the New York banks, the outside banks would doubtless have lent more largely directly to borrowers in New York when the demand for loans was slight at home, but it is not reasonable to think that money thus invested would have by any means equalled balances deposited in New York in excess of legal reserve requirements But the chief evil of interest upon bankers' deposits was of a different character The interest-paying banks were unable to maintain large reserves and at the same time realize a profit from the use of the funds thus attracted. Particularly was this the case when the accumulation of such funds was only temporary The extra supply of money to be lent forced down rates, and, as rates fell, more and more had to be lent by the banks in order even to equal the interest which they had contracted to pay In the years before 1873 the banks paid as much as 4 per cent for bankers' deposits, a rate which, relative to lending rates at that time, is not far from the 2 per cent rate of a later period. If the banks receiving these deposits had followed the practice of European central banks and had paid no interest, they could have kept a large reserve and still have earned a satisfactory profit. But, unfortunately, this was not the policy which was adopted, although the mere fact that a number of banks in New York and not a single bank, as in European countries, secured these bankers' deposits, did not change the nature of the obligation or responsibility. New York bank loans regularly expanded with every increase in the receipt of deposits from out of town banks Year after year the loans of the banks followed the same course, advancing in the early months of the year and undergoing some decline in the spring, then rising to the highest level of the year in July, only to be followed by contraction which as regularly brought loans to their lowest level in October The following table shows the movement of loans, deposits, and cash of the New York clearing-house banks at selected dates in 1872.

[In millions]

	Loans	Deposits	Specie	Legals
Jan 1	$270	$200	$25	$40
Mar 4	282	210	18	44
Apr 22	273	195	18	40
June 3	284	226	21	53
June 17	288	228	20	55
July 22	297	247	29	53
Aug 12	299	237	18	54
Aug 19	295	235	20	52
Sept 2	288	219	16	49
Sept 23	280	201	12	44
Sept 30	272	195	11	45
Oct 7	269	186	10	42
Oct 14	268	189	12	45

Since the movement of loans and of reserves was in close correspondence with known movements of bankers' deposits it is therefore to be expected that changes in the operations of the seven banks will account for the bulk of these fluctuations. As an illustration the following table is presented showing the loans of the New York banks, those of the seven banks, and those of the remaining banks on July 29 and October 7, 1872.

[In millions]

1872	60 banks	7 banks	53 banks
July 29	$295	$90	$205
Oct 7	269	71	198

It will be observed that the loan contraction of the seven banks makes up $19,000,000 out of a total of $26,000,000 The seven banks reduced their loans by 21 per cent, a proportion which would be still greater if the security holdings of the banks were not included with loans in the weekly New York bank statement The bond holdings of the seven banks were set down in the comptroller's return for October 3, 1872, at $10,000,000, and, as a large portion of them were held for circulation, it is reasonable to assume that the amount had not greatly changed during the short interval covered in the table Upon this assumption, the loans of the seven banks were $80,000,000 in July and $61,000,000 in October, showing a contraction of 24 per cent. In the case of the other banks the contraction was less than 3½ per cent, and, omitting bonds, it was only slightly more than 4 per cent. Evidently the banks holding bankers' deposits lent to an excessive extent upon the basis of the resources thus secured, even though it was perfectly apparent that they were available but for a very short time. It should also be noted that neither the industrial nor commercial business which centered in New York was of a nature to require temporarily large accommodation at the particular time when the bankers' deposits were large The loans which were made, therefore, were largely in connection with stock-exchange dealings The interest-paying banks were all known as Wall street institutions They favored stock-exchange loans, especially call loans, because they were regarded as peculiarly liquid, and also, it may be suspected, because there is an almost indefinite hunger for loans in that quarter. This practice agreed with the view still commonly held, that call loans are the only proper basis for the use of funds subject to unexpected withdrawal. How far in emergencies this view is sound will be examined in our analysis of successive crises. Here it may be noted that even the seasonal requirements of normal years could not be met without severe strain and high rates for loans. In July and August speculation in securities flourished upon the basis of cheap money. Prices advanced to levels which could not be maintained, only to fall in September and October to equally temporary low levels. Even though the banks were able to liquidate their loans to some extent, this system created opportunities for speculative manipulation which were a source of loss to many and which cast not a little discredit upon American financial methods.

THE NEW YORK MONEY MARKET IN 1872–73

At this point it will be of advantage to follow the course of the New York money market during the summer and autumn of 1872 There was a slow but continuous increase in loans from $273 000,000 in April to $299,000,000 on August 12. Continued ease prevailed, and shortly after the middle of the month it was reported that "the money market for August has been unusually quiet, with an ample supply of money on call and seeking investments in commercial paper and in railroad securities. The rates for loans on call have been as low as 4 per cent, and freely offered at 5 or 6 per cent "[a]

The withdrawal of money for crop-moving purposes then began, accompanied by the usual contraction of loans In the course of the six weeks to September 22 the banks lost $10,000,000 in legal-tender notes, and loans were reduced by $18,500,000 Writing on this date, it was reported in the monthly financial review in the Bankers' Magazine that "the quiet of summer in the money market has been succeeded by a period of increasing activity, culminating in great excitement during the past week The usual demand from the West for currency to move the autumnal crops had already reduced the deposits and the reserve of our city banks by several millions, when an unscrupulous combination of designing stock operators seized the opportunity to further their own ends by the endeavor to bring about a panic, in which they very nearly succeeded This trickery was attempted at the same period of last year and produced then similar results.

"The bank returns show a line of deposits some $36,000,000 less than at this time in 1871, with a reduction of $14,000,000 of currency and legal tenders, while the crops

[a] Bankers' Magazine, September, 1872, p 236

of the interior are larger this year than last The weekly statement exhibits a deficiency in the legal reserve of $332,475 below the required 25 per cent In the corresponding week of last year the banks held an excess of $1,168,250

"Rates for money have increased very considerably, as high as one-half per cent having in some cases been paid for the temporary wants of needy borrowers in carrying stocks On the best classes of loans 6 to 7 per cent per annum is paid." [a]

The following week witnessed a further contraction of $8,000,000 in loans The pressure to sell on the stock exchange became general, and complete demoralization of the money market was threatened At this point the Government came to the relief of the banks by the sale of gold and the purchase of bonds to the amount of $5,000,000 of each. This assistance was sufficient to enable the banks to meet further demands upon them without very much further loss in their reserves, since the crop-moving requirements were nearly at an end. Referring once more to the monthly report in the Bankers' Magazine, we find that "the extreme stringency which existed at this time of last month has given place to a condition of the money market which is comparatively one of ease. It has been brought about by the sale of gold and purchase of government bonds by the Secretary of the Treasury to the extent of $5,000,000 of each—an action which, though affording a timely and welcome relief to banks and business men, is a measure of doubtful expediency and likely to be

[a] Ibid , October, 1872, p 316

but temporary in its good effects Under a proper sense of duty on the part of our city banks no such adventitious aid should have been needed. They should have been prepared for the inevitable autumnal reduction of balances belonging to their western correspondents by holding much larger reserves. But the pernicious practice of allowing interest on current deposits impels their employment in the kindred evil of call loans, and these made to stock speculators, too often reckless and unprincipled, subject our money market to violent disturbances, deprive the business community of accommodations justly their due, increase largely the lists of failures, and foster that growing mania for gambling which is one of the worst features of the day "[a]

This disturbance and strain in the money market was clearly caused by the close use by the banks of the funds which they received from outside institutions But as further evidence the following table is instructive:

[In millions]

	Country banks		Reserve city banks		New York banks	
	Cash	Deposits with agents	Cash	Deposits with agents	Cash	Due to banks
1872						
June 10	$44	$57	$45	$33	$65	$78
Oct 3	46	52	38	28	45	56

The course of events in 1872 indicated clearly that the country banks would rely entirely upon their balances with city banks and might even strengthen their cash

[a] Ibid , November, 1872, p 396

reserves in an emergency The banks in the reserve cities paid out $7,000,000 from their own reserves, but shifted a considerable part of the burden to New York by reducing their deposits at that center by $5,000,000 The New York banks paid out $20,000,000, a loss almost equaling the reduction in the amount due to other banks. Upon them rested the burden of finding very nearly all the cash required for crop-moving purposes, and there was every probability that in an emergency the other banks would resort even more exclusively to the withdrawal of their funds deposited in New York.

Although the stringency was considerably relieved in October, it did not entirely disappear until after the beginning of the following year, being prolonged beyond the usual term. But though at length the return flow of money from the interior became normal in volume, the proportion of bank notes to legal tenders was unusually large An opportunity was thus afforded for the exercise of a wise policy of conservatism by the banks Most of the money coming to the city from the interior was sent to the seven banks, which were at the same time the redemption agents of their banking depositors It would have been a simple matter for the depository banks to have required at least the redemption of the notes of those banks for which they were the redemption agents It would have involved no direct payments of cash but simply a cancellation of the deposits of their correspondents to an amount equivalent to the notes retired. But this policy would, of course, have diminished the available funds of the depository banks. The action taken in disposing of the accumulation of bank notes was of an entirely different nature In the Commercial and Financial Chronicle of January 18, 1873, it was reported that "some of the city banks have been selling national bank notes for greenbacks to the brokers at one-fourth per cent discount, and these brokers sell them again at one-eighth per cent to supply country banks" In his annual report for 1872 the Secretary of the Treasury had observed that the "redemption of the national currency is too formidable and expensive to be adopted by any bank or association of banks." It would, however, seem that the New York banks might have been reasonably expected to resort to occasional redemption rather than to the sale of surplus notes at a discount This episode affords striking confirmation of the opinion of a banking authority that where thousands of banks issue notes no effective redemption can be secured unless each bank is forbidden to pay out the notes of other banks.[a]

The customary midwinter ease in the money market was cut short at an unusually early date in 1873. The withdrawal of funds by interior banks was large and so also was the resulting contraction of loans in New York City During March and April loans were reduced by $21,000,000, and then stood very nearly at the level at which they had been in the previous October. Both the unsatisfactory situation and remedies therefor were clearly set forth in the Bankers' Magazine for May and June, 1873, from which the following extracts are taken:

> The month has been remarkably stringent in its money features, producing heavy losses to borrowers, and resulting in the failures of several

[a] C. F. Dunbar, Theory and History of Banking, p 73

firms heretofore possessing large capital and good credit Among these suspensions are Messrs Barton & Allen, on the 16th instant, Brownell & Bro on the 17th, and Lockwood & Co on the 18th The rates prevailing for money in April have been quite as severe in Wall street as at any previous period. The enlarged volume of stocks and bonds on the market, rapidly increasing during the last two years, has demanded fresh capital to sustain prices and the market This capital has been liberally supplied from foreign and domestic sources, thereby creating higher prices At the same time the stock exchange and its members have absorbed a large portion of the capital which is demanded for the legitimate wants of trade and commerce The country bankers, far and near, have been importuned to place their cash balances in Wall street, instead of keeping them at home, the promise of high rates of interest creating inducements for the transfer of capital to New York Country bankers in former days kept from $10,000 to $100,000 on hand in their vaults to meet the ordinary cash demands of the day Gradually, this "ready cash," instead of being kept dead in their vaults, has been largely transferred to NewYork, where 4, 5, or 6 per cent interest paid to the owners, would make these funds "active" instead of "dead" The principle is a vicious one, because the same money serves a double purpose, but at great risk The exchange transactions with New York are so heavy and so constant, that balances in Wall street are by the country banker considered as cash in hand The result has been that these immense accumulations of capital owned in the South and West, instead of being "cash on hand," are loaned out "on call" by the city banker, thereby contributing to a fatal inflation of prices The country banks thereby contribute indirectly to the stock gambling in New York in order to realize interest on their daily balances here * * * The obvious necessity prevailing to place these accumulated country funds in "loans on call" (loans on stock), instead of commercial paper, so as to be ready at a moment's warning, for the country drafts, acts doubly It encourages stock gambling and carries prices above real values, at the same time the legitimate demands of trade are denied, and the merchant and manufacturer suffer because they can not compete with the stock operator in the rates for money The merchant can afford to pay 6 per cent, rarely more, per annum The stock operator who bids for a rise in market values, offers 6 per cent per month in many instances Even this is not a maximum in Wall street In the month of April current, millions have been loaned at one-eighth to one-half per cent per day for carrying loans, and money was scarce (or not attainable) at that One of the firms recently suspended announced that they had paid, between March 1 and April 16, $50,000 in extra interest

Is it surprising, with such prospects for money, that capital concentrates here from the wilds of Maine, the recesses of Connecticut, the prairies of the West, or the tobacco fields of the South to be used at 1 or 2 per cent per month, instead of 6 per cent at home?

Is it surprising that the bubble will burst occasionally and drive into common ruin the speculators for a rise in stocks or for a corner in some great staple of commerce?

We caution our country bankers to keep a healthy reserve at home, and not to trust too large a fund in Wall street "on call."[a]

The month of April was among the most stringent in its money features, and has been followed by more moderate rates for money in Wall street. The terms to borrowers remain severe to those who are compelled to resort to brokers. The banks have apparently increased their loans to the extent of nine millions since the close of April, but are yet several millions below the loan column of January and February. There were some indications, at the first of the month, of a panic in New York, brought on by the failure of one of the national banks and by rumors of weakness in others. There have been several heavy mercantile failures during the month, showing recklessness in credits and overtrading on limited capitals.

The banking movement at New York indicates expansion, prompted by the pressing demand for money from merchants and brokers. Now, that the pressure is over, it would be well for the banks to curtail their loan column at the rate of $1,000,000 per week for three months, in order to strengthen their legal tenders, which are now $20,000,000 too low, or $43,000,000 instead of $63,000,000.[b]

That caution and even a reversal of the customary policy of the banks was to be desired was clearly perceived. In the Chronicle for June 7, 1873, it was observed that the "summer torpor has fairly taken possession of Wall street, and some of the banks are yielding to the temptation to make time loans running into October and November and even longer. The leading institutions have made such large profits during the past half year that they ought to be content to adopt a conservative policy, even if they thereby sacrifice some future gain, and one of the evident requirements of a conservative, safe policy is the strengthening of reserves. Our bank officers will do well to look over some of their old reports and observe how much more ample a few years ago were the

[a] Bankers' Magazine, May, 1873, p. 916.

[b] Ibid., June, 1873, p. 996.

reserves which they used to keep than those of more recent times"

The usual return of money from the interior set in at the end of April and again the banks were afforded an opportunity to exhibit caution, but little heed was paid to the warnings of recent experience Legal-tender holdings increased until on August 4 they stood at $50,000,000, contrasted with $55,000,000 at the same time in the previous year. Specie holdings were, however, larger than in 1872, so that the total reserves of the banks were nearly the same in the two years. As to loans, no appreciable change in the policy of the banks is to be observed, and on August 4 they stood at $290,000,000, an increase of $21,000,000 from the low point in April. Deposit liabilities were then $3,000,000 less than in the previous year, but when account is taken of the larger amount of gold in the total reserves of the banks, it will be seen that they were by no means in a stronger position Had nothing unusual happened there would unquestionably have been a repetition of the high rates and general financial disturbance which had characterized the autumn of 1872.

During the winter and spring of 1873 fears had been frequently expressed that a crisis was imminent, but from the end of June there seems to have been a general feeling that the situation was improving The excess of imports over exports was considerably less than at the same time in the previous year. Gold exports were upon a reduced scale, and, though more discrimination was being exercised, the sale of American railway bonds in Europe had improved. The corn and wheat crops of the year were abundant, and a large European demand was assured Grain began to move in volume at an unusually early date—by the beginning of September—and though the consequent withdrawals of money from New York in the first two weeks of the month were unusually large, it was believed that this was a favorable influence, as it would probably mean that the crop movement would be spread over a longer interval than in the previous year.

It seems to be invariably the case that the outbreak of a crisis comes as a surprise to the business community, and the crisis of 1873 was no exception to this rule, but the astonishing suddenness of the explosion, which came in the third week of September, can not be urged as a sufficient excuse for the inability of the banks to cope with its banking consequences They had had ample experience that the reserves which they were accustomed to hold were insufficient to meet even ordinary requirements, yet there was only too much truth in the caustic observation in the monthly review in the Bankers' Magazine for July "that the ordinary course of events will doubtless prevail; full sail will be carried as if summer were to last forever, when the now plethoric accounts are diminished by their owners, sharp and sudden calls will derange not merely stock speculation, but legitimate business throughout the country." [a]

More than a month before the outbreak of the crisis the first shipments of currency to the interior for crop-moving

[a] Bankers' Magazine, August, 1873, p 156.

purposes began, and, as in other years, they were the signal for loan contraction The following table shows the condition of the clearing-house banks as a whole, the 53 banks, and the 7 banks, for August 16 and September 13, 1873:

[In millions]

	The 60 clearing-house banks		53 banks		7 banks	
	Aug 16	Sept 13	Aug 16	Sept 13	Aug 16	Sept 13
Loans	$292 6	$284 5	$206 4	$202 4	$86 2	$82 1
Specie	27 6	20 4	21 1	15 2	6 5	5 2
Legal tenders	47 6	36 7	28 1	23 8	19 5	12 9
Circulation	27 2	27 4	19 8	20 0	7 4	7 4
Deposits	234 9	207 3	146 9	131 2	88 0	76 1
Surplus reserve	9 7	—1 6	7 5	1 2	2 2	—2 8

A reduction in loans of $8,000,000 was distributed equally between the two groups of banks, but relative to their total loans it was more than twice as great in the case of the 7 banks. The loss in specie was said to have been due to payments to the Government in connection with the Geneva Award, and the contribution of the seven banks did not exceed their proportion of the total specie holdings of the banks On August 16, before the crop-moving period began, it will be noted that the surplus reserve of the 7 banks was somewhat less in proportion to their liabilities than was the case with the other banks. On September 13 the banks as a whole were below the 25 per cent requirement, showing a deficiency of $1,600,000, but the 53 banks still had a surplus of $1,200,000, while the deficiency of the 7 banks was $2,800,000 From the returns to the Comptroller of the Currency, which happen to have been made on September 12, we find that the 7 banks held net bankers' deposits of $53,500,000, with but $12,000,000 of legal tenders and $4,600,000 in specie, while the other banks, with net bankers' deposits of $20,000,000, had almost the same amount of legal tenders and $10,000,000 in specie. It will thus be seen that in mid-August, before the withdrawals of money to the interior began, the banks which were certain to experience the greatest loss on that account were somewhat weaker than the other banks. A month later, the eve of the crisis, found these banks, which were chiefly responsible for the maintenance of the credit machinery of the country, distinctly less well supplied with cash than those banks whose operations were of a purely local character. It is not surprising, therefore, that the shock of the crisis soon forced the interest-paying banks to resort for aid to their more conservative neighbors.

THE OUTBREAK OF THE CRISIS

Two failures which preceded the crisis deserve mention because they were due to the same causes as those of more importance which came a little later. The New York Warehouse and Security Company was forced to suspend on September 8. Organized to make advances on grain and produce, it had been induced to finance the Missouri, Kansas and Texas Railroad. On Saturday, September 13, came the failure of the important banking house of Kenyon, Cox & Co., owing to indorsements on $1,500,000 of the paper of the Canada Southern Railroad. These failures, while causing considerable disturbance in the stock market, were not regarded as of far-reaching importance. The disasters and panic of the last three days of the following week have been described by many later writers, but a contemporary account will best serve to picture the situation which had to be faced by those responsible for the working of the credit machinery of the country. For this reason copious extracts from the weekly money market summary of the Commercial and Financial Chronicle are appended

The disturbances of last week on the annoucement of the failure of the New York Warehouse and Security Company, which were not regarded at the time as having any general significance, have this week been followed by one of the most serious financial crises ever known in our market. For the prime cause of these difficulties it is necessary to go back a few months and bring to mind the excessive tightness of our money market, which prevailed without interruption from September, 1872, to May, 1873, at times almost prohibiting the sale of new railroad bonds, and requiring the issue of large amounts of railroad paper for the prosecution of the several enterprises Together with this, and partly connected with it, came the failures of quite a number of smaller railroad companies to pay their interest, causing a feeling of distrust and aversion toward new railroad bonds, which has been quite perceptible for some months past Under these circumstances several of the banking houses negotiating large railroad loans, or intimately connected with the building of the roads, became heavily responsible to their respective companies by the indorsement of notes, or by borrowing largely on call loans secured by pledge of the railroad securities as collateral In this delicate situation the equilibrium was liable to be violently disturbed, as subsequent events have most unfortunately proved

The first shock came with the suspension on Saturday, 13th instant, of the well-known stock-brokerage house of Kenyon, Cox & Co , in which Daniel Drew is a general partner, the cause being that the firm were indorsers on about $1,500,000 of Canada Southern Railway paper, a part of which fell due on the 15th, and they were either unable or unwilling to assume the sole responsibility of paying it This suspension, although important in stock circles, was of far less general influence than that of Messrs Jay Cooke & Co , which occurred on Thursday, and of Fisk & Hatch, which was announced on Friday morning, and followed by the failures of a number of smaller stock-brokerage firms during the day The immediate cause of Messrs Jay Cooke & Co 's suspension was the large advances made by the Philadelphia house to the Northern Pacific Railroad, which together with a heavy drain of late from their depositors so reduced their cash resources that they were unable to continue The excitement and general distrust which followed this suspension caused a general and rapid calling in of loans, and precipitated the misfortune of Messrs Fisk & Hatch, and with the great fall in stocks produced the other disasters It seems much more proper to refer to these disasters as temporary suspensions rather than failures, and there is scarcely a doubt that most of the firms will be able to settle their affairs and resume business in a short time, their resources and those of their individual partners being known in many cases to be very large

The excitement in Wall street and vicinity was intense, and was heightened by a run on the Fourth National Bank and the Union Trust Company, the bank remaining open after its usual hours and meeting every demand, and the trust company paying depositors during the day, and being reported abundantly able to meet its liabilities, provided money could be obtained on first-class securities

The bank officers have been in council, and will take measures to furnish every possible relief to the market, and it is expected that the Secretary of the Treasury will, if possible, use a part of his currency reserve to purchase 5-20 bonds, or will otherwise give assistance to the banks At the close of business there was a more hopeful feeling and a belief on the part of many that the worst of the panic had been seen [a]

Amidst the great confusion and excitement which has been prevalent in financial circles since the date of our last report, and the occurrence of important events crowding one upon another in rapid succession, it is somewhat difficult to give a review of the past week which shall be at all satisfactory

On Saturday morning, 20th instant, the markets opened with wild excitement, in consequence of the numerous suspensions of banking and brokerage firms on the previous day, and the closing of the Union Trust Company and the National Bank of the Commonwealth that (Saturday) morning The suspension of the trust company was alleged to be caused by its inability to get call loans paid in, or of realizing or borrowing on securities, but in addition to its other troubles a defalcation of its secretary, Mr Carleton, was discovered to the extent of about $500,000, and the company was placed in the hands of Mr E B Wesley as receiver, who has not yet made a report, but promises a favorable one soon Among the most important loans of the company was one to the Lake Shore and Michigan Southern Railroad for $1,750,000, and which falls due, we believe, in January next

The failure of the Commonwealth Bank was occasioned by permitting a banking firm to overdraw their account some $200,000, and the bank has also gone into a receiver's hands If the accounts be true, it appears that the depositors both in the bank and trust company will be almost or

[a] Commercial and Financial Chronicle, September 20, 1873, p 382.

wholly free from loss whenever the market becomes settled so that securities can be sold at a fair price

At the Stock Exchange excitement was so high and prices were declining so rapidly that the governing committee met about 11 o'clock a m and decided to close the exchange immediately until further notice, which was accordingly done This was a coup d'état, and at the time was considered by some members to be rather a high-handed proceeding, though under the light of subsequent events it has met the unqualified approval of the whole business community [a]

THE CLOSING OF THE STOCK EXCHANGE.

The Stock Exchange remained closed for ten days, until September 30, an event which was wholly unprecedented and which was not found necessary in later crises. Not unnaturally the impression has been drawn that the situation in 1873 was peculiarly desperate, but such a conclusion, so far as it is based upon the closing of the Stock Exchange, rests upon a misunderstanding of the real occasion for that drastic measure. It was a result of a cumbersome mode of transacting business, which required the co-operation of the banks in ways which were often illegal and which absorbed a disproportionate share of their credit facilities. The method of daily stock delivery peculiar to American exchanges always causes trouble in time of crisis, though this difficulty has been greatly diminished since the establishment of the Stock Exchange clearing house in 1892. In 1873 every transaction on the exchange involved a payment with a certified check The method of business was thus described in a contemporary journal

From the comments made upon the cases which the panic has brought to light of brokers' "overdrafts" it is evident that the public knows very little of the system upon which Wall street houses transact business and

[a] Ibid , September 27, p 410

effect daily "clearances" of an enormous amount of stock * * * Temporary "overdrafts" are the rule and not the exception with most of the banks in the vicinity of the Stock Exchange No other way has yet been devised through which a broker's "clearances" can be effected Most houses with an "average deposit" of from $10,000 to $20,000 in bank have to receive and deliver from $100,000 to $500,000 worth of stock or gold per diem, larger houses, proportionately larger values * * * Almost every banker or broker in good credit has an arrangement, definite or implied, with his bank, by which he is allowed to largely overdraw his balance—in payment for blocks of stock—with the understanding that before 3 p m of the same day he shall deposit the certified checks of other people in amount sufficient for the redemption of his own checks and the maintenance of a respectable "balance" On the latter the bank makes its profit Large houses often open accounts of this sort with several banks at once * * * The whole system is perilous and illegal * * * When, as now, they suspend this usage, all business has to stop [a]

On September 24 the stock exchange committee sent the following communication to the committee of the clearing house.

The great obstacle we have to deal with in resuming the operations of the Stock Exchange is * * * the mode of settling our transactions As long as the banks on whom checks are drawn are distrustful of each other, so long will a condition of unreasoning panic continue, and the demand on all sides will be for "greenbacks" rather than for "certified checks," which may turn out worthless within twenty-four hours after they have been accepted in payment To reopen the Stock Exchange under this condition of affairs would simply, therefore, be the inauguration of a run upon the banks for legal tenders, with what results you are better qualified to judge than ourselves * * * The true plan, in the present emergency, in our opinion, is that those banks who are content to make clearances with each other, should, to the extent of their associated capital, guarantee the payment of checks certified by the banks allowed to enter the clearing house * * * It is necessary to have the moral courage to sacrifice the weak members of your present association, rather than to have all the banks of New York suffer the disgrace of a suspension of payments [b]

With reference to this proposal, it was observed by the Times:

This, we submit, is neither reasonable nor, under the trying circumstances of the day, to be expected The banks cleared last week an average

[a] New York Tribune, September 24, 1873
[b] New York Times, September 25, 1873

of $109,000,000 per day The last of the brokers' checks were cleared on Monday of this week, when the total clearings fell to $83,000,000 On yesterday (Tuesday) the total fell to $49,000,000, this morning to $45,000,000 The question, therefore, recurs, Is it right that, after the Stock Exchange is reopened, the associated banks should (in violation of law, so far as the national banks are concerned) certify for $50,000,000 or $60,000,000 a day? The mere statement of the case supplies the answer * * * The sooner the clearing house stops clearing and certifying for the Stock Exchange the better, forcing the exchange to provide other means of clearing among themselves [a]

The reply of the clearing-house committee was equally unfavorable. They refused the request with the laconic observation that it was too exclusively to the convenience and safety of the exchange [b]

The disturbing consequences of our system of dealings on the Stock Exchange will be seen in the course of later crises Here it may be noted that it tends to create an exaggerated idea both in other countries as well as at home of the seriousness of American crises The Stock Exchange was at length reopened on September 30, though at first only a moderate business could be carried on, as the banks refused to overcertify checks for the brokers, but with the resumption of monetary ease the banks resumed their former relations with them

GOVERNMENT ASSISTANCE.

The Secretary of the Treasury was strongly urged to intervene to relieve both the foreign and the domestic exchange situation, but he wisely refused to strain if not exceed his lawful authority.[c] Government assistance was limited to the redemption of bonds in currency, offers being accepted at prices not exceeding par in gold During the week beginning Saturday, September 20,

[a] Ibid , September 25 [b] Ibid , September 28. [c] See p. 322.

more than $27,000,000 in excess of receipts was paid out at the subtreasury in New York, but not all of this amount was a net addition to the available supply of money. Rather more than $17,000,000 was in exchange for certificates of deposit which by the act of June 8, 1872, were issued to national banks in denominations of not less than $5,000 upon the deposit in the Treasury of an equivalent amount of legal tender notes The purchases of bonds, including the premium paid, set free $12,966,000 in currency, while ordinary receipts and disbursements very nearly balanced.[a]

Further assistance was beyond the power of the Treasury, unless the $34,000,000 of legal-tender notes retired in 1866 and 1867 were to be reissued, as its currency hold-

[a] The receipts and payments on all accounts at the subtreasury in New York between September 20 and September 27, 1873, were—

Receipts	
Transfers from depositary banks (currency)	$1,249,985 80
Transfers from treasury offices—	
Currency	730,000 00
Coin	1,513,615 39
Duties on imports, etc (coin)	2,535,458 12
Miscellaneous collections (currency)	139,617 28
Total receipts	6,168,676.59
Payments	
Treasury warrants paid—	
Currency	1,356,741 92
Coin	1,822,763 47
Certificates of deposit redeemed (currency)	17,475,000 00
Bonds purchased—	
Principal (currency)	11,708,100 00
Premium (currency)	1,255,582 93
Interest (coin)	200,922 31
Total payments	33,819,110 63

This statement was prepared by the Treasury Department at the request of the writer

ings, not including those held for the redemption of certificates, were exhausted This expedient had been resorted to earlier in the year to meet a temporary deficiency in funds, but, though strongly urged by some of the distressed financiers in New York, the President and the Secretary of the Treasury refused their consent In the second week of October, however, the Treasury, again on account of the deficiency in revenue, began to entrench upon the so-called "currency reserve," but the payments at that time were not large and had no influence upon the monetary situation.

Even the $13,000,000 of currency paid out by the Treasury were of slight service in relieving the situation The purchased bonds came almost entirely from the savings banks, and they were not willing to deposit the proceeds with the clearing-house banks. It would have been far more satisfactory had the money been deposited with the banks by the Treasury, but at this period such deposits were not customary beyond the amount required to facilitate government business It is somewhat surprising to find that the United States bonds on hand, held by the New York national banks, amounting to about $3,500,000, were not returned to the Government in exchange for currency. These bonds, however, were widely scattered among the 50 national banks Only two of the banks held any considerable amount of them, and as they were perhaps the two strongest banks in the city it may be presumed that they felt that they had contributed sufficiently to the relief of the general situation in joining the currency pool described on a subsequent page

THE EFFECT OF THE PANIC ON THE NEW YORK BANKS.

We now return to our subject proper and follow the effects of the panic upon the banks On Saturday, September 20, two trust companies, after withstanding runs for a short time, were obliged to close their doors One national bank also failed The two trust companies were able to resume—one on October 15 and the other early in December. The bank was liquidated with no loss to creditors. Its solvency had been long in question, and its business was of small proportions, with loans in the neighborhood of $2,000,000 Its failure, therefore, was not one of the serious factors in the situation The trouble of the trust companies had more important immediate consequences. Their reserves were principally in the form of deposits with New York national banks, and in their unavailing effort to meet the runs upon themselves they had drawn out considerable amounts of money from the banks Reports of withdrawals by individual depositors from the banks generally are also found in the newspapers of the day, but in the case of but one bank, the Fourth National, were these withdrawals sufficient in size to reach the proportions of a run Distrust of this bank was excited because of its large dealings with brokers, the numerous failures and suspensions among whom gave rise to a fear that the bank must have been compromised. The Fourth National Bank was at that time one of the largest banks in the city, having deposits of $30,000,000, almost equally divided between individual and bankers' deposits Distrust of this bank was, therefore, a most serious matter Finally, the banks were receiving urgent demands for funds by telegraph from their banking cor-

6158—10——4

respondents in all parts of the country Private bankers, such as Jay Cooke & Co., seem to have held at least relatively larger deposits payable on demand both from individuals and banks than is now customary.[a] Moreover, outside banks seem to have lent considerable sums in New York directly to brokers, as well as through the medium of their reserve agents The failures and suspensions of bankers and brokers therefore weakened the out of town banks directly, to say nothing of the alarm which was excited among their own depositors Recourse to deposits with their reserve agents was therefore in some instances necessary and in others was far from being a product of unnecessary fear.

The effects of these various demands upon the banks in New York can not be exactly determined since the weekly bank statement shows only the average condition of the banks for the week ending with Friday night The statement for September 20, therefore, probably shows something like the actual condition of the banks on Tuesday or Wednesday, just before the panic began It is, however, inserted here as better than no statement whatever:

	Amount	Changes from previous week	
		Decrease	Increase
Loans	$278,421,700	$6,114 550	
Deposits	198,040,100	9 277 400	
Circulation	27,414,200		$30,800
Specie	18 844 800	1,597,700	
Legal tenders	34 307,900	2,409,300	
Reserve percentage	23 03		
Reserve deficit	$3 211,075		1,695,050

[a] Bankers' Magazine, November, 1873, p 320.

CLEARING-HOUSE LOAN CERTIFICATES

There can be no doubt that the very considerable contraction of $6,114,000 in loans was far less than that which had actually taken place, and this is also true regarding changes in other important items in the statement. But to allay the panic it was absolutely necessary to secure the cessation of further contraction. Nothing could be more certain than that the continuance of loans was necessary, not only to prevent the spread of failure to other branches of trade but also to save the banks themselves from loss and even bankruptcy. The stock-exchange situation was such that it would have been worse than useless to attempt to reduce appreciably the amount of call loans. Outside bankers might follow that course, but for the banks of the city it was both their duty and their interest to sustain the local situation and, so far as possible, to prevent further failures The necessity for the adoption of this policy was clearly recognized, and on Saturday, September 20, the following arrangements were adopted to meet the situation by the New York banks in the Clearing House Association:

> That in order to enable the banks of the association to afford additional assistance to the financial community, and also for the purpose of facilitating the settlement of the exchanges between the banks, it is proposed that any bank in the Clearing House Association may, at its option, deposit with a committee of five persons, to be appointed for that purpose, an amount of bills receivable or other securities, to be approved by said committee, who shall be authorized to issue thereupon to said depositing bank certificates of deposit bearing interest at 7 per cent per annum, in denominations of $5,000 and $10,000, such as may be desired, to an amount not in excess of 75 per cent of the securities in bills renewable so deposited, except that when the securities deposited shall consist of either United States stock or gold certificates the certificates of deposit may be issued upon

the par value of such securities These certificates may be used in settlement of balances at the clearing house for a period not to extend beyond November 1, and they shall be received by creditor banks during that period daily in the same proportion as they bear to the aggregate amount of the debtor balance paid at the clearing house The interest which may accrue upon these certificates shall, on November 1 or sooner, should the certificates be all redeemed, be refunded and apportioned among the banks which shall have held them during that time The securities deposited with the committee as above named shall be held by them as a special deposit, pledged for the redemption of the certificates issued thereon The committee shall be authorized to exchange any portion of the said securities for an equal amount of others, to be approved by them, at the request of the depositing bank, and shall have power to demand additional security, either by an exchange or an increased amount, at their discretion The amount of certificates which this committee may issue, as above, shall not exceed $10,000,000 The banks shall report to the manager of the clearing house every morning at 10 a m the amount of certificates issued by them This arrangement shall be binding upon the clearing house Association when assented to by three-fourths of its members

That in order to accomplish the purposes set forth in this agreement the legal tender belonging to the associated banks shall be considered and treated as a common fund, held for mutual aid and protection, and the committee appointed shall have power to equalize the same by assessment or otherwise, at their discretion For this purpose a statement shall be made to the committee of the condition of such bank on the morning of every day, before the opening of business, which shall be sent with the exchanges to the manager of the clearing house, specifying the following items

"(1) Loans and discounts, (2) amount of loan certificates, (3) amount of United States certificates of deposit and legal-tender notes, (4) amount of deposit, deducting therefrom the amount of special gold deposits

"That the bank to which loan certificates may be issued be charged, in addition to 7 per cent interest, one-quarter of 1 per cent to defray the expenses consequent upon carrying out this plan

"F D TAPPEN,
"*President of Clearing House* "[a]

These arrangements were virtually the same as those which had been adopted and which had proved strikingly successful in 1860 and again in 1861.[b] It will be ob-

[a] Commercial and Financial Chronicle, September 27, 1873

[b] Loan certificates were also issued in 1863 and in 1864, but apparently for special purposes of no general importance

served that two fairly distinct powers were given the clearing-house committee The right to issue clearing-house loan certificates, and control over the currency portion of the reserves of the banks The loan certificates could be used solely in settling balances between the banks, though of course no obstacle was placed in the way of a bank which might choose to meet its unfavorable balances in the usual way by cash payments This arrangement was devised after the crisis of 1857,[a] according to tradition by George S. Coe, of whom we shall hear much a little later. The purpose of the certificate was to remove certain serious difficulties which had become generally recognized during that crisis. The banks had pursued a policy of loan contraction which ultimately led to general suspension, because it had proved impossible to secure any agreement among them [b] The banks which were prepared to assist the business community with loans could not do so because they would be certain to be found with unfavorable clearing-house balances in favor of the banks which followed a more selfish course. The loan certificate provided a means of payment other than cash, and what was more important, it took away the temptation from any single bank to seek to strengthen itself at the expense of its fellows, and rendered each bank willing to assist the community with loans to the extent of its power.

The use of certificates did not diminish in the slightest degree the obligation to pay cash to depositors on demand. On previous occasions its use had not led to the suspen-

[a] See note, p 419

[b] C F Dunbar, Economic Essays, pp 278–83

sion of cash payments, and although suspension followed within a few days after the issue of the certificates in 1873, it can not be too strongly insisted that their use had no direct bearing upon that unfortunate step [a]

In addition to the arrangement for the use of loan certificates, provision was also made for what was called the equalization of reserves. This provision was an essential part of the arrangement devised in 1860 to meet crisis conditions, and it requires especial attention because this is the only crisis since the organization of the national banking system during which it was adopted along with the issue of the clearing-house loan certificates.

The banks were not, of course, equally strong in reserve at the time the loan certificates were authorized. From that moment they would be unable to strengthen themselves aside from the receipt of money from depositors except in so far as the other banks should choose to meet unfavorable balances in cash Moreover, the withdrawals of cash by depositors would not fall evenly upon the banks Some would find their reserves falling away rapidly with no adequate means of replenishing them The enforced suspension of individual banks would pretty certainly involve the other banks in its train Finally, it would not be impossible for a bank to induce friendly depositors to present checks on other banks directly for cash payment, instead of depositing them for collection through the clearing house and probable payment in loan certificates The arrangement for equalizing reserves therefore

[a] In the later crises of 1893 and 1907 there was, as we shall see, a close connection between the issue of the certificates and suspension See pp 182 and 272

diminished the likelihood of the banks' working at cross purposes—a danger which the use of clearing-house certificates alone can not entirely remove.

These arrangements had enabled the banks to pass through periods of severe strain in 1860 and in 1861 without suspension In both instances the use of the loan certificate was followed immediately by an increase in the loans of the banks, and in no short time by an increase in their reserves. The situation in 1873 was more serious, and as events proved, the reserve strength of the banks, while sufficient to carry them through the worst of the storm, was not enough to enable them to avoid the resort to suspension

The opinion has been expressed by a high authority that these arrangements should have been adopted on Thursday, and that the delay of two days involved serious consequences which might have been averted [a] The impending failure of Jay Cooke & Co seems to have been disclosed to certain New York bankers on Wednesday,[b] and it is difficult to see how its seriousness can have been underestimated But the Clearing House Association's officers were entirely from the more conservative mercantile banks, and very likely they did not at first perceive the gravity of the situation, and probably knew nothing of the Cooke failure until it occurred

Let us consider once more the condition of the banks on September 20, the day when the clearing-house loan certificates were authorized. They held $18,800,000 in specie, but this specie was useless in meeting the require-

[a] Dunbar, Theory and History of Banking, p 84

[b] F Oberholtzer, Life of Jay Cooke, Vol II, p 422

ments of ordinary depositors From the total of 198 millions of deposits we may offset the specie holdings, leaving 180 millions of deposits payable in legal-tender notes Against this liability the banks held $34,300,000 in greenbacks, or 19 1 per cent But as the return was for the average condition for the week the banks must have been in a considerably less satisfactory condition than is indicated by this statement In conclusion, it should be remembered that the banks entered upon this struggle with panic conditions with no means of adding to their cash resources They could not increase their note issues; the money paid out by the Treasury in the purchase of bonds did not reach the banks; and gold imports were of slight service, because gold was not the medium of the ordinary business of the country.

On Monday, September 22, the first business day under the régime of clearing-house loan certificates and of the greenback pooling agreement, it soon became evident that the worst stage of the panic had been passed Notwithstanding temporary relapses upon the announcement of further failures on this and the two following days, improvement was reasonably steady and unquestioned The banks took out loan certificates freely, and on Wednesday the ten millions authorized were entirely exhausted. The drastic contraction of loans which had taken place during the previous week was over. Runs upon particular banks in the Clearing House Association ceased, since now the reserves of all the banks were at the disposal of any threatened institution. The banks in general, however, experienced some further loss of cash from individual depositors whose alarm was too extreme to be allayed by the clearest evidence of the continuance of normal banking operations. More considerable withdrawals, in some instances reaching the proportions of runs, were reported by the savings banks These banks, of course, carried little or no cash reserves, and the withdrawal by them of money to their credit with the clearing-house banks must have been an important factor in the depletion of their stores of cash By resorting to their legal privilege of requiring notice from depositors, the savings banks were soon able to remove themselves as a disturbing force from the field of action

Had all the New York banks been purely local institutions, with no responsibilities to the rest of the country, there can be little doubt that they would have been able to weather the storm without further difficulty But the most considerable withdrawals of currency which they had to meet came from the out-of-town banks, and demands from that quarter showed no signs of diminishing, but rather increased day by day. During the turmoil of Friday and Saturday reports were current that money was not being shipped to interior banks.[a] Amid the rush of business during those two days it may well have happened that shipments of currency were delayed, but at the beginning of the following week it is entirely reasonable to conclude that the New York banks were fully meeting their obligations to their banking correspondents when we find Chicago papers mentioning liberal remittances from New York to that city and to

[a] See Chicago Tribune, September 24, 1873

other centers[a] Unfortunately, the New York banks were unable to continue this wise and salutary policy for many days. Meeting every demand from their depositors, they had already during the first three days of this week done much to restore confidence, but at the close of business on Wednesday, September 24, they were left with a supply of greenbacks so scanty that they could hardly hope to maintain payments until with the restoration of confidence the normal course of currency movements would bring money to their depleted reserves

The actual condition of the banks at this time (Wednesday, September 24) is fairly well indicated by taking the bank statement showing average conditions for the week ending Friday, September 26, though, if anything, it probably presents a stronger condition than was actually the case The following table shows the condition of the New York banks for the week ending September 26, 1873.

		Changes from previous week (decrease)
Loans	$266 811 800	$11 609,900
Specie	12,937,300	5,907,500
Legals	21,229,100	13 078 800
Deposits	174,527,800	23 512 300
Circulation	27,327,600	86,600
Reserve deficit	16,297,450	[a] 13,076,375
Reserve percentage	16 97	

[a] Increase

In analyzing the changes shown by this table, account must be taken of the elimination of the failed Commonwealth Bank The contraction of loans shown by the

[a] See Chicago Tribune, September 24, and also New York Tribune, September 23

table should be reduced by $1,900,000, but the net contraction of $9,700,000 is large, though most if not all of it belonged properly to the previous week All reports agree that the banks resumed lending operations upon the issue of clearing-house loan certificates The absence of the Commonwealth Bank doubtless accounts for the reduction of $86,000 in circulation, as the circulation of that bank was $230,000 It was not a time when the banks would be likely to keep any of their notes out of circulation. The deposits of the Commonwealth Bank were $1,692,000, specie holdings $15,800, and their legal tenders $476,600—amounts which do not appreciably affect conclusions drawn from the bank statement of the week The reduction of more than one-third in reserves, especially in legal tenders, may be looked at from two points of view. It shows the enormous extent of the demands which had been met by the banks, and credit should certainly be given the clearing-house committee for the brave effort which was made to meet every obligation of the members of the Clearing-House Association But the proportion of reserve was reduced in one week from 23 per cent to 16 97 per cent, and if we take the proportion of currency to deposits, less the amount of specie, it was reduced from 19.1 per cent to 13.1 per cent

SUSPENSION IN NEW YORK.

It is reasonable to believe that success would have crowned the efforts of the clearing-house committee to handle the situation if the reserves at their disposal had been somewhat greater at the beginning of the disturbance. If they had been able to draw upon any outside funds, it is probable that they would have persisted in the policy of unrestricted payments Had the Treasury deposited the $13,000,000 which was used in the purchase of bonds, something would have been gained The relief which had been experienced at the beginning of the week, when the banks proved able to continue payments, was so great that the public, unaware of the depletion of the reserve did not see the necessity of resorting to further measures—measures which could not fail to disturb trade and weaken confidence. But the banks were clearly at the end of their resources, and the step taken on Wednesday, September 24, seems amply justified. Another issue of $10,000,000 of clearing-house loan certificates was authorized—a measure which introduced no change in the policy hitherto followed.[a] In addition the following momentous resolution was adopted:

> That all checks when certified by any bank shall be first stamped or written "Payable through the Clearing House"

The adoption of this resolution involved the partial suspension of cash payments by the banks It did not signify that no money whatever would be paid out to depositors, but it placed the dwindling supply of currency more absolutely within the control of the clearing-house committee In later crises this restriction of cash payments has been carried to extremes, and the banks have not thereafter allowed their reserves to fall away, but have even greatly increased them with little regard to or per-

[a]Another issue must have been authorized later, as the maximum amount outstanding, on October 3, was $22,410,000 This was equal to 8 35 per cent of the loans of the banks, and may be compared with the maximum issue of $88,420,000 on Dec 16, 1907, which was 7.52 per cent of loans at that time

haps better realization of the effect on the business community. In 1873 money continued to be paid out by the banks—indeed almost as freely as before—especially to the banking depositors of the banks That the reserves were used freely is shown by the following table which contains the bank statement from September 27 to November 8, the entire period during which its publication was discontinued: [a]

	Loans	Specie	Legal tenders	Deposits.	Circulation
Sept 27	$266,811,800	$12,937 300	$21,229,100	$174,527,800	$27,327 600
Oct 4	268,408,700	10,635 500	12,012,700	156,402,300	27,425,900
Oct 11	265,593,900	11,919,900	10,178 800	156,004,600	24,451 600
Oct 18	261 366,100	13 388,500	6 280,500	153,794,900	27,453 400
Oct 25	254,896,200	13,270,600	8 777 700	150 397,700	27,422,300
Nov 1	253,232,400	14,972,600	14 724,900	155,844,200	27,413 700
Nov 8	249,277,300	16,878,000	21,040,200	157,967,500	27,434,800

The bank statement of October 4 showed a loss of $9,000,000 of currency and of some $2,000,000 in specie During the following two weeks there was a further loss of currency to the amount of $6,000,000, the statement of October 18 showing only $6,280,500 of legal tenders Owing to gold imports, the specie holdings had somewhat increased and amounted to $13,338,000. There was then a reserve deficit of $25,648,000, exceeding by nearly $6,000,000 the actual reserve of $19,664,000. The proportion of the total reserve to liabilities was only 10 85 per cent, to deposits alone 12 79 per cent, and the proportion of greenbacks to deposits, less specie held, was only 4.47 per cent. On October 14 the legal-tender reserve was at the lowest point, at $5,800,000, having been

[a] This table is taken from the Bankers' Magazine for May, 1875, p. 857.

reduced from $34,000,000 on September 20[a] The currency movement then turned in favor of the banks, at first slowly, but by the end of the month rapidly, and by the middle of November the banks were again above their reserve requirements.

In the subsequent crises of 1893 and 1907 the banks followed an entirely different course after cash payments were restricted, and bent every energy to the immediate strengthening of their reserves. It is this difference in policy that gives importance to the study of the crisis in 1873 In making free use of their reserves the clearing-house committee exhibited a determination and strength of purpose which can not be too highly praised. As will be seen in our study of the course of later crises, the banks, when they suspended in 1873, were far less well supplied with funds and were also unable to secure additional currency from any source. In 1907 suspension was more complete and continued for a longer period than in 1873, and its disturbing effects upon the trade of the country seem to have been far more serious. Further comparison must be deferred to a later stage in this investigation, but with this end in view it will be seen that a detailed analysis of the course of the crisis of 1873 after suspension is of the utmost importance

THE CURRENCY PREMIUM.

The first and most immediate consequence of partial suspension by the New York banks was the appearance of a premium upon currency in terms of certified checks

[a] See p 94

The rumor that this action was under discussion by the clearing-house authorities is said to have caused the premium to appear late on Wednesday, but the first quotation which found its way into the daily journals was for Thursday, September 25, when the premium was reported as ranging from one-half to 3½ per cent The following table presents the currency premium for each day during its continuance, showing the highest and lowest quotations

Date	Quotations	Date	Quotations
Sept 25	½-3½	Oct 9	½-1¼
26	1½-4	10	½-1
27	2-4	11	¼-⅝
28	Sunday	12	Sunday
29	2-5	13	¼-½
30	2-4	14	¼-½
Oct 1	2-3½	15	½-1
2	1-3	16	Close at 1/16
3	¼-1½	17	⅛-½
4	¼-1 [a]	18	1/16-½
5	Sunday	19	Sunday
6	½-1	20	⅛-¼
7	¾-1¼	21	Nominal
8	½-1¼	22	⅛-¼ [b]

[a] In Philadelphia 3-4 [b] Bank notes at par

[This table is taken in the main from reports in the New York Tribune and Times, these failing, from telegraphic reports in the Boston Advertiser and the Chicago Tribune.]

The fluctuation in rates on some days was often considerable. It is possible that the lower rate may refer to the price paid by brokers for currency and the higher rate to the price at which they sold it to customers. There were, however, wide differences both in supply and demand from hour to hour, and especially high rates were regularly paid for currency in quantity. It will be observed that the premium ruled at a fairly high rate for some ten days, followed by a week during which rates were in the neighborhood of 1 per cent and then by another week when the rates were nominal As a positive factor in the situation the currency premium had a duration of less than three weeks.

FOREIGN EXCHANGE.

The course of both the foreign and domestic exchanges during crises is exceedingly difficult to follow and to explain Their derangement has an immediate and far-reaching effect upon the movement of commodities between different parts of the country and for export, and if continued for any length of time leads to the serious interruption of the ordinary productive activities of the people In the case of the crisis of 1873, unlike that in 1857, the disturbance of the foreign exchange market was of short duration. On Friday, September 19, it was reported that the market was demoralized, and on Saturday that foreign exchange was blocked, and for several days during the following week newspaper reports agree that mercantile bills were practically unsaleable It was stated that foreign exchange dealers could not dispose of their own drafts on London, and that they were unwilling to take the risk of purchasing bills in the disturbed state of affairs. By the end of the week, however, conditions became more satisfactory, and on Friday, September 25, $2,500,000 was taken from the Bank of England for export to the United States This was the beginning of a considerable movement which continued until the end of October, a total of $15,000,000 being sent to the United States from Europe This inflow of gold in itself was of less importance than upon other occasions of crisis, because the business of the country was being carried on upon an inconvertible paper basis, but it is an indication that the blockade in the foreign exchanges had been effectively broken.

It remains, however, to determine just what had brought about this improvement in the foreign exchange situation The view has gained ground in recent years that the currency premium which has appeared in our successive crises has been a chief factor in stimulating gold imports, and consequently in bringing about the continuance of dealings in foreign exchange In 1873 no expression of this opinion has been discovered, and it may be asserted with confidence that at no time has the currency premium exerted more than a secondary influence on the course of foreign exchange dealings.

Comparatively little capital has been employed in this business by American foreign exchange houses, and until recently the banks did not engage directly in such operations at all. Commercial bills drawn against American exports are regularly discounted at once in Europe, and against the credits thus secured abroad drafts are drawn and sold here so far as the demand allows The banks appear as a factor in these dealings when the funds of the exchange dealers are not sufficient to meet the temporary excess of bills purchased over drafts sold, or in the case of gold imports during the time the gold is in transit. At the outbreak of a crisis, due to domestic causes, the demand for drafts is certain to fall off, and if the exchange houses are to purchase bills and import gold the banks must supply the funds during the period of shipment. It has already been pointed out that the banks were probably not making any new loans during the latter part of the week ending September 20, and those of the first part of the following week probably served only to satisfy the most urgent needs of their customers and check liquidation. But the issue of a second ten millions of clearing-house loan certificates, authorized on Wednesday, September 24, seems to have enabled the banks to do more than that, since the bank statement of October 4 shows an increase in loans of some $2,000,000 The advances of the banks enabled the exchange houses to resume the purchase of bills, thus preventing the threatened cessation of commodity exports. The currency premium had no direct bearing on the matter, exchange rates and the gold premium moved up and down with changes in the currency premium, since they were both expressed in terms of depreciated certified checks [a]

The temporary blockade in foreign exchange was chiefly felt in the grain and produce markets From Chicago, on Friday, September 19, it was reported that "the shipping movement was partially paralyzed by the news from New York that sterling exchange was unnegotiable "[b] Through the following week the situation remained serious. The movement of wheat to the Atlantic ports fell off, and in consequence the elevators and stock yards became crowded to their utmost capacity, and

[a] For a further discussion of this matter, see pp 191 and 282.

[b] Chicago Tribune, September 20, 1875

shipments from primary markets were necessarily refused by the railroads[a] The price of wheat fell off sharply—from $1.13 on September 19 to 90 cents on September 24. With the resumption of foreign-exchange dealings at the end of the week shipments were renewed, and the wheat quotation was again above $1 on September 29. Cotton was not affected so seriously by the foreign-exchange situation, other causes contributing to the sharp decline in its price from 19¼ to 17¼ cents per pound. The movement of the crop was only just beginning, and of course difficulties of storage were absent

SUSPENSION THROUGHOUT THE COUNTRY.

The maintenance of the usual system of payments between different parts of the country is a problem wholly unlike that of the foreign exchanges Continuance of cash payments by the New York banks, rather than the continuance of loans, is the essential requirement Local business can be carried on after a fashion with certified checks payable only through the clearing house, and foreign-exchange transactions, except when gold is being exported, may be characterized as a local business. If, however, the banks of the money centers refuse or even delay the shipment of funds deposited with them, the thousands of country banks will inevitably discontinue remittances upon items sent to them for collection. But is the reverse equally inevitable? If the initiative is taken by the country banks, is that sufficient reason for the discontinuance or restriction of the shipments of money to the interior by the banks of

[a] Chicago Tribune, September 25, 1875

the money centers? The answer is most certainly and decidedly in the negative. The banks in the money centers reap great advantages from their position as clearing centers and as reserve agents. They incur a responsibility for maintaining the credit situation which does not rest upon the other banks.

Finally, what has been said of money centers generally in relation to the country banks applies with even less qualification to the responsibilities of the New York banks, to the banks of other money centers, and, indeed, to the banks of the entire country There is always a chance that the New York banks, by meeting every demand upon them for cash, may be able to reestablish the ordinary course of payments between banks in different parts of the country, while nothing that the country banks and those of the secondary money centers may do can possibly bring this about It follows, therefore, that even though in 1873, or on later occasions, some of the banks outside New York may have restricted payments before the suspension in New York, the general dislocation of the domestic exchanges is properly to be attributed to the banks of that city A danger, therefore, which had been merely threatening became a reality at the moment the action of the clearing-house banks on Wednesday, September 24, became generally known. Similar steps were immediately taken in most of the secondary money centers. In Boston, Philadelphia, Baltimore, Washington, New Orleans, Cincinnati, and St. Louis the issue of clearing-house loan certificates, and at the same time the use of certified checks, payable through the clearing house, were sanctioned.[a] We have already seen that the use of loan certificates does not necessarily involve suspension, but the fact that both measures were taken together in many places not unnaturally gave rise to the erroneous impression that suspension is an inevitable consequence of the issue of loan certificates. Moreover in many cities, Chicago being the most important, as well as by the country banks generally, suspension of cash payments was quite as complete, even though they did not resort to the loan certificate. In many instances the banks made public the reasons which led them to restrict payments, and as they afford a clear idea of the situation as it presented itself in different parts of the country they are here given in some detail

SAVANNAH —The Chamber of Commerce, September 26, held an adjourned meeting at 10 o'clock at night to receive the report of its committee, who presented the following

Resolved, That the banks and banking houses of Savannah will only meet demands of depositors by certification of checks, to be used as the necessities of the holders may require, until the temporary difficulties are removed, and until exchange can be negotiated or currency be received to move the crops

The banks are acting according to this resolution

NEW ORLEANS —At a meeting of all the bank presidents in New Orleans, September 25, it was resolved to pay no check for more than $100 All larger checks are to be certified, and the arrangement to continue thirty days This action is considered precautionary to prevent a drain The merchants generally approve of the course the banks have taken

The following address was issued by the banks of this city

The undersigned, incorporated banks and bankers of the city of New Orleans, desire to inform the community of the motives which actuate them in partially suspending payment of currency upon their demand

[a] For resolutions and statistical data regarding the issue of loan certificates in all these cities except Washington see James G Cannon, Clearing-Houses pp 91–7 For Washington the return to the Comptroller for October 13, gives an issue of $28,000 It is in the case of that city the only reference I have found

obligations, owing to a partial suspension of currency payments by the associated banks of New York and other northern cities, and the consequent refusal of the western and other banks to receive checks on New York, as is the regular course in the settlement of collections made here for their account It is ascertained that a very large remittance of currency hence has been made upon peremptory orders within the past five days To such an extent indeed has this prevailed that at the same rate only a few days must elapse before our vaults and the community would be entirely depleted of the means essential to the ordinary movement of trade At the present moment foreign exchange is unsalable in New York, and as we derive from this source our main supply of currency we are now thus deprived of the only means of restoring the amounts lost by shipments to the West and the interior We have therefore taken this step as a means of self-protection, and for the benefit of the agricultural as well as the commercial interests, and as the only means through which the incoming crops can be moved without ruinous sacrifice in prices The duration of this protective policy is limited to a period of thirty days, during which time we are confident that the daily receipts of cotton and sugar will afford us a prompt and ready relief, and compel currency to seek this market

MARYLAND —Officers of the associated banks of Baltimore met September 25, and resolved, in view of the present financial situation, not to pay out money on checks except what may be required for legitimate business purposes, the banks to certify all good checks which can be used in business transactions It is confidently believed here that the banks in the city were never in a sounder condition than at present, and their action this afternoon is recognized as a prudent precaution against any panic The president of the German Savings Bank states that deposits are in excess of the amounts drawn from the bank Mercantile and commercial interests of the city, while experiencing to some degree the general pressure and tightness in money, are regarded as being on a safe and sound basis, no failures being at present anticipated As elsewhere, trade is very limited, no heavy transactions taking place The feeling to-day, sympathizing with the favorable dispatches from New York, is much better than for several days previous, and it is confidently expected that business will soon revive

ST LOUIS, MO , *September 25.*—A slight run having been made on the banks of St Louis on the 25th of September, it was decided at a meeting of bankers to suspend the payment of checks or drafts, either in currency or exchange, until the excitement in the East subsides and the former condition of the markets is restored Shipments of flour to the East having been virtually suspended by the recent advance in railroad freights, the board of directors of the Merchants' Exchange have petitioned railroad companies to restore the old rate during the present financial troubles

OHIO —The Cincinnati Clearing-House Association has adopted the following resolution

"*Resolved,* That for the protection of our commercial interests, and for the purpose of preventing a drain of currency from the banks and bankers of this city, we do hereby agree to adopt substantially the plan adopted in New York, viz They will not pay out currency on checks except for small sums, to be optional with the banks upon whom they are drawn, but they will certify checks drawn on balances in their hands, payable through the clearing house only "

Each member of the Clearing-House Association is required to deposit such sum, in approved securities, as will at all times cover the amount of his clearings Government bonds are received at their par value Railroad and other stock and bonds and bills receivable are received at 75 per cent of the value fixed on them by the committee Loan certificates are issued by the committee, which can only be used in the settlement of balances between the banks, and are not negotiable The banks have since resumed currency payments as usual

RHODE ISLAND —An adjourned meeting of the Providence banks, September 30, received and adopted the report of a committee recommending a liberal policy on the part of banks toward each other and customers, that each bank should request its depositors to draw checks payable through the clearing house, and should certify checks payable through the clearing house, that deposits made in banks in currency be paid out to such depositors in currency, and that deposits made in certified checks be paid in kind The Providence banks are in a generally sound and strong condition

NASHVILLE —The national banks of Nashville, four in number, in view of the present state of financial affairs, have agreed to suspend currency payments on all balances exceeding $200 The board of trade, at a large and full meeting, unanimously approved of the course of the banks, and adopted a resolution that merchants and business men would continue to deposit with and aid the banks by every means in their power A general good feeling prevails among business men, and there are no symptoms of a panic [a]

The following news items are taken from the Boston Advertiser and the Chicago Tribune:

INDIANAPOLIS, *September 26* —The clearing house adopts suspension of currency payments for two days

PHILADELPHIA, *September 26* —The clearing house resolves that the banks will not pay out any more currency except what is actually needed for the payment of wages

DUBUQUE, IOWA, *September 27* —Only one national bank is meeting its demands in full in currency, one other has suspended payment entirely, a third pays in bills receivable, and small amounts in currency

---

[a] Bankers' Magazine, November, 1873, pp 383-393

KNOXVILLE, TENN, *September 27*—Banks here suspended currency payments

NEWPORT, *September 29.*—All the banks suspend currency payments

LOWELL, *September 29*—Decision to limit currency payments to $50, unless in cases of strong necessity The $200,000 due on pay rolls this week will be amply provided for

CONCORD, N H, *September 29*—Banks limit currency payments to small amounts

CAIRO, ILL, *September 29*—Adopts Cincinnati plan of suspension

WORCESTER, MASS, *September 29*—No concerted action, but banks "will avoid any obvious attempt to draw away greenbacks to New York, by paying large demands from out of town in cashiers' checks on Boston or New York"

HARRISBURG, PA, *September 28*—Banks and savings institutions agree to suspend currency payments

LOUISVILLE, *September 29*—A clearing house formed and a majority of the banks resolve to limit currency payments to small amounts

ALBANY, *September 29*—Banks working under New York plan

KANSAS CITY, *September 25*—Banks resolve that "we decline payments of checks or debts over our counters either in money or exchange, second, that clearing-house balances shall be carried to the extent of 75 per cent of approved collaterals

DAVENPORT, IOWA, *September 26*—Banks limit currency payments to $100

LEAVENWORTH, KANS, *September 26*—Six banks agree to suspend currency payments

Finally attention is called to the following reports of the action of the Chicago banks

The clearing-house association has voted [September 24] to recommend the suspension of currency payments on any large demands made upon them either from the country banks or over their counters [a]

Since Monday (September 22) or Tuesday last some of the banks of this city which have large deposits from country banks have been unable to return those balances in currency as fast as they were drawn for. * * * Other banks, and by far the larger number, having to deal only with city depositors, have been paying all demands upon them, both over the counter and at the clearing house

The banks vary largely as to what is a "small check," some pay $25, some $1,000, some 25 or 30 per cent of depositor's account The great difficulty is that the Chicago banks are not united, but rather are trying to get the advantage of each other [b]

[a] Chicago Tribune, September 25 [b] Ibid, September 26

Chicago bankers, on the evening of September 26, met and refused to issue clearing-house certificates, but appointed a committee on the question [a]

The action taken by the Boston banks is particularly instructive. The banks of that city were not subject to such heavy demands for crop-moving purposes from their banking correspondents as were those of New York and of the western and southern cities. They were also in a fairly strong position at the beginning of the crisis, having some $10,000,000 in cash against $62,000,000 of deposits. Payments were continued after suspension in New York, with the consequence that Boston exchange at once commanded a premium in New York, and was being eagerly purchased. On this account the banks on September 27 adopted a plan similar to that which had been adopted in New York, but with no provision for the equalization of reserves.

With the close of the week ending September 27 partial suspension had taken place throughout the country, aside from the Pacific coast, where the banks were upon a gold basis, and where general business was largely independent of that in the rest of the country. Up to the time of suspension there had been no failures of consequence in general business, and no failures of banks outside of New York, except those in Philadelphia and Washington, in connection with the failure of Jay Cooke & Co Confidence in the banks had not been seriously weakened, and there were few reports of runs and of hoarding by individuals outside of New York The course of trade had not as yet been seriously disturbed except in the grain and produce

[a] Ibid, September 27

markets in Chicago. With the beginning of the following week newspapers began to refer to "the late panic," and with reason, there was no further panic during 1873, though the crisis had only begun and although the effects of suspension which had been brought about by the panic had yet to be experienced There is every reason therefore to accept the explanation put forward by the banks that suspension was due to the action of the New York banks, action which, as we have already seen, was due to the lack of any adequate reserve in New York at the beginning of the crisis

HOARDING.

When once the banks had resorted to suspension, various causes of disturbance, till then of minor importance, became serious. The amount of actual money required for a given volume of transactions was greatly increased. Uncertain whether the banks would provide the money which they might shortly need, many persons began to discontinue paying into the banks cash received in the course of their daily business. On September 30, for example, one of the Boston banks reported that many of their customers were depositing their currency in their own safes [a] The currency premium also tended to keep money from finding its way into banks Many retail shops in New York, it was said, sold to brokers their receipts in currency Positive hoarding also seems to be increased by suspension, even though some money is brought into use by the possibility of realizing a profit from its sale at a premium. In 1873 at any rate the

[a] Boston Advertiser, September 30, 1873

amount of money thus brought to light was unquestionably more than offset by the amounts which were locked up in savings banks. In New York alone the savings banks were estimated to have held from $13,000,000 to $20,000,000, and they were severely criticised for withholding this money from the channels of trade[a] Such criticisms would have been well founded if the commercial banks had not resorted to suspension. The savings banks, having required thirty days' notice from depositors, were properly justified in holding themselves ready to meet the demands of those depositors who had already given notice

Aside from the savings banks, very little was said about the hoarding of currency, but there is direct evidence that as in later crises it threatened to assume alarming proportions Fortunately the banks, at least those at New York, adopted the only wise and effective remedy. Money was paid out freely, and the hoarding propensity vanished On October 13 and on November 1 the Comptroller of the Currency asked for special reports of the condition of the national banks, and thus secured a mass of statistical data showing the monetary effects of the crisis which is unique in banking history It is much to be regretted that this precedent was not followed in later crises On September 12, the date of the regular returns of the national banks, they held $112,958,000 in legal-tender notes. On October 13 they held $86,435,000, a loss of $26,523,000, or more than 23 per cent On November 1 they held $100,722,000, a gain of $14,287,000. More

[a] Commercial and Financial Chronicle, October 18, New York Tribune, October 20 and 21, Boston Advertiser, October 15

than half the loss had been recovered When it is remembered that this was the crop-moving period, it will be seen that no considerable amount of money lost by the banks was then being hoarded by depositors

The date of the first of these special reports, October 13, happened to have been at the moment when the banks were at the lowest point in reserves From about the middle of October money began to flow back into the banks, and by the close of the month the resumption of normal relations between banks and depositors was almost completely reestablished throughout the country As a seriously disturbing influence, suspension continued for less than three weeks.

The return of money to the banks and the resumption of cash payments may be due to influences quite opposite in nature The complete prostration of business may diminish the use for money outside the banks, and also the requirements of borrowers for loans This is the undesirable avenue of escape from suspension when it is prolonged over a considerable period of time, so that the dislocation of the domestic exchanges places a serious check upon the movement of commodities between different parts of the country An instance of this nature will be afforded in the case of the crisis of 1907 In 1873 it is not unlikely that suspension would have been thus prolonged had not the New York banks continued to meet their obligations to the utmost limit of their reserves As has already been stated, money was shipped to the banks of the interior in large quantities after the resort to partial suspension, and this action had the most reassuring effects on the banks and the people elsewhere. Currency began to be sent to New York by banks in other parts of the country as early as the first week in October On October 3 it was even reported that receipts had exceeded the amount which was required for the needs of the out-of-town banks Resumption came gradually and not at the same moment throughout the country, but by the end of October it was virtually complete except in a few Southern cities.

PAY ROLL DIFFICULTIES.

The most immediate effect of partial suspension is the difficulty of securing money for various purposes, especially for pay rolls In 1873 there were numerous reports from different parts of the country of inability to secure money for this purpose, though trouble on this account was probably much less than in later crises, because of the custom of paying wages monthly, which generally prevailed at that time It is, however, a cause of trouble which may be largely removed by means of substitutes for money, such as certified checks and local script of various kinds Were trade purely local it is probable that it would take but a short time for a community to adjust itself to suspension, if not without inconvenience, at least sufficiently well to permit the continuance of ordinary business payments

The following news items will serve to illustrate the difficulties which arose from the refusal of the banks to supply currency to their depositors, though it should be noted that in many instances of the shutting down of factories other causes were also potent It is not always certain that the lack of currency was due to the suspension of the banks. Inability to secure loans or to make collections may in many cases have deprived producers of the expected bank balances which would have given them the right to demand currency

In the Boston Advertiser for September 30 it was reported that

E Howard & Co (watch and clock makers) had closed part of their works Unable to make New York collections or to obtain Boston accommodations without great difficulty, "and being unwilling to swerve from the long-established practice of meeting their heavy pay-roll obligations weekly, they have decided to give a portion of their hands a fortnight release from labor" The American Watch Company, of Waltham, also discharged one-sixth of its force (150 in all) on September 29, "on account of the unsettled condition of the money market" J P Squire & Co discharged 100 men on Saturday (September 27), "because of the general troubles in financial matters." At Taunton banks have suspended temporarily "The firms having large pay rolls feel the contraction the most"

The following dispatches from a number of widely separated cities are taken from the Chicago Tribune:

TOLEDO, *September 29*—The various manufacturing establishments about town report some embarrassment caused by the crisis, such as difficulty in obtaining money to pay their hands, and the large tobacco factories have not been able to ship for four or five days on account of their inability to procure currency to purchase stamps It may be necessary to dress up the stock again before shipping, as it will not sell readily after a prolonged stay at the factory in packages About 40,000 pounds of "fine cut" has accumulated —*Chicago Tribune, September 30*

ST LOUIS, *September 30*—On account of the scarcity of currency, one prominent lumber firm suspended operations to-day, and discharged their men, and one or two other establishments will do the same if money is not easier within two days —*Chicago Tribune, October 1*

PITTSBURG, *October 3*—A meeting of manufacturers resolved, "That in order that the employee and employer may each contribute to the best interests of this community, and relieve our moneyed institutions from the excessive drain of currency, we commend that the manufacturers only make payment not to exceed one-half of the amount to our employees on each pay day on and after this date until the currency and exchange of the country assume their normal condition"—*Chicago Tribune, October 4*

CLEVELAND, *October 5*—No manufacturers are embarrassed so far as can be seen. All the heaviest ones are paying in full in cash, a few paying half and two-thirds in cash, the balance in orders on stores—*Chicago Tribune, October 6*

BALTIMORE, *October 6*—Some factories discharged a portion of their hands, others paid half wages in cash and rest in due bills The bills have been generally paid —*Chicago Tribune, October 7*

Finally, attention is called to a number of items of a somewhat later date from the New York Tribune

PHILADELPHIA, *October 11*—A number of Frankford cotton mills are running on half time in consequence of falling off of orders and difficulty of procuring currency to pay wages —*New York Tribune, October 13*

PITTSBURG, *October 14*—Report from Brady's Bend to effect that extensive ironworks had closed, also the cotton mills in Allegheny, ostensibly for repairs "It is feared that unless the banks resume their discount business many business interests will be seriously crippled"—*New York Tribune, October 15*

At Johnstown, Pa, the Cambria Iron Works has given notice to employees that the company finds it impossible to make collections or to sell for cash or to raise money in any other way to make the usual monthly cash payments, and gives notice of intention to pay as soon as possible "While the company will guarantee to employees all necessary supplies to the extent of their earnings, no regular cash payments need be expected until cash can be obtained for products of the works"

On Monday of last week (October 20) the Pittston and Elmira Coal Company suspended because of lack of money to pay its workmen On Thursday arrangements were made, and work was resumed to-day (October 27)

At Newburgh the "steam mills" have stopped (October 25), owing to the money stringency Four hundred persons are thrown out of work —*New York Tribune, October 27*

UTICA, *October 27*—The Remington gun factory at Ilion has been seriously embarrassed in obtaining currency to pay off its hands "There has been very little trouble of that kind in this city (Utica), as the banks have done all that lay in their power to accommodate business men, and have been materially aided by the Savings Bank of Utica, which has deposits exceeding $3,000,000 and supplies large amounts of currency to the banks of discount —*New York Tribune, October 28, 1873*

ROCHESTER, *October 28*—There has been some difficulty among Rochester manufacturers on one or two occasions in getting currency to pay their help, but in no case has there been more than two or three days' delay in payment The banks discount very little, but in other ways have done all they could to facilitate business

At Auburn there is great complaint of scarcity of money, "but, with the exception of one or two instances at the beginning of the panic, the banks have been able to furnish currency enough to pay off the operators employed in the workshops" The Frisbie steam fire-engine works are running on short time Plenty of orders, but no collections, "and the company finds it difficult to get money to pay off their hands. The engines are sold on long credit to corporations, and, while the securities are ample, it is impossible to negotiate them for money" Other manufactories closed or curtailed for same reason —*New York Tribune, October 30, 1873*

PROVIDENCE, *October 28*—J Y Smith, ex-governor and leading cotton manufacturer, said that "there has been a good deal of difficulty—now in part past—in getting currency to pay wages, but our mills have paid fully in cash, and promptly"—*New York Tribune, October 31*

Taken together these reports seem to indicate a serious state of affairs, but it must be remembered that they are the most definite examples of pay-roll trouble which have been found in two New York newspapers and in one Boston and one Chicago journal The impression left upon the mind from the examination of contemporary newspapers is that upon the whole the banks generally supplied at least the more urgent requirements of their depositors Pay-roll difficulties were certainly of short duration, disappearing shortly after the middle of October. Their place was taken by far more serious causes of trouble, which were not, however, of a banking nature. It would seem fairly certain that the following statement from the Boston Advertiser of October 22 was true for the country generally:

"The financial disturbances have but just reached the large New England manufactories. Great concerns that had to pay out thousands of dollars to hundreds of employees found it difficult then to get the money with which to cancel their pay-rolls, but most of them, in one way or another, did it But now stock has piled up, and curtailment has become necessary"

It is not possible at this distant date to make any estimate of the extent to which various local substitutes for money were made use of Scattered references to such devices, especially to those issued by municipalities, appear here and there in the newspapers, but they do not seem to have been so generally issued as in 1893 or 1907.[a]

THE DOMESTIC EXCHANGES

A far more serious cause of disturbance from the suspension of payments is the dislocation of the domestic exchanges In making payments at a distance local substitutes for money will not serve When the banks in one locality refuse to remit to banks elsewhere upon drafts and checks sent to them for payment business must soon come to a standstill. The sudden and general trade prostration which can be brought about by this means is within the recollection of all from recent experience In 1873 the dislocation of the domestic exchanges could not have had so serious effects as at present because of the much less complete development of economic interdependence between different parts of the country. But after making every allowance on this account, there can be no question that the dislocation of the domestic exchanges, with its resulting trade consequences, was far less complete than in later crises The exchanges were indeed deranged for a time, but they were never completely blocked, except in Chicago, and serious derangement continued for but a few days at the end of September

[a] See Chicago Tribune September 30, October 3 and 24, also New York Times, October 1

and the beginning of October. There were very few references to the matter in the newspapers of the time, and still more seldom is it mentioned among the chief causes of difficulty The following are the most definite references to the effect of the dislocation of the exchanges which I have found.

We learn that one effect of the present trouble has been to put a considerable check on the remittances of country tradesmen to the centers of wholesale trade This is probably not because there is less money in the country to send, or because the retail merchants are unable to remit The result of the practice, however, is detrimental to business, and checks the recovery from the panic, without helping those who cease remitting [a]

"The effect of the financial panic on the transportation business has been very serious Railroad freight on all the principal lines from New York to the West has fallen off since the beginning of the panic from 25 to 50 per cent" Especially the west-bound freight "The eastern-bound freight, which consists mainly of grain, has not been so seriously affected as yet, but unless western buyers, who are compelled to pay greenbacks for grain, are supplied by the banks with something besides certified checks, they say that the movement of produce eastward will soon cease [b]

In reducing to a minimum both the period and the effects of the suspension, all credit should be given to the clearing-house committee and to the more conservative New York banks, which upheld it in its policy of meeting from the combined reserves of the members of the association the demands made upon the interest-paying banks by their banking depositors Restrictions on cash payments in New York were confined chiefly, if not entirely, to dealings with local individual depositors; the banks elsewhere, finding that their requirements were being met, soon began to resume the ordinary course of business [c]

[a] Boston Advertiser October 1, 1873

[b] New York Tribune, October 16, 1873

[c] See p 71

As in the case of pay rolls, the impression which is derived from the examination of the newspapers of the time is, that though the dislocation of the domestic exchanges caused much inconvenience it did not lead to the serious interruption of business activities It was not until nearly the end of October, when the suspension of payments was already a thing of the past, that reports of the actual curtailment of production became a subject of daily report in the newspapers At that time the more permanent causes of business depression were beginning to make themselves felt The transition from business activity was gradual and seems to have extended beyond the close of the year There was no sudden and universal trade prostration such as occurred in November and December, 1907, lasting during the period of suspension and then followed by considerable recovery to a condition of less severe though more prolonged depression. It is, therefore, reasonable to conclude that the temporary suspension of payments in 1873 had relatively little influence upon the course of trade The weekly review of the dry goods trade in the Commercial and Financial Chronicle illustrates both the effects of suspension upon trade and the gradual appearance of trade depression, owing to the generally unsound condition of affairs throughout the country As the course of events is not within the recollection of many readers, copious extracts have been taken from it

REVIEW OF THE DRY GOODS TRADE

FRIDAY, P M , *September 26, 1873*

There has been a fair jobbing trade in progress during the past week despite the unfavorable condition of affairs in Wall street It was not expected that the monetary disturbances would have much effect upon trade in this branch, but as the panic continues and becomes more wide-spread, the difficulty in effecting exchanges with the country is acting as a check upon further operations There is a large indebtedness on the part of the country merchants to this market just now, and some fears are entertained for the safety of collections which should be coming in largely during the next thirty days Some of our largest dry goods houses have asked their customers to ship currency instead of exchange, to relieve the city banks, and if this request be granted it will prove beneficial to the trade in a very marked degree

FRIDAY, P M, *October 3, 1873*

The week opened with comparatively little business doing, owing to the prolonged financial disturbances Dealers from the interior were distrustful of the future, and limited their purchases to actual wants, which prevented the jobbing houses from doing a very heavy business and restricted the aggregate movement of the week There was no feeling of insecurity on the part of the trade here until Wednesday, when the suspension of the house of Paton & Co was announced, and the news came so unexpectedly as to create a very doubtful feeling among many of the trade regarding what might follow This firm has been long established, and had a reputation for financial stability second to none in the market It seems, from a statement by the firm, that their suspension was due solely to the monetary stringency, which prevented them from negotiating their paper for the last thirty days, and although such assistance was offered them by outside parties as would, under ordinary circumstances, have enabled them to weather the storm, they were unable to avail themselves of it now, and were, therefore, forced to suspend temporarily It is generally believed, however, that they will be able to resume business within a very brief time We hear of no other failures, nor do the trade anticipate any

FRIDAY, P M, *October 10, 1873*

Closely following our last report came the suspension of Messrs Peake, Opdycke & Co, jobbers, and although this suspension was not entirely unlooked for, its announcement did not fail to produce some effect upon the market, and to cause a slight feeling of distrust in the trade as to the stability of other houses There has been an improvement of the exchanges with the interior since our last, and this fact helps the feeling at the close The dullness and depression are looked upon by the trade as but temporary, and in view of the activity of our export trade and the liberal demand existing in the interior for all classes of goods, the probabilities are that there will be a liberal movement later on in the season Settlements between agents and jobbers are reported as being promptly made

FRIDAY, P M, *October 17, 1873*

The financial condition of the dry goods trade seems to have improved somewhat during the past week, and there is a steadier feeling than at the time of our last report Jobbers, as a rule, are meeting their paper with a good degree of promptness, and where they ask for accommodations the commission houses generally show a disposition to accommodate them The banks are rather more liberal with these houses, and are thus relieving the pressure considerably Remittances from the interior, which are pretty liberal at this season of the year, are coming forward promptly, and many of the country merchants are discounting their bills to aid jobbers through the trying period

FRIDAY, P M, *October 24, 1873*

The current week has been about the dullest of the season in the dry goods market, and there is very little news to note in connection with any line of fabrics The jobbing trade has been for the most part restricted to the requirements of retailers in near-by localities, the merchants in more distant sections having already laid in pretty full supplies for their early trade It is greatly to be regretted that the season which opened so auspiciously, and with such brilliant prospects, should have been interrupted as this has been, but a very hopeful feature is the present reduced condition of stocks, which results from the liberal sales effected early in the season Prices are now held pretty steadily, and the reduced production of nearly all classes of goods is likely to prove beneficial to the trade by preventing an accumulation of stock and a break in prices Reports from the manufacturing centers show that nearly all the mills, both cotton and woolen, are running on reduced time, while some of the largest corporations are preparing to stop entirely Collections are fair, but, while the stringency is somewhat relieved, there is far from being an easy feeling in the market

FRIDAY, P M, *October 31, 1873*

There has been no general improvement in trade during the past week, but a steady jobbing distribution was effected, and the indebtedness of buyers being met, as the rule with a good deal of promptness, the feeling and prospects were becoming rather more encouraging On Tuesday the trade were excited over the rumored suspension of the Messrs A & W Sprague, of Rhode Island, and their agents here, Messrs Hoyt, Sprague & Co Confidence was somewhat restored on Wednesday by the authoritative denial of the rumor, but was lost again on Thursday, when it became known that Messrs Hoyt, Sprague & Co had notified their bank to pay no more of their paper The Messrs Sprague, of Providence, have not, up to the hour of this writing, suspended, but are waiting the action of the Providence banks, which have promised to come to their aid with $1,000,000 Should they be thus assisted, they will probably be able to weather the storm, but otherwise their suspension seems likely The Messrs Sprague control some 280,000 spindles in Rhode Island and other States, and employ in the manufacture of textiles probably not less than 10,000 men Their interests are very extended, and are not confined to dry goods alone, although the bulk of their assets are probably in cotton mills and machinery The suspension of Messrs Hoyt, Sprague & Co was not a thorough surprise, but its occurrence has a generally depressing effect, and destroys confidence in the stability of other houses There seems to be no immediate prospects of other suspensions, payments being met with a fair degree of promptness by both retailers and jobbers

FRIDAY, P M, *November 7, 1873*

Trade has been stagnant for a week past, the attention of all classes of dealers being given more to the financial position of the market than to the transaction of business At the opening nothing definite was known relative to the A & W. Sprague Manufacturing Company, of Providence, or to their agents here, Messrs Hoyt, Sprague & Co The suspension of these concerns having become a settled fact, however, and their statements showing a large excess of good substantial assets over their liabilities, the uneasiness caused by their suspension was gradually decreased toward the close, and the interest now mainly centers upon the action of their creditors, who are endeavoring to devise some satisfactory means of settling up the affairs, so as to allow the concerns to proceed with their business There has been considerable excitement during the week over the rumors regarding Messrs H B Claflin & Co, but as this firm showed assets about 40 per cent in excess of their liabilities, and only asked their creditors for an average extension of four and one-half months on open accounts, which was promptly granted, the excitement has subsided Messrs Peake, Opdycke & Co have resumed business, and while the position of finances generally is liable to render temporary suspension necessary with any of our dry-goods houses, it seems to be the prevailing opinion that the trade, as the rule, are entirely solvent, and that no serious panic in this branch need be feared

The liberal auction offerings of last week, and the fact that importers as well as domestic houses were pressing goods upon the market at public sale, had the effect of drawing a large attendance of buyers from the interior into this market, but their presence has not been marked by any increase in the distribution through regular channels and the week has been one of extreme dullness, with prices somewhat unsettled and rather favoring buyers

It does not fall within the scope of this investigation to follow the industrial history of either this or later crises, except in so far as may be necessary for the proper understanding of banking problems After the beginning of November the course of the crisis was determined by influences entirely outside the field of banking operations The return flow of money to the banks, which began in the third week of October, was accelerated by the depres-

Name and location of bank	Date of organization	Capital stock	Receiver appointed	Total assets	Offset allowed and settled	Loss on assets compounded or sold under order of court
Washington D C	July 16 1863	$500 000	Sept 19 1873	$ 173 [illegible]	$ 80 [illegible]55	$ 65 [illegible]
Commonwealth New York N Y	July 1 1865	50 000	Sept 2 1873	66 509	368 991	589 [illegible]
Bank Petersburg Va	Sept 1 1865	400 000	Sept 25 1873	1 013 841	103 842	616 642
Petersburg Va	July 1 1865	200 000	do	272 634	3 [illegible]25	146 764
Mansfield Ohio	May 24 1864	100 000	Oct 18 1873	296 910	5 735	182 231
[illegible] Banking Association New Orleans La	May 2 1871	600 000	Oct 23 1873	1 431 055	8 964	715 564
Carlisle Pa	July 7 1863	50 000	Oct 4 1873	115 304	7 008	5 291
Anderson Ind	July 31 1863	50 000	Nov 23 1873	335 [illegible]	10 [illegible] 0	235 127
Topeka Kans	Aug 23 1866	100 000	Dec 10 1873	203 098	26 951	118 083
Norfolk Va	Feb 23 186[illegible]	100 000	June 3 1874	217 912	2 101	55 [illegible]

(To face page 81.)

Name and location of bank	d.
First National Bank, Washington D C	5
National Bank of the Commonwealth, New York N Y	
Merchants' National Bank, Petersburg, Va	
First National Bank, Petersburg, Va	
First National Bank, Mansfield, Ohio	
New Orleans National Banking Association New Orleans, La	
First National Bank, Carlisle, Pa	
First National Bank, Anderson, Ind	
First National Bank, Topeka, Kans	
First National Bank Norfolk, Va	

6158—10 (To face page 81.)

sion in general business, which diminished requirements for its use in general circulation The returns to the Comptroller of the Currency of the condition of the banks on December 26 found them with a reserve $28,000,000 above that held on September 12, and greater than they had held at any time since June, 1871. There were also few banking failures either during or after the first outbreak of the crisis, and none of them were of great importance.

The accompanying table, taken from the more comprehensive tables which regularly appear in the reports of the Comptroller of the Currency, shows the results of the liquidation of the banks which failed during the panic and the year which followed

All of the failures which occurred during the crisis were, as was observed by the Comptroller of the Currency, due to "the criminal mismanagement of their officers or to the neglect or violation of the national-bank act on the part of their directors."[a]

It would not be difficult to find many quite normal periods during which both the number of failures and the losses of creditors were far more considerable than in 1873 The solvency of the banks was at no time in question The defects in the banking system which were disclosed were in its organization It was made painfully evident that there was nowhere any reserve power with which to meet an emergency Moreover, the banks were in what was for them a normal condition of strength at the time The breakdown of the credit

[a] Report of the Comptroller of the Currency, 1873, p xxxv

machinery of the country could not be attributed to any unaccustomed lack of preparation The defects which appeared were characteristic of the system, and they have reappeared with similar consequences upon every occasion of severe financial strain down to the present. The purely banking aspects of the crisis of 1873 may, therefore, be regarded as having practical significance, similar to that which may be derived from more recent experience

ANALYSIS OF BANK RETURNS

In order to avoid an interruption of the narrative of the course of the crisis during what may be called its "banking stage," detailed analysis of the condition of the banks has been deferred for separate treatment. It is a matter which deserves particular attention, since, as has already been stated, the statistical data is far more extensive than that which we have for the later crises of 1893 and 1907, and influences affecting the position of the banks were sufficiently similar in the three instances to render any conclusions at which we may arrive from a study of the earlier crisis of something more than merely antiquarian interest. Abstracts of the regular return of September 12 and the two special returns for October 13 and November 1 are presented in the accompanying table The special reports included only the more important items of bank reserves and liabilities, and consequently the statements do not balance That of November 1 is of importance because it shows the rapid recovery of the banks, but requires no special analysis Attention will be given chiefly to the changes which

Abstracts of the reports of condition of national banks on September [illegible], October [illegible], and November [illegible], arranged by [illegible]

SEPTEMBER [illegible]

	New York City (... banks)	Other redemption cities (... banks)
RESOURCES.		
Loans and discounts	[illegible]	[illegible]
Overdrafts	[illegible]	[illegible]
United States bonds to secure circulation	[illegible]	[illegible]
United States bonds to secure deposits	[illegible]	[illegible]
United States bonds and securities on hand	[illegible]	[illegible]
Other stocks, bonds, and mortgages	[illegible]	[illegible]
Due from redeeming and reserve agents	[illegible]	[illegible]
Due from other national banks	[illegible]	[illegible]
Due from other banks and bankers	[illegible]	[illegible]
Real estate, furniture, and fixtures	[illegible]	[illegible]
Current expenses	[illegible]	[illegible]
Premiums	[illegible]	[illegible]
Checks and other cash items	[illegible]	[illegible]
Bills of other national banks	[illegible]	[illegible]
Bills of State banks	[illegible]	[illegible]
Fractional currency	[illegible]	[illegible]
Specie	[illegible]	[illegible]
Legal tender notes	[illegible]	[illegible]
United States certificates of deposit	[illegible]	[illegible]
Clearing-house certificates	[illegible]	75 000 00
Total	[illegible]	480 356 658 65
LIABILITIES.		
Capital stock	[illegible]	64 985 00
Surplus fund	[illegible]	[illegible]
Undivided profits	[illegible]	[illegible]
National bank notes outstanding	[illegible]	[illegible]
State bank notes outstanding	[illegible]	[illegible]
Dividends unpaid	[illegible]	[illegible]
Individual deposits	[illegible]	[illegible]
United States deposits	[illegible]	[illegible]
Deposits of United States disbursing officers	[illegible]	[illegible]
Due to national banks	[illegible]	[illegible]
Due to other banks and bankers	[illegible]	[illegible]
Notes and bills rediscounted	[illegible]	[illegible]
Bills payable	[illegible]	[illegible]
Total	[illegible]	480 356 658 65

SEPT. [illegible]

	Country banks
RESOURCES.	
Loans and discounts	[illegible]
Overdrafts	[illegible]
United States bonds to secure circulation	[illegible]
United States bonds to secure deposits	[illegible]
United States bonds on hand	[illegible]
Other stocks, bonds, and mortgages	[illegible]
Due from redeeming and reserve agents	[illegible]
Due from other national banks	[illegible]
Due from other banks and bankers	[illegible]
Real estate, furniture, and fixtures	[illegible]
Current expenses	[illegible]
Premiums	[illegible]
Checks and other cash items	[illegible]
Bills of other national banks	[illegible]
Bills of State banks	[illegible]
Fractional currency	[illegible]
Specie	[illegible]
Legal tender notes	[illegible]
United States certificates of deposit	[illegible]
Total	[illegible]
LIABILITIES.	
Capital stock	[illegible]
Surplus fund	[illegible]
Undivided profits	[illegible]
National bank notes outstanding	[illegible]
State bank notes outstanding	[illegible]
Dividends unpaid	[illegible]
Individual deposits	[illegible]
United States deposits	[illegible]
Deposits of United States disbursing officers	[illegible]
Due to national banks	[illegible]
Due to other banks and bankers	[illegible]
Notes and bills rediscounted	[illegible]
Bills payable	[illegible]
Total	[illegible]

OCTOBER [illegible] AND NOVEMBER [illegible]

	New York City (Oct.)	New York City (Nov.) (48 banks)	Other redemption cities (Oct.) (79 banks)	Other redemption cities (Nov.) (79 banks)	Country banks (Oct.) (1,346 banks)	Country banks (Nov.)
RESOURCES.						
Loans and discounts	[illegible]	[illegible]	[illegible]	[illegible]	[illegible]	[illegible]
Overdrafts	[illegible]	[illegible]	[illegible]	[illegible]	[illegible]	[illegible]
United States bonds on hand	[illegible]	[illegible]	993 850 00	[illegible]	[illegible]	[illegible]
Other stocks, bonds, and mortgages	[illegible]	[illegible]	[illegible]	[illegible]	[illegible]	[illegible]
Due from approved reserve agents	[illegible]	[illegible]	[illegible]	[illegible]	[illegible]	[illegible]
Due from other banks and bankers	[illegible]	[illegible]	[illegible]	[illegible]	[illegible]	[illegible]
Real estate, furniture, and fixtures	[illegible]	[illegible]	[illegible]	[illegible]	[illegible]	[illegible]
Specie	[illegible]	[illegible]	[illegible]	[illegible]	[illegible]	[illegible]
Legal tender notes	[illegible]	[illegible]	[illegible]	[illegible]	[illegible]	[illegible]
United States certificates of deposit	[illegible]	[illegible]	[illegible]	[illegible]	[illegible]	[illegible]
Total	[illegible]	[illegible]	[illegible]	[illegible]	[illegible]	[illegible]
LIABILITIES.						
Capital stock	[illegible]	[illegible]	[illegible]	[illegible]	[illegible]	[illegible]
Circulation outstanding	[illegible]	[illegible]	[illegible]	[illegible]	[illegible]	[illegible]
Deposits	[illegible]	[illegible]	[illegible]	[illegible]	[illegible]	[illegible]
Total	[illegible]	[illegible]	[illegible]	[illegible]	[illegible]	[illegible]

	Oct 13 (179 banks
CES	
	$222,351,70
	25,182,23
and	1,695,65
mortgages	4,959,71
leeming and reserve	
	16,118,68
and bankers	12,578 34
ouse	17,066,38
	4,199,30
	585 01
	1 714,69
	1,566 24
	28,242 16
of deposit	3,150,00
ficates	9 547 47
	348,957 62
TIES	
	126,172,565
ding	78,090,059
	148 081,974
kers	46 017 750
	398,362,348

occurred between September 12 and October 13 The following table shows the changes in loans for the banks as a whole for the three groups of banks:

[In millions]

	Country banks	Reserve city banks	Banks in New York	Total
Sept 12, 1873	$478 5	$262 5	$199 2	$940 2
Oct 13, 1873	455 8	247 5	179 1	882 4
Nov 1, 1873	442 0	242 2	169 1	853 4

The contraction of loans to October 13 may be taken as representing the extent of contraction which was due to and which in turn contributed to the severe financial strain of the crisis The further contraction to November 1 represented the diminishing requirements of business owing to trade depression [a] By the banks as a whole loans were reduced by $58,000,000 before October 13, or slightly more than 5 per cent. This contraction was general, both the country banks and those in reserve cities showing a contraction of about 5 per cent and those in New York a more considerable contraction of 10 per cent The most severe contraction among city banks was in Chicago, where, doubtless owing to the decision of the banks not to issue clearing-house loan certificates, loans were reduced from $25,300,000 on September 12 to $19,000,000 on October 13,

In this, as in other American crises, a somewhat exaggerated opinion became current as to the extent to which the banks required borrowers to liquidate their loans.

[a] During the last two weeks of October there were many newspaper reports of a more liberal loan policy being adopted by the banks

Difficulty experienced in disposing of commercial paper through note brokers and the high rates for call loans seem to have been the grounds for this erroneous impression. Under our banking system borrowers unable to dispose of their paper through note brokers in times of crisis resort more largely to the particular banks which hold their accounts than is usual at other times This shifting of loan relationships gives rise to an impression of wholesale contraction which the statistics of the total loans of the banks show to be unfounded

In the particular case of call loans also contraction is more apparent than real. On September 12 of the total loans of $199,000,000 of the New York banks, $60,800,000 were demand loans On October 13 these loans had been reduced only $4,600,000, about 7½ per cent; while the $139,000,000 of other loans had been reduced to $123,000,000, nearly 12 per cent. These figures would seem to show that call loans are even less liquid than other classes of loans in an emergency, a view which, though wholly at variance with generally accepted banking opinion, will be borne out by our experience in later crises [a] Explanation is simple When a few banks demand the payment of call loans, the brokers to whom they are principally made secure loans elsewhere, and the banks calling the loans are paid The total volume of call loans is not much changed Within narrow limits it may be possible to reduce the aggregate of such loans by the sale of securities to persons able to pay for them outright It is also possible to secure additional margins from customers

---

[a] See p 301

for whom brokers are carrying securities. But when all banks call their loans, they cease to be convertible to any considerable extent into money Purchasers who might be able to pay for securities outright become frightened, and little or no contraction takes place, while panic and alarm are generally increased The contraction of call loans is indeed wholly incommensurate with the commotion in the stock market which characterizes our crises There are only two kinds of loans which can be regarded as in any considerable measure liquid during an emergency Loans made to those engaged in the final stages of production of commodities which are required for individual consumption may be reduced, as such producers curtail production and dispose of their supplies of the finished product Such curtailment in production, however, is likely to make it necessary for producers at the earlier stages to increase loans on account of inability to make expected sales Holdings of foreign bills are probably the only asset which may be liquidated without serious inconvenience to the country involved in the throes of a crisis, but this is a kind of investment which has not been held by our banks After all, it should be remembered that the primary object of liquid assets is to enable particular banks to meet unusual requirements in ordinary times, not to provide the banks as a whole with money in emergencies It is then the business of the banks to continue and even to increase their loans to the business community, and to rely upon their reserves of cash to meet money requirements.

From this point it will be of advantage to study the operations of the banks by groups, and attention is first called to the condition of the country banks as shown in the following table

RESOURCES

[In millions.]

	Sept. 12	Oct. 13	Nov. 1
Loans	$478.0	$455.0	$442.0
Specie	2.0	2.0	2.0
Legals	45.0	48.0	49.0
Bank notes	8.5	9.8	9.0
Due from reserve agents	64.0	38.0	36.0
Due from other banks	21.0	17.0	18.0
LIABILITIES			
Circulation	$233.0	$235.0	$236.0
Deposits	296.0	251.0	239.0
Due to banks	13.0	19.0	15.0

General deposits of the country banks between September 12 and October 13 were reduced by $45,000,000, of which $23,000,000 are accounted for by loan contraction and $8,000,000 by the increase in circulation and the amounts due to other banks. At the same time the banks had actually increased their cash holdings by $3,000,000 in the form of legal-tender notes and $1,000,000 in the notes of other banks They had shifted more than the entire burden of supplying the demands of their depositors for cash, as far as they were met at all, upon the other banks. Deposits with reserve agents were reduced from $64,000,000 to $38,000,000, and amounts due from other banks had also been reduced by $4,000,000. The country banks can not be held guiltless of unnecessarily strengthening themselves and causing needless strain in the money centers [a] On the other hand, the experience of previous years afforded ample evidence that the country banks would adopt this policy, and the city banks should have held themselves in readiness to meet the obligations which they had incurred in becoming reserve agents.

The following table shows the condition of the reserve city banks, not including those of New York·

RESOURCES

[In millions]

	Sept 12	Oct 13	Nov 1
Loans	$262 0	$245 0	$244 0
Specie	3 0	3 0	3 0
Legals	36 0	31 0	36 0
Bank notes	5 0	4 0	5 0
Due from reserve agents	32 0	16 0	16 0
Due from other banks	14 0	12 0	14 0
Clearing-house exchanges	21 0	17 0	21 0
Clearing-house loan certificates	....	9 5	11 4

LIABILITIES

	Sept 12	Oct 13	Nov 1
Circulation	$78 0	$78 0	$78 0
Deposits	175 0	148 0	151 0
Due to other banks	59 0	46 0	50 0

The reduction in deposits, amounting to $40,000,000 ($27,000,000 in the case of general deposits and $13,000,000 in the case of bankers' deposits), was due in part to loan contraction of $17,000,000, to a reduction of $4,000,000 in clearing-house exchanges, and of $2,000,000 in the amount due other banks, a total of $23,000,000 In cash and bank notes these banks suffered a loss of only

[a] But see what is said on the subject on p 305

$5,000,000, while they drew on their reserve agents in New York for one-half of their deposits, which fell from $32,000,000 to $16,000,000 In cash reserves the reserve city banks slightly increased the ratio to their demand liabilities Hardly more than the country banks did these banks rely on their own stores of cash to meet the emergency. There were, of course, wide differences among the banks of the different cities as to the extent to which they used their own reserves and reduced deposits in New York. The most serious offender was Chicago, the banks of which positively increased their cash and bank-note holdings from $5,700,000 to $6,300,000 and reduced their New York balances from $3,500,000 to $1,600,000.

From the preceding tables the extent to which the New York banks alone were required to meet the emergency has been evident enough, but it will be even more clearly seen from the following statement of the condition of the New York banks

RESOURCES

[In millions]

	Sept 12	Oct 13	Nov 1
Loans	$199 0	$179 0	$168 0
Specie	14 5	10 0	11 0
Legals	32 0	6 5	15 6
Bank notes	2 6	4 0	5 5
Due from other banks	18 0	16 6	17 3
Clearing-house exchanges	68 0	41 0	57 0
Clearing-house loan certificates	-------	16 2	15 9

LIABILITIES

Circulation	$27 0	$27 0	$27 0
Deposits	168 0	131 0	149 0
Due to other banks	90 3	55 4	54 2

General deposits were reduced by $37,000,000 and bankers' deposits by $35,000,000. Of this total of $72,000,000 some $27,000,000 are accounted for by the smaller clearing-house exchanges and $20,000,000 by the contraction of loans The remaining $25,000,000 are rather more than accounted for by the loss of $4,500,000 in specie and of some $25,000,000 in legal-tender notes. The reduction in general deposits may be reasonably supposed to be explained by the loan contraction and the smaller clearing-house exchanges, that of bankers' balances was due to the shipment of currency, a conclusion which is in accord with the statements of the clearing-house loan committee regarding the matter [a]

THE WISE POLICY OF THE NEW YORK BANKS

In comparison with the banks in the reserve cities, the New York banks responded remarkably well to the demands made upon them, and if comparison be made with the hoarding policy pursued by the New York banks themselves during the crises of 1893 and 1907, the contrast is both astonishing and disheartening The explanation of the difference is simple It was due to the adoption of the provision for equalizing reserves and to the bold and fearless fashion in which the clearing-house committee exercised the power which was placed in its hands. In consenting to the arrangement the conservatively managed banks exhibited a praiseworthy willingness to act for the common good, inasmuch as the demands for money were almost wholly upon the

[a] See p 93

banks which had accumulated bankers' deposits by the offer of interest, and which were at the same time the greatest lenders on the stock exchange The clearing-house committee determined to meet the obligation of a few of their members to the banks of the country, and to accomplish this purpose took money from the reserves of the banks whose business was of a purely local character. From about the middle of October proposals to bring the arrangement to an end were urged by some of the banks, but the committee manfully opposed such action until the beginning of November, when a common policy was no longer necessary During the continuance of the arrangement the banks were converted, to all intents and purposes, into a central bank, which, although without power to issue notes, was in other respects more powerful than a European central bank, because it included virtually all the banking power of the city

The situation which confronted the New York banks at the beginning of the crisis and the methods of handling it are clearly set forth in the report of a special committee of the clearing house which was appointed during the crisis to consider reforms in banking methods. It is hardly too much to say that this report is the ablest document which has ever appeared in the course of our banking history It was largely, if not wholly, the work of the chairman of the committee, George S Coe, who for more than forty years was a leading figure in the financial world of New York He is said to have devised the clearing-house loan certificate, and he took a leading part in the formation of the banking syndicate which took successive blocks of government bonds in the latter part of 1861. The report is so important, both in its narrative of certain aspects of the crisis and on account of the reforms suggested, that it has seemed proper to insert it in the text rather than to relegate it to an appendix.

NEW YORK CLEARING-HOUSE REPORT, NOVEMBER 11, 1873

The committee appointed by the New York Clearing-House Association "to carefully consider and report what reforms are required in the practical operations of banks with each other and with the public to increase the security of their business," respectfully reports

That in order to reach the object sought by the resolution it is necessary briefly to review the condition and practical working of the banking system in this city before the commencement of the late panic

Banks are the natural depositories of the current capital of the nation, passing into and out of active industry and commerce The balances held by them are for the time specially reserved by their owners from permanent investment and kept subject to immediate command They constitute a main portion of the wealth of the community which is not yet ready to be consolidated into fixed capital or immovable forms The custodians of such funds are consequently bound by the very nature of their trust to preserve them in their integrity and to apply them only in such ways as will prevent them from falling into inactivity, and also to hold such proportion in ready cash in hand as long experience has proved to be necessary to meet immediate demands in every possible emergency And it may be confidently affirmed that a bank or banker who faithfully meets all these obligations renders a full equivalent for any benefits which can be honorably derived from the custody of such a trust

No institution can, in the long run, purchase deposits of money payable on demand of the owners and at the same time secure to itself a just and proper compensation for the business without violating some of the conditions indispensable to the public safety It must either use them in ways that are illegitimate and perilous or use them in excess This has been abundantly proved by innumerable instances in years past, and the practice of paying interest for such deposits was unanimously condemned by the bank officers in 1857 as one of the principal causes of the panic at that period, for the reasons given in a printed report, of which a copy is annexed hereto, and to which, with the consequent resolutions of the associated banks then adopted, your committee most respectfully invite attention

The creation of many new institutions, since the late civil war began, which have considered it expedient to purchase public favor, and thus divert to themselves business from established channels, has revived the custom of paying interest upon deposits, and has also led some of the older banks, in self-defense, to yield more or less to the pressure in the same direction, while it has induced others to adopt newer methods of obtaining patronage equally pernicious

And thus a sharp and degrading competition has not only prevailed among banks in this city, but has been excited, as a necessary consequence, in other places, where the far-reaching enterprise of some of our associates has led them in pursuit of business, not only from institutions but from all classes of society Banks throughout the country have been aroused to enlist in the same destructive practices toward each other and in defense of their various localities A premium has been unnecessarily given for business which, left to itself, would fall without cost into its natural channels and adjust itself to such localities as the convenience of the people and the best interests of the country require

Without such rivalry the resources of the nation would be so diffused among the banks as to give increased financial strength and stability to every part, and not only remove a great cause of irritation, but add to the comfort, efficiency, and profit of all

The evil results of paying interest upon current deposits, avowed when the internal commerce of the nation was conducted upon a specie basis, are greatly aggravated when it is carried on by an irredeemable currency, which has a fixed and invariable volume, and which flows to and from the commercial center with the changes of the seasons Such a currency is superabundant in summer, and instead of being then naturally absorbed and diminished by redemption, it accumulates in banks, which can not keep it idle without loss of the interest paid to its owners Legitimate commerce does not then demand it It is still subject to instant call There is consequently no resource but to loan it in Wall street upon stocks and bonds, in doing which so much of the nation's movable capital passes for the time into fixed and immovable forms of investment and its essential character is instantly changed Loans are made with facility upon securities which have no strictly commercial quality, new and unnecessary enterprises are encouraged, wild speculations are stimulated, and the thoughtless and unwary are betrayed into ruinous operations The autumnal demand finds the resources of the nation unnaturally diverted from their legitimate channels, and they can only be turned back with difficulty and public embarrassment Such has been our well-known experience year after year Interest upon money has, as a consequence, fluctuated widely from 3 and 4 per cent per annum in summer to 15 and 20 per cent in the fall and winter upon commercial paper, and upon stocks at times to one-half and even 1 per cent a day Vicissitudes like these are utterly destructive to all legitimate commerce, and institutions whose operations tend to such results are enemies to the public welfare

Deposits which are derived from strictly commercial operations can not fluctuate so widely from time to time as to produce disturbance in the community, and banks which confine their business to them as they naturally arise are always reliable and regular in their treatment of their dealers and can be conducted with ease and comfort to their managers and safety to the public On the contrary, deposits which are purchased by payment of interest or otherwise, and which must, therefore, of necessity be largely loaned "on demand," are the cause of continual agitation and solicitude to those who hold them in charge They are certain to be withdrawn at the season of the year and at the moment most inconvenient to the banks and to their dealers This fact is best illustrated by the following figures

The average deposits of the 60 clearing-house banks for ten weeks from July 5 to September 6 were		$232, 228, 000
The lowest amount reached since the panic was		143 170, 000
Showing a total reduction of		89, 058, 000
Of the above amount during the ten weeks, 12 interest-paying banks held	$111, 585, 000	
The lowest total reached by them since the panic	52, 669 000	
Showing a loss in 12 banks of		58, 916, 000
In the other 48 banks		30, 142, 000

and were it not for the fact that several of the 48 banks are more or less involved in the same practice, this disparity would be still more apparent

When the late panic commenced, the sixty banks composing the New York clearing house were indebted for about $200,000,000 of deposits Of this amount three institutions (paying interest to their country depositors) owed about $50,000,000, and including these, 12 banks of similar character owed obout $100,000,000, that is to say, 12 institutions held one-half of the aggregate deposits, and the other 48, their associates, the other half The proportionate reserve of legal-tender notes in the associated banks was also greatly in favor of the latter number, for the obvious reason, that banks which pay interest upon money can least bear to have any amount of it idle The active demand first came, as it usually comes, for that portion of deposits due to country banks, who, in addition to their annual necessities, had been disturbed by failures of several city bankers, holding large balances of money due to the interior These deposits were to a great extent loaned upon stocks and bonds in Wall street, payable "on call," with the confident belief that they were there earning more than the interest paid for securing them, and were available as promised But, from the very nature of the case, the rapid withdrawal of deposits from the banks made the 'call" from every direction simultaneous, and closed every resource from which the "street" derived its power to respond Borrowers upon stocks were deprived both of their facilities of borrowing and of all power to sell their securities The necessary result occurred Banks which found themselves in this dilemma had no alternative but to ask the assistance of their associates, and the conflagration was so rapid and violent that every consideration of fraternal sympathy, self-preservation, and public safety compelled a general and earnest cooperation, and the majority, who had for long years conducted their business upon sound principles, and who had patiently submitted to the loss of valuable accounts, drawn from them by their associates, by practices against which they had continually protested, instantly responded to the call by placing their resources at command of those who had done so much toward producing the calamity, making common cause, the weak with the strong, to avert a universal catastrophe.

An expedient was found by which the stronger banks placed themselves under the unequal burden and equalized the pressure by gathering in their resources and placing them at the disposal of the weaker, who were thus furnished with means to meet the demands of their depositors and to save themselves from public exposure and their dealers in city and country from disaster and ruin Meanwhile the public confidence in institutions had become so greatly impaired that the "legal-tender reserve" was reduced from $34,000,000, on September 20, to $5,800,000 on October 14—an amount of ready money never before paid out in the same time Interior banks, whose ready means in hand had always been merely nominal, but whose resources consisted chiefly of credits upon the books of interest-paying banks in the principal cities, were under the necessity of calling back their deposits in a medium never before required, and to these the associated banks were asked to respond, as well as to the demands of timid dealers at home

Your committee take this occasion to congratulate the associated banks upon the liberal and excellent spirit in which this crisis has been met, and upon the happy escape from a most imminent danger which threatened them, and with them the country at large It is not too much to say that, had it been less boldly, promptly, or unanimously encountered, the results must have been more disastrous and widespread than any that have occurred during the present generation

While the banks have intelligently recognized the errors of their associates, by which the late financial complications were aggravated and the community imperiled, there has been no disposition whatever to deal in harsh reproaches On the contrary, the magnitude of the trust is deeply felt, and the utmost good feeling prevails, an earnest desire and a unanimous determination are expressed on every side to reform existing abuses and to reorganize the clearing house upon a basis of mutual support and uniformity of business

Late experience has again demonstrated the fact that the banks in the association are necessarily dependent one upon the other in times of peril, as well as in the trusts which the large operations of the clearing house daily impose, and that the entire body inevitably suffers from the errors and indiscretions of a single member No institution, therefore, has a moral right to conduct its affairs with the public in defiance of the general conviction of its associates, or to introduce private terms of dealing with its customers which are in conflict with the best interests of all Bank officers have no right to be sharp personal competitors for public patronage, nor merely laborers for dividends on behalf of a limited constituency They are in a most important sense trustees for the whole community, and public administrators of great interests, which forbid the least departure from principles which long experience has sanctified

With these general considerations, your committee proceed to the more practical question submitted to them, viz "What reforms are required in the operations of banks with each other and the public to increase the security of their business," and, first, and most prominent, they recommend that the banks entirely discontinue the payment of interest upon deposits, whether directly or indirectly

THE RESERVE

The requirement of a "legal reserve" is now engaging special public attention, and much impatience is expressed at the law which compels banks to hold a definite ratio of legal-tender notes to liabilities The practical difficulty consists in attaching a rigid and inflexible rule of law to a mobile fund, which is held for the purpose of meeting sudden contingencies, and which is, therefore, in its very nature, a variable quantity It is impossible clearly to prescribe by statute the circumstances or the exact periods during which the reserve should be increased or diminished There seems an intrinsic absurdity in a law requiring that a "reserve" must be always kept, which was created on purpose to be used, or that a bank officer who draws upon his reserve, under circumstances for which it was intended, is false to the oath which he takes to obey the law But the fact that a military commander can not be definitely instructed when he may employ his reserve force, is not regarded as a reason why that important portion of an army organization should be abandoned, or be reduced in number or efficiency So long as bank debts are subject to cash payments, so long must the obligation be either imposed or assumed of keeping sufficient cash in hand to pay whatever portion can possibly be presented It must always be remembered that in the absence of any important central institution, such as exists in other commercial nations, the associated banks are the last resort in this country, in times of financial extremity, and upon their stability and sound conduct the national prosperity greatly depends In claiming for them that in taking faithful care of the active capital of the nation with which they are intrusted they render a full and equitable compensation for its proper use, your committee point to the consequent and paramount duty of the banks to hold such proportion of that fund in actual possession in cash as the extremest needs may demand

It has been suggested that the federal principle which our association has applied to banking, through the use of "loan certificates" in two important crises, might be used effectively in regular business, by keeping two separate accounts, viz, "cash" and "bank credit," each payable in kind, to avoid a "run" upon banks in times of panic, and much speculative study throughout the world is given to the question how the idea of "clearing," as used through banks, may be indefinitely extended to effect the smaller exchanges of the community, so as to dispense in a great measure with large reserves of ready money But in the present condition of economic science, and especially in this important exigency, your committee recommend that we accept the teachings of practical experience, and pursue the well-beaten track which trade and commerce universally recognize

Experience of older commercial nations has shown that the volume of "reserve" should be in the proportion of one-fourth to one-third the direct liabilities of a bank, and whenever it is there found receding from this amount restrictive measures are taken to replenish it Our own association in 1857 established a minimum ratio of 20 per cent in coin, which was for the time carefully observed, and again in 1860 increased this minimum to 25 per cent The present abnormal condition of the currency increases the difficulty inherent in this subject The law permits the reserve to consist of coin and legal-tender notes, and at the same time compels banks to receive as money the notes of national banks, which in legal payments are not money, so that for practical uses as "reserve," we are troubled by a species of money which is above, and by another which is below, the standard quality And it affords a striking commentary upon our present anomalous condition that the money of the world, which is now freely coming into the country from legitimate commerce, can not be absorbed into our banking system, but is necessarily repelled as a cause of serious embarrassment The opinion that has largely prevailed that because the business of this country is now conducted upon a basis of irredeemable paper, that therefore there can be no suspension of payments, has been most effectually dispelled, and the contrary is established, that a currency, from its nature, limited in volume, is subject to sudden and special dangers, and therefore requires special protection Recent experience has shown how rapidly $34,000,000 may be withdrawn from our associated institutions, and for practical uses how inadequate is the reserve held by country banks That reserve, as fixed by law, is 15 per cent of liabilities, and three-fifths of it may consist of deposits in banks in the larger cities, who may subdivide it by placing one-half their own reserves in banks in the city of New York, where again it is subject to a further reduction, from the fact that these last are only required to hold 25 per cent of their own liabilities, of which these deposits form part The aggregate held by all the national banks of the United States does not finally much exceed 10 per cent of their direct liabilities, without reference to the large amount of debt which is otherwise dependent upon the same reserves When we consider that a portion of this final reserve may consist of coin, which, under present circumstances, has no practical power in an extremity, and a further fact that the interest-paying banks, which have always held the larger part of those reserves, have been forced by their position continually to disregard the law, it is manifest that the requirement, in its real operation, has not worked against the public welfare, or against the true interests of the banks themselves

The abandonment of the practice of paying interest upon deposits will remove a great inducement to divide these reserves between cash in hand and deposits in cities, and make the banks throughout the country what they should always be, financial outposts to strengthen the general situation The associated banks of New York, the ultimate resource in financial emergencies, are deprived by usury laws of the power, which is so effectively used by the principal banks in Europe, of protecting or augmenting their resources by adjusting the rate of interest to the necessities of the occasion—a power which, if practicable, Congress might safely confer upon the clearing-house committee, in consultation with the Secretary of the Treasury, with great advantage to the country, as also the power of deciding when the time or the emergency has arisen in which the public interest requires a relaxation of a rigid legal requirement in respect to the reserve to be held by banks in New York City

If the legal or financial necessity exists to maintain a certain reserve, it is manifestly the duty of every institution to carry its just proportion, and no bank, whether incorporated under national or state law, can honorably evade its full share of this burden

Your committee therefore recommend that all the associated banks, while they strictly follow the requirements of the national currency act, by keeping on hand, either in coin or legal-tender notes, an amount not less than 25 per cent of their total liabilities to the public, be required always to hold at least 15 per cent in legal-tender notes, subject only to such modifications as the clearing-house committee may, from time to time, unanimously determine

A suggestion has been made, which your committee consider worthy of notice, because it has heretofore proved an important restriction to excessive expansion, and because it may assist in preventing many of the evils referred to, that no institution be allowed to loan more than two and a half times its capital and surplus

CERTIFICATION OF CHECKS

The practice of certifying checks upon banks as "good" has proved a great public convenience, and has for that reason grown into extensive use

Your committee approach its consideration with some embarrassment. The custom originated in the natural inquiry of bank tellers respecting the standing and credit of their dealers, and for many years it had little significance, otherwise than as giving clerical information Checks so marked were not regarded as binding upon institutions in the nature of an official acceptance, and were, therefore, not entered upon their books It was only since about the year 1850 that a new and influential institution deemed it expedient to define the character of an act then vague and uncertain, by charging such checks to the accounts of their drawers, since when they have been legally regarded as formal obligations, and have become the medium of the most important transactions If such writing certified to a real fact, that the bank actually had in possession, and due from it to the drawer of the check, the stated sum which it thus agreed to transfer to another party, no possible injury, but great good, would ensue But when a bank binds itself to transfer what it has not, but only expects to have, it assumes for its dealers, without reason, all the contingencies incident to human transactions, and places its shareholders under perils which they never intended to assume

The power of certifying checks is necessarily intrusted to clerks or subordinate officers, who are employed to perform the ordinary and more mechanical duties of the bank, and who are supposed to be strictly limited in giving to every dealer only what has before been received from him And the power of bestowing credit is reserved for abler and more experienced men, themselves personally identified with the interests they administer, who gravely deliberate upon every transaction, and decide with the light of their united wisdom But the practice of certifying uncovered checks, as pursued in some institutions, entirely reverses this established order, and while the responsible council is carefully deliberating over smaller credits, a noncommissioned officer is freely bestowing them in larger volumes, without security, upon comparatively irresponsible men. So extensively has this practice been pursued by several institutions that the amount of such checks, which have passed daily through the clearing house, has reached in some instances to twice and three times, and in one or two, to four and five times their capital stock, and this through long periods of time

Every bank in the association is directly involved in the risks attending this practice It multiplies excessively the sums which such institutions pass through the clearing house, and the consequent balances of the exchanges with their associates, which the capital of such banks can never adequately guarantee

The most striking commentary upon the danger of this practice was afforded during the late panic by the dealer of a bank who had largely received such favors and who, seeing by its application to others that his own checks were in peril, declined, under advice of counsel, to cover them by a deposit until otherwise assured that the bank could respond to these very obligations

No sufficient reason, in the opinion of your committee, can be given why a corporation should place itself without compensation and special security between two parties dealing with each other and become the guarantor of either in transactions entirely personal to themselves simply because one or the other is a depositor in the institution We have already stated that the safe custody of money payable "on demand" is full compensation for its legitimate use, and the risks attending such a business are all that properly appertain to the profession of a banker And if the rule be invariably observed of certifying checks only when the drawer has the full amount at his credit in the bank no one can be injured or offended when he is treated in all respects like every other of his fellow dealers The restriction suggested will work favorably to every interest—to the banks, their shareholders, and their associates—by diminishing the risks now so widely incurred, and it also conforms to and confirms the law which Congress has established upon this subject in respect to national banks

Your committee therefore recommend that in no case shall a check or other obligation be certified by a bank unless the amount of it is first found regularly entered to the credit of the dealer upon the books of the institution

INDIRECT EXCHANGES

A custom has grown up among the associated banks, and has greatly increased within the last few years, of engrafting upon themselves and thus admitting to the benefits of the clearing house, other institutions and individuals who, while not eligible to regular membership, participate in all its advantages without sharing its expenses, incurring its responsibilities, or submitting to its regulations Over all these the association has no possible control They consist of banks and corporations of various character and objects in this city and vicinity, many of whom attract to themselves deposits of active capital from the commercial community by extraordinary rewards and use it for purposes and enterprises which are illegitimate in regular banking The associated banks thus find themselves surrounded by diligent competitors in their proper business, which increase their risks, while they lean upon them for support By keeping a satisfactory balance in bank, for which interest is frequently paid, these institutions avoid the necessity of any money reserve whatever and not only invest all the resources at their command in profitable or unprofitable enterprises, but have a claim upon their patron bank for assistance in time of need The banks are thus deprived of a large portion of commercial deposits that would naturally come to them and incur increased and indefinite risks, and the public are unconsciously placing their ready means where they are subject to unusual hazards

Any bank in the city worthy of public confidence may become a regular member of the Clearing-House Association, and the banks which compose it are bound, in duty to themselves and to the public, to withhold the special support of this body from any who can not submit to or safely pass through the necessary examination which entitles them to credit And your committee can see no valid reason why banks outside this city should receive the benefit of the New York clearing house when they share none of its burdens and submit to none of its regulations

They therefore recommend that no bank shall receive upon deposit from its city dealers checks or drafts other than upon banks members of this association

RECEIVING OUT-OF-TOWN CHECKS AS CASH DEPOSITS

Among the various devices introduced to attract mercantile accounts and to secure deposits of country banks is that of receiving and crediting immediately as cash checks and drafts upon places outside this city, a practice which was commenced as a special inducement by one institution, but which, as the natural consequence of unfair competition, has been followed and extended by others until it embraces points far and near throughout the whole country It has been carried on with such utter disregard of the laws of exchange and of the time necessary to effect returns that the former and regular methods of making payments in and remittances to this city is greatly changed Interior merchants finding that checks upon their own localities are readily accepted as cash in New York prefer that mode of payment, and they are naturally encouraged to do so by their banks at home, who receive the benefit, so that our own institutions are not only deprived of deposits which by the laws of trade naturally belong to them, but they are daily encumbered by a miscellaneous mass of checks, which occasion serious embarrassment, loss of time, great risk, clerical labor, and expense of collecting, entirely caused by this unnecessary diversion of business from its natural courses Some of the interest-paying institutions which have by this expedient enlarged their correspondence with interior banks have, with them, adopted peculiar methods of facilitating such collections, which they regard as advantageous to themselves, but by which they are continually extending this evil City merchants, whose business is chiefly with the country, now accept such checks freely from their customers, because their banks will accept them from them, and many of the accounts which, from their amount, dealers regard as very valuable to their banks the latter find by experience to result in actual loss Instead of being the natural depositories of country banks for the business of legitimate commercial exchanges in the city, such banks are thus made ours. The subject is the cause of continual irritation and discord between banks and their customers and between the banks themselves.

Your committee, in considering this evil, can perceive no remedy but by its total abolition, and they therefore recommend that the clearing-house committee be required to establish monthly a schedule of minimum rates at which the associated banks shall receive on deposit checks and drafts upon places out of this city, and to which every bank shall be bound strictly to adhere.

Having now considered the prominent evils which exist, the removal of which your committee consider as indispensable to the harmonious intercourse between banks bound together by common interests, and having recommended for their removal—

1. That payment of interest upon deposits, either directly or indirectly, be entirely prohibited.

2. That each bank, while it observes the requirements of the law of Congress respecting a reserve fund, be required to carry at all times an amount of legal-tender notes equal to at least 15 per cent of its liabilities to the public.

3. That no bank shall certify a check as good until the full amount of it shall appear upon its books from a deposit, regularly entered to the credit of the drawer.

4. That no check or draft shall be received by a bank upon deposit at par as cash, drawn otherwise than upon one of the banks composing the Clearing-House Association.

5. That all checks and drafts upon places out of the city of New York shall only be taken at rates of discount established monthly by the clearing-house committee.

They now proceed to state how the observance of these rules may be effectively secured. It is well known that in some of these the sentiment of the association has been repeatedly expressed and resolutions of reform have been adopted, but which have gradually fallen into neglect.

Your committee believe that late occurrences have produced a deeper conviction, both in the association and in the public mind, of the inter-dependence of the banks upon each other, and of the wrong which any one member imposes upon the entire body, by unsound or irregular practices. They, however, recommend as an effectual security for the future:

That the constitution of the clearing house be changed into articles of association, which shall be signed by the officers of every bank, or member, and ratified by its board of directors. And your committee respectfully submit for consideration the accompanying instrument, which has been compiled from the present constitution of the Clearing-House Association, with such changes and amendments as present circumstances have suggested.

Your committee also recommend that the clearing-house committee shall procure a tablet, containing in large and very legible impressions, the rules which are to be observed by each member in dealing with the public, as follows

RULES

OF THE

ASSOCIATED BANKS

OF THE CITY OF NEW YORK

WITH THEIR DEALERS

---

1 No bank shall pay, or procure to be paid, interest upon deposits

2 No check shall be certified until the full amount is first deposited

3 Checks upon associated banks only received on deposit

4 Checks upon places out of New York City received at rates of discount fixed by clearing-house committee

5 Checks will be taken at depositor's risk and collected through the clearing house

6 Checks not good will be returned to the depositor the day following

---

BANKS NOT STRICTLY OBSERVING THESE RULES WILL BE EXCLUDED FROM THE CLEARING-HOUSE ASSOCIATION

These shall be appropriately framed and always kept conspicuously suspended in the banking room of each institution for public information.

With these regulations the public are always informed of the terms upon which alone they may conduct their business uniformly with every bank that has the facilities and the support of the Clearing-House Association. With these always in view, no person worthy of credit at a bank can ever ask a deviation from them, and no institution can retain the confidence of any respectable dealer after it is thus known to have compromised its integrity.

By these important changes many of the evils which have grown up in the business community and which have their origin in the vicious practices of banks will expire, the banks will resume their rightful position as safe and substantial supports of legitimate commerce, and their officers will be relieved from the anxieties which, in the present unnecessary competition, continually pursue them

All which is respectfully submitted by—

Committee
- GEORGE S COE, *President American Exchange National Bank*
- W. L JENKINS, *President Bank of America.*
- J M MORRISON, *President Manhattan Bank*
- MOSES TAYLOR, *President National City Bank*
- F D TAPPEN, *President Gallatin National Bank*
- JOHN E WILLIAMS, *President Metropolitan National Bank*
- J L EVERETT, *Cashier National Broadway Bank*
- ROBERT BUCK, *Cashier Pacific Bank*
- JOHN Q JONES, *President Chemical National Bank*

NO CHANGE IN BANKING METHODS

In emphasizing the inadequacy of the reserves of the banks this report was in accord with the best opinion of the time Comparatively little reference was made to the currency system as a cause of trouble, or to its modification as a possible remedy. It seems to have been felt that the banking system as it was was essentially workable if the banks were prepared to conduct their affairs in a conservative way. It is also significant that this committee did not seek to shift the responsibility upon the banks outside New York, as has been attempted in some explanations of later crises We have seen that the country banks and those of the reserve cities might have shown more moderation in their withdrawals from New York. Doubtless the framer of the report perceived that no other course could be expected, since united action is out of the question among hundreds of banks widely separated from each other both by distance and circumstances. The report clearly recognized that the New York banks are the center of our banking system, and that the obligation rests upon them to be constantly in position to meet emergencies. However important the results which may be expected from changes in our system of note issue, it may be suggested that this remedy has been given too exclusive attention in recent years. The older view of 1873, that our reserve system is unsatisfactory, may well receive careful consideration.

The report of the clearing-house committee seems to have been received with general approval, both by bankers and by the public,[a] but it led to no immediate change in banking methods. It was considered at a meeting of the banks on Thursday, November 21, and the adoption of its principal recommendation, that interest on deposits be prohibited, was favored by about three-fourths of the banks. It was felt, however, that a unanimous agreement was necessary to secure its effective adoption. At a subsequent meeting, on November 28, the committee was discharged at its own request, and a second committee was appointed representing views opposed to those advocated in the report. This action was rightly assumed to mean the indefinite postponement of the question, and in fact no report was ever presented by the second committee.

Of the various reforms urged in the report all except that regarding interest upon deposits have been embodied more or less completely in general banking practice. A specific penalty for the overcertification of checks in the national banking law of 1882 did something to check that dangerous practice, the organization of the stock exchange clearing house in 1892 did more, and for many years overcertification has ceased to be a serious menace to the credit structure. The recommendation of the committee that

[a] Commercial and Financial Chronicle, November 22, 1873, p. 677.

collection charges be imposed upon the checks and drafts of out-of-town institutions was adopted in 1899—a proposal unlike the others, in that it was likely to be a source of profit to the banks. The matter of clearing for institutions not members of the clearing house was taken up in 1902 in the case of the trust companies But so far as the banks were concerned, no change in methods followed directly as a result of the experience gained during the crisis of 1873

LEGISLATION AFTER THE CRISIS

Both the Secretary of the Treasury and the Comptroller of the Currency in their reports for 1873 commented adversely upon the practice of paying interest upon deposits and upon the insufficiency of the reserves of the banks.[a] The long session of Congress which followed the crisis was largely devoted to banking and currency problems, but with results on the banking side which were of slight practical importance The redemption system through reserve agents in the money centers had not even served to remove from circulation notes which were no longer fit for use Redemption at Washington by means of a 5 per cent fund deposited with the Treasury therefore met with general favor. In connection with this change it was also agreed without much opposition that the banks should be relieved from the requirement of holding reserves against their circulation This change in itself, however, would have reduced the total reserves of the banks, and after the recent experience of the crisis no one was pre-

[a] See Appendix, Notes A and B, pp 321 and 332

pared to contend that the reserves were too large. It was therefore proposed that the banks be required to hold the same proportion of reserve as formerly against deposits, but that it should be held entirely in their own vaults By this change the required cash reserve of all the banks except those in New York would have been increased considerably more than the amount set free by the removal of the requirement of a reserve against circulation As a slight concession to the banks it was also provided that the 5 per cent fund should be counted as a part of the required reserve These purely banking provisions were accepted without much discussion both in the House, in which the bill originated, and also in the Senate In both branches attention was almost wholly concentrated upon those provisions of the bill which related to the amount of bank notes and of greenbacks which should be issued. The House bill was an inflation measure, pure and simple. It restored the limit of $400,000,000 for the greenbacks, the limit which in a separate measure was vetoed by President Grant It also provided for "free banking," as it was then generally designated; that is, it removed the limit upon the total amount of circulation which the banks might issue [a] In the Senate the bill was radically modified The issue of greenbacks was fixed at $382,000,000, the amount then in circulation, and in connection with the provision for free banking the requirement was added that greenbacks should be retired automatically to the

[a] See Congressional Record, 1873–74, p 1007, for the bill as reported to the House by the Committee on Banking, and p 3023 for its form as passed by the House

amount of 25 per cent of any future increase in bank notes [a] In conference the provision requiring the banks to hold their reserves entirely in their own vaults was sacrificed in order to conciliate the opponents of contraction; but the proportion of greenbacks to be retired was increased to 37½ per cent [b] This conference report was not accepted by the House, and a second conference was ordered It was apparent that no measure looking toward resumption through the gradual retirement of a portion of the greenbacks could be passed But, apparently in order to show some results for their months of effort, the second conference committee brought in a report in which free banking was given up and in which the only provision regarding greenbacks was to fix their amount at $382,000,000 The only change affecting circulation was to increase the amount to be withdrawn from banks issuing more than their proper quota from $25,000,000 to $55,000,000 The provision requiring the reserves of the banks against deposits to be held in their own vaults was not restored.[c] In this form the bill was passed and became law on June 10, 1874 Whether the provision requiring banks to hold their entire reserve was desirable may be open to question, but it has seemed advisable to place on record the peculiar set of circumstances which brought about a reduction in the reserves required by the banks so shortly after their inadequacy had been made evident by the crisis of 1873

[a] See Congressional Record, 1873–74, p 3835. The Finance Committee proposed a retirement of 50 per cent, but an amendment was passed reducing this to 25 per cent (p 3806)

[b] Congressional Record, pp 4852–4853

[c] See Congressional Record, p. 5310

CHAPTER II.

THE PANIC OF MAY, 1884

It will not be necessary to devote much space to the panic of 1884, inasmuch as the financial disturbance was wholly confined to New York, and in its banking aspects was of an unusually simple and definite nature The events which preceded the panic were quite unlike those which preceded the crisis of 1873, or indeed crises in general A period of economic activity began in 1879 and culminated in 1882. During much of 1883 and the early part of 1884 there was a slow but general decline in most branches of trade, marked by some curtailment in production, and an increase in the number of failures, including a number of railroad receiverships, but more strikingly by a fall in prices of commodities and securities The price of steel rails, for example, dropped from $71 at the beginning of 1880 to $35 at the close of 1883 The price of standard railway stocks in 1883 declined from 10 to 20 per cent. But the apparent strength of the banks was not weakened by these unfavorable business conditions The expansion of loans which had been rapid from the beginning of 1879 continued, but at a much less rapid rate. In cash reserves the banks, especially those in New York, improved their condition, and the crop-moving requirements of 1883 were met with little or none of the usual advance in rates for loans

The strength of the banks in cash reserves, however, was due to an artificial cause—the monthly addition of two million silver dollars under the provisions of the

Bland-Allison Act. This increment was hardly observed while business was active, though it doubtless prevented the country from retaining so large a proportion of gold in circulation as would otherwise have been the case. But when business became depressed, the effects of the silver issues became more marked The outflow of gold being offset by the silver, the banks did not experience that reduction in reserves which would have led to an advance in the rates for loans in the money centers. Moreover, the silver issues were at least a contributing cause of the distrust of American securities in Europe which led to their return to this country in considerable quantities for some months before the panic.

To these sales were attributed the enormous exports of gold in March and April, 1884, which amounted to nearly $30,000,000. Notwithstanding this loss from gold exports, it was not until the beginning of May that the reserves of the New York banks were reduced to a point below that at the same time in the previous year The statement for May 3 showed a surplus reserve of only $806,000 compared with $1,604,000 on May 5, 1883. Money was, however, flowing into the banks from the country, and it was thought that the loss from gold exports was nearly at an end. There had been no appreciable advance in rates for loans or contraction in their volume during the winter and early spring. The continued fall in security values, therefore, must be ascribed to other than banking causes

At length the strain of successive breaks in prices on the stock exchange brought about the downfall of a number of speculators whose plans might have proved successful if general conditions had been such as to lead to a rise in security values. Within little more than a week an astonishing series of instances of fraud and defalcation, unexampled in our history, were brought to light. On Thursday, May 8, the failure of the brokerage firm of Grant & Ward was announced—a firm better known for its personnel than for the scope of its business operations with the public. The failure was unusually disastrous, the firm having assets of less than $700,000 against liabilities of more than $16,000,000, and was highly discreditable to all concerned except the senior partner. This failure involved the Marine National Bank, whose president was a partner in Grant & Ward The direct cause of failure of the bank was the illegal certification of a check for $750,000 for the above-named firm. The bank was of secondary importance, however, having a capital of $400,000 and deposits of about $5,000,000. It had little or no business as a reserve agent, since its bankers' deposits amounted to less than $400,000 In liquidation, its creditors ultimately received 83 465 per cent of their claims This failure, together with various unfavorable influences of a more general nature, caused a considerable further decline in the stock market The banks, however, were not affected, and the rates for the various classes of loans were advanced but slightly, those for call loans being from 3 to 4 per cent, for time loans from 4 to 4½ per cent, and 5 to 5½ per cent on commercial paper. The following week opened with rumors of impending failures, which shortly became realities On Wednesday, May 13, it became known that the president of the Second National Bank had stolen over $3,000,000 of securities from its vaults, and a little later the suspension of the Metropolitan Bank was also announced[a] As in the case of the crisis of 1873, the narrative of the events at the height of the panic is taken from the Commercial and Financial Chronicle.

THE MONEY MARKET AND FINANCIAL SITUATION

Financial circles have passed through an excited week, marked by many disasters and full of disturbing features The failure last week of the Marine Bank and of Grant & Ward, together with the developments to which this gave rise, created serious distrust, which was deepened when it was announced Saturday afternoon that the Northwestern Car Company, in which Senator Sabin, of Minnesota, was the controlling spirit, had been placed in the hands of a receiver Consequently, an uneasy feeling prevailed on our stock exchange at the opening of business on Monday, and the fear was freely expressed that other institutions and firms would be found to be in an equally precarious condition Prices reflected this fear in a pretty general decline through the day The uneasiness increased rather than diminished during Tuesday, and when it appeared on Wednesday morning that a defalcation of three millions had been detected in the Second National Bank, confidence entirely disappeared It was apparent then—even before the opening of the exchange—that only very little more was needed to precipitate a panic and a wholesale destruction of values The final shock came in the failure of several brokerage and banking firms and in the suspension of the Metropolitan National Bank Then the wildest kind of a panic raged, and securities were thrown overboard regardless of price

To add further to the discomfiture of dealers, money became exceedingly stringent, and at one time commanded as much as 4 per cent for 24 hours' use This caused a further sacrifice of stocks, since few could afford to pay the high rate asked The exorbitant charge was, of course, the direct result of the distrust prevailing, since there was no actual scarcity There was no improvement until it was understood in the afternoon that the banks had taken action similar to that of 1873, and that no further bank suspensions were therefore likely At the close of the business on that day the disasters included Metropolitan Bank, Atlantic State Bank (Brooklyn), Hotchkiss, Burnham & Co , Hatch & Foote, Nelson Robinson & Co , O M Bogart & Co , Donnell, Lawson & Simpson, Goffe & Randle, J C Williams.

[a] See Appendix, Note C, pp 345–350, for an account of the causes of the difficulties of these New York banks taken from the Report of the Comptroller of the Currency for 1884.

The improvement noted at the close on Wednesday made headway on Thursday, when it appeared that the Metropolitan Bank, through the aid of the clearing house, would be enabled to resume at once, and that the Second National Bank was experiencing no difficulty whatever in meeting all payments, the deficit having been made good in full by the father of the president of the bank The failure in the morning of A W Dimock & Co had comparatively little effect upon the market (though it caused a fall of 64 per cent in Bankers' and Merchants' Telegraph stock), but the unexpected suspension of Messrs Fisk & Hatch late in the afternoon was a complete setback, and again threw things into confusion Friday morning the closing of the Newark Savings Institution was another unfavorable feature, but it was soon seen that this was connected with the suspension of Fisk & Hatch, and a more hopeful view of the situation prevailed No further failures occurring, the market improved in tone, and late in the day a pretty substantial recovery took place, which was furthered by the relaxation in the rates for money

We have thus briefly reviewed each day's events, because of their great importance and because of the bearing they have had upon the general commercial and financial situation To state briefly the causes of the disturbance in the market, it may be said that they were strictly due to a complete loss of confidence, not so much in the market prices of securities as in the stability and soundness of various institutions and firms The difficulty of obtaining ready cash, as a result of disquietude prevailing, also contributed to intensify the troubles that had developed It is to this latter fact, namely, the desire to realize and obtain cash, that the large decline on Thursday and Friday of nearly 7 per cent on United States Government bonds is to be attributed There was no loss of confidence in the value of these, nor was there in good railroad bonds and stocks

One result of the phenomenal and temporary rise in the rates for money was to bring a vast amount of foreign capital promptly to the market Some of it was sent here to buy stocks at their depressed prices, and more to loan on stocks or any other good securities at the high rates of interest The effect of this was to completely turn the foreign exchanges which had been running so heavily against us for the last three months Large amounts of loan bills and bankers' demand bills on London came on to the market, and on Thursday rates for sterling dropped 1 cent on the pound and on Friday 2 cents more The supplies of available funds furnished by this means, together with relief afforded by the banks in the Clearing House Association adopting the same plan of issuing clearing-house certificates for use in the settlement of their clearings as in 1873, already alluded to, had the effect to overcome the pinch for money, and the result was that at the close of business on Friday money on call had dropped to 5 and 6 per cent per annum [a]

[a] Commercial and Financial Chronicle, May 16, 1884, p 589

In the temporary squeeze for money, resulting from the above causes, there was of course less business done in other classes of loans than those on stocks, but the evidence that there was no loss of confidence in values of other kinds of collateral nor in mercantile credit at large was shown by the fact that while money was loaning at 3 and even 4 per cent per day for use in connection with stock speculations, the rates for mercantile discounts remained nominally unchanged at 4½ and 5 per cent per annum on first-class indorsed paper for two and four months, and 5½ and 6 per cent for single-name paper [a]

It will be seen that the steps taken to allay alarm were immediate and effective During the following week the panic entirely subsided A good detailed account of the action taken by the clearing house in assisting the Metropolitan Bank, as well as of the use made of loan certificates, is given in the following extracts taken from the annual report for 1884 of the Comptroller of the Currency, Henry W Cannon:

The suspension of the Metropolitan National Bank on May 14 caused great excitement All stocks and securities called upon the New York Stock Exchange were greatly depreciated under the pressure to sell, and it was practically impossible for the banks to collect their call loans, as their borrowers could not obtain money by sale of their securities except at ruinous rates, neither could they borrow elsewhere, and it was impracticable and impolitic to throw the mass of securities held as collateral to the call loans of the associated banks upon the market If it had been done, it is probable that a suspension of gold and currency payments by the banks throughout the country would have followed the general panic that would have ensued In this emergency the members of the New York Clearing House Association, realizing that an immediate demand for deposits would be made by their country correspondents, called a meeting at the clearing house on the afternoon of May 14, and the following plan for settling balances at the clearing house was unanimously adopted

"*Resolved*, That, in view of the present crisis, the banks in this association, for the purpose of sustaining each other and the business community, resolve that a committee of five be appointed by the chair to receive from banks members of the association bills receivable and other securities to be approved by said committee, who shall be authorized to issue therefor to such depositing banks certificates of deposit bearing interest at 6 per cent per annum not in excess of 75 per cent of the securities or bills receivable so deposited, except in case of United States bonds, and said certificates shall be received in settlement of balances at the clearing house"

[a] Commercial and Financial Chronicle, May 16, 1884, p 582

After consultation with the officers and directors of the Metropolitan National Bank a committee of examination was appointed to visit the bank and to ascertain if some plan could not be arranged to permit it to open again for business The greater part of the securities of the bank were found to be of such a character that loan certificates could safely be issued upon them, and in this way the Metropolitan National was enabled to resume business on May 15 and settle its balances at the clearing house The prompt action of the members of the associated banks and the resumption of the Metropolitan National Bank greatly assisted in allaying excitement and staying the panic, and although confidence was not immediately restored, and although the banks in the city of New York were largely drawn upon by their country correspondents, reducing their reserve for a time below the 25 per cent limit prescribed by law, and although, on account of the great depreciation of values and the stringency of the money market occasioned by the want of confidence, other failures of state banks, private bankers, and mercantile firms occurred in New York and throughout the country, there was no suspension of gold and currency payments at any point, and the issue of loan certificates was confined to the banks of New York City, which were soon enabled to collect their loans and make good their reserves [a]

Upon learning of the defalcation at the Second National Bank on May 14, and when it was apparent that a financial crisis was imminent in the city of New York, the Comptroller ordered expert and reliable examiners to the assistance of the national-bank examiner stationed at New York in order to protect the public The examiners were instructed to exercise the utmost caution and vigilance, and to visit any of the national banks that appeared to be in trouble or where violations of law or irregularities were suspected They were especially instructed to report any criminal irregularities or violations of section 5209 Before permitting the Second National Bank, whose president had misappropriated over three millions of its funds, to open for business, the defalcation was made good under the supervision of the examiner The plan of resumption for the Metropolitan National Bank, by obtaining loan certificates of the New York Clearing House Association upon its securities, was also submitted by the examiner in charge of the bank to the Comptroller, the examiner remaining in charge until the plan was carried into effect and the bank permitted to resume [b]

The success which crowned the efforts of the banks in dealing with this crisis affords convincing evidence that if clearing-house loan certificates are to be issued at all, they should be issued at the beginning of a disturbance. Local runs on the banks did not become severe, because

[a] Report of the Comptroller of the Currency, 1884, p 33 [b] Ibid , p 36.

announcement was made that assistance would be granted at the moment when the disasters which might have weakened general confidence became known to the public It was also a favorable circumstance that the panic came in the spring rather than in the autumn Crop-moving requirements were months away and the normal movement of money was in favor of New York. The danger which confronted the banks was therefore confined to withdrawals which might be made on account of the loss of confidence Having made arrangements which reduced that danger to a minimum, the banks endured calmly a moderate loss of cash from their reserves and were able to go through the disturbance without suspending payments

Looking below the surface, we shall discover in a mild form the same elements of weakness which caused suspension in 1873. The Second National Bank was a purely local institution, having no bankers' deposits whatever On the other hand, about $7,000,000, nearly two-thirds of the total deposits of the Metropolitan Bank, were due to other banks Had the clearing house not acted with admirable promptness in coming to its assistance there is little question that out-of-town banks would have become alarmed for their deposits, not only in this bank but for those in the banks generally. Even as it was, the customary inflow of funds from the interior, which had been going on for some weeks, was instantly reversed during the panic week. According to the returns collected from the banks by the Financial Chronicle regarding the movements of money to and from the interior, there was a gain of nearly $3,800,000 for the week ending Friday, May 9. In the following week it was reported that "the exchanges at interior points have been deranged by the existing condition of affairs, St. Louis falling to par against 90 cents per $1,000 premium, and Chicago being nominally 80 cents per $1,000 discount against 60 cents premium These rates indicate the calling of balances from New York, due to the bank failures and the disturbed credit." [a] The loss of the banks as reported for the week ending May 16 was $1,107,000, and in the following week there was a further loss of $2,300,000 After that date, with the renewal of confidence, the normal movement in favor of New York was resumed The actual loss of cash by the New York banks was, however, far greater than the amount of the reported withdrawals by country banks Between May 10 and May 24 the reserve of the banks fell from $86,000,000 to $67,000,000, and although deposits were reduced by considerable contraction in loans, a surplus reserve of $4,400,000 was converted into a deficit of $6,600,000. The comparatively slight reserves of the New York banks, and hence their small resisting power, could not be disguised, even though they succeeded in passing through the strain of this panic Had there been numerous failures among country banks (the failure of the Pennsylvania Bank in Pittsburg, owing to dishonesty, disclosed by the collapse of a speculative movement in oil, was the only important banking failure outside of New York), or had the disasters in New York occurred during the crop-moving period, there is every probability that the banks would have drifted into suspension

Notwithstanding the liberal issue of loan certificates, the banks contracted their loans to a noticeable extent,

[a] See Commercial and Financial Chronicle, May 31, 1884, p 583

from $333,000,000 on May 10 to $313,000,000 on May 24. That this contraction was not accompanied by extraordinarily high rates for loans except during the very height of the panic may be explained by the entrance of country banks into the market for commercial paper from which the New York banks had virtually withdrawn [a]

Further evidence of the strain upon New York banks is afforded by the two returns of the national banks to the Comptroller of the Currency on April 24 and June 20. As the first of these returns was made before the crisis, while money was coming to New York from the country, and as the second was made after withdrawals had ceased and money had begun to be sent back to New York, they may be taken to represent, at least roughly, the changes in the amount of bankers' balances due to the crisis. The following table shows the principal items of reserves and liabilities of the New York national banks on the dates mentioned above.

[In million dollars]

	April 24	June 20
RESOURCES		
Loans	$250	$209
Due from banks	20	19
Clearing-house loan certificates		10 3
Clearing-house exchanges and cash items	64	53
Cash reserve	74	67
LIABILITIES		
Individual deposits	231	203
Due to national banks	95	71
Due to other banks	37	28
Clearing-house loan certificates		11 9

This table shows changes which are unlike in many respects those which occurred in the crisis of 1873 and,

[a] See Commercial and Financial Chronicle, May 31, 1884, p 632

as we shall see, unlike those in later crises In the first place, it will be observed that while the reduction in bankers' deposits was large, amounting to $33,000,000, on the other side of the account the banks experienced a loss of cash of only $7,000,000. This seeming contradiction of the view so frequently expressed in these pages that bankers' deposits are reduced primarily by withdrawals of cash requires explanation In this particular instance the out-of-town banks lent largely in the New York market, and the credits thus secured by borrowers would serve to diminish bankers' deposits and increase individual deposits, which would then be canceled by the liquidation of New York bank loans That this was the case is evident from the slight change in the amount of individual deposits, there being a reduction of only $28,000,000, while the diminution in loans and clearing-house exchanges amounted to $52,000,000. The shifting of loans from the New York banks to the out-of-town banks would result in large unfavorable balances for those banks holding large bankers' deposits, unless the borrowers from the country banks also happened to be depositors with them The disturbance due to the shifting of loans would, however, be much less than when the country banks actually withdrew funds, since the unfavorable clearing-house balance could be met by the resort to clearing-house loan certificates After this explanation, it will cause no surprise to find that the greater part of the certificates taken out, aside from those issued for the Metropolitan Bank, were taken out by the banks having large bankers' deposits. Only 20 of the 82 clearing-house banks took out certificates, and several of the banks did not use them [a] It was because the strain remained purely local that the use of loan certificates alone proved sufficient to meet the emergency.

The experience derived from this panic directed attention once more to plans for strengthening permanently the credit fabric through clearing-house action. George S Coe in a notable address reaffirmed the suggestions made in the clearing-house report of 1873, and a committee was appointed which reported favorably upon the proposal to prohibit interest upon deposits, the representative of only one bank dissenting. Both the address and the report of the committee will be found in the appendix [b] The opposition of a few banks was, however, again effective, though the interest-paying banks seem to have agreed upon a uniform rate of 2 per cent upon country balances.[c]

As in the case of the crisis of 1873, the Comptroller of the Currency formulated a number of suggestions based upon the experience of the banks during the panic. Those portions of his report bearing on this subject will be found included in the appendix. The danger of over-certification was emphasized, and the creation of a stock-exchange clearing house urged.[d] Difficulties in securing adequate information through examination were pointed

[a] See Appendix, Note C, pp. 350–353, for details, including forms and statistical information, regarding the issue of clearing-house certificates in 1884.

[b] Appendix, Note D, pp 371–386, and also Commercial and Financial Chronicle, May 31, 1884, pp 632–633.

[c] See Banker's Magazine, November, 1884, p 390.

[d] See Appendix, Note C, pp. 353–359

out, and, finally, the evil effects of interest on bankers' deposits were indicated; but the difficulty of securing effective action seemed insurmountable to the Comptroller.[a] Finally, it may be noted that little or no reference was made by anyone to changes in the system of note issue. The discontinuance of the silver purchases was the one currency matter to which much attention was given.

It remains to call attention to a precedent which was made, if not established, during this crisis, a precedent which was to have far-reaching consequences, although its significance was not perceived at the time or subsequently. The arrangements of the clearing house, when clearing-house loan certificates were issued, were unlike in one most important respect those adopted in 1873 and on earlier occasions. No provision was included for the equalization of the reserves of the banks. Opposition to this measure was so widespread that it does not appear that it was even formally considered. The ground of this opposition can be readily understood In 1873 the noninterest-paying banks entered into the arrangement in expectation of securing a clearing-house rule against the practice of paying interest on deposits, but their efforts had resulted in failure. Some of them had employed their reserves for the common good most reluctantly in 1873, and the feeling against a similar proposal in 1884 was naturally far stronger and more general Moreover, the working of the pooling agreement in 1873 had occasioned heartburnings which had not entirely disappeared with the lapse of time. It was believed, and doubtless

[a] See Appendix, Note C, pp 359–370

with reason, that some of the banks had evaded the obligations of the pooling agreement. It was said that some of the banks had encouraged special currency deposits, so as not to be obliged to turn money into the common fund. Further, as the arrangement had not included bank notes, banks exchanged greenbacks for notes in order either to increase their holdings of cash or to secure money for payment over the counter. Here we come upon an objection to the pooling arrangement which doubtless had much weight with the specially strong banks, although it was more apparent than real. In order to supply the pressing requirements of some banks, others who believed that they would have been able to meet all the demands of their depositors were obliged to restrict payments That such an expectation would have proved illusory later experience affords ample proof. When a large number of the banks in any locality suspend, the others can not escape adopting the same course.[a] But in 1884 it was a belief the erroneousness of which had not been made evident by recent experience.

The following news items regarding the pooling arrangement in 1873 are instructive, though they go too far in attributing the restriction of payments to that device·

When the question of "pooling" the greenbacks came up, one or more of the banks strongest in legal tenders, especially the Chemical, demurred, and substantially refused to enter into what they regarded as an inequitable arrangement The solemn assurance that they would be expelled from the association if they persisted in that position brought them to terms, and they will now all stand or fall together —*New York Tribune, September 26, 1873*

There is a very early prospect of putting an end to the "pooling" arrangement for greenbacks Many of the old and prudently managed banks down, and nearly all the small banks up town, are restive under the arrangement and desire the liberty of managing their own greenbacks, as well as national bank notes, in their own way, and to receive and pay them out

[a] See p 181

across their counters Their receipts, they very properly urge, can not be made free, as before the suspension, so long as there is a discount on bank checks in Wall street, and while they have no anxiety about breaking up the arrangement for certifying checks payable through the clearing house, and settling daily balances in relief certificates * * * they do insist on the resumption in notes * * * across their own counters It is further urged that this license need not necessarily create embarrassing discriminations among the different banks in the clearing house All will be left to settle the order of business with their own dealers If any of them are unable to send currency to their country bank correspondents where such correspondents have a claim upon them for notes in place of certified checks to pay debts in New York, they will have to buy the notes or sell their gold reserve for notes Should the Gold Room persist in buying and selling and settling daily balances exclusively in certified checks, the gold can be sold for notes to * * * any other responsible bullion and bank-note broker on the street The belief now prevails, however, that currency, on the resumption of currency payments in New York, will come from the West as rapidly as it will go to the South, and large sums of greenbacks now withheld in New York and the East will soon return to the general banking employment —*New York Times, October 10, 1873*

The banking movement is reported better from the clearing house, but the precise position of the Associated Banks is withheld from the public The clearing house, it is rumored, has under control only $6,605,000 greenbacks to-day, but the belief is that double this sum in greenbacks and national bank notes is actually held in bank, in one way or another The circumstance that pains are taken by certain of the well-to-do and strong banks to keep down the scaling process, to the support of their less prudent neighbors, is only another argument in favor with doing away with the pooling and scaling order at the clearing house, to which we may add the additional and very forcible argument that bank checks have fallen to one-fourth to one-half per cent for currency, owing to the accession of greenbacks and nationals by express and the appearance of numerous and very considerable Treasury warrants * * * in the mails from Washington and the West —*New York Times, October 18, 1873*

There is less difficulty about paying out currency when wanted for pay rolls at home, or remittances to the country banks near by, and while the majority of the clearing-house banks persist in what is known as the pooling and scaling process in the matter of greenbacks, these notes have been freely thrown upon the street, and sold for bank checks, not only by outside parties, receiving them by express or otherwise, but by some of the stronger banks themselves, the latter having vainly protested against the folly as well as injustice of the process referred to, to the support of the weaker banks, none of which would be suffered to fail, but some of which fear the liquidation of their deposits, in case greenback payments become the rule in place of the exception among the other banks —*New York Times, October 20, 1873*

One of the reasons given [for dissolving the pooling agreement] is that some of the banks evade the obligation * * * For example, * * * [some banks] which receive greenbacks in the ordinary course of business * * * instead of placing them in the "pool," enter them in their respective books as "special deposits," sacred to the exclusive draft of the depositor, when in reality they are used as the banks deem most convenient Again, these latter banks secure greenbacks * * * and exchange them for national-bank notes, and pay these over the counter * * * Up to the present time checks for the pay rolls of manufacturers have been the only large sums cashed by a certain class of banks, but it is expected that the banks will take some action this week to effect a formal resumption of payments. * * * Some feeling exists on the subject of these payments, inasmuch as a number of the banks in Western cities have resumed, while New York has not formally done so as yet —*New York Tribune, October 21, 1873.*

It may be assumed that the question of general currency payments * * * is about to solve itself Most of the banks are paying on all demands, when preferred to the certification of checks, and the difference against the checks of other banks that, from their position, decline to pay out large sums in currency is only one-fourth to one-eighth per cent in exchange for greenbacks or nationals Some of the first-class of banks are not only helping their neighbors to greenbacks and sending currency to their country correspondents, but they are paying their debtor balances at the clearing house, as a matter of choice, in greenbacks in place of relief certificates —*New York Times, October 23, 1873*

If the emergency in 1884 had been more serious or prolonged the need of some arrangement for equalizing reserves when loan certificates were issued would probably have been made apparent. But as the banks were able to handle the situation successfully both in 1884 and in 1890 with the loan certificate alone, the original complementary device of equalization came in the course of time to be not only disregarded, but entirely forgotten The result has been, as we shall see, to convert the clearing-house loan certificate into an instrument which inevitably and immediately leads to the suspension of payments by the banks. But this is a matter which can only be explained at a later stage in this investigation.

6158—10——9

CHAPTER III

FINANCIAL STRINGENCY IN 1890

No changes in banking methods or in legislation were made as a consequence of the experience afforded by the panic in 1884 In 1887, however, the provisions of the national banking law [a] regarding reserve cities were somewhat modified, but it was a change which does not seem to have been made so much for banking reasons as to satisfy the ambitious desires of the bankers and people of certain cities. Instead of designating the cities by name it was provided that cities with a minimum population of 50,000 [b] might upon the application of three-fourths of the banks established in them, become reserve cities, and that cities with a minimum population of 200,000 might similarly become central reserve cities

Chicago and St Louis at once elected to become central reserve cities, but no other cities have followed their example. The number of reserve cities has slowly increased until at present there are 46, contrasted with the 13 (not including Chicago and St Louis) reserve cities before 1887 This change in the law did not involve any essential modification in the national banking system The increased number of reserve cities has simply kept pace with the growth of population in different sections As regards the two additional central reserve cities, the

[a] Act of March 3, 1887

[b] Reduced to 25,000 by the act of March 3, 1903

immediate effects at any rate, were much less important than has been generally supposed. At that time the Chicago and St Louis banks controlled only 5 per cent of the total resources of the national banks of the country and their bankers' deposits amounted to only $34,000,000, compared with $145,000,000 held by the New York banks. Moreover, the Chicago and St Louis banks did not discontinue the practice of keeping large balances in New York even though they could no longer be included as a part of their required reserves In the case of the Chicago banks, for example, in March, 1887, just before they ceased to be reserve cities, the amount due from reserve agents was nearly $7,000,000, and the amount due from other banks was nearly $5,000,000. In the following return for May the amount due Chicago banks from other banks had increased to $10,000,000. Evidently the considerable addition to this item was due to the continuance of balances in New York which could no longer appear under the rubric "Due from reserve agents."

In the course of time the banks of Chicago and St. Louis have largely increased the amount of their bankers' deposits and also its proportion contrasted with New York In May, 1890, the New York banks owed other national banks $124,000,000, those of Chicago and St. Louis $35,000,000. In May, 1908, these deposits of the New York banks had increased to $294,000,000, those of the two other central reserve cities to $178,000,000 The central position of the New York banks has not, however, been greatly changed in consequence of the increasing importance of the Chicago and St. Louis banks as reserve agents Their balances in New York continue to be large and are drawn down in every emergency.[a] In May, 1908, for example, the amount due to the banks of Chicago and St Louis from other national banks was $79,000,000, while the similar item for the New York banks was but $44,000,000, although their total resources were then two and one half times as large as those of the Chicago and St Louis banks. That a large portion of the amount due to the banks of the two western central reserve cities consists of balances with the New York banks is well known, though no figures of its exact amount are available.

Large New York balances are necessary because New York remains the clearing house of the country In this connection certain statistics gathered by the Comptroller of the Currency in 1889, 1890, and 1891 are of interest. From information provided by 3,329 of the 3,438 national banks, it was found that in 1890 all but three drew drafts upon New York, and that the total amount of such drafts was 61.31 per cent of all the drafts drawn upon all the banks of the country. The amount drawn upon the Chicago banks was but 9 82 per cent of the total The Chicago banks drew upon New York for $222,000,000, and were drawn upon in return for but $82,000.[b] These figures show very clearly how indispensable is the maintenance of cash payments by the New York banks if the dislocation of the domestic exchanges

[a] In recent years investments in the New York call-loan market by the banks of other cities have become large, they are reduced in emergencies to an even greater extent than balances The effect on the New York banks is similar See p 229

[b] See Report of the Comptroller of the Currency, 1891, pp 16–23, and ibid, 1892, pp 24–31

is to be avoided. Even if every bank were required to keep its entire reserve in its own vaults, though the likelihood of suspension in New York might be diminished, the certainty that general suspension would follow suspension in New York would remain.

One further matter regarding the relative position of the New York, Chicago, and St. Louis banks may be noticed. With few exceptions all our crises, panics, and periods of less severe monetary stringency have occurred in the autumn, when the western banks, through the sale of the cereal crops, were in a position to withdraw large sums of money from the East In normal course credits from the sale of agricultural products will serve to meet purchases of eastern and imported manufactures, which will be spread over the autumn and winter months. But for a short period in October and November the western banks are in position to draw for more money than the course of trade will permit them to retain permanently, and this power they have been disposed to exercise in emergencies

In both the instances of financial strain which have been examined, the causes of the disturbance were primarily of domestic origin In 1873 the unwillingness of Europe to take indefinite quantities of our securities was after all a minor factor, and in 1884 the return of American securities before the May panic was the result of developments which had taken place in this country. We have now to consider a crisis in which the United States participated, to a somewhat greater extent at least, as a passive sharer in a disturbance the causes of which were in other parts of the world.

It became evident in 1893 that the beginnings of much unsound business activity were of long standing, but in 1890 the condition of affairs had not reached that unstable condition which renders a transition to depression inevitable. The painful consequences of an even more unstable business situation would probably have been delayed as a result of the abundant harvests of 1889, which, as the yield elsewhere was below the average, made it possible for the United States to increase exports very materially over the amount in the years immediately preceding. For the year ending June 30, 1889, merchandise imports of $742,000,000 exceeded exports by nearly $3,000,000, while in the following year exports of $857,000,000 exceeded imports by $68,000,000, and gold exports fell from $49,000,000 to $4,000,000. The yield of the crops of 1890 was less satisfactory, but the prices at which they were marketed were appreciably better. It is probable that nothing more than the usual monetary stringency would have occurred in the autumn of 1890 had this country been able to escape from the effects of the collapse of the speculative movement in England which culminated in the Baring failure in November. Sufficient reason for this belief is afforded by the continuance of business activity without serious interruption and the speedy return to normal banking conditions which was reached before the end of the year. There was no accumulation of money in the banks or decline in the demand for loans such as marks a period of general business reaction and trade depression. Aside from the stock exchange and the banks of the eastern money centers the disturbance did not reach an acute stage.

From about the beginning of 1886 there was a steady increase in the volume of bank loans extending pretty generally throughout the country. In New York this upward movement was never very rapid and it did not continue beyond the spring of 1889. Further increase in that center was checked by declining cash reserves During the first half of 1890 the banks were regularly from ten to fifteen million dollars below the reserve at the same time in the previous year. Explanation of this uncomfortable situation is simple. It was due to the smaller amount of bankers' deposits which provide so large a proportion of the resources of the New York banks. The amount due to the banks reached its highest point in February, 1889, at $145,000,000. At the same time in the following year it was only $132,000,000, and there was about the same relative difference at corresponding dates in other seasons of the two years

Declining bankers' balances in New York may be due to either one of two causes which are quite different in nature. At times out-of-town banks lend largely in New York, a condition which has been very common in recent years In that case the amount of money in the possession of the New York banks is not appreciably affected. Bankers' deposits are reduced, but individual deposits become correspondingly greater. It may happen, however, that interior banks find full employment for their funds at home This was the situation of affairs in 1889 and 1890, when active business in the West and South taxed the banking resources of those sections, leaving no surplus for deposit in New York beyond the amount which could be included as a part of the required reserve. The reduction in bankers' deposits, therefore, tended to reduce to an equivalent extent the amount of money in the New York banks It did not, however, tend to diminish the probable requirements of the interior banks for a supply of money for crop-moving purposes On the contrary, such demands were likely to increase on account of the greater activity in the West and South as far as it led to an increase in agricultural production.

Only one course was open to the New York banks if they were to maintain themselves in a position at least as strong as in 1887 or 1888 By reducing the average volume of loans by an amount several times greater than the loss in reserves deposits would have been canceled sufficiently to give them the same surplus reserve which they had had in previous years The average volume of loans was indeed some $10,000,000 less in the first half of 1890 than at the same time in 1889, but this contraction was not sufficient to offset in deposits the amount of the loss in reserve. Consequently the surplus reserve in New York was in general distinctly less than in the previous year. In lieu of adequate contraction the banks seem to have adopted the illusory policy of increasing the amount of their call loans relative to the total of their loans In the absence of statistical evidence it can not be positively asserted that the amount of call loans was actually increased, but this is a matter of secondary importance. It is certain that the banks were lending more nearly to the limit set by reserve requirements and that whenever their reserve fell off even slightly they resorted to call-loan contraction Rates for these loans consequently became subject to increasingly violent fluctuations Between July, 1889, and July, 1890, the loans of the clearing-house banks were continually in the neighborhood of $400,000,000 When they were a few million dollars above that amount call-loan rates were moderate, when a few million dollars below, they were advanced to painfully high levels

Notwithstanding smaller reserves and more frequent fluctuations in rates, the course of the securitiy markets during the winter and spring of 1890 was not unlike that in previous years The month of May, as usual, found quotations at the highest level since the beginning of the year, though not at so high a point as in 1889. This was probably because of the comparative scarcity of loanable funds The normal June increase in the reserves of the banks was accompanied by a downward tendency in the rates for loans, but although there were almost no unfavorable railway or trade developments, there was a distinct pause in the upward movement on the stock exchange There was almost no change in the volume of loans during the month, and the speculative movement seemed to be subsiding The cessation of the foreign demand for American securities rather than any positively unfavorable development in this country seems to have been the occasion of this change in speculative feeling, and before the beginning of July the sale of American securities by London became the controlling factor in the situation For a number of years English capitalists and banking houses had been indulging in venturesome foreign investments, especially in South America. During the summer of 1890 London was selling good securities in order to carry the load of investments of a less desirable description. These sales caused foreign exchange rates to turn persistently against the United States, and between the middle of June and the second week of August gold was exported to the amount of $15,250,000, equal to about one-seventh of the reserve of the New York banks at that time. As a result of this gold movement the reserves of the banks were somewhat less at the beginning of the crop-moving period in August than they had been at the end of June, a quite exceptional condition.

The following table shows the changes in the condition of the New York banks from June 28 till August 9, 1890, and also the weekly fluctuations in call-loan rates.

New York bank statement

[In millions.]

1890	Loans	Cash	Net deposit	Surplus reserve	Call-loan rates
June 28	$397.1	$108.0	$405.5	$6.6	4½-10
July 5	404.6	106.5	414.3	3.8	2 - 9
12	403.0	110.3	415.9	6.4	3 - 8
19	402.3	109.2	414.3	5.7	2 - 6
26	400.0	108.3	408.9	6.1	2½- 6
Aug. 2	401.4	112.9	415.0	8.9	2 - 6
9	406.1	103.3	407.9	1.3	3 -20

On June 28, with a reserve of $108,000,000, the banks had a surplus reserve of $6,600,000, while on August 9 their reserve was reduced to $103,000,000 and the surplus was only $1,300,000. During July the Treasury had paid out $4,000,000 in excess of its receipts, and the reported movement of money between New York banks and the interior showed a net balance of nearly $4,000,000 in favor of the metropolis. It should be added that there was no appreciable change in the reserves of the banks until the week ending August 9. This was because $8,500,000 of the $15,250,000 of gold exports were taken during the last week of July and the first week of August.

While London sales of American securities were the fundamental cause of this movement, the banks might probably have prevented some of the outflow had they pursued a more conservative lending policy Low rates for call loans during July and the increase in loans at the beginning of August facilitated the transfer of securities to this country. A declining stock market was prevented in July (indeed the quotation for some securities then reached the highest level of the year) with the result of making inevitable a vastly more serious collapse in August and September. Moreover, then as now it was customary for foreign exchange dealers to draw anticipatory bills of exchange to be met with cotton and grain bills later in the season In the summer of 1890 such bills were not drawn because interest rates were higher in London than in New York. In this connection it is worthy of note that gold shipments came to an end as soon as there was an advance in the rates for loans in New York.

It is indeed true that the bank statement for August 2 showed that the banks had a considerable surplus reserve, but that alone was not sufficient ground for the policy pursued. The necessity of sending large amounts of money to the interior was realized, but instead of declining to increase loans altogether the banks simply discriminated in favor of call loans. The policy of the banks was thus described in the Chronicle for August 2

> Another element of uncertainty has affected our money market this week The large export of gold with the prospect before us of more to follow disturbs all calculations Gold exports are, of course, a material loss even if regarded simply as a question of the quantity of our currency for early fall requirements, for evidently it is no gain in exchanging $5,000,000 of silver certificates a month for $10,000,000 of gold It may be said that the flow of gold is not likely to continue long, but in the meantime the loss is sufficiently large to make an impression upon the bank reserves, Hence it is that money on time is firmer this week (although a large amount of currency has been paid out by the Treasury on account of bond purchases), while on call it is easier The most liberal lenders for from day to day money are the banks As their reserves are low, as they are being drawn upon for the gold exports, and as they are liable to be further drawn upon for crop purposes, the officers prefer to keep their money within control, which they could not do if loaned on time Some of our largest trust companies also refuse to put out their money otherwise than on call, but they are companies that do not disturb call money except when there is some material change in the market
>
> As already stated, the rates for call money have for the reasons mentioned been easier this week So far as reported for bankers' balances the extremes have been 6 per cent and 2 per cent, the average being 4 per cent The banks and trust companies have loaned at 4 per cent as the minimum, many, however, getting 4½ per cent [a]

Within less than three weeks from the date of the report quoted above call loans were advanced to 186 per cent and the stock market was in a turmoil. Not a single failure had occurred Nothing had happened except that the reserves of the New York banks had been reduced by entirely normal causes from $103,000,000 on August 9 to $95,000,000 on August 23, and the banks were below reserve requirements, $2,800,000 To meet this situation the banks were resorting to call-loan contraction, or at least they were attempting such contraction Notwith-

[a] The Commercial and Financial Chronicle, August 2, 1890, p 124.

standing the efforts made by the banks to secure the "money" which they fancied they had "kept within control," they were only able to reduce their loans by $8,500,000 during the two weeks after August 9, when they were at their highest point. Aside from the gold exports, the movements of money had not been at all unusual The reported shipments to the interior between August 1 and August 22, accounted for a net loss of $4,100,000, contrasted with $4,200,000, the year before. The disappearance of the surplus reserve was the signal for an attempt to liquidate call loans—loans which should not have been made. Even the contraction which was brought about was probably in no small degree due to the diminution in the amount of time loans, since the banks almost entirely ceased making loans on time and many of those made in previous months must have come to maturity The commotion in the money market and on the stock exchange was wholly unnecessary. It indicated on the part of the banks and the public an increasing tendency to regard the 25 per cent reserve as an irreducible minimum and not as a resource to be held in ordinary times for use in emergencies. Moreover, although crop-moving requirements were only beginning, and although it was certain that a large amount of money must be sent away from New York in the course of succeeding weeks, every one was aware that there were ample funds available in the United States Treasury and that they would be placed at the disposal of the banks

As early as 1882 surplus revenue became a factor in the finances of the Government, but at that time there was an ample amount of bonds outstanding which were redeemable at par. Momentarily reduced after the panic of 1884, the revenues of the Government soon reached even more formidable proportions than ever before In 1887 there were no more bonds outstanding which were redeemable at par, and further liquidation of the debt involved purchases at a premium in the open market After some hesitation this policy was adopted, but, as was proper, the Treasury endeavored to secure the bonds upon terms as favorable as possible to the Government. The bulk of the bond purchases, therefore, were made at times when the money market was in a stringent condition, when holders were most willing to dispose of their bonds, or further delay was inexpedient. During the seven months from July, 1889, to February, 1890, the Treasury paid out some $42,000,000 more than it received, having purchased bonds to the amount of more than $70,000,000. In the succeeding five months to July the Treasury increased its cash holdings by more than $18,000,000, its moderate bond purchases being largely offset by the withdrawal of government deposits from the banks It then held some $250,000,000, including the gold reserve of $100,000,000 and some $21,000,000 of more or less unavailable fractional silver coin About $54,000,000 of the remainder consisted of the bank-note redemption fund which had been transferred to the general fund of the Treasury by the act of July 14, 1890 This money was not a recent accumulation and, in fact, had been much greater in previous years. It will be seen, then, that aside from the $18,000,000 withdrawn between February and July, the

Treasury surplus was not a fund the building up of which had had any influence in bringing about the actual money-market conditions which prevailed in the summer of 1890. Moreover, any payments by the Treasury in excess of the $18,000,000 would be in the nature of a windfall for the banks

The relief which the market expected from the Treasury was slow in making its appearance, though not on account of any unwillingness or delay on the part of the Secretary of the Treasury to make use of the government funds On Tuesday, August 18, the Treasury offered to redeem $15,000,000 4½ per cent bonds with interest to May 31, 1891 This offer not proving attractive to holders of bonds, on Thursday it was announced that the Treasury would redeem $20,000,000 of the 4½ per cents, prepaying the entire interest to the maturity of the bonds on August 31, 1891 It was on this day that call loans had advanced to one-half of 1 per cent a day, and the stock market was threatened with complete demoralization Upon the announcement of this liberal offer of the Treasury trouble was largely allayed, the banks discontinued their efforts at wholesale contraction, and quotations on the stock exchange regained some of their loss The whole episode illustrates the groundlessness of the disturbance, since the amount of money actually secured from the Treasury by the New York banks was inconsiderable. Only $9,000,000 of bonds were presented for payment up to the end of the month, and the amount actually received by the New York banks was by no means so large as this, as many holders were scattered throughout the country.

Treasury operations for the month as a whole set free only $7,500,000 Further efforts were evidently required, and on August 30 the Treasury offered to take another $20,000,000 of the 4½ per cent bonds on the same terms as before. On September 6 the Treasury offered also to prepay the interest of the 4 per cent bonds up to and including July 1, 1891, amounting to $23,000,000. It is worthy of note, however, that not all of the holders made the necessary application for the interest upon these bonds Notwithstanding these various devices, the Treasury was not paying out money rapidly enough to prevent further reduction in the reserves of the New York banks The following table shows the course of events as reflected by the bank statement and call-loan rates for the period under review, and carries on the record to the close of September

New York Bank Statement

[In millions]

	Loans	Reserve	Net deposits	Surplus reserve	Call-loan rates
1890					
Aug 9	$406 1	$103 2	$407 9	$1 3	3–20
16	402 2	99 2	399 5	— 6	3–25
23	397 7	94 9	389 5	— 2 5	3–189
30	392 5	95 6	385 1	— 5	2–15
Sept 6	395 0	95 7	388 4	— 1 4	3–12
13	393 2	92 5	388 3	— 3 3	3–189
20	392 6	99 4	390 0	1 9	2–96
27	394 0	115 8	406 8	14 1	2–6

For two weeks after the stringency in August the reserves remained almost stationary, but in the week ending September 13 there was a loss of $3,500,000, and the reserve deficit of $3,300,000 was the most considerable of the year up to that time The banks again resorted to loan contraction, and the high rates of August once more became a factor in the situation As one writer expressed it, "The stock market was almost strangled by the restriction in the money market" The fall in security quotations was even greater and more general than in August At length the hand of the Secretary of the Treasury was clearly forced Four per cent bonds had been purchased for the sinking fund in July at prices ranging from 122.26 to 124 On Monday, September 17, the Treasury invited offers of bonds to the amount of $16,000,000, and accepted nearly $17,000,000 at prices ranging from 125 to 126¾, calling for a disbursement of more than $21,000,000 These bonds were largely supplied by a New York syndicate, and the money received in payment went directly into the banks, accounting for the enormous increase in the reserves from $92,000,000 on September 13 to $115,000,000 on September 27.[a] The net addition to the money in circulation secured from the Treasury during September reached the enormous total of $57,887,000, and for the three months from July 1 nearly $70,000,000 had been secured from that source

Upon the basis of the money thus secured the loans of the banks began to increase and ease was restored Between September 20 and October 11 the loans of the New York banks increased from $394,000,000 to $407,000,000,

[a] For a circumstantial statement from a generally conservative source to the effect that the bonds were held by a group of operators engaged in manipulating the market, see Bankers' Magazine for October, 1890, p 248

and stocks recovered some of their September loss Crop-moving requirements were, however, causing the reserve to fall away once more, and on October 15 it was $15,000,000 below the figure for September 27, and again the banks were below the required reserve by $349,000.

Loan contraction once more became the order of the day, but on this occasion pressure upon borrowers was not carried to the extremes which had characterized August and September During the three weeks ending November 8, loans were reduced a little more than $7,000,000, and the highest rate quoted on any one day for call loans was 30 per cent There was a further decline on the stock exchange, but at no time was panic threatened London sales of American securities were an important factor during these weeks and contributed largely to the fall in quotations which was particularly severe in standard stocks, many of which reached the lowest level of the year.

These recurring periods of monetary stringency were due almost wholly to domestic causes, only indirectly and to a relatively small extent were they the result of the European situation. Even the fall in the prices of securities was probably quite as largely due to loan contraction as to London sales Gold exports of the early summer had to some extent depleted the reserves of the banks, but the loss from withdrawals for crop moving purposes was of much greater magnitude. But these withdrawals, it should be noted, were not by any means of an unusual character Between July 1 and November 8, 1889, the reported net shipments of currency to the interior from New York were $35,500,000. For the same period in 1890 they amounted to $34,900,000 The conclusion can not be escaped that an insufficient reserve in New York during the first half of the year was the inevitable cause of the disturbance in the summer and autumn months

We now enter upon the final stage of the monetary disturbance of this eventful year Up to the second week of November there had been no important failures, either banking or mercantile. But the decline on the stock exchange had carried quotations below the level reached during the panic of 1884. It was evident that further decline could hardly fail to bring about extensive failures and undermine general confidence This was the general situation on Friday, November 7, when the Bank of England advanced its rate of discount from 5 per cent to 6 per cent. An advance of 1 per cent in the Bank of England rate is according to custom, but as the rate is seldom changed, except at the regular meeting of the directors on Thursday, this action naturally gave rise to a general feeling of apprehension and alarm. On the following day the New York bank statement showed a decrease of $4,254,000 in the reserve and a reserve deficit of $3,544,000 From this point the narrative of the course of events is taken from the annual review of the Commercial and Financial Chronicle for 1890

During the week of the crisis the record was substantially as follows

On Monday, November 10, there was heavy London selling and great depression, and the death of Mr James Struthers occurred at the stock board and caused an adjournment for half an hour about noon, money was one-half per cent a day plus interest On Tuesday, the 11th, London advices were strong, as the Bank of England obtained a loan of £3,000,000 gold from the Bank of France, but the Villard stocks broke badly, and Decker, Howell & Co.'s failure was announced about 2 p. m., the Bank of North America being also involved. The clearing-house committee then met and resolved to issue clearing-house certificates, and this relieved the banks, though the news of this issue was not known till after business hours. Messrs. Charles M. Whitney & Co., bankers, failed, and also Mr. David Richmond, an old member of the stock exchange. On Wednesday, the 12th, the tone was much improved, money relaxed with the knowledge that clearing-house certificates were issued. Messrs. J. C. Walcott & Co., stock brokers, suspended; the North River Bank closed. On Thursday, the 13th, the feeling was still better, but the North American Company's stock fell from 16 to 7, recovering slightly afterwards, and the market resisted very well; the Bank of England rate remained at 6 per cent, which was encouraging. On Friday, the 14th, the market was weak and sensitive, but without special features. On Saturday, the 15th, early cables from London announced the embarrassment of Baring Brothers & Co., and this led to a feeling of panic at the stock board, and the sales in two hours of business reached 424,000 shares. On Monday, the 17th, the failure of Mills, Robeson & Smith was announced, occasioned by the forgeries of A. H. Smith, carried on for some years by raising the face value of stock certificates; Messrs. Randall & Wierum and Gregory & Ballou suspended; the Bank of Commerce passed its resolution against the contraction of loans and took out $500,000 in clearing-house certificates—the resolution said: "In the opinion of this board expansion is the heroic remedy for present ills rather than unceasing contraction;" money was at one-half per cent a day and the depression was great. On Tuesday, the 18th, Messrs. P. W. Gallaudet & Co. failed, and it was made known also that the North River Bank could not open, but must go to receiver. On Thursday, the 20th, Barker Brothers & Co. failed in Philadelphia, but this did not affect the market greatly, although they were involved in large financial operations with several railroads; the Bank of England rate remained unchanged at 6 per cent and the tone in stocks was getting perceptibly stronger. On Friday there was a very sharp improvement, and many stocks rebounded from the depression, which had been severe until Wednesday; the tone was almost buoyant, and although the feeling was not fully maintained the general market in the next week ending November 29 was very strong and leading stocks advanced from 5 to 8 points.[a]

The disturbance, it will be noted, was of short duration and did not at any time get beyond control. The prompt action taken by the clearing-house authorities did much to prevent the spread of panic. It is not improbable that

[a] Commercial and Financial Chronicle, January 3, 1891, p. 16.

some intimation of impending trouble in London may have been conveyed to bankers in New York As in 1884, no provision for equalizing reserves was adopted. When the issue of loan certificates was authorized on both occasions they were intended to meet the requirements of particular institutions rather than a general situation In spite of the issue of certificates, loans which had been reduced by $5,500,000 for the week ending November 15 were reduced still further in the two following weeks by $8,700,000 There seems to have been some hesitation among the banks to take out certificates from the fear that such action would be regarded as a confession of weakness. A striking example of a more far-seeing view was afforded by the Bank of Commerce, one of the strongest banks in the city at that time. On Monday, November 17, the following resolution, presented by Mr A A Low and seconded by Mr J. P. Morgan, was passed by the directors.

Resolved, That the directors of this bank desire to express their entire approval of the action of the Clearing House Association in so promptly providing for the issue of the clearing-house certificates against satisfactory collateral

Resolved, That the officers of this bank are directed to invite the consideration of the national and state banks, associated as members of the clearing house, to a policy of forbearance in respect to all loans with parties in good standing, extending such indulgence as circumstances may warrant, to the end that all the banks and trust companies in the city may not be simultaneously calling on their customers for money at a moment when all are reluctant to lend

In the opinion of this board, expansion is the heroic remedy for present ills, rather than unceasing contraction—necessary alike for the promotion of confidence and the maintenance of the value of all assets in possession of our moneyed institutions

Resolved, That in furtherance of the above, the officers be and are hereby directed to apply for clearing-house certificates to such an extent as may from time to time be deemed advisable [a]

[a] Bankers' Magazine, May, 1891, p 417

These resolutions emphasize one of the two specifics for the proper treatment of a panic—the continuance of loans to solvent borrowers A second equally important specific is the prompt payment by the banks of every demand by depositors for cash In this particular instance the banks were not subjected to a severe test of their ability and willingness to apply this remedy Withdrawals by no class of depositors went beyond normal requirements and the reserves of the banks did not undergo any material change The contraction in loans did not occasion any such degree of stock-market strain as had occurred in August and September. Rates went to the same high level of 186 per cent, but the period of high rates was somewhat shorter than in September Within a week after the announcement of the Baring failure on November 15, call-loan rates were quoted between 2 per cent and 5 per cent Large purchases were being made by investors, and the stock market was reported as steady, strong, and almost buoyant Although call-loan rates were not constantly maintained at this extremely low level, it is still within the truth to say that after November 20 the monetary situation ceased to be a serious factor in the stock market or elsewhere [a]

The following table shows the course of events as reflected by the bank statement and call-loan rates between November 1 and December 15, 1890.

[a] There was a flurry in the money market on December 8, and call loans, largely through manipulation, again rose to 186 per cent, but in the course of the day fell again to 6 per cent

New York bank statement

[In millions]

	Loans	Reserve	Deposits	Surplus reserve	Call-loan rates
1890					
Nov 1	$399 8	$99 9	$396 3	$0 7	3 - 30
8	398 9	95 6	392 3	-2 6	3 - 25
15	393 3	95 8	386 6	- 8	2½- 186
22	387 3	95 5	381 7	1	2 - 186
29	384 5	95 0	378 6	4	2 - 8
Dec 5	386 5	91 8	376 9	-2 4	3 - 15
11	386 0	94 8	376 7	6	2 - 186
18	386 4	99 6	380 3	4 5	2 - 6

The banks of Philadelphia and Boston also resorted to the issue of clearing-house certificates. In these cities, as well as in New York, the primary object was to meet the requirements of particular banks A detailed account of the issue of loan certificates in 1890 appeared in the report of the Comptroller of the Currency for 1891 and will be found in the appendix [a]

As in 1884, the issue of loan certificates was not followed by the suspension of payments by the banks One episode which occurred early in December, however, affords evidence of the danger of suspension if no provision is adopted for the equalizing of reserves when loan certificates are issued. The course of the later crises gives significance to the following account taken from the Commercial and Financial Chronicle.

A feature which has caused some remark this week has been the payment at the subtreasury over the counter in gold coin and notes of about two-thirds of the disbursement made by the Government on account of bond purchases, instead of the checks taking the usual course and being collected through the clearing house This change is thought by some to indicate

[a] Appendix, Note E, pp 387–392

that the money received is to be hoarded by the people and companies who sold the bonds, and not to go into banks That may be true in a measure But as a further explanation, we would state that this method of collecting government checks has for a number of weeks been in operation, it having been practiced by our clearing-house banks Indeed, this practice explains in part the recent large increase in loan certificates These certificates are used, of course, to pay debtor balances at the clearing house These balances are not perfectly natural, that is to say, they occur through a withholding of all subtreasury checks from the clearings and collecting them, as stated, in gold over the subtreasury counter The result is that the banks show an adverse balance at the clearing house, to pay which it uses a small amount of loan certificates, the receipts from the Treasury, however, reenforce its gold reserve This process, to be sure, makes no one richer or poorer, but it affords currency for the supply of the demand from the interior without exhausting the banks which ship it [a]

By the means above described weak banks could gain cash and meet unfavorable clearing-house balances, which would otherwise have been smaller, by issues of certificates, and strong banks could diminish favorable balances which might only be met with certificates from other banks The cashing of checks by depositors over the counters of banks of which they were not depositors at the instance of their own banks would be simply another step in the same direction Working at cross purposes among the banks might easily become almost as serious as if loan certificates had not been issued, and the banks would soon inevitably drift into suspension

Foreign exchange rates followed the normal autumn course, illustrating the strength of the American position during that season of the year Notwithstanding the sales of American securities in London, there was no gold export movement after the middle of August The advance of the Bank of England rate to 6 per cent on November 5 and the Baring disclosures caused rates to rise,

[a] Commercial and Financial Chronicle, December 13, 1890, p 808

but not to the export point The advance was but momentary; rates soon fell below par, and in the second week of December nearly $5,000,000 was taken from the Bank of England for export to the United States

The ordinary money requirements of this year were, as we have seen, entirely provided by the Treasury. Between July and December the cash reserves of the national banks were reduced by less than $3,000,000, from $280,900,000 to $278,000,000 As in other years, this slight loss was more than shifted to the city institutions The reserves of the New York banks were reduced $4,600,000, those of Chicago and St Louis $2,500,000, and those of other reserve cities $1,500,000, a total of $8,600,000, while the reserves of the country banks were increased $6,700,000 Again, the fundamental characteristic of our banking system was illustrated, that for any extraordinary cash requirements the reserves of the country banks are an unused asset. Evidence was again given which should have brought home to city institutions the heavy responsibility which they incurred in attracting the reserves of other banks.

During the same months of 1889, there was comparatively little financial disturbance, although the reserves of the banks fell off more than $24,000,000 Explanation of the difference is to be found in the loan and deposit situation. In 1889 the ratio between deposits and the reserve was such as to make it possible for the banks to increase loans In 1890 loan expansion had gone beyond the permanently available resources of the banks. The difficulty which was encountered in carrying through a very moderate amount of loan contraction was evidence, not that the community needed additional credit, but that business was already extended beyond the limits of safety set by adequate supplies of working capital

Although the reported net shipments of the New York banks to the interior between July and the end of December were more than $50,000,000, the amount of bankers' deposits held by them was reduced but slightly, from $170,000,000 to $153,000,000, between July 18 and December 19 A number of possible explanations of this unusual result may be mentioned The trade relations of the rest of the country with the East may have given western and southern banks a favorable balance of payments, and the investment of eastern capital in the West may have contributed to this result In the second place, the bonds purchased by the Government were to some extent held outside of New York, though the immediate payments made by the Treasury may have been made through the New York banks Again, loans of outside banks in New York, if liquidated, would provide the means for drawing funds from that city. This last factor has become of enormous importance in quite recent years. It was not mentioned in 1890, and was not probably important, as the western and southern banks were then hardly able to satisfy the requirements of local borrowers. Finally, the banks seem to have rediscounted freely at the eastern money centers The amount of rediscounts and bills payable increased from $22,000,000 to $37,000,000 between July and December, the most considerable increase which had occurred at any time since the organization of the national banks In 1873 there was no increase whatever in these items, and in 1884 there was an increase of only $4,000,000

The assistance afforded the money market by the Treasury was a subject which was much discussed, and upon which quite opposite opinions were expressed. That it was proper for the Treasury to restore to general circulation money which it had recently withdrawn was not questioned From this position many, including the Secretary of the Treasury, went on to the conclusion that a treasury surplus was a desirable means for safeguarding the credit structure of the country. This view was expressed in the annual report of the Secretary of the Treasury for 1890, extracts from which containing the account of the Treasury operations during the year will be found in the Appendix.[a] It is unquestionable that a supply of money, whatever its source, is of the very greatest utility in an emergency, but it is a far cry to the conclusion that the Government rather than the banks is the organ which should provide this resource The unfavorable effects of treasury assistance were thus set forth in the Chronicle

> The time was when our banks provided beforehand for the fall trade, and so trimmed their sails, if we may be permitted to use the expression, through the summer months as to avert a storm by preparing themselves for the crop demand Of late years they have looked to the Treasury wholly, and have gone through the summer trenching on their reserves regardless of any increased drain sure to come later on [b]

New York bankers denied strenuously the justice of this criticism. The president of the Park Bank, one of

---

[a] Appendix, Note F, pp 393–399

[b] Commercial and Financial Chronicle, December 6, 1890, p 754

the largest holders of bankers' deposits, asserted that, "we always prepare ourselves carefully for the fall demand for money for the movement of the crops * * * and keep our loans and reserves throughout the summer for this purpose" The cashier of another almost equally important bank observed "that as far as we know the banks of this city do not intend to make their calculations relying on the Treasurer of the United States for assistance in perfecting the same, nor do we consider they should or that it would be wise to do so" [a]

We may accept the contention of the bankers that the Treasury surplus had had no influence upon their reserve policy, but for a reason less complimentary to their sagacity than those which they put forward In years when there was no available surplus in the Treasury we have seen that the New York banks failed to carry an adequate reserve, and there is every reason to suppose that had there been no surplus in 1890 the banks would have carried a full line of credit, and that their reserves would not have been more adequate. We may therefore accept the view of the Secretary of the Treasury that the government surplus would serve to supply means for crop-moving purposes which the New York banks would not have been able to supply without general financial disturbance On the other hand, the Treasury surplus was by no means a solid foundation for the credit structure It could not be expected that there would always be a government surplus, but while it continued the necessity

[a] For these and other similar opinions expressed by various New York bankers, see David Kinley, The Independent Treasury of the United States, p 293

of making provision for emergencies was far removed from the banks Very likely the banks might not have provided these means at once, but the likelihood that they would ever come to a proper understanding of their responsibilities was distant so long as the surplus remained.

In only one direction did the experience of the year bring about a change in banking practice, and that was of secondary importance. It will be remembered that the three banks which became involved in difficulties in November were all state institutions The clearing-house rule requiring all members to hold a 25 per cent cash reserve had not been strictly adhered to for many years by a large number of the state banks in the association. Since more than three-fourths of the clearing-house banks were national banks, it was not a difficult matter to secure action looking toward a more rigorous rule.[a] This, however, did not in itself serve to increase greatly the power of the New York banks in an emergency. The resources of the state banks were less than one-sixth those of the national banks, and they were engaged in a purely local business This action of the clearing house was probably a result of the increasing tendency to regard the 25 per cent reserve as a permanent requirement, not to be reduced in any circumstances The acceptance of such a belief was certain to involve trouble in an emergency if it did not lead the banks to maintain considerably more than the minimum requirement in ordinary times, so as to have a large amount of free cash to meet extraordinary occasions.

[a] Bankers' Magazine, March, 1891, p 673

A much more fundamental change in the organization in the New York money market came with the establishment of the stock-exchange clearing house in May, 1892. It led to a very considerable reduction in the clearing-house exchanges of the banks and also, and more important, in the volume of certified checks. Over-certification ceased to be a factor of the first magnitude in the banking methods of the city. Had not this arrangement for stock-exchange dealings been set up, it is probable that it would have been necessary to close the stock exchange in 1893 and in 1907, and it is also probable that the volume of business transacted in the years after 1897 could not have been handled.

CHAPTER IV.

THE CRISIS OF 1893.

In previous chapters attention has been centered upon the New York banks because their operations were the most important banking factors both before and during the emergencies which have been analyzed. We have seen that the New York banks did not normally maintain the large reserves which the responsibilities of their position demanded We have also seen that the methods of handling difficult situations were upon the whole wise and adequate for the purposes in view, so far as the means of the banks allowed. We now approach a crisis which, so far as it was due to banking causes, was a result of banking operations in other parts of the country The strain upon the New York banks was not on that account less severe, but, though they were not as strong in cash reserves at the time as the responsibilities of their position demanded, they were far more amply provided with cash than has been customary in periods of active business either before or since On the other hand, we shall find that in handling the situation there was an absence of the intelligent and bold action which did so much to extricate the banks from a situation of equal if not greater seriousness in 1873.

MONETARY AND BANKING MOVEMENTS, 1890–1893

The course of events between the panic of 1890 and the crisis of 1893 centers about the monetary history of the period. The crisis itself was a result of complex causes, among which the monetary situation was by no means certainly the most important This is especially true of the causes of the long years of depression which followed its outbreak. Among these causes may be mentioned unremunerative prices for agricultural staples, and the heavy load of farm-mortgage indebtedness, also railway receiverships, which were due to the oversanguine estimates of the future and reckless financing of the wildest sort Even the unsatisfactory banking position at the time of the crisis seems to have been far less a product of monetary conditions than has been usually supposed. At the risk of exaggerating the importance of the monetary influences it will, nevertheless, be convenient to make that history the point of departure in the study of the course of events which preceded the crisis of 1893

Almost exactly $100,000,000 had been added to the money supply of the country during the last six months of 1890, and all of this increment was, as we have seen, outside the banks at the time of the December return to the Comptroller of the Currency. With the end of the crop-moving period there came the usual return flow of money to the banks—a movement which was accelerated by the moderate decline in business activity during the winter and spring of 1891 The strengthening of bank reserves which would have been thus brought about was in a measure offset by gold exports to the unusual amount of $53,000,000 during the first six months of the year This outflow was due to a number of causes and not a simple result of the silver-purchase law, as some zealous advocates of the gold standard were inclined to argue.

Depression and credit contraction had gone much further in Europe than in this country, and as a natural consequence there was a considerable decline in merchandise exports relative to imports Between January and July, 1891, there was an excess of merchandise imports of $14,000,000, which, together with the course of foreign dealings in our securities, affords adequate explanation of the movement of gold If the currency situation exerted any influence, it was indirect and remote. Had the currency been susceptible to contraction through internal causes it does not follow that gold would not have gone out, since the banks could have endured a considerable additional loss of cash without such a contraction of credit and advance in rates as might have influenced appreciably the course of business dealings.

In itself the loss of the gold would not have been a serious matter if it had involved an equivalent contraction in the amount of money in the country, since business requirements were upon a smaller scale than at the same time in the previous year. A part of the loss, however, was offset by issues of treasury notes in payment for silver bullion. Moreover, Treasury operations, far from taking money from circulation as in previous years, added about $9,000,000 to the amount afloat in the country. Government expenditure had at length overtaken revenue and even gone beyond it a little, and this remained the constant situation of the Treasury throughout the period to the crisis As a result of all these various influences, there was a net contraction of only $29,000,000 in the money in circulation between January and July, 1891.

For the banks the immediate consequence of the partial failure of the currency to contract was favorable. Between December and July their cash reserve increased about $32,000,000, and as there was only a moderate increase in loans the proportion of cash to deposit liabilities was somewhat improved. But the price which was paid for the temporary ease thus secured was a heavy one—the weakening of the gold foundation of the monetary system of the country Contraction, always painful, would have been comparatively easy during a period of moderate decline in business activities As it was, the deterioration in the quality of the money in the country through the loss of gold was intensified by additional amounts of every other kind of money of which the circulating medium was composed

Fears of the possible effects of continued gold exports were soon removed in consequence of the bumper crops of 1891, which were sold in unexampled quantity and at high prices in Europe, where there had been a complete failure of harvests in south Russia and less than an average crop elsewhere During the six months to January, 1892, net gold imports were $34,000,000 and, together with various other influences affecting different elements of the money supply, brought about an increase of $89,000,000 in the amount of money in circulation. It is not surprising in these circumstances that no trouble was experienced in New York during the crop-moving months.

The foreign demand for wheat stimulated a renewal of business and speculative activity, which continued to the outbreak of the crisis of 1893. In the stock market the invigorating influence first made itself felt, and a buoyant market characterized the later months of the year. The loans of the New York banks, which had been stationary during the spring and summer, began to increase, and, notwithstanding the autumn requirements of the interior banks, no very great advance in rates for loans occurred In the country generally the renewal of activity was a marked feature of the opening months of 1892 The stimulation of the foreign demand for our staple agricultural products did not, however, lead to anything like the rapid advance which occurred either in 1880 or in 1898 A prolonged upward movement was subject to a number of adverse influences. The disturbances in 1890 had not been severe enough to clear the ground of all unsound undertakings. Moreover, Europe was still plunged in depression, made all the more profound by the necessity of paying dearly for its food supply. Payment was made immediately in cash, but in large measure ultimate payment was made by the return of American securities held abroad. Finally as in Europe there was no business and speculative activity, with its accompanying credit expansion, corresponding to what was taking place in this country, there was a relatively high level of prices here, which stimulated merchandise imports and influenced the export trade adversely

As a result of these various influences foreign exchange rates were almost constantly against this country during 1892, and only in October and November were gold imports in excess of exports The net loss from gold exports during the year amounted to $50,000,000. There was, however, no diminution in the amount of money in circulation, but, rather, an increase of $22,000,000 In addition to silver issues and excess Treasury payments there was also an increase of $8,000,000 in the note issues of the banks With the cessation of government purchases the price of bonds had fallen enough to make it profitable for banks to take out additional circulation During the year there was a notable increase in bank loans, but the greater requirements for reserves and the increased amount of money required outside the banks on account of more active business did not exhaust the cash resources and lending power of the banks, and no pressure was experienced in the money centers during the crop-moving period Continued monetary ease was secured at the price of a still further deterioration in the quality of the money supply of the country

Before the close of 1892 another factor appeared in the gold-movement situation—the return of American securities, owing to doubt among European investors of our intention and ability to maintain the gold standard. This influence, together with an increasingly unfavorable merchandise balance, caused gold to flow out in unexampled quantities, beginning with an export of $11,000,000 in December, 1892. During the first five months of 1893 the net loss was nearly $60,000,000 Even this drain did not greatly reduce the available stock of money in circulation, silver issues, Treasury payments, increased circulation, and domestic gold production offsetting all but $14,000,000 of the loss. Taking the entire period from January, 1891, to June, 1893, there was an increase of $68,000,000 in the estimated amount of money in circulation It will thus be seen that the money available for use had not been reduced and that, however undesirable from a monetary point of view, considered simply on the banking side, there was no reason why the banks should have found themselves at the beginning of the crisis poorly supplied with cash reserves

Contrasting the reserves of the banks in December, 1891, with those of December, 1892, there was an increase of $8,000,000, while the money in circulation increased about $37,000,000 Nearly $30,000,000, therefore, either was absorbed by banks outside the national system or went into every-day use in consequence of increasing population and greater business activity The return for March, 1893, showed a loss of $4,000,000 in cash reserves, while there was a falling off in the total amount in circulation of $11,000,000 Between March and May the banks gained more than $8,000,000, and the total of money in circulation was stationary There can be little doubt that the cash holdings of the banks would not have been as large as they were in May, 1893, if that contraction in the currency had taken place which was needed to place it upon a solid foundation It is possible, however, that the gradual inflation of the currency may have weakened the banks indirectly On account of abundant cash reserves, the banks may have extended credit more freely during 1891 and 1892 than they would otherwise have consented to do. Between May, 1891, and September, 1892, the loans of the national banks increased from $1,969,000,000 to $2,171,000,000. This increase was very general in all parts of the country. During the following eight months to May, 1893, there was a slight contraction of $10,000,000 The banks of the New England and Middle Atlantic States had reduced their loans by $35,000,000; in the Southern States loans were stationary, while in the North Central and Western States there was a further increase of $25,000,000.

This movement of bank loans clearly reflected the situation in different parts of the country The West had been most influenced by the profitable export trade of 1891, and business and speculative activities in that part of the country continued up to the outbreak of the crisis In the East the cotton industry was unusually profitable in 1892, but in other lines there was only a moderate improvement In the case of the railroads, while their gross earnings increased there was some falling off in net earnings. For this reason and because of the sales of securities held in Europe, the stock market during 1892 was in general dull and quotations for standard securities ruled lower at the end than at the beginning of the year. There was therefore only a moderate increase in the loans of the New York banks during the year, although the rates for call loans were abnormally low. Activity on the stock exchange was largely in connection with speculation in industrial companies and the financing of various combinations. Finally it may be noted that the increase in loans, taking the country as a whole, was not greater than at many other periods of active business in our history and that the change in the proportion of reserves was not such as to weaken the banks very materially In May, 1891, the proportion of cash reserves to deposit liabilities was 16 6 per cent, in 1892 it was 18 4 per cent, and in 1893 it was 16 9 per cent The statistical position of the banks was, therefore, reasonably satisfactory.

On the other hand it became evident during the crisis that the banks had been carrying a large amount of loans which should have been long since written off or at least written down. These loans had been made in many instances before the panic in 1890, and in part they had been made more recently, serving to bolster up weak enterprises and to make an already unhealthy situation more unsound. In the Southern States real estate speculation in town lots and mineral lands seems to have been the most unsound element in the situation. There was comparatively little speculation in agricultural lands because the cotton crop of 1891 was not so exceptionally remunerative as had been the case with the cereal crops in the Northwest It is possible that but for the silver issues the banks might have enforced a more rigorous policy against the renewal of loans and might not have increased the total of loans to so considerable an extent as they actually did. On the other hand the country banks, which were chiefly responsible for loan expansion, were well above their reserve requirements, and if there had been less money in the country it might have happened that something like the same amount of credit expansion would have occurred upon smaller reserves. In that case deposits with reserve agents would not have been so large, and it is, therefore, in the operations of the city banks, if anywhere, that we must look for the banking effects of the silver issues. Fortunately, the regular returns of the banks give a clear answer to this question. The loans of the New York national banks were $365,000,000 in May, 1892, and in March, 1893, they had been reduced to $323,000,000, and in May to $307,000,000. In Boston there was a reduction during the same period from $156,000,000 to $142,000,000, and in most of the other reserve cities there was also some contraction, or at most a very moderate increase In the eastern money centers the unsatisfactory monetary situation seems in some measure to have exerted a restraining influence. During 1892 the low rates for loans were a clear indication that the banks would have been glad to lend more than the demand of borrowers made possible. The situation was in marked contrast to the months preceding other crises when every available credit resource at the money centers has been stretched to the extreme limits of safety and beyond For these reasons the opinion may be ventured that the silver issues were not an important factor in determining either the course of trade or the operations of the banks during the period which preceded the crisis of 1893.

THE FIRST STAGE OF THE CRISIS.

We must now follow the course of the New York money market during the months which immediately preceded the crisis. The usual return flow of money from the interior was not much below the normal during the winter of 1893, but it did not avail to increase the reserves of the banks on account of the enormous gold exports During January, however, loans increased at a slightly more rapid rate than in 1892, but in February sufficient impression had been made upon the reserves of the banks to lead to some loan contraction and a slightly higher level of rates. These factors, however, had little to do with the first serious disturbance of the year which came with the failure of the Philadelphia and Reading Railroad on February 26 This railroad had taken the lead in absorbing coal lands and had also ventured into the New England railroad field Both enterprises were far beyond the available capital of the company and its downfall was directly due to the weight of an enormous floating debt. The immediate effects of the Reading failure were comparatively moderate, but it gave rise to doubts of other companies, particularly of the industrials, and the course of the stock market was depressed and downward throughout March and April. To this tendency high average call loan rates and the continued contraction of bank loans, of course, contributed

The course of the banking operations of the New York banks during the first four months of this and the preceding year is shown in the following table.

New York bank statement

	Loans	Net deposits	Reserve	Surplus reserve
1893				
Jan 7	$441 000,000	$455,000,000	$122,000 000	$8 900 000
Feb 4	465,000,000	495,000,000	142,000,000	18,600,000
Mar 4	453,000,000	462,000,000	122 000,000	6,500,000
Apr 1	433 000,000	439,000,000	120,000,000	10 600 000
May 6	425,000,000	433 000 000	121,000,000	12,800,000
1892				
Jan 9	444 000,000	477,000 000	138,000,000	18,900,000
Feb 6	460,000 000	515,000,000	162,000 000	33 000,000
Mar 5	488,000 000	533,000,000	154,000,000	21 200,000
Apr 2	489,000 000	528,000,000	150 000,000	18,000,000
May 7	493,000,000	531,000,000	147 000 000	14,800,000

It will be noted that at the beginning of February, 1893, the banks held a surplus reserve of $18,600,000 contrasted with $33,000,000 in February, 1892 The statement for the first week in May, 1893, shows a surplus of $12,800,000, only $2,000,000 less than that in May, 1892. This comparatively good showing had been secured, notwithstanding a loss in cash of $21,000,000 in 1893 as compared with only $15,000,000 in 1892 It had been secured through the contraction of loans from $465,000,000 to $425,000,000 while in the previous year loans had been increased by $33,000,000 This contraction in loans had been carried out slowly and steadily and with comparatively little difficulty. It involved loss to holders of securities, especially those of the more speculative variety, but even in this respect it served a good purpose, since the condition of many corporations warranted a far greater decline than had actually taken place Painful evidence of this fact was afforded by the disastrous failure of the National Cordage Company early in May The course of events of which that failure was a determining factor was thus described in The Commercial and Financial Chronicle:

> Again our market has passed through a severe stock panic, and again the prodigious vitality of bankers and brokers has been abundantly demonstrated On such an enormous and precipitate shrinkage in values it is very remarkable that so few houses have failed, and those that were compelled to suspend were more or less loaded up with the stocks of those companies which proved to be the bane of the market
>
> A stock dividend of 100 per cent in January and a receiver in May—this is the brief statement of a method of financiering which has lead up to and precipitated one of the worst stock panics of short duration that we have ever known in this city The story is almost a counterpart to that of Philadelphia and Reading, which paid 5 per cent on its preferred income bonds just before going into receivers' hands It may not be possible to prevent such methods altogether, but the public should get a clear idea of what terrible disaster is brought to thousands of innocent holders of

stocks and bonds, and the parties engaged in this sort of financial operation ought not to be held up as heroes of the day, although they may have personal integrity.

The open-market rates for call loans during the week on stock and bond collateral have ranged from 4 to 40 per cent, the average being 6 per cent To-day rates on call were 6 to 40 per cent Commercial paper quoted at 6 to 9 per cent [a]

Again, if we inquire how far the currency situation had anything to do with the course of events up to this time, the answer is clear that its influence was extremely slight It was argued at the time that fears for the maintenance of the gold standard frightened investors and deprived worthy enterprises of additional capital But the enterprises which had failed were not worthy, and there were many more whose situation would have been made worse rather than better by additional capital, and an even greater number whose further expansion would have served only to provide facilities for the production of commodities already in excess of profitable demand It was also argued that business was being deprived of needed circulating capital through wholesale credit contraction by the banks, but the returns of the national banks, at least, show that there had been no contraction whatever For the banks as a whole, between March 6 and May 4, there had been a slight increase of $3,000,000 In New York there had been a contraction of $16,000,000, in Boston $4,000,000, and in Chicago $4,000,000 In the country at large there was therefor an expansion of at least $27,000,000 up to the 1st of May. Finally, it may be observed, that a situation which demands constantly increasing credits to prevent collapse is certain to arrive

[a] The Commercial and Financial Chronicle, May 6, 1893, p 743

at that state in any case, and that delay can hardly be expected to improve matters

There is also no evidence of any general distrust of the banks up to this time The total amount of money held by the banks, as we have seen, had increased somewhat—from $314,000,000 to $323,000,000—and in the case of the New York banks from $94,500,000 to $98,000,000. There was, however, one change of a most unusual character disclosed by the returns of the banks for May. The amount due from reserve agents was reduced from $202,000,000 to $174,000,000, and in the case of the New York banks from $137,000,000 to $114,000,000 Changes in this item involve, usually, a shifting of cash holdings between the banks, but, as was noted above, the New York banks increased their cash holdings by $3,500,000. Explanation of this apparent anomaly is simple. The balance of payments for commodities was in favor of New York, and the rest of the country, particularly the West and South, was paying for the enormous imports of commodities which had taken place during preceding months. In other words, the gold exports were in the last analysis due to the obligations of the people generally and not those of dealers in New York City. Another indication that the balance of payments between New York and the rest of the country was in favor of New York may be mentioned: Drafts on New York received in payment for commodities would increase individual deposits and diminish bankers' deposits. Some such influence is suggested by the fact that, though loans were reduced by $16,000,000 and clearing-house exchanges by $11,000,000, there was a positive increase in individual deposits. The result of all these changes was to place the New York banks in a vastly stronger position in May than in March. The proportion of reserve to net deposits had increased from 26.34 per cent to 28.52 per cent, and the proportion of bankers' deposits to total deposits had diminished

THE SECOND STAGE OF THE CRISIS.

Following the stock market collapse of May 4 the market was irregular and dull throughout the remainder of the month. The lending rates of the banks were moderate, but a further decline in the volume of loans continued, and on May 27 they stood at $415,000,000, some $10,000,000 less than at the beginning of the month. In the meantime, the banks had been receiving large amounts of money from the interior, and, notwithstanding continued gold exports, the reserves rose from $121,000,000 to $134,000,000. The position of the banks, therefore, at the end of May had distinctly improved, they were, in fact, stronger than at the same time in the previous year, as is evident from the following table:

New York Bank Statement

	May 27 1893	May 28, 1892
Loans	$415,801,000	$488,000 000
Deposits	436 724 000	536,000 000
Reserve	134 621,000	158 000 000
Surplus reserve	25 439,000	24,600,000
Per cent of reserve	30 82	29 58

During the following week there was a loss of $5,700,000 in reserves, principally on account of gold exports, which excited no particular alarm, but the loss for the week ending June 10 was not only more considerable—nearly $10,000,000—but it was also the beginning of an entirely new stage in the crisis. Up to this time receipts of cash from the interior had been fairly large For the week ending June 2 the reported movements of money between the New York banks and the interior showed a net gain of $2,500,000; but the following week shipments were over $8,000,000 and were nearly as much for the week ending June 16 In the three weeks ending with June 17 the reserve of the New York banks was reduced from $134,000,000 to $110,000,000 and the surplus reserve fell from $24,600,000 to $8,700,000.

The cause of this abrupt change was certainly not in any definite way connected with the silver situation. Information that the administration would move for the repeal of the Sherman silver purchase act had already been made public The withdrawal of money from New York was directly due to the failure and suspension of large numbers of banks, both state and national, and of private bankers in the West and South Nineteen national banks were placed in the hands of receivers during May and June, and the number of state and private banks which fell was even greater. The causes of these failures were in most instances, as was pointed out by the Comptroller of the Currency, due to "violations of law and imprudent methods of banking, and the closing of them was only hastened by the general condition of financial affairs Some failed because of criminal acts on the part of the officials in charge and others because of the lack of proper comprehension of the purposes of a bank."[a] Quite apart from mismanagement it was inevitable that some banks should have gone to the wall in consequence of the many mercantile failures, 3,401 in number, with liabilities of $169,000,000, which occurred during the period from January to July, 1893 These failures exceeded both in number and in the amount of liabilities those which had occurred in any other period of equal length in our history. Bank suspensions were almost as numerous as bank failures and seemed to have been due to a greater variety of causes. In some instances banks were forced to suspend temporarily because of the distrust excited by the failure of banks in their neighborhood. In other instances it was on account of the distance which separated banks from their reserve agents [b]

In the eastern money centers bank failures and suspensions were attributed almost entirely to the silver influence. But it is to be noted that they occurred principally in the West and Southwest, where there is no evidence that people were distrustful of silver money Had the monetary influence been potent, we should expect to find numerous failures in the eastern States and also some discrimination on the part of depositors between the different kinds of money in circulation Distrust of the solvency of the banks rather than dissatisfaction with the circulating medium was clearly the direct cause which brought about runs upon banks and the numerous failures and suspensions.

[a] Report of the Comptroller of the Currency for 1893, p 10

[b] For a list of suspended banks, with dates of suspension and resumption, see Comptroller's Report for 1893, p 78

So far as the national banks were concerned it mattered little that the relative number of disasters among them was considerably less than among state institutions. The spread of distrust and the contagion of panic are essentially products of unreasoning fear. Moreover, the national banks of the cities held large balances of state as well as of national banks, and to call home some portion of these balances was in the circumstances the natural and proper course for the country banks

One element of weakness in the situation had disappeared. With the shipment of $1,000,000 on June 6 gold exports ceased, and from that time to the end of the crisis foreign exchange rates never fell to a point which suggested the likelihood of the renewal of the movement Indeed $500,000 was engaged from London for export to the United States on June 21. But the peculiar seriousness of the situation was at once recognized by the New York banks Never since the establishment of the national banking system had they been confronted with a like situation—widespread distrust of the solvency of their banks among the people in entire sections of the country. The ability of the New York banks to maintain payments was not as yet in question But though no bank in the city was in difficulty and there was still a surplus reserve on June 17 of $8,700,000, the machinery for the issue of clearing-house loan certificates was set up on the 15th of June.

The New York banks had never resorted to the issue of clearing-house loan certificates at so early a stage in any previous crisis. The following statement, taken from the

Commercial and Financial Chronicle, clearly sets forth the considerations which led to this wise action

Much interest has been taken in the decision of the New York clearing-house banks to issue clearing-house certificates if the need for so doing arises The statement issued by the banks on June 10 showed a heavy reduction in the reserve, owing to withdrawals for the West, and this week, as already said, the shipments to the interior have been remarkably large, the disturbed state of affairs in certain sections leading financial institutions there to increase their cash resources The agreement of the New York banks to issue clearing-house certificates is a precautionary measure, which will tend to prevent contraction of loans if this drain goes on, at the same time showing the confidence the banks have in one another More than this, it will be useful in inducing the clearing-house associations of other cities to take some similar course of united action None of the certificates have thus far been issued [a]

Suspension of cash payments was not at that time associated in the mind of anyone with the issue of clearing-house loan certificates, and there is no evidence whatever, beyond the vague recollections of bankers at the present time, that suspension was immediately resorted to by the banks Nowhere in contemporary journals has there been found a single reference to refusal or delay on the part of banks in meeting the demands of depositors for cash. If such occurred, it must have been exceptional and a result of the timidity of individual bankers. The issue of clearing-house loan certificates does not seem to have changed in the slightest degree the relations between banks and their depositors This point is of the very utmost importance, because in 1907, as we shall see later, the tradition seems to have become established among New York banks that the issue of clearing-house loan certificates and the suspension of cash payments are virtually one and the same thing

[a] Commercial and Financial Chronicle, June 17, 1893, p 1000

After the authorization of clearing-house loan certificates the reserves of the New York banks continued to fall away, the loss between June 17 and July 8 amounting to nearly $16,000,000, making a total loss since the beginning of the movement of $40,000,000 Loans also were further reduced during the week ending June 24 by nearly $5,000,000, but during the two following weeks there was an increase of nearly $13,000,000. Money had become extremely stringent owing to the normal heavy requirements at the close of the half year, and from June 29 a number of banks took out a large amount of certificates and offered to lend freely. The bank statement for July 8 found the banks for the first time during the crisis below reserve requirements with a deficiency of $5,082,000. During the following week loans were reduced $5,000,000 and there was no appreciable change in reserve There was a loss of only $323,000 and the reserve deficiency was reduced to $4,269,000. For the first time since the beginning of June reported movements of currency were in favor of the New York banks. The situation at that time was such as to give rise to hopes that the worst of the crisis was over. The prospects for the repeal of the silver-purchase law were good Reports of runs upon banks in different parts of the country were less frequent and during the second week of July the number of failures was comparatively small

The middle of July may properly be regarded as the end of the second stage of this crisis In its first stage the disturbance was largely confined to New York and was marked by the Reading and Cordage failures, a general decline in the stock market, the steady contraction of loans, and improvement in the position of the New York banks. During the second stage there was no serious disturbance in New York, but the reserves of the banks were reduced by $40,000,000 on account of the withdrawal of money by banking depositors in the West and South Serious strain had been met boldly and successfully, and had no further banking failures occurred it is probable that, with the general trade depression which was setting in, the reserves of the banks would soon have reached large proportions On July 12 the national banks made their usual returns to the Comptroller of the Currency, thus providing data for the analysis of the effects of the crisis upon the banks during this second stage of its course The following table shows the condition of all the banks and the various groups of banks on May 4 and July 12, 1893

	Loans	Net deposits	Cash reserve	Ratio to liabilities	Total reserve with agents	Ratio to liabilities
All banks						
May 4	[a] 2,162	1,910.0	323.0	17.0	504.0	26.4
July 12	2,020	1,674.0	289.0	17.2	456.0	27.2
Country banks						
May 4	1,196	970.0	109.0	11.2	120.0	24.4
July 12	1,108	864.0	114.8	13.3	110.0	26.8
Reserve city banks						
May 4	526	464.0	78.8	16.87	55.5	28.5
July 12	497	404.0	68.4	16.93	48.5	29.2
St Louis						
May 4	32	27.7	5.9	21.4	----------	----------
July 12	26	19.9	4.5	22.6	----------	----------
Chicago						
May 4	96	99.6	29.3	29.4	----------	----------
July 12	82	81.3	24.9	30.6	----------	----------
New York						
May 4	307	345.0	98.4	28.5	----------	----------
July 12	308	304.0	77.0	25.3	----------	----------

[a] Numbers, except ratios, represent million-dollar units

The contraction in loans amounting to $142,000,000, nearly 7 per cent of the total, was more considerable than in 1873 or in 1907 With the exception of the New York banks which increased loans $1,300,000 the banks everywhere resorted to contraction. By this means, and through the reduction of deposits with agents and the loss of cash, net deposits were reduced by $236,000,000, or about 12 per cent All classes of banks were able to reduce deposit liabilities Notwithstanding the loss of $34,000,000 in cash the banks were able to increase slightly the ratio of cash to net deposits from 17 per cent to 17.2 per cent The country banks, as in 1873, positively increased their cash holdings The banks of the reserve cities and those of Chicago and St. Louis experienced some loss, but still increased slightly the proportion of cash to net deposits. All banks, therefore, except those of New York are found with a higher reserve ratio at the end than at the beginning of the two months of financial strain. About two-thirds of the cash loss fell upon the New York banks, and the ratio of their reserve to net deposits was reduced from 28.5 per cent to 25 3 per cent While the causes of the disturbance were, in many ways, unlike those which brought about the crisis of 1873, banking movements had taken almost exactly the same course The banks in all parts of the country were relying upon the New York banks to supply them with the bulk of the money withdrawn by depositors, and by loan contraction were positively strengthening themselves. Reliance upon the New York banks seems to have been even greater than is disclosed by the figures which we have analyzed Between

May 4 and July 12 the bills payable and the notes rediscounted of the national banks had increased from $40,000,000 to $61,000,000, and it is reasonably certain that by far the greater part of this increase represented advances made by New York banks to banks in the West and South. Advances of this kind explain the comparatively small reduction in the bankers' deposits in New York City which, between May and July, notwithstanding enormous shipments of cash, were only reduced by $6,000,000.[a]

It will accordingly be recognized that up to this time the New York banks had fully lived up to the most exacting requirements which the responsibilities of their position as central reserve agents placed upon them, and that they had made a vastly better showing than the banks in the other central reserve cities, Chicago and St. Louis.

THE THIRD STAGE OF THE CRISIS

During the third week of July a second wave of distrust of the banks spread over the West and South. More than half of the Denver banks suspended and there were scattered failures at many points. The withdrawal of funds from New York was at once resumed and the reported net loss for the week ending July 22 was $2,800,000. The bank statement for the week, reflecting earlier conditions, showed a gain in reserve of $2,100,000 and through

[a] Reduction in net deposits of the New York banks was chiefly in individual deposits, which were $286,000,000 on May 4 and $246,000,000 on July 12. This reduction is to be accounted for chiefly by the smaller clearing-house exchanges, which were $74,000,000 in May and $65,000,000 in July, but, as clearing-house loan certificates were included in this item for the returns in 1893, the real reduction in clearing-house exchanges was in the neighborhood of $30,000,000.

the cancellation of deposit liabilities, resulting from a contraction of $4,300,000 in loans, the reserve deficit was reduced to $1,256,000 Early in the following week came bank failures in Chicago, Indianapolis, Milwaukee, Louisville, and smaller places, and the net shipments of the New York banks were $7,800,000 A customary feature of our crises was also announced, the Erie Railroad went into the hands of receivers Beset with fears of other receiverships and with high call-loan rates the stock exchange suffered the worst decline of the year The following account of the course of events during the week is taken from the Commercial and Financial Chronicle·

Our markets have been more disturbed and excited this week than at any time this year The situation looked unpromising when the week opened, and became daily more unsettled until Thursday, when there was a decided improvement, but yesterday the situation was again somewhat less favorable Monday and Tuesday an unusual number of failures among our banks and private firms were reported in various parts of the country, but especially in the West, some of them being concerns of long standing and held in high repute On those days, too, rumors became hourly more distinct respecting the difficulties Erie's floating debt was causing the management and the probability of its becoming needful to put the road into the hands of receivers Tuesday afternoon the announcement was made that receivers for the company had been appointed On Wednesday the failures referred to, the Erie receivership, and the state of the money market caused an unsettled and feverish opening, which conditions were used, and used most effectually, by those seeking to break prices, values of all the leading stocks gradually melting away This decline was favored by the fact that the outside public having money to invest either looked upon the Erie receivership as a more disturbing affair than the step warranted, or else were discouraged by the frequent flurries and declines in prices which have occurred of late, and so for the time being kept off the market The next day, Thursday, the outlook, as already stated, was much brighter, and so it was yesterday, though there was some reaction from the previous day, a further large break in General Electric stock being a disturbing feature

Money on call representing bankers' balances was not stringent until Wednesday The loans early in the week were from 6 to 2 per cent, the latter figure being recorded on Monday after the inquiry for the day had been satisfied and there seemed to be an abundance offered The demand for currency for shipment to the West, stimulated by the failure of the "Mitchell" bank at Milwaukee and of banks at Louisville and Indianapolis, was urgent on Tuesday, and on the following day a calling in of loans by some of the banks and trust companies in this city and in Brooklyn created a disturbance in the money market, while the fall in stock values induced discrimination against collateral, and the rate was advanced to three-sixteenths of 1 per cent and interest, equal to about 74 per cent per annum, and large amounts were loaned at one-eighth of 1 per cent and interest, equal to 51 per cent per annum On Thursday there was an early demand for money which caused 51 per cent to be again recorded, but in the afternoon the rate fell to 6 per cent Yesterday the course was much the same, the range being 51 and 2 per cent, with the close at the lowest figure The average for the week was probably about 10 per cent Renewals were at from 6 to 8, and while banks and trust companies quoted 6, very little was loaned over the counter at this figure, and the institutions that had money to loan offered it in the stock exchange Time contracts continue in urgent demand and good rates are bid, but the supply is small and chiefly confined to private sources Neither banks nor trust companies are making loans on time, but it is probable that a few of the insurance companies and other corporations have yielded to the importunities of brokers The basis of the business is 6 per cent, in addition 1 per cent commission is paid for thirty days, 1½ per cent for sixty days, and 2 per cent for four months Scarcely anything is done in commercial paper, and the few transactions made are at such rates as can be agreed upon Many of the jobbing commission houses are advising the mills with which they do business to shut down, as it is impossible at present to make advances, and many of the mills at the East are consequently closing [a]

The bank statement showed a loss in reserve of $5,100,000, and a somewhat greater reduction in deposits, as loans were reduced $2,700,000 There was an increase in the reserve deficit of from $1,300,000 to $4,300,000, and the actual condition of the banks was certainly even more unfavorable than this showing of average conditions.

We have now reached the crucial stage in this long period of financial strain, by far the most prolonged which the country has experienced in modern times Suddenly and unexpectedly the banks throughout the country, be-

[a] Commercial and Financial Chronicle, July 29, 1893, p 162.

ginning with those in New York, partially suspended cash payments. The immediate consequences of this unfortunate step were serious, and it also had the more permanent result of giving rise to an expectation of suspension upon future occasions of difficulty, which was the most serious cause of weakness disclosed during the financial disturbance of 1907 The general situation, therefore, at the time of suspension must be considered with great care

In some respects affairs were in a more critical state than in June, in other respects the situation was distinctly more satisfactory The number of bank failures was not greater than those which had occurred during the two worst weeks in June. There were, however, a greater number of prominent city institutions involved and the number of suspensions was considerably greater; 33 national banks suspended between July 14 and August 1. Thereafter, the number of failures and suspensions was small and included no important banks, and the opinion was current even then that the difficulty from this source was largely a thing of the past. Moreover, there was no evidence of any sudden increase of panic at the beginning of August, and the demand for currency from New York was apparently no greater than that which had come during the second and third weeks of June So far as the New York banks in relation to interior institutions were concerned, the situation was similar and there was no reason to believe that the continued demand for shipments of currency to the interior would not be discontinued in the course of time in August, just as had been the case in July.

The disturbance on the stock exchange following the Erie failure may seem to have involved an element of weakness not present in June, but in fact the decline on the stock exchange strengthened the situation from a purely banking point of view. Foreign purchases of our securities were made in large quantity during the week ending with July 29, and these purchases continued throughout the month of August. Attractive bargains in shares were not the only cause of these purchases. Foreign observers had become convinced that the silver-purchase law would be repealed at the impending session of Congress, and were, therefore, confident of the future value of our securities.[a]

There was, as we have seen, not a little exaggeration of the influence of silver money in bringing on the crisis. After the outbreak of the crisis it is, however, clear that the silver issues became a vastly more seriously disturbing factor. The difficulty of the Treasury in maintaining the gold standard was vastly increased, and the suspension of gold payments became imminent. Although the prospective repeal of the law could not serve to bring about renewed business activity, it did enable us to secure temporary assistance from Europe, which

[a] After another severe decline in prices at the stock exchange this week our market has been supported by the purchases of foreign buyers. This is a most hopeful sign, and it indicates that in London they consider the repeal of our silver law a foregone conclusion. Nor is it the first time that the foreigners have been able to take a clearer view of our affairs than we could get at home, for some weeks past their financial newspapers have been speaking of the repeal of our silver law as a necessity that would force itself upon us sooner or later, and their bankers are apparently willing to back up the opinion by taking some of our securities at the low prices now ruling.—The Commercial and Financial Chronicle, July 29, 1893, p. 171.

was of the utmost banking importance during the short acute stage of the crisis.

Between the middle of June and the end of July gold had been imported at New York to the amount of more than $5,000,000 [a] It had come in small consignments and from a great variety of sources During the week ending July 29 gold began to move toward this country in quantity, between $2,000,000 and $3,000,000 being engaged for shipment, and during the following week more than $10,000,000 was secured The fall in exchange rates which made this possible was due to foreign purchases of our securities and also to a decline in merchandise imports and an increase in exports Further importations were expected, and in fact occurred It will therefore be seen that the New York banks could look forward to a supply of gold to take the place, at least in part, of shipments to the interior

Two further favorable elements in the situation may be noted, though they were of minor importance. The savings banks decided to enforce the legal notice for withdrawal of deposits, taking this wise action before any considerable withdrawals had been made Finally, the Chicago banks for the first time in their history authorized on July 26 the issue of clearing-house loan certificates.

SUSPENSION OF PAYMENTS

While the general situation was thus on the whole such as to give ground for hope of improvement, there was

[a] More gold would have arrived during the month if the banks had adopted a liberal loan policy, enabling exchange dealers to purchase commercial bills more freely and to finance the gold while in transit (See p 191.)

one further serious element of weakness in the situation. When the withdrawals from New York began in June, the banks were well above reserve requirements, having a surplus of over $24,000,000 At the beginning of the second period of strain they were slightly below reserve requirements, and the bank statement of August 5 found them with a reserve deficit of $14,017,000 During the week the banks had lost $12,000,000 in reserve and had slightly increased loans by $2,200,000 This statement of average conditions probably represents something like the actual situation of the banks on Tuesday or Wednesday, when the banks resorted to suspension.

Two reasons may be advanced for this action It may have been thought that a further depletion in the reserve might cause general loss of confidence in the New York banks, but this is a superficial reason at best. There is no evidence that depositors had become distrustful of the banks, and had this been feared the banks might have adopted the expedient resorted to in 1873—the discontinuance of the publication of the bank statement altogether The real reason for suspension was that which was pointed out in the report of the clearing-house committee of 1873. The drain had not fallen equally upon the banks We have no means of knowing the exact position of the few large banks which held the bulk of bankers' deposits at this time, but there can be no doubt that they must have suffered a far more serious loss of reserve than that of the banks taken as a whole [a]

[a] The last statement of condition of the individual banks appeared on June 10. The subject is considered at greater length in connection with the crisis of 1907, for which the available data are more complete. (See p 266.)

Suspension was at no time complete, and in explaining its extent bankers gave indirect but convincing evidence that the deficiency in the reserves of particular banks rather than a small total reserve was the cause of the restriction of cash payments It was stated that the banks were continuing to ship currency to interior institutions drawing upon their cash balances, and that refusal applied only to the payment upon drafts remitted to them in the course of current business dealings These drafts, it was pointed out, did not enable the banks to secure money from the banks on which they were drawn, since a bank when it had a favorable clearing-house balance could only get loan certificates. This was indeed true During July 78 per cent of the balances between the banks were settled with the certificates, and in August 95 per cent. Doubtless during the weeks of most acute strain, in the latter part of July, virtually all balances were settled in this way

Here we find the connection between the issue of clearing-house loan certificates and suspension. A bank which received many drafts could not pay out cash indefinitely if it was unable to secure any money from the banks on which the drafts were drawn While only a few banks were taking out certificates and the bulk of payments was made in money, no difficulty was experienced; but as soon as all the banks made use of that medium, the suspension of the banks which had large numbers of correspondents soon became inevitable The further contention of bankers that they had not suspended since they had only refused to honor drafts was untenable. The clearing-house loan certificate was a device which the banks themselves had adopted and they had failed to provide any means for preventing its use leading to partial suspension The contention of some bankers that they had suspended because they had no money to pay out was doubtless true of a few banks, but for that very reason other banks must have been all the stronger, probably well above their required reserve.

That the arrangement for equalizing the reserves adopted in 1873 would in this instance have availed to prevent suspension is highly probable, indeed, a practical certainty. Events proved that the banks had maintained payments up to the very last of the succession of disasters with the results of which they had been contending. During August the number of bank failures was not large and none of them was of great importance We can not, of course, know how soon money would have begun to flow back to New York, but certainly the suspension of payments could hardly have hastened the movement. From the beginning of September the reported movements of currency showed a gain for the New York banks and for the week ending September 16 the gain was no less than $8,000,000 One month more of drain, therefore, was the most that the banks would have been obliged to endure, and for the needs of that month the banks would not, as in 1873, have been confined to the single resource of the $79,000,000 of cash on hand. Gold in quantity had been engaged prior to suspension and continued to come in thereafter, the total gold imports between the first of August and the middle of September reaching the unexampled amount of more than

$40,000,000. How far this movement was due to suspension and the currency premium will be discussed in subsequent pages [a] All authorities agree that much of the gold would have been secured in any case, and there is ground for the opinion that the amount sent was independent of suspension altogether Still another influence upon the money supply should be noted. The banks had begun to take the necessary steps to secure additional bank-note circulation. The addition to the money supply thus secured was, of course, widely diffused among the banks of the country, but to some extent it served to diminish the withdrawals of funds from the money centers. The gain from this source was small, but still it was a gain—$5,000,000 in July and $15,000,000 in August—and it might have been considerably greater if the large New York banks holding bankers' deposits had chosen to take out circulation to anything like the amount their capital permitted. Finally, excess Treasury payments added $9,000,000 to the money in circulation during the month of August From all these various sources, together with the continued silver purchases, the money in circulation, that is, in use and in the banks, increased $17,000,000 in July and nearly $70,000,000 in August

Although the banks probably held less money at the end than at the beginning of the period, it is evident that they were not obliged to meet the situation with such rigid cash reserves as to have made the continuance of payments an obviously hopeless endeavor.

---

[a] See p 191

The probability that the equalization of reserves would have served to prevent suspension in 1893 brings up the question whether the banks might have been reasonably expected to resort to the arrangement in this emergency. At first sight it seems unreasonable to expect banks which reap no advantage from bankers' deposits to employ their reserves to meet needs with which they are not directly concerned. On the other hand, all the banks agree upon and benefit by the use of the clearing-house loan certificate. It is a device which enables the banks to meet the demand for loans, and as the loans of the New York banks are principally to local borrowers it is the local situation that is thus relieved. This is the proper policy for banks in any community, but it should not be carried out at the cost of the rest of the country or be allowed to overshadow all other responsibilities The continuance of loans enables the banks to escape almost inevitable loss from failures of customers through the sudden contraction of credit, and also enables them to earn profits for their shareholders Individually all the New York banks reap an advantage not only from the clearing-house loan certificate but also from the position of New York as the money center of the country, and anything which undermines its reputation for strength is harmful to all Finally, profits are not sacrificed when reserves are equalized, as the reserve is not a source of profit, it is a foundation of credit and a resource for emergencies. The use of a reserve does not in any way reduce the gains of a bank from its loans or other profitable operations. The objection to equalization is simply the natural objection to assisting those who should have assisted themselves, it rests upon a sound basis of human experience, but it does not follow that the refusal to cooperate must be absolute It may be conditional upon amendment. This was the attitude of the more conservative banks in 1873, but, as often happens, their hopes of amendment were not realized They proposed an indirect remedy, the prohibition of the payment of interest on bankers' deposits A more direct remedy would be secured through the insistence, by clearing-house authorities and the public, that banks holding these highly explosive bankers' deposits should hold larger reserves in normal times than are held by the banks carrying on a purely local business.

The value of large reserves was clearly shown in the second stage of this crisis. At the beginning of June the large banks were unusually strong in reserve, and they were able to withstand the strain which followed the first series of bank failures. Had their reserves been somewhat larger, so as to have enabled them to go on for a very few weeks more, it is highly probable that even without equalization suspension would not have occurred.

THE CURRENCY PREMIUM.

The banks were not able for any length of time to confine suspension within the narrow limits of a refusal to honor drafts with cash payments. A beginning once made, they found themselves confronted with a situation which compelled more complete suspension Currency went to a premium, and thereupon money was withheld by many depositors whose business brought to them a constant stream of money Moreover, depositors of the "baser" sort began to withdraw, upon various pretexts, larger amounts of money than were needed for their normal requirements, in order to secure the profit from their sale.

The following table presents the highest and lowest quotations at which purchases were made by brokers, and also similar quotations of sales by them during each day throughout the period of the continuance of the currency premium.

The currency premuum

	Buying rates	Selling rates
Aug 3	¾ to 1	2
4	½ to 1	2
5	1	2
7	½ to 2	3 to 3½
8	½ to 3	4
9	3	4
10	2 to 3	4
11	½	3
12	1	1½ to 2½
14	1 to 1½	2 to 3
15	1 to 1½	1½ to 3
16	1½	2 to 2½
17	1½ to 2½	3
18	2½	[a] 3
19	3	4
21	1½ to 2½	2¾
22	1½ to 2	2½
23	½	[b] 2 to 2½
24	1	1½ to 2
25	1	[c] 1½
26	½	1 to 1¼
28	¼	¾
29	¼	½
30		½
31	(d)	(d)
Sept 1	⅜	½ to ⅝
2		¼ to ⅜

[a] Gold ½ to 2
[b] Gold 1½
[c] Gold 1¼
[d] Premium reported practically disappeared.

This table may be taken as indicating with a fair degree of exactness the general course of the currency premium, but it is probable that purchases and sales were made on some days above or below the rates given. There were of course no official quotations, and somewhat different rates were found on some days in the two journals (New York Evening Post and the New York Tribune) from which the table was made up[a] Rates were regularly higher for small bills than for other kinds of money and the purchase price of gold was subject to especially wide fluctuations, because it was received irregularly and in large quantities, on the particular days of the arrival of European steamers The premium continued for thirty days, contrasting with twenty-eight days in 1873 The range of quotations was similar in the two years but rates continued upon a high level for a longer period of time in 1893, rates of 1 per cent or more being quoted for sixteen days in 1873 and for twenty-three days in 1893, and above 2 per cent on only eight days in the first instance and twenty-one days in the second

During the first ten days of the currency premium interior banks were reported to have been large purchasers Then the premium declined, owing to a smaller demand which was confined largely to those requiring money for pay-roll purposes On August 19 the premium again rose to its maximum point of 4 per cent in consequence of the renewal of purchases by banks.

[a] The Commercial and Financial Chronicle mentions 5 per cent as having been paid for currency, but does not give the exact date (See issue of Aug 12, 1893, p 232)

The reported movements of currency between the New York banks and the interior, and the condition of the banks as shown by the weekly statements, do not help greatly in interpreting the fluctuations in the premium, but they do serve to explain its sudden disappearance at the beginning of September During each of the first two weeks of August there were net shipments of money to the interior of a little more than $5,000,000, and for the third week $6,000,000, for the last week of the month, $2,000,000; and for the week ending September 2, less than $1,000,000 [a] In the following week there was a slight gain for the New York banks, which was the beginning of a long-continued movement of funds to the city The reserves of the banks were reduced by $2,700,000 for the week ending August 12, but there was an increase in loans largely made for facilitating gold imports Deposits were reduced but slightly and the reserve deficit was then $16,545,000, and the ratio of reserve to deposit liabilities was 20 55 per cent During the following week the reserve was increased $8,400,000. There was a slight reduction in loans and the reserve deficit was reduced to $12,000,000. During the two following weeks to September 2 the reserve increased $12,000,000, loans were reduced by $6,000,000, and the reserve deficit was brought down to $1,500,000 The next week the statement showed a surplus reserve of nearly $3,000,000, and as it was based on rising averages

[a] The reported movements of currency are not official, and do not provide any evidence of the extent to which the banks supplied correspondents with funds, because a part of the amount reported was currency purchased at a premium for outside banks

we may be certain that at the beginning of this week the banks had acquired at least the 25 per cent reserve. They then removed all restrictions upon payments, thus bringing about the disappearance of the currency premium Whatever excuses may be made for suspension it was wholly without good cause that the banks persisted in this policy while their reserves were increasing in the rapid fashion which marked the last two weeks of August

In 1873 the currency premium was of short duration, because the New York banks continued to meet all demands of banking correspondents and thus maintained confidence until the natural return flow of money served to build up depleted reserves In 1893 the response to demands for currency by interior institutions was less complete,[a] and the restoration of reserves was secured in another way—by enormous gold imports During the four weeks ending September 2 over $40,000,000 of gold was imported to New York from Europe These imports

[a] The bank statement for the week ending August 19 showed an increase of $4,000,000 in the reserve held If allowance is made for the effect of the average method, it seems probable that the banks did not allow their reserves to decline at all after cash payments were restricted The following table shows the changes in the condition of the banks just before and during suspension

	Loans	Net deposits	Reserve	Reserve deficit
July 29	$406 500 000	$382,200,000	$91 200 000	$4,300 000
Aug 5	408 700,000	372,900 000	79,200,000	14 000,000
12	411,800,000	372,200,000	76 500 000	16 500,000
19	406 500 000	370,300,000	80 500 000	12,000,000
26	403 600,000	370 500,000	85,900,000	6,700,000
Sept 2	400 200 000	374,000,000	91 900,000	1,600,000
9	397,000,000	373,800,000	96 400,000	[a] 3,000,000

[a] Surplus

greatly exceeded the amount of money which was sent from New York to the rest of the country and explain the rapid increase in reserves of the banks during the period of the currency premium

THE CAUSES OF GOLD IMPORTS

The enormous influx of gold established a strong prima facie case for the influence of the currency premium upon the movement Moreover, practically no gold was engaged for import after the disappearance of the currency premium, the gold which was received during the latter part of the month being largely for special purposes, such as the $1,200,000 which arrived on September 20 in transit to the West Indies Finally, during the entire continuance of suspension exchange rates were far above the normal gold import point and at times even above the export point On the other hand at least $14,000,000 was engaged before there was any currency premium and throughout the month real bills provided a large part of the means for securing the gold that was imported. During July and August merchandise exports exceeded imports by more than $21,000,000 contrasted with an excess of imports of $13,000,000 during the same period in 1892. European purchases of securities at the end of July and during much of August also provided a large amount of sight exchange In continuing exchange dealings and securing gold imports through these bills the extension of loans by the banks was essential The process was thus described:

The clearing-house loan committee have issued $9,300,000 loan certificates this week, and the amount now outstanding is $34,550,000 A large proportion of these new certificates have been issued to aid the foreign bankers in importing gold The bankers deposit collateral with their banks and borrow the money on the security for a fixed period at an agreed-upon rate The bank obtains loan certificates against this collateral and when the gold arrives the loan will be repaid, the collateral released, and the certificates canceled [a]

Some gold was secured before suspension through sterling loans in London, and it is only to the extent that the amount of such loans was increased by suspension over what would otherwise have been made that the currency premium was a factor in the movement of gold The conditions of this problem can be stated, although no definite answer can be given Before suspension higher interest rates in New York than in London made the negotiation of sterling loans profitable, though the operation was subject to possible loss, since exchange rates were low and might advance before the maturity of the bills The difference in lending rates between New York and London was favorable to such dealings throughout July and August, but the successive advances in the Bank of England rate between August 3 and August 24 from 2½ to 5 per cent, while the money stringency was diminishing in New York, tended to reduce this advantage. With the appearance of the currency premium the immediate profits of importers on gold previously engaged were large, and this unexpected profit stimulated arrangements for further shipments through sterling loans. But exchange rates also advanced, and were within a week at the gold export point, thus offsetting a part of the profit from the operation. A premium of at least 1 per cent was then necessary to give the importers the ordinary profit from the transaction During the greater part of the

[a] The Commercial and Financial Chronicle, August 5, 1893, p 196

month the published quotations were above this point, but after gold came in quantity it seems to have been difficult to secure sales at these terms Moreover, the importer had to take account of a possible fall or disappearance of the premium. He might sell the gold for delivery on arrival, but this was an arrangement which was not at all times possible Finally, suspension seems to have caused some diminution in the volume of real bills, since it interrupted somewhat the movements of grain and cotton The problem of the influence of the currency premium is obviously, therefore, one of extreme complexity, regarding which it is probable that opinions of exchange experts at the time would have been widely at variance. Upon the whole it would seem safe to conclude that the currency premium was only an influence of minor importance in bringing about the gold movement The following extracts from the weekly review of the foreign exchange market, taken from the Commercial and Financial Chronicle, while they may not enable the reader to follow the course of exchange, will serve to illustrate the great complexity of the influences at work:

Our foreign exchange market was unsettled early in the week, lower on Wednesday, and firmer at the close The offerings were largely from the arbitrage houses, with a fair supply of commercial bills, but there was a steady demand to remit for prospective imports of gold, which caused a reaction on Thursday, and long sterling was then affected by the advance in the discount rate in London [a]

Our foreign exchange market has been almost entirely dominated this week by the premium on gold in transit and by the advance in the open market and the official discount rate in London The premium upon gold enhanced the value of the metal in New York, so as to make possible, if not profitable, the import of gold This was true, although on Thursday rates for sight bills and cable transfers were not only above the normal gold-

[a] The Commercial and Financial Chronicle, August 5, 1893, p 196

importing point, but very near that at which gold has been exported The premium here on gold ranged, as already stated, from 1½ to 2 per cent after Tuesday, the average being equal to about 7 to 8½ cents per pound sterling, but on Thursday afternoon there were indications of a smaller premium, and yesterday afternoon the best bid for gold was one-half of 1 per cent, with offerings at 1 per cent [a]

Foreign exchange has been unsettled this week by the varying premiums for gold and currency, and on Tuesday and Wednesday there were frequent changes by some of the leading drawers The market was also influenced by dearer discounts in London, which indicated a possible advance in the bank minimum Commercial bills have been scarce, the movement of cotton and grain being interrupted by the stringency in money, and arbitrage operations have had little or no effect On Thursday it was stated that bids could not be obtained for gold for gold to arrive within ten days, but the bidding was chiefly for gold on the spot, and 1½ per cent and upward was paid for such metal Those who were importing generally had gold on hand, which they sold at the ruling premium, and the profit enabled further speculative importations to be made [b]

Our foreign exchange market has again tended downward, chiefly by reason of the varying premium on gold on the spot and to arrive, other influences operating have been the renewal of sterling loans, the dearer discount rate in London, and fairly liberal supplies of commercial bills drawn against grain exports The market was firm on Monday, unsettled and lower on Tuesday, active, closing easier, on Wednesday, and dull and steady on Thursday, with short rates affected by the advance in the Bank of England rates of discount [c]

Our foreign exchange market was firm on Monday although business was light On the following day the tone was easier in consequence of the absence of a premium for spot gold, and the market was also influenced by offerings of commercial bills against grain and provisions, and on Wednesday there was a good supply of drafts against securities bought for London and Amsterdam account The market was dull and steady on Thursday and slightly influenced by easier discounts in London [d]

One further result of the currency premium was the direct importation of gold by interior banks, especially by those of Chicago. Instead of disposing of commercial bills to foreign exchange houses in New York, they were used to secure gold in London, which was shipped di-

[a] The Commercial and Financial Chronicle, August 12, 1893, p 232

[b] Ibid, August 19, 1893, p 273

[c] Ibid, August 26, 1893, p 321

[d] Ibid, September 2, 1893, pp 356–357.

rectly to the various banks engaging in the operation. Had the usual practice been followed, the banks would have simply increased their unavailable balances in New York It is obvious that this had no effect upon the aggregate amount of gold sent to the United States

SUSPENSION AND HOARDING

As in the case of gold imports, the effect of the premium on currency upon the domestic money supply can not be determined exactly There were reports of money being brought to brokers which had obviously been kept by its owners for a long time before the outbreak of the crisis and also of money which had been probably withdrawn from banks by frightened depositors But as early as August 16[a] it was reported by brokers that they were no longer getting hoarded money, but were purchasing from retail shopkeepers and from persons who had succeeded in extracting money from the banks A suspicious increase in the amount of money which small clothing manufacturers asked for, ostensibly for payroll purposes, was observed at certain of the New York banks More generally it was found that depositors were not paying into their banks customary amounts of currency

While it is possible, though not probable, that the currency premium increased the domestic money supply,[b] it is certain that it vastly increased the amount of money required for a given volume of transactions Evidence for this conclusion is found in the apparent dearth of

[a] See New York Evening Post, August 16, 1893

[b] It was estimated that not more than $15,000,000 was purchased during the continuance of the premium (See p 426)

money which followed immediately the announcement that banks had restricted payments The serious significance of the premium on currency was not at first clearly recognized. Upon its first appearance it was observed in the Chronicle.

A little incident of the week, typical of the times, has been the effort to establish a premium on small note currency We do not look upon the effort as important, how far the transactions have been made for effect and how far they are real it would be difficult to say [a]

A week later the subject is treated in a fashion which is in amusing contrast·

Other than the President's message and the meeting of Congress, which we have remarked upon in a subsequent column, the premium on gold and currency that has prevailed has been the important topic This feature in the situation we referred to last week when it had developed only very moderate proportions From that beginning, however, the demand for currency gradually grew more urgent, the premium rising as high even as 5 per cent, disclosing a marked scarcity of currency, not alone in this city but very noticeable at Philadelphia and Boston in the East and Chicago and other centers in the West All kinds of currency were in request, including even standard silver dollars Foreign bankers also report that 1½ to 2 per cent was paid for gold to arrive Of course, the gold import movement had been affected by these operations, which in turn have raised foreign exchange rates materially, since the premium paid raises the power of exchange and consequently the point at which gold can be imported at a profit Thursday, however, there were decided indications that the transactions in currency had culminated On that day the supply was increased by large offerings and the demand slackened Yesterday the same conditions continued to prevail, and the premium on currency dropped to 1½ and 2 per cent [b]

Suspension in New York had necessarily involved suspension throughout the country, and thereupon the dearth of money became the most striking feature of the crisis, one which came home directly to the mass of the people and which was remembered long after the exact

[a] Commercial and Financial Chronicle, August 5, 1893, p 196
[b] Ibid , August 12, 1893, p 232

course of the crisis had been forgotten Few observers seem to have perceived that the dearth of money was a consequence and not a cause of suspension, with the result that power to issue notes in large quantities has become the accepted panacea for meeting the difficulties with which banks are confronted during emergencies It was estimated that something like $300,000,000 in money and substitutes for money were added to the supply outside the banks during August, and it was, therefore, urged that it was necessary to give the banks power to issue notes to something like that amount in order to enable them to cope with similar situations in the future Not having this power, it was also generally felt that suspension by the banks was unavoidable and due to no fault on their part

Moreover, estimates of money requirements during this crisis were very greatly exaggerated In a pamphlet published and widely circulated by the Sound Currency Committee of the Reform Club it was assumed that the reduction of about $200,000,000 in the deposits of the national banks between May and July represented withdrawals of cash We have already seen that the decline in deposits was due principally to loan contraction and to the withdrawal of money from reserve agents, and only to an insignificant extent was it a result of the withdrawal of money from the banks. In the second place, issues of clearing-house loan certificates were frequently regarded as an addition to the circulating medium The maximum amount of the certificates in the United States at any one time was probably in the neighborhood of $60,000,000, but they were simply loans between banks, and had all the certificates been retired there would not have been a penny less in the banks taken as a whole. To some extent their use might have enabled the banks to pay out more cash from their reserves than they otherwise might have been disposed to relinquish, but as they resorted to suspension before reserves were seriously depleted, even this possibility was not realized

Various substitutes for money were utilized to meet the situation which the banks had brought about by refusing to use their own stores of cash Clearing-house certificates (not clearing-house loan certificates) were issued in many towns, especially in the Southeastern States Cashiers' checks in convenient denominations seem to have been used in all parts of the country In factory towns pay checks became an acceptable part of the circulating medium [a]

Some hoarding had certainly taken place before the beginning of August, but it was largely confined to those parts of the South and West where there had been numerous bank failures and suspensions The disappearance of money after the beginning of August can not properly be characterized as hoarding People naturally refrain from paying money into the banks after the banks have begun to place restrictions upon its withdrawal. The various substitutes for money served in a measure to take the place of money which would have moved into and out of the banks in ordinary course had they not resorted to suspension

[a] For an account of these and other substitutes for money see The Currency Famine of 1893, by J DeWitt Warner, in Sound Currency, vol 2, No 6, and in Sound Currency Year Book, 1896, pp 341 to 356

The following extract, taken from the pamphlet already referred to, is entirely accurate as to the course of events, but places the cart directly before the horse in its explanation of the phenomena

Then developed the feature that will forever characterize the stringency of 1893—instructive to those who have not already learned how immaterial is any ordinary supply of legal currency when compared with credit in its various forms—the real currency of the country * * * Almost between morning and night the scramble for currency had begun and culminated all over the country, and the preposterous bulk of our circulating medium had been swallowed up as effectually as, in a scarcely less brief period, gold and silver had disappeared before the premiun on specie a generation before Currency was hoarded until it became so scarce that it had to be bought as merchandise at a premium of 1 to 3 per cent in checks payable through the clearing house, and to enable their families to meet petty bills at the summer resorts the merchants and professional men of the cities were forced to purchase and send by express packages of bills or coin, while savings banks hawked their government bond investments about the money centers in a vain effort to secure currency [a]

THE EFFECT OF SUSPENSION ON TRADE

The effect of suspension upon the trade of the country was similar to that which was analyzed in the case of the crisis of 1873, though in some respects the general economic situation was different. In 1873 the banks restricted payments almost at the beginning of the disturbance, while in 1893 that step was taken only after some months of struggle with adverse circumstances. In 1873 suspension was one of the initial causes interrupting the normal course of business. In 1893 it was rather of the nature of a last straw added to the burdens resting on the business community It is not possible, therefore, to determine with any degree of accuracy the relative effects

[a] The Currency Famine of 1893, by J DeWitt Warner, in Sound Currency, vol 2, No 6, and in Sound Currency Year Book, 1896, p 340

of suspension during these two crises. Mercantile failures and the curtailment of production had marked the course of previous months [a] And even if the banks had maintained payments, it is reasonably certain that August would have witnessed further decline in general business activities Moreover, partial general suspension may have enabled some banks which might have failed or suspended completely to escape those misfortunes It is also possible that more drastic loan contraction would have been enforced by the banks if they had been exerting every effort to maintain cash payments.

There is, however, evidence that suspension was a potent factor accentuating the depression in trade which characterized the month of August It increased the general feeling of distrust which, as always in a crisis, does so much to bring about greater inactivity than the actual condition of affairs warrants A more definite consequence was the difficulty in securing money for pay rolls, which led to the temporary shutting down of many factories Finally, it deranged the exchanges between different parts of the country, causing a slackening in the movement of commodities and needless delays in collections which were already slow on account of the general situation

The preponderant result of these various influences was certainly unfavorable Perhaps the best indication is to be found in the returns of railway gross earnings, which are presented in the following table.

[a] For the effect of the crisis upon manufacturing industries before the beginning of August see Bradstreet's, August 12, 1893, p 502

Railway gross earnings.[a]

	1893.	1892.	Per cent increase (+) or decrease (−).
March	$61,900,000	$58,700,000	+ 5.53
April	56,000,000	54,100,000	+ 3.42
May	65,000,000	60,300,000	+ 7.8
June	59,500,000	57,800,000	+ 2.97
July	56,800,000	59,700,000	− 4.85
August	54,700,000	63,100,000	−13.29
September	58,200,000	64,900,000	−10.35
October	64,000,000	67,400,000	− 5
November	56,700,000	63,100,000	− 8.7
December	48,000,000	56,300,000	−14.75

It will be observed that the crisis did not cause a falling off in earnings until July. The loss of nearly 5 per cent in that month was followed by one of more than 13 per cent in August. Doubtless the loss for the latter part of July was considerably greater than that for the month taken as a whole. But when every allowance has been made there can be no question that the greater loss in August earnings reflects a far more unsatisfactory volume of trade during that month. The September returns showed some improvement over the previous month, as did also those of October, but the percentage of loss in earnings increased once more in November and was at the highest point of the year in December. The December return was, aside from the fact of one less working day, an indication of the long period of trade depression which was to follow. Much of the decline in August, with the subsequent partial recovery, can only be ascribed to the trade paralysis produced by the financial

[a] The Commercial and Financial Chronicle, February 25, 1894, p. 328.

situation at that time The situation was described as follows in the Chronicle:

> The month of August will long remain memorable as one of the most remarkable in our industrial history Never before has there been such a sudden and striking cessation of industrial activity Nor was any section of the country exempt from the paralysis, mills, factories, furnaces, mines nearly everywhere shut down in large numbers, and commerce and enterprise were arrested in an extraordinary and unprecedented degree The complete unsettlement of confidence and the derangement of our financial machinery, which made it almost impossible to obtain loans or sell domestic exchange and which put money to a premium over checks, had the effect of stopping the wheels of industry and of contracting production and consumption within the narrowest limits, so that our internal trade was reduced to very small proportions—in fact, was brought almost to a standstill—and hundreds of thousands of men thrown out of employment [a]

Another indication of the course of trade was furnished by the figures of clearing-house transactions, not including New York, where financial operations are a predominant factor. These returns show a loss for June of 10 per cent, of 15 per cent for July, and of no less than 29 8 per cent for August. During the succeeding three months there was some improvement, followed by a further decline, as in the case of railway earnings in December

During July the newspapers had contained many reports of the closing of factories on account of failures, inability to make collections, or to procure credits from the banks In August these causes were mentioned in some instances, but the most frequently assigned cause of the shutting down of factories was inability to procure money for pay rolls The impression derived from an examination of contemporary journals is that this difficulty was more general and more severely felt than in

[a] The Commercial and Financial Chronicle, September 16, 1893, p 446

1873 But there are reasons which render such a conclusion far from certain, and even less certain the conclusion that the banks restricted payments more generally The number of factories had of course greatly increased during the interval between the two crises, and it is also probable that the news service had become more complete The weekly payment of wages had become more general, thus increasing the requirements of employers Finally, the resort to various substitutes for money, which was far more general in 1893, may indicate more general restriction of payments by the banks, but, on the other hand, it may simply mean that employers had found a way out of the difficulty. Inability to secure currency certainly did not continue through an appreciably longer interval in 1893 than in 1873. As early as August 18 reports of the reopening of factories began to appear in the daily journals, and though reports of the shutting down of factories continued for some days, by the end of the month the tide had turned strongly in the opposite direction The banks removed the restrictions upon cash payments, gradually reaching complete resumption early in September, and the simultaneous renewal of business activities affords striking evidence of the disturbing effect which had been brought about by suspension

THE DOMESTIC EXCHANGES.

The domestic exchanges had been deranged at various points before the New York banks suspended at the beginning of August. In Omaha, for example, it was reported that "the failure of seven banks in Nebraska makes Omaha banks rather more conservative, and they now refuse country checks except for collection."[a] A little later it was reported in Philadelphia that "banks are husbanding currency very carefully, some of them having been obliged to pay $5 per 1,000 exchange on New York."[b] After the beginning of August reports of difficulties of this kind became general and rates of exchange on New York became almost prohibitive in many parts of the country. The following table, compiled from Bradstreet's, shows the course of exchange on New York at a number of important points throughout the country between July 29 and September 9, 1893.

	Boston	Philadelphia
July 29	35 to 45 cents discount	$10 premium
Aug 5	$1 to $2 premium	$10 premium
12	$1 to $2 premium	$10 to $15 discount
19	$1 25 to $2 premium	$15 to $20 discount
26	90 cents to $1 premium	$8 75 discount
Sept 2	15 to 20 cents premium	75 cents to $1 premium
9	20 to 25 cents discount	50 cents premium

	Chicago	St Louis
July 29	$3 discount	$3 discount
Aug 5	$7 to $10 discount	$4 25 discount
12	$25 to $30 discount	$7 50 discount
19	$15 discount	$7 50 discount
26	$5 discount	$4 discount
Sept 2	$5 discount	Par
9	50 cents premium	90 cents premium

[a] Bradstreet's, July 8, 1893, p. 431.
[b] Bradstreet's, July 22, 1893

	Cincinnati.	Kansas City.
July 29	50 cents discount	$1.75 discount.
Aug. 5	$1 discount	$1.50 discount.
12	$4 to $5 discount	$2 discount.
19	$3 to $6 discount	$3 discount.
26	$5 discount	$3 discount.
Sept. 2	Par to 50 cents discount	Par.
9	Par	50 cents premium.
	Minneapolis.	**New Orleans.**
July 29	$2 discount	Par.
Aug. 5	$10 discount	$1.50 discount.
12	$10 discount	$1.50 discount.
19	$15 discount	$5 discount.
26	$5 discount	$1 discount.
Sept. 2	$1 discount	$10 premium.
9	Par	$1.50 premium.
	Charleston.	**San Francisco.**
July 29	$1.25 premium	$3.50 premium.
Aug. 5	$2.50 premium	$1.25 premium.
12	$2.50 premium	75 cents discount.
19	$2.50 premium	$1.25 premium.
26	$10 to $15 discount	Par.
Sept. 2	$10 to $13 discount	$1.25 premium.
9	$10 to $13 discount	$3 premium.

An analysis of the various influences which affect domestic exchange rates under the régime of suspension will be found in the chapter on the crisis of 1907.[a] Here it will be sufficient to note that they were generally at a discount which was in most instances abnormally low. The most striking example was Chicago, where a rate of $30 per $1,000 was quoted at one time. These rates, however abnormal, merely indicate the dislocated condition

[a] See p. 291.

of the domestic exchanges They do not measure the extent of the dislocation and still less do they measure its effect upon the trade of the country The published rates apply chiefly to business between banks and furnish no indication of the treatment which was accorded drafts on distant places when paid into the banks by depositors. Drafts were often of little or no utility to the holder because the banks refused to take them except at a ruinous discount or for collection. Exchange between different parts of the country, at least between the more important cities, does not seem to have been at any time completely blocked It was, however, deranged to such an extent as to interfere seriously with the ordinary movement of commodities The banking situation in general and the dislocation of the exchanges in particular seem to have been the influences which made the first two weeks of August the worst period of the crisis in general trade The condition of affairs may be judged from the following extracts from Bradstreet's for the weeks ending August 5 and 12.

While special telegrams from many points South and West report a more hopeful feeling in financial and commercial circles, due to the increased currency issue by New York national banks, the gold afloat for the United States, and in the expectation that Congress will promptly repeal the compulsory purchase of silver clause of the Sherman Act, the week has, on the whole, brought more unfavorable features in the apparent hoarding and scarcity of currency East and West, the near approach of the demand for funds to "move the crops," the increase in the shut-down movement by manufacturers in New England, Middle and Central Western States, and the clog to trade shown by prohibitive rates for New York exchange at centers East, West, and Northwest * * * Chicago packers and grain shippers selling to interior eastern points, having been unable to sell their New York exchange, are ordering the currency to pay for stuff shipped direct by express, thus doing away with banks At New York credit of both banks and commercial interests is unimpaired, but actual money is scarce and commands a premium The arrival of gold in transit is expected to clear the atmosphere and relieve pressure Demands for actual currency from all quarters on New York are pressing The scarcity of small notes and silver dollars is a feature Banks are generally refusing or complying only partially with requests for large sums * * *

Money remains stringent at Boston, Hartford, Providence, and Philadelphia, with a depressing effect on business There is a smaller volume of orders being received at Baltimore, and banks are not meeting the out of town demand for currency Currency is scarce at Pittsburg also, but at Buffalo banks are refusing to ship currency west, while having sufficient for local demand Trade there is dull, and savings banks profess not to need the sixty-day rule [a]

The irrational but widespread hoarding of currency has compelled jobbers and manufacturers in many instances to do business more nearly than ever on a cash basis, which has resulted in a further restriction of trade throughout the country This is accompanied by such signs of aggravation as increased difficulty in disposing of commercial paper, a still greater scarcity of currency at larger centers, and a shut-down movement among industrial establishments, the latter, together with curtailment of forces in that and in commercial lines, points to the enforced idleness of nearly 1,000,000 wage-earners within the past two months, as compared with not more than 400,000 at the close of 1884, the previous year of greatest business depression The week's bank clearings total is the smallest of recent years—$802,000,000—17 per cent less than last week and 20 per cent less than in the week of 1892 * * *

A hand to mouth demand for staples is reported from Boston, many leading industries have shut down, currency is scarcer, commercial paper is ignored, and general business rather more clogged than last week, all of which applies as well to New York, Philadelphia, Baltimore, and Pittsburg

Philadelphia banks request customers to stamp checks "payable through the clearing house" Baltimore distillers experience difficulty in getting currency to buy revenue stamps, while jobbers there report salesmen returning, owing to lack of orders Pittsburg hopes for greater ease in its local money market, now that the clearing house will issue certificates At Buffalo banks continue to pursue a very cautious policy, and many merchants are stamping checks "payable through the clearing house" * * *

Increased demands from country banks make currency scarcer at Cleveland and Cincinnati, where previous dullness is intensified Business at Louisville is almost at a standstill, banks declining to receive country checks even for collection, and preferring not to handle New York exchange General trade is almost on a cash basis at Indianapolis, and reduced in volume, which is also true at Milwaukee Chicago bankers are

---

[a] Bradstreet's, August 5, 1893, p 495

hopeful, owing to the heavy gold importations, but orders left with jobbers are held awaiting crop advices, some of the latter being doubtful St Paul, Minneapolis, and Duluth jobbers are doing a hand to mouth business, awaiting a change in the situation. St Louis reports a shrinkage in the volume of sales of dry goods and hardware, while at Omaha banking accommodations and the volume of trade continue in reduced volume Live stock receipts are smaller, with higher prices, and the corn crop is damaged in western Nebraska [a]

The first faint signs of recovery were observed during the third week of August, and by the beginning of September the reaction from extreme depression was unmistakable The passage by the House of Representatives on August 28 of the bill repealing the silver purchase clause of the act of 1890 did much to restore confidence, but the restoration of banking facilities did far more to start the wheels of industry. The domestic exchanges resumed their normal course, and no further difficulty was experienced in securing money for pay rolls Unfavorable banking influences which had been at work long before the beginning of August also disappeared. The banks began to make loans more freely, and though the total volume of loans seems to have been still further reduced, contraction was no longer drastic, and where business needs appeared loans were increased.

Contraction in loans was perhaps the most striking feature of this crisis. From their maximum amount of $2,161,000,000 on May 4 loans of the national banks were reduced on July 12 to $2,020,000,000, and on October 4 to $1,843,000,000, a total contraction of $318,000,000, or more than 14 7 per cent. In 1873 loans had been reduced but 5 per cent, and in 1907 the reduction was only 2 per cent. The long period over which the financial disturbance

[a] Bradstreet's, August 12, 1893, p 511.

extended accounts in some measure for this unsatisfactory showing in 1893; it simply reflects in part the inevitable diminution in business dealings which would have taken place sooner or later quite apart from banking and monetary causes It can not be questioned, however, that the banks in many parts of the country caused needless damage to their customers by a ruthless policy of loan contraction. Nowhere is this more clearly evident than in Chicago, a central reserve city with responsibilities to the community at large which are not incurred by purely local banks. The Chicago banks reduced loans from $96,800,000 on May 4 to $82,400,000 on July 12, and to $73,500,000 on October 4. No sound reason can be given for such drastic contraction, but it is explained by the failure of the Chicago banks to make use of clearing-house loan certificates.[a] They were far stronger in July than in May and had still further strengthened themselves in October, and there is no indication that they had allowed their reserve to decline appreciably during the interval Each bank pursuing its own selfish policy, all were forced to contract loans, thus increasing the strain upon their own customers and in some measure increasing the burdens upon the banks in New York.

After the beginning of September the course of the crisis of 1893 was no longer a banking affair. As always, when general trade depression sets in, the banks soon found themselves with an abundant supply of funds and

[a] The issue of clearing house loan certificates in Chicago was authorized on July 26, but none were taken out by the banks After the partial suspension which came in the following week they were no longer necessary.

in position to lend far beyond the requirements of borrowers. On October 4 the cash reserves of the banks were $346,000,000, contrasted with $289,000,000 on July 12. At the earlier date the reserves of the banks were not at the low point reached in August, and the flow of money to the banks in September must have been far greater than this increase The next return on December 19 found the banks with cash reserves of $414,000,000, an increase since July of $125,000,000 This rapid return of money to the banks suggests the very obvious conclusion that the withdrawal of money in June and July was not due to deep-seated doubts of the solvency of the banks in general, but was due rather to a temporary wave of distrust which might have been successfully overcome by a bolder policy in the use of reserves

NO CHANGES IN BANKING METHODS OR LEGISLATION.

The experience derived from this crisis led to no changes whatever either in banking methods or in legislation The silver question drew away men's minds from any consideration of the questions raised by earlier crises. Whether the banks through their own efforts might not place themselves in a better position to meet future emergencies does not seem to have been discussed. Both bankers and the public seem to have been well satisfied with the showing made by the banks, especially by those of New York; and indeed if comparison be made with the policy adopted by the Chicago banks, the banks of the metropolis met the situation in a creditable fashion.

There was, however, evidence of a willingness to adopt suspension in emergencies, which is in striking contrast to the healthy critical attitude of both bankers and the public in 1873.

It is difficult to imagine a more weak and pusilanimous attitude than that which found expression in the following passage from Bradstreet's:

> Since the present financial complications began the New York associated banks have virtually acted as one institution in all matters of vital moment The services they have rendered, not only to the business community at New York but to the banks and commercial interests of the entire country, can not be overestimated The situation has constantly been one of danger and difficulty, and could only be met by extraordinary measures The banks here have been called on to supply funds for the whole country, and did so unhesitatingly until it became necessary to put a check upon a movement which depleted the reserves upon which the banking facilities of the entire United States depend The restricting of the facility with which bank credits could be converted into cash served the purpose It tended to make the hoarding of money expensive, and at the same time prevented individuals from utilizing the banks for the purpose of speculating in currency It was a useful and salutary move and will in the end aid in bringing about a restoration of confidence and a normal condition of credit Attacks upon the banks for the restriction thus exercised may be founded in ignorance of the real principles, but they tend to do a great deal of mischief and to create a state of public feeling which it is eminently desirable should be avoided These considerations apply with added force to the manifestations of hostility toward the New York banks and their course by a certain element in Congress The banks have been supporting the credit of the country and checking the symptoms of the panic, and ill-informed criticism upon their methods have no excuse at a juncture of this gravity[a]

It may, however, be observed once more that the New York banks had met successfully but one part of their responsibilities to the community The need for larger reserves by the banks holding bankers' deposits or some method for making use of the entire store of cash held by the banks was just as clearly shown by the course of

[a] Bradstreet's, August 26, 1893, p 534

the crisis as were the good results of the liberal loan policy which was adopted

Neither the Secretary of the Treasury nor the Comptroller of the Currency made any important recommendations in their annual reports which followed this crisis,[a] their comparatively recent entrance into these offices being perhaps a sufficient reason. The Comptroller of the Currency contented himself with an argument backed up with statistics to show that the number of suspensions and failures among national banks was far less numerous than among state institutions [b] This was indeed true, though the statistics were in some respects not comparable, to say nothing of some special circumstances which accounted in a measure for the relatively poor showing of the state institutions [c]

The showing made by the national banks was in any event far from satisfactory There were 65 failures during the year, only 13 banks paid all claims in full, and but 9 of them were able to meet the interest obligation during the period of liquidation Claims against all failed banks amounted to $14,434,105, and $9,778,449 was paid. The cause of failure and also of suspension in

[a] On account of the absence of a contemporary narrative of the crisis in government reports, considerable portions of an article by Mr A D Noyes have been reprinted in the Appendix See Note I, pp 413-427

[b] See report of the Comptroller of the Currency, 1893, p 13

[c] The figures for the state banks included every kind of banking institution, even private banks Moreover, the number of state banks was relatively large in the West and Southwest, where failures of all kinds of banks were most numerous Finally the state banks were relatively of small size and the mortality among the smaller banks was particularly great among both national and state banks.

some instances might probably have been removed by more efficient examination and more rigorous enforcement of the law by the Comptroller of the Currency.[a]

In later years, as we have seen, the most dramatic and striking episode of the crisis—the dearth of currency—became an important influence in directing attention exclusively to various devices for a less rigid system of note issue as a resource for future emergencies That by such means the ability of the banks to cope with crises would be increased is not questioned, but, after all, such proposals do not go to the root of the matter Unless associated with more conservative management it is highly probable that enlarged power to issue notes would be used in such a fashion in the years before crises as to place the banks in an extremely hazardous position through more unrestrained extension of credit than would otherwise have been granted

While there may be room for differences of opinion as to the teaching of this crisis with regard to the need and effects of a more liberal power of note issue, in another direction an inference was drawn which was wholly without foundation and which had the most unfortunate effect upon the course of events in 1907 With the lapse of time recollections of the exact course of the crisis became vague, and gradually the view seems to have become established among bankers that the issue of clearing-house loan certificates inevitably and immediately involves suspension and the currency premium. These

[a] See Appendix, Note G, pp 400-405, for a detailed account of failures and suspensions during 1893, taken from the Comptroller's Report for 1893.

aspects of the crisis were remembered, but it was forgotten that certificates had been in use for six weeks before suspension occurred, and that 1873 was the only other occasion when their use had involved suspension We have seen that suspension may occur when loan certificates are being used, but there is strong ground for the opinion that on those occasions suspension would have come earlier had their issue not been authorized Without the certificate each bank would most certainly have pursued in 1893 the policy of loan contraction, just as was the case in 1857 Disastrous failures among brokers and business houses would inevitably have followed, the banks would have suffered loss from the nonpayment of loans, and doubts of their solvency would have been engendered with consequent runs and inevitable suspension. General loan contraction spells general insolvency, while a relatively stable volume of loans secured through the use of loan certificates may or may not enable the banks to escape suspension Never until 1907 did the issue of loan certificates and suspension come at the same moment, and then it was due more than anything else to the utterly unfounded notion that the use of the one had involved the other in previous emergencies [a]

The issue of clearing-house loan certificates was not more general in 1893 than in 1873, and though the amount issued was greater it was not so large in proportion to the volume of banking business.[b] The period of strain was,

[a] See p 257

[b] For an account of the issue of loan certificates in 1893 the reader is referred to Note H in the Appendix containing the report of the New York clearing house loan committee and extracts from the Report of the Comptroller of the Currency for 1893 See pp 406–412 below

however, unusually long, and consequently the use of the certificates in quantity was more protracted than on former occasions To this may perhaps be attributed the weakening of the disinclination of many of the banks to take them out. In 1907, on the authorization of their issue, they were immediately taken out by practically all the banks having to meet unfavorable balances. In these circumstances, as we shall see in the following chapter, immediate suspension became inevitable

CHAPTER V.

THE CRISIS OF 1907

The same elements of weakness have been uniformly disclosed by the analysis of the experiences of the national banks during successive periods of financial strain The normal condition of the banks was one of lack of preparation for emergencies. No adequate lending power or surplus cash reserve was available at any time except during periods of trade depression when the banks were unable to find borrowers for all the loans they were prepared to make. This unsatisfactory situation was, however, not clearly recognized Minor causes of difficulty absorbed the attention both of bankers and of the public. It was felt that the banks had to work under unfavorable conditions, for the results of which they were not responsible, and the conclusion was generally drawn that no blame rested upon them In 1873, for example, the currency was inconvertible and depreciated, and the banks could not increase their available cash reserve by the acquisition of gold During the eighties and early nineties silver purchases weakened the monetary structure and bred distrust of American securities at home and in foreign countries For our purposes, therefore, we are fortunate in being provided with a crisis which was preceded by no legislation or monetary conditions unfavorable to sound banking. On the contrary, these influences tended to strengthen the banks in very definite ways

BANKING MOVEMENTS, 1897–1907.

At the beginning of the ten years of business activity which culminated in 1907 the banks were in an exceedingly strong condition, as is usually the case at the end of a long period of depression During the four years following the crisis of 1893 the loans, deposits, and cash reserves of the banks fluctuated within narrow limits, reflecting the stagnant condition of trade On October 5, 1897, against net deposits of $2,195,000,000 the national banks held a cash reserve of $388,900,000, giving them the tolerably high ratio of 17 7 per cent to deposit liabilities Their loans also must have been of high average quality after four years of thoroughgoing liquidation and recuperation in the business world.

Beginning with the autumn of 1897, the cash reserves of the banks increased rapidly At first the gain was due to gold imports secured through abnormally large grain exports to Europe, and afterwards on account of increasing gold production, of which the United States acquired a considerable share A further gain was secured indirectly as a result of the currency act of 1900. That measure made the issue of bank notes somewhat more profitable to the banks, and between February 13, 1900, and August 22, 1907, bank-note circulation rose from $204,900,000 to $551,900,000 By this means nearly $350,000,000 was provided to meet the hand-to-hand needs of the people for money and to supply the reserve requirements of state banks and trust companies. The national banks were consequently enabled to secure and retain a larger portion of the other kinds of money in the country—those kinds which could be included as a part of their own reserves As a result of these various influences, the cash holdings of the national banks increased from $388,900,000 on October 5, 1897, to $701,600,000 on October 22, 1907.

With this increase of nearly $313,000,000 in their cash reserves it would have been possible for the banks to have nearly doubled their productive investments without diminishing the ratio of cash to deposit liabilities As a matter of fact, these investments were increased far more than this—from $2,661,000,000 to $6,334,000,000. This increase was roughly paralleled by the increase in net deposit liabilities, which advanced from $2,195,000,000 to $5,256,000,000, and the ratio of the cash reserve to deposit liabilities was reduced from 17.7 per cent to 13.3 per cent.

The following table shows the changes in loans, net deposits (not including government deposits), cash reserves, and reserve ratio at the time of the early autumn return of the condition of the national banks from 1897 to 1907:

[Amounts expressed in millions]

	Loans	Net deposits	Cash reserve	Ratio to net deposits
				Per cent
Oct 5, 1897	$2 066	$2 179	$388 9	17 9
Sept 20, 1898	2,172	2,404	420 7	17 5
Sept 7, 1899	2 496	2,952	466 3	15 8
Sept 5, 1900	2,686	3 187	518 5	16 2
Sept 30, 1901	3 018	3,554	539 5	15 2
Sept 15, 1902	3 280	3,720	508 0	13 7
Sept 9, 1903	3 481	3 863	554 3	14 3
Sept 6 1904	3,726	4,400	661 5	15 0
Aug 25, 1905	3,998	4 735	665 6	14 3
Sept 4 1906	4,298	4 927	626 0	12 7
Aug 22, 1907	4,678	5,256	701 6	13 3

Every year witnessed an increase in loans (that for the last year of the series being the most considerable) and also in deposit liabilities Cash reserves showed a gain, except in 1902 and 1906, but the reserve ratio was subject to greater fluctuation Between 1897 and 1902 the decline was continuous, with the exception of 1900, when the banks enjoyed the benefit of the change in the requirement as to note issue from 90 per cent to the full par value of the bonds deposited as security By 1902 the banks had evidently approached as near to legal-reserve requirements as they felt was consistent with safety, and thereafter loans and deposit liabilities were kept roughly within limits determined by the amount of cash holdings It will be noted that in 1902 the banks were little above, and in 1906 somewhat below the ratio of reserve on August 22, 1907, the date of the last return before the crisis. That the banks were slightly stronger in cash in 1907 than in 1906 may be in part due to the earlier date of the return of 1907, nearly two weeks earlier than that for the corresponding period in 1906 It is evident, however, that the banks were at least in, what was for them, a quite normal condition of strength just before the beginning of the crisis But this was not on account of any exercise of restraint in making loans, since the increase during the previous twelve months was greater than for any other year of the period under review. Finally, it may be noted that the proportion of reserve to deposit liabilities which had become customary was distinctly less than it was during the years before either the crisis of 1873 or that of 1893

Analysis of the condition of the banks by groups does not give different results in the case of the country banks and those of reserve cities. The net deposits of the country banks increased without interruption from

$963,000,000 on October 3, 1897, to $2,527,000,000 on August 22, 1907. Aside from a slight loss in 1900, cash reserves also showed a gain in every year, rising from $111,000,000 in 1897 to $199,600,000 in 1907. The reserve ratio, which was 11.6 per cent at the outset, declined rapidly and was constantly in the neighborhood of 7.5 per cent from 1902 onward; in 1906 it was 7.5 per cent; in 1907, 7.6 per cent.

In the reserve cities also deposits increased with the exception of a single year, 1903, rising from $586,000,000 to $1,423,000,000. Cash reserves increased, except in 1902, advancing from $94,000,000 in 1897 to $190,000,000 in 1907. The reserve ratio was 17.8 per cent at the outset, but was in the neighborhood of 12½ per cent from 1901 onward. In 1906 it was 12.1 per cent, in 1907 it was 13.4 per cent.

The condition of the banks in the central reserve cities presents greater individual differences. In St. Louis both deposits and reserves increased regularly with the exception of 1900—the former from $33,000,000 to $116,000,000, the latter from $8,200,000 to $29,200,000. The reserve ratio of the St. Louis banks was below 25 per cent even in 1897 and was above that point in only one year, 1905. In 1906 it was 24 per cent and in 1907 23.5 per cent. In Chicago deposits fell off somewhat in two years, 1900 and 1906, but increased from $105,700,000 in 1897 to $262,900,000 in 1907. The reserve underwent greater fluctuation, falling in 1899, 1902, and 1906, but, taking the period as a whole, was increased from $38,000,000 to $66,000,000. Beginning with a high reserve ratio of 36 per cent in 1897 the Chicago banks soon broke away from the traditionally ample reserve which had characterized the banks of the city. In 1899 the reserve was 25.4 per cent, in 1902 only 21.9 per cent, and thereafter every autumn return showed a deficiency until 1907, when the banks held a cash reserve equal to 25.3 per cent of their deposit liabilities

Leaving the New York banks out of consideration, every group of banks except those of St Louis was in a slightly stronger condition in 1907 than in 1906, and all, judged by the average of the preceding half dozen years, were in a normal condition of strength, but as their condition was somewhat less strong than at the time of the reports immediately preceding the financial crises of former years, it should have been evident that in case of an emergency the pressure upon the banks of New York would be even greater than in the past.

The position of the New York banks is so important a factor in our banking system that their condition at the time of each autumn report is appended in the following table

[Amounts expressed in millions]

	Loans	Net deposits	Cash reserve	Ratio to deposits
				Per cent
Oct 5, 1897	$408	$506 8	$136 5	27 0
Sept 20, 1898	441	596 0	152 7	25 6
Sept 7 1899	541	707 7	177 6	25 1
Sept 5, 1900	569	769 6	213 4	27 8
Sept 30, 1901	611	811 3	215 6	26 6
Sept 15 1902	607	753 4	184 3	24 6
Sept 9, 1903	631	741 0	203 1	27 5
Sept 6 1904	807	1 034 3	287 9	27 8
Aug 25, 1905	805	993 8	253 2	25 6
Sept 4, 1906	702	827 4	199 2	24 2
Aug 22 1907	713	825 7	218 8	26 5

It will be observed that the upward tendency of loans was not so marked in New York as in the case of the banks in general. The $408,000,000 of New York bank loans in 1897 was nearly 20 per cent of all the loans of the national banks, while the $712,000,000 of loans in 1907 was just above 15 per cent of the total. Fluctuations in all the various items, except the reserve ratio, were no less wide [a] than for the various groups of banks or for the banks taken as a whole. Even at the beginning of the period the New York banks were able to find borrowers for all they were prepared to lend, and throughout the period they were evidently handling their loan account so as to keep just above the 25 per cent requirement against deposits They did no more than maintain the reserve position which previous experience had clearly shown to be inadequate, although the burden resting upon them through the relatively greater expansion elsewhere tended to increase

As in the case of cash reserves, that portion of the reserves of the country and reserve city banks deposited with agents increased during the period under review, but not so rapidly as the increase in deposit liability The deposited reserves of the country banks were $192,500,000 in 1897, and $420,000,000 in 1907, while those of reserve city banks increased from $104,500,000 to $194,000,000.[b]

[a] The enormous increase in reserve and loans in 1904 was a result of the decline in trade which marked that year Loans were made at such abnormally low rates in New York that outside banks and the trust companies of the city found it to their advantage to increase their balances with the banks, upon which they received a return of 2 per cent

[b] With the return for April, 1902, statements of reserves for country and reserve city banks in the reports of the Comptroller of the Currency do not include deposits in excess of the amount which each bank can include

The failure of this portion of the reserves of these banks to increase as rapidly as the growth of their net deposits would not, however, tend to diminish appreciably the extent of the withdrawals in an emergency, since the determining factors at such a time would be the state of the cash reserves and the degree of confidence in their reserve agents

A more significant indication of the situation as regards deposited reserves is afforded by the following table, which shows the gross and net amounts due other national banks by the national banks of the three central reserve cities.

[Expressed in millions]

	St Louis		Chicago		New York	
	Gross	Net	Gross	Net	Gross	Net
Oct 5, 1897	$14 0	$5 8	$47 5	$21 7	$184 0	$155 0
Sept 4, 1906	41 5	20 7	117 2	69 0	297 5	243 8
Aug 22 1907	52 3	30 3	115 8	76 7	259 3	213 8

New York still maintained its commanding position as a debtor of national banks The comparatively unfavorable showing for New York for August, 1907, seems to have been due to special temporary influences, for in January of that year the deposits due other banks held by those in Chicago and St Louis were only $100,000,000 compared with $262,000,000 in the case of New York Balances with New York banks are subject to wide fluctuations from day to day, on account of the enormous settlements for outside banks which regularly take place in that city. There had been no marked change in the

as a part of its reserves, but the total deposits are given here because they convey a better idea of the basis upon which the banks were working and also of the responsibilities of the banks which are reserve agents.

proportion of deposits due to national banks compared with the total deposits of the New York banks. They were 30 per cent of the total in 1897, nearly as much in 1906, and 27 per cent in 1907. For Chicago and St Louis the relative importance of bankers' deposits to total deposits was at all times considerably greater than in New York.[a] But for reasons explained in a previous chapter little attention need be given to the condition of the banks of those cities [b] So far as the national banks are concerned, then, the statistical position had undergone only one change for the worse—namely, the smaller cash reserves of the banks in the country, the reserve cities, and also Chicago. The New York banks were comparatively as strong as in the past and under no greater relative obligations to other national banks. They might, however, reasonably have expected somewhat greater withdrawals in an emergency, because of the smaller cash reserve ratio of all the other banks in the system, through the probable difference on this account was not remarkably great

STATE BANKS AND TRUST COMPANIES.

In the analysis of previous crises it has not seemed necessary to include any detailed reference to credit institutions under state laws. Even as late as 1893 the resources of state banks and trust companies were but little more than half those of the national banks, and the deposits of state institutions in the national banks of the money centers were a correspondingly small item relative to the deposits of national banks with their reserve agents

[a] Banks in Chicago and St Louis whose business is to be purely local are almost invariably organized under state laws

[b] See p 125

During the ten years from 1897 the growth of banking institutions under state laws was remarkably rapid The total resources of state banks and trust companies were reported at $1,981,000 in 1897 and at $7,290,000 in 1907, compared with $3,563,000 and $8,470,000 in the case of the national banks

This startling increase among banking institutions outside the national system greatly complicates the problem of legislation designed to improve the national banking system. But in following the course of the crisis of 1907 only two matters need be considered—the growth of deposits in national banks, due to state institutions, and the relations between trust companies and banks in New York City

On October 2, 1897, the net amount due from national banks to state banks of all kinds was only $185,600,000, on August 22, 1907, it was $646,000,000 Of course, much of this amount was the result of current dealings between the banks, but by far the greater portion was made up of the reserves of these state institutions, which even in the cities held much smaller amounts of cash than the national banks In particular the increase in the deposits of state banks and trust companies held by the New York banks was most striking and might well have been considered alarming. The following table tells the story·

[Expressed in millions]

	Oct 2, 1897	Sept 4, 1906	Aug 22, 1907
Net deposits due national banks	$155 0	$264 3	$213 8
Net deposits due state banks, trust companies, etc.	75 9	202 1	196 3

From a little more than one-third the aggregate of bankers' deposits in 1897, the deposits due state institutions had become in 1907 almost equal to those due the national banks. The aggregate of bankers' deposits had also become a slightly larger part of the total deposits of the New York banks, but the real importance of this growth is due to the fact that the cash reserves of the state banks and trust companies were notoriously inadequate. Even more than the national banks were these state institutions certain to be obliged to draw down their deposits in an emergency. That these deposits should have been acquired with eagerness and without the slightest unfavorable criticism from the public is indeed strange The state banks and trust companies were from time to time the subjects of unfavorable comment, and efforts were made looking toward the maintenance by them of larger cash holdings, but that the receipt of enormous deposits from these institutions subjected the national banks holding them to serious dangers was not apparently given a thought At any rate, the banks holding these deposits did not build up reserves any larger than they would have carried had they been received from that class of conservative individuals who habitually maintain large balances with their banks Even if the brunt of the storm in the autumn of 1907 had not struck the trust companies, it is certain that their requirements would have been relatively greater than those of the national banks having deposits with reserve agents.

The growth of state banks in New York City was not relatively more rapid than that of the national banks, but that of the trust companies was vastly, even dramatically, greater. In January, 1898, the loans of the trust companies were about $180,000,000, considerably less than half those of the national banks In August, 1907, their loans had increased to $610,000,000, compared with $712,000,000 for the national banks at the same date.

The growth of the purely banking business of the New York trust companies subjected the banks to an unprecedented amount of competition, but it can not be said to have brought about any appreciable change in the character of their operations, nor did it involve any change in the proportion of their cash reserves to deposit liabilities. In times of moderate strain the clearing-house banks were often enabled by means of the trust companies to make a better showing in the weekly bank statements than would otherwise have been the case As the business of the trust companies was chiefly local, they were not subject to seasonal withdrawals of cash, and their lending power was, therefore, more nearly the same throughout the year. An increase in rates for loans in New York was usually followed by a shifting of loans from banks to trust companies By this means the deposit liabilities of the clearing-house banks were reduced, thus enabling them to preserve the cherished 25 per cent reserve ratio. The resort to this device was, of course, greatly simplified through the close affiliations between some of the large banks and trust companies, and it was so much in evidence during the years before the crisis that the surplus reserve became quite as much an object of mirth as of confidence.

ELEMENTS OF WEAKNESS IN THE NEW YORK MONEY MARKET.

The ease with which the growth of the trust companies made possible the shifting of tens of millions of loans and deposit liabilities seems to have obscured the essential unsoundness of the situation. If, for any reason, it should become necessary for the trust companies to contract their banking operations, it would obviously be necessary for the banks to shoulder the burden in order to save the local situation. In the past the banks could carry through some slight curtailment of loans in an emergency without involving the business community in disaster. The course of the panic of 1907 was to show that in an emergency the New York national banks, in addition to being obliged to meet heavy withdrawals of cash, must also make a positive increase in their loans

Another development of this period requires attention because it tended to increase the sensitiveness of the New York money market in times of moderate strain and because it created a serious element of weakness in emergencies The consolidation of corporations together with other influences tended toward the concentration of all kinds of financial transactions in New York, and among them the business of making loans Outside banks, including those of Canada, came to supply an increasingly large though variable portion of the funds available for loans. No exact statistics are to be had, but it was estimated that in 1906 the loans of outside banks in New York were no less than $300,000,000.[a] An analogous development has taken place in London through the lending by foreign banks in that market. Now, to maintain payments in these circumstances and to prevent extreme fluctuations in the rates for loans are extremely difficult matters. The outside banks feel no responsibility for the course of the market. They will naturally withdraw from it when affairs at home require more of their funds or when they have come to distrust its future. It therefore becomes necessary for the local banks in the money center to be able at all times to shoulder at least a part of the loans which may be liquidated by outside banks, and also to supply the cash which they thus secure the power to draw away.

Another somewhat analogous banking development must also be noted. We have already seen that no part of our foreign trade is financed on this side. Imports are secured through commercial letters of credit, and bills against exports are regularly discounted in Europe. Anticipatory bills also have long been in use by means of which immediate credits are secured against exports of future months. During the years of active business after 1897 another device was, if not for the first time put into use, at least utilized to an extent hitherto unknown—the finance bill. Like other bills in form, it was made possible by the hypothecation of American securities to bankers in foreign countries. The extent to which such bills were drawn can not be determined

[a] A. D. Noyes, Forty Years of American Finance, p. 356.

exactly, but more than once the credit secured in this way amounted to several hundreds of millions of dollars. In 1906 the maximum was reached, and it was generally believed that finance bills to the amount of $400,000,000 or $500,000,000 had been drawn At the time of the crisis of 1907 the amount of these bills was, as we shall see, comparatively small, but their extensive use in earlier years illustrates the tendency in the New York money market to employ not only its own resources to the limits fixed by law, but also to exhaust every other source of credit, both domestic and foreign, leaving nothing in reserve for emergencies.

Taking all these influences together it is evident that the New York money market was far more subject to severe strain than at any time covered by this investigation To the possibility of withdrawals by outside banks must be added the danger of withdrawals by a large group of local institutions, the trust companies. Moreover, there was the possibility that the contraction of loans by outside banks, trust companies, and foreign lenders might come together, creating a situation which would be extremely difficult to handle successfully in any case and well nigh impossible if in normal times the important clearing-house banks failed to exercise great caution and maintain large reserves

THE POLICY OF THE TREASURY.

Some of the influences which have been just described weakened the New York money market in ways for which the national banks were not responsible But there was another influence, potent during this period, which tended positively to encourage unsound banking—a large government surplus. The disposition of the government surplus both in this and other periods has varied with successive Secretaries of the Treasury. Between 1900 and 1907 deposits of the Government with the banks rather than bond purchases were constantly favored. No banking objection can be made to this practice if all funds immediately upon their receipt are thus deposited, but in place of that policy a sort of grandfatherly attitude toward the banks was adopted, especially by Secretary Shaw. It does not fall within the scope of this investigation to consider the numerous devices which were made use of by him to relieve the money market. They are summarized as follows in an admirable study of the relations between "The Treasury and the Banks," by Prof A. P Andrew:

> Mr Shaw's administration of the Treasury was marked by at least six significant departures from the paths of his predecessors (I) He placed government money with the banks upon other security than government bonds, (II) he exempted the banks from maintaining the legal reserve against government deposits, (III) he transferred to the banks public money which had already been turned into the Treasury, (IV) he artificially stimulated the importation of gold, (V) he deliberately withdrew money from the banks in certain seasons in order to redeposit it later, and (VI) he forced alternately the enlargement and retirement of the note issue by changing his orders about deposit security as he saw fit [a]

Whether the operations of the Treasury were a fundamental influence tending to weaken the credit situation may, however, be doubted After all, the course of the New York money market was not very different from what it had been in the years before the crises of 1873 and 1893, when there was no government surplus With

[a] The Quarterly Journal of Economics, August, 1907, p 559.

the exception of a few months before the crisis of 1893, when, on account of the silver situation, the business atmosphere was tinged with unusual caution, the New York banks have always lent to the full extent of their resources, even though a part of them was but temporarily at their disposal The Treasury surplus is indeed a stumbling block in the way of any proper realization of the necessity of maintaining a large available reserve, but that such a reserve would have been held between 1900 and 1907, had there been no surplus, is extremely doubtful.

THE ULTIMATE RESERVE.

As in our analysis of the banking position before 1873, it will be necessary to carry one step further the search for the whereabouts of the ultimate reserve in our banking system Throughout the period covered by this study a few of the New York banks have held the bulk of bankers' deposits, the majority of the banks being engaged in purely local business. In 1907 this concentration was but little greater than in 1873, though on account of the magnitude of bankers' deposits the banks holding them had become more conspicuous and attracted much more public attention Instead of the seven banks of 1873, there were in 1907 and the years immediately preceding six banks which regularly held about three-fourths of all bankers' deposits. These banks, in the order of their importance, were the City, the Bank of Commerce, the First, the Park, the Chase, and the Hanover national banks. The following table shows the condition of all the 38 New

York national banks, the 6 banks, and the other 32 banks on August 22, 1907:

[Expressed in millions.]

	Thirty-eight banks.	The six banks.	Thirty-two banks.
Capital	$114.6	$71.0	$43.6
Surplus and undivided profits	140.2	80.4	59.8
Individual deposits	532.6	285.1	247.5
Due to national banks	259.3	168.6	90.7
Due to other banks	206.1	158.6	47.5
Loans	712.6	417.4	295.2
Due from national banks	45.5	19.1	26.4
Due from other banks	9.7	3.9	5.8
Clearing-house exchanges and other cash items	131.0	79.0	52.0
Cash reserve	218.8	140.7	78.1
Total resources	1,364.0	836.0	528.0
Net bankers' deposits	410.2	304.2	106.0

Comparison with the similar table for 1873 [a] shows that remarkable changes had taken place in the position of the banks holding bankers' deposits. In 1873 the seven banks controlled only about 30 per cent of the resources of all the New York national banks. In 1907 the six banks controlled over 60 per cent of the total. The change in capital and surplus was equally noteworthy—from less than 24 per cent to nearly 60 per cent. Other items tell the same story. Individual deposits had increased from less than 20 to more than 54 per cent and loans from about one-third to nearly three-fifths. Finally, the cash reserve had increased from less than two-fifths to about two-thirds that held by all the banks.

This growth of the banks holding bankers' deposits was in keeping with their responsibilities and had a double

[a] See p. 17.

significance. The ability of the other banks to assist the six banks in an emergency, as was done in 1873, was clearly very much lessened, at the same time the power of the six banks, taken together, to cope with an emergency was vastly increased. It can not be doubted that any agreement upon a common policy in times of difficulty could be carried through by them, even without the co-operation of the other banks. In 1873 the seven banks were weak because they were carrying on business almost entirely with bankers' deposits. In 1907 they were weak taken singly, but acting together they would have wielded a banking power sufficient, it may be readily believed, for almost any emergency

The improvement in the position of the banks responsible for bankers' deposits, however, may be easily overestimated The greater capital and surplus in themselves did little except to give slightly greater confidence to depositors, and this gain was perhaps offset by more general knowledge that some of these banks were controlled by various financial groups whose principal interests were not in banking pure and simple The large loan account of these banks did not strengthen them as it would have done in 1873, since, on account of the entrance of outside lenders into the market, these banks were certain to be obliged to increase rather than decrease their loans in an emergency The only certain resource for banks holding large bankers' deposits is a large cash reserve, and that was as conspicuously lacking in 1907 as it had been in 1873. In both years net bankers' deposits were more than twice the cash reserves of these banks, and their proportion of cash to net deposits, like that of the purely local banks, was but slightly above the 25 per cent required by law.

The power of the banks holding bankers' deposits to restrain the various dangerous influences which have been analyzed was not great Their situation in this respect is not unlike that of the great European central banks When, for example, in London the reserves of the other banks are increasing or foreign bankers are investing more largely in loans in the London market, the Bank of England can do little more than husband its own resources Similarly, the New York banks holding bankers' deposits can not check the resort to finance bills or the entrance of outside banks into the market for loans, but they can maintain large reserves, and so long as they are permitted to hold the position of central reserve agents it is not unreasonable to expect that they should do so

That the banks which held the reserves of other banks were in no position to meet an emergency was clear from the course of the money market during nearly every year between 1900 and 1907 As in other periods of active business, loans were increased in summer, only to be followed by disturbing contraction and high rates in autumn It has indeed been urged in defense of the banks that, though these temporary fluctuations might have been prevented by them, the proper and effective remedy was through changes in legislation. The erratic withdrawal and return of money to the channels of trade through the operations of the Treas-

6158—10——16

ury and the system of note issue were certainly in part responsible But, quite apart from these causes of temporary difficulty, it is clear that the banks were not strong enough to meet the more occasional, but also more severe, requirements of an emergency. Their responsibility at such a time was in no way connected either with the system of note issue or the movements of government funds Trust company balances afford an excellent example The deposits of the trust companies with the national banks increased steadily with the growth of their banking operations Most of them were city institutions, subject to no seasonal variations in the requirements of their depositors for cash, but as few of the trust companies held cash reserves, in receiving deposits from them the banks were assuming a risk of a particularly explosive character But they did not on this account maintain reserves proportionately greater than those held in former years. It is therefore difficult to escape the conclusion that, if all government funds had been deposited with the banks upon their receipt, loans would have been still further increased in those months, when, in fact, money was withdrawn from the market by the Government. Legislative changes may remove obstacles to sound banking, but they can not take its place altogether.

INDICATIONS OF APPROACHING REACTION.

The failure of the banks holding the ultimate reserve of the country to live up to the responsibilities of their position is evident in still another direction. While the exact moment of the outbreak of the crisis of 1907 could not be foreseen, the imminence of a period of trade reaction had been for many months so probable that precautionary measures might reasonably have been expected from these banks, if not from the banks and the public in general. A short account of the course of events during 1906 and 1907 down to the outbreak of the crisis will afford ample evidence of the obvious need of caution and will also serve as an introduction to the narrative of the crisis itself.

After the San Francisco earthquake on April 18, 1906, eighteen months before the crisis, there were indications in plenty that the pace was too rapid and that the equilibrium of economic forces was becoming increasingly unstable That catastrophe destroyed an immense amount of capital, a loss which, through insurance, was widely distributed, but even if it had not occurred it is certain that demand for additional capital was outstripping current savings seeking investment Increasing difficulty was experienced in marketing securities of the very highest class. By some journalists and others eagerly searching for objections to a prevailing tendency this difficulty was attributed to the activities of the national and state governments designed to regulate corporations, but it can hardly be supposed that this superficial view blinded those in responsible positions in the financial world The strain upon capital was worldwide, and in the United States municipal bonds whose sale would have been stimulated by distrust of business corporations could only be marketed when offered at lower prices or a higher rate of interest

Whatever the causes, the inability to secure capital by the sale of securities in a period of active business should have been enough in itself to inspire unusual caution in the management of banking institutions. When corporations of the highest standing are obliged to resort to short-term notes it may be assumed without question that other corporations are expanding upon an insufficient foundation of working capital, that current obligations are increasing, and that bank credits are being used to their utmost extent. This probability might well have been recognized as a certainty when it appeared that during the latter half of 1906 and the first eight months of 1907 the loans of the national banks had increased more rapidly than at any time in the history of the system.

Increasing tension in New York, whenever comparatively slight contraction in loans took place, was another indication pointing to the same condition of affairs It suggested that there were few persons in the community with idle funds available to take over either the loans or the collateral of borrowers, and that, consequently, any considerable liquidation of loans would be difficult, and, if carried through rapidly, disastrous.

Another indication of the approach of a period of declining activity in trade was the increasing ratio of costs reported in many industries. This is probably one of the most fundamental causes of industrial reaction and the necessity for an occasional period of recuperation During the ten years before 1907 production in many branches had more than doubled, as, for example—coal, iron, and also railroad traffic A far more rapid increase in the number employed in such occupations was made than was compatible with the maintenance of industrial efficiency The incompetent could hold places because there were none to fill their positions, and there was no time to acquire skill by those capable of acquiring it

As a result of these and other causes which might be mentioned there could be no doubt that the United States, like other countries, was about to pass through a period of reaction, though the exact moment of its beginning could not be foreseen and might largely be determined by fortuitous circumstances It was so probable that with each month of 1906 and 1907 the exercise of increasing caution might well have been expected in all responsible circles.

Little heed seems to have been given to these warning signs, but much was made of every straw which suggested a possible further advance. On July 31, 1906, dividends were resumed on the common stock of the United States Steel Corporation, and on August 18 the Union Pacific dividend was advanced from 6 to 10 per cent, and dividends were begun at the rate of 5 per cent on the shares of the Southern Pacific Railroad Events seem to have proved conclusively the ability of these companies to earn the dividends which were then declared, but nevertheless, coming when it did, this action exercised an unfortunate general influence It gave encouragement to the unbridled optimism which was already too much in evidence. It was preceded and followed by a speculative movement on the stock exchange which was made possible through credits granted by the banks upon the foundation of the usual summer inflow of funds from the interior. The unsoundness of the situation was shown during the first half of September, when loan contraction of only $27,000,000 brought call-loan rates on successive days to 40, 30, and 25 per cent. Relief was secured in two ways—through the intervention of the Secretary of the Treasury and through foreign exchange operations. During September and October the money in circulation increased nearly $100,000,000. Treasury holdings were reduced $23,000,000 by deposits in the banks State and other bonds were accepted as security for such deposits on condition that the banks should use the released United States bonds as a basis for further issues of notes Nearly $54,000,000 was secured through gold imports, which were brought about primarily by means of the negotiation of finance bills, though the movement was slightly facilitated by the deposit of government funds in the banks against gold engagements By these means after the middle of September the New York banks were enabled to meet further crop-moving requirements without any considerable loss in cash. Loan contraction ceased and there was even some slight increase. The one apparent gain was to enable the bull movement on the stock exchange to continue through the autumn months. The last month of the year, however, was marked by a return of stringent monetary conditions and a declining stock market. In January came the usual return flow of money to New York and temporary ease, but the stock market was then overshadowed by an influence which made liquidation necessary and upon an extensive scale

Owing principally to the enormous exports of gold to the United States secured by means of finance bills, the Bank of England on October 11 advanced its rate from 4 to 5 per cent, and followed this action on Friday, October 19, by an advance to 6 per cent, a rate which had been reached only three times before during twenty years. At the same time the bank intimated to the London financial world that the acceptance of American finance bills was a menace to the stability of the London market, against which the bank would throw the full weight of its power and influence. From that time the further negotiation of finance bills was at an end, and as those drawn in earlier months matured payment was exacted, except where by previous arrangement a single renewal had been provided for. From December, 1906, the liquidation of these bills was the most potent single factor in the situation So long as it was possible to transfer loans to the banks in New York no great difficulty was experienced, but toward the end of February it became necessary for the banks to contract loans to an extent about equal to the increase which had been made during the first weeks of the year. The double process of liquidation soon culminated in the so-called "rich men's panic" of March, 1907 Never before or since have such severe declines taken place on the New York stock exchange The most notable decline was in the case of Union Pacific shares, which fell over 50 points within less than two weeks Probably no one security had been used so extensively as collateral in finance-bill operations.

Some recovery took place at the end of March and in subsequent months, though a succession of unfavorable influences prevented any active speculative movement. Copper had advanced to the extraordinary high price of 26 cents a pound at the beginning of 1907, reflecting in part conditions of demand and supply and in part manipulation of the market for the metal It was held stubbornly at that price, although demand fell off sharply and stocks accumulated. At length in July some concession was made in price without, however, stimulating demand. Thereafter the price fell rapidly and was only 13 cents at the beginning of October. Even with the price cut in half, the demand for copper was sluggish, and it became clear that the diminishing consumption of copper was the fundamental factor in the situation. Copper shares, which had advanced with the price of copper, fell sharply though hardly enough to discount fully market conditions

Another significant occurrence was the failure on June 28 of New York City's offering of $29,000,000 of 4 per cent bonds, the applications for which aggregated only a little more than $2,000,000 Finally, it may be mentioned that the gain in railroad net earnings was not proportionate to that in gross earnings and that during three of the first nine months of the year there was a positive decline.

While the course of prices on the stock exchange after the March panic was upward, the market manifested great sensitiveness at all times. Early in August came another decline, which wiped out more than the gain of the preceding months. This August decline was the only episode during the year which can be ascribed in part at least to governmental activities designed to restrain corporations It followed hard upon the $29,000,000 fine imposed upon the Standard Oil Company, which, coming at a time when the market was not strong, may be properly regarded as occasioning the sharp decline which followed its announcement Had the crisis come at that time it might have been argued with some plausibility that if not caused it was at least precipitated by this rather spectacular exercise of judicial power. But the crisis came more than two months later, and therefore it can have been at most a contributing and not an immediate cause There is, however, reason to hold that this and all other governmental activities which had the control of corporations as their object did quite as much good as harm from a purely financial point of view

Government interference in the affairs of corporations may have caused some depreciation in their securities and might also have caused plans for the investment of capital and earnings in the improvement of corporate properties to be deferred. But there was no diminution in the demand of corporations for additional capital so that it becomes necessary to show that there were savings seeking investment which would have been available but for alarm as to the future returns from investments in corporations There is, however, no evidence whatever that there was available idle capital either in this country or elsewhere in 1907. On account of the increased cost of living and the growth of extravagant expenditure it is probable that there had been a relative decline in new savings, and as borrowers of all kinds had difficulty in securing capital the contention that governmental activities were the controlling factor in the situation falls to the ground

On the other hand, in so far as government policies tended to check speculation and suggested the need of caution they served a most useful purpose Had stocks advanced rather than declined in August it is quite certain that the banks and the business community would have been far less able to withstand the approaching shock than they actually were in October The situation was in many respects similar to that just before the panic in May, 1884, although in the earlier year in addition to successive declines on the stock exchange there had been considerable trade reaction. In 1907 the outlook for the future was not promising in many basic industries, but there had been no positive reaction except in the case of copper.

Stock exchange liquidation in March and August had vastly improved the credit situation as contrasted with the previous year. There was no serious monetary strain in New York during August and September, although the amount of money in circulation increased far less than in previous years We have already seen that the New York banks on August 22 were in slightly better shape than at about the same time in 1906 As the next report to the Comptroller of the Currency was not made until December, the condition of the banks in general just before and during the greater part of the crisis can not be analyzed In the case of the New York banks resort may be made to the weekly bank statement The following table shows the condition of the banks on August

24 and just before the outbreak of the crisis on October 19, figures for corresponding dates for the previous year are also included·

New York bank statement

[Expressed in millions]

	1907		1906	
	Aug 24	Oct 19	Aug 23	Oct 20
Loans	$1,088 0	$1,076 0	$1,071 0	$1,082 0
Deposits	1,048 0	1,025 0	1,053 0	1 062 0
Reserve	272 0	267 0	267 0	271 0
Surplus reserve	9 9	11 2	4 2	6 2

In 1906, notwithstanding large gold imports and aid from the Government, the banks with difficulty were able to maintain a surplus reserve In 1907 there had been no gold imports, and the release of money by the Treasury had been no greater in amount and a relatively small part of it had been secured by the New York banks. The surplus reserve was larger in August of the crisis year, and notwithstanding a slight loss in cash, was increased somewhat during the two months preceding the beginning of the panic.

But it was the foreign exchange situation in which there was by far the greatest improvement in October, 1907, contrasted with the same month of 1906. It is true that exchange rates during the first three weeks of October were in the neighborhood of the export point This was due to European sales of American securities, which were largely sold as a result of a severe crisis in Amsterdam and Hamburg. On October 19 $1,500,000 was engaged for shipment to Germany. There were, however, no finance bills approaching maturity, and an unusually small amount of anticipatory bills had been drawn, so that as soon as grain and cotton should begin to move in quantity it was certain that exchange would rule strongly in favor of this country

After the August decline on the stock exchange a number of unfavorable events served to weaken confidence The most important of these were the disclosures regarding the affairs of the New York street railway companies, which culminated in the appointment of receivers toward the end of September There is, however, no evidence that distrust of the solvency of the banks either in New York or elsewhere had been excited. During the crisis distrust rapidly developed, but this was owing to causes similar to those which had produced the same effect in other crises and can be naturally accounted for by the events which marked its beginning

THE BEGINNING OF THE CRISIS.

The initial episode of the crisis was, as has often happened in previous instances, insignificant enough Copper was, as we have seen, the one branch of industry in which a positive decline had taken place No time could possibly have been chosen so unfavorable for venturesome attempts at manipulation either of copper itself or of the shares of copper companies It happened that the particular disaster which precipitated the crisis was a copper gamble, the outcome of which would ordinarily have had no public importance.

An unsuccessful attempt to corner the stock of a copper company of secondary importance involved certain brokerage firms, including that of the brothers of Mr. F. A. Heinze, who at the beginning of the year had become president of the Mercantile National Bank by securing a majority of its stock Mr. Heinze had acquired a large fortune from highly spectacular operations in Montana copper properties, and distrust of his methods led many depositors to withdraw their accounts after the change of management. The diminishing resources of the bank seem to have been used to an increasing extent in the furtherance of copper enterprises and speculation, and the failure of the copper corner brought matters to a head. The bank was unable to meet unfavorable balances at the clearing house, which assumed large proportions because alarmed depositors were shifting their accounts to other banks. A request for assistance from the clearing house was granted after an examination to determine the solvency of the bank and upon condition that the president and entire board of directors should resign On October 21 the bank began business under a new management and thereafter ceased to be a disturbing factor in the situation, though, it may be added, in January it was deemed advisable to close the bank for liquidation.

While the reorganization of the Mercantile Bank was being carried out the clearing house was given an opportunity to intervene in the affairs of certain other banks whose management had long been regarded with distrust. One of the directors of the Mercantile Bank was

C. F Morse, whose activities in the industrial and banking world had been of an extreme character, even when judged by American speculative standards. He first became prominent as a promoter of the American Ice Company, an enterprise disastrous to its shareholders, and in recent years had been actively engaged in the formation of a combination of shipping companies engaged in the Atlantic coasting trade For a number of years he had been one of the largest owners of shares in New York banks, but, it is important to observe, only in banks of moderate size. He was a director in seven banks, over three of which he seems to have exercised complete control In securing this chain of banks the shares of one bank, along with other collateral, were used as a security for loans with which to purchase shares in another bank, and so on in succession, while the various banks were efficient instruments in the furtherance of other enterprises Morse had long been regarded with distrust in banking circles, and a clearing-house investigation of his methods had been made as early as 1902, but it led to no definite action His connection with the Mercantile Bank seems to have frightened depositors in his other banks, the most important of which was the National Bank of North America, and two of them were obliged to appeal to the clearing house for aid on October 19. Assistance was granted upon condition that Morse should retire altogether from banking in New York Much the same course was taken with Messrs. E. R and O. F. Thomas, who were associated with the Heinzes, and were the chief owners of the Mechanics and Traders

Bank, a state institution in the clearing house, and the Consolidated Bank, which was not a member of the association. Taken together, five banks, members of the clearing house, were concerned, three of which were national and two state banks, and also three banking institutions outside the association, a national, a state bank, and a trust company. The total deposits of the five banks on October 12 were only $56,000,000, and those of the entire number only $71,000,000. It was not, therefore, a very difficult matter to afford them the assistance they required. Various clearing-house banks subscribed to a fund of $10,000,000 to be used if necessary, and on Monday, October 21, it may be said that the clearing house had completed the work of putting its affairs in order. It is to be noted that there had been nothing in the nature of a crisis up to this time, although the difficulties of these banks doubtless gave rise to a vague feeling of distrust, which speedily assumed dangerous proportions when it became known that certain far more important banking institutions were also in need of assistance.

The narrative of the crisis may with advantage be interrupted at this point to call attention to the significance of this Heinze-Morse episode as an example of a deep-seated cause of weakness in the financial system of the country. National banks are not allowed to open branch offices, and most of the states have enacted similar legislation. Consequently, banks are numerous, nearly 16,000, not including savings banks, and are generally of small size. While this system of independent local banks has very great advantages, it has also certain serious, though not incurable, disadvantages Few banks are large enough to be the principal interest of those who own and control them Upon the whole the system has not worked badly, since the directorate has commonly included capable men from various occupations, but danger arises when an individual or group of closely associated individuals gains control of a bank for the purpose of furthering private undertakings. This danger is of course vastly more serious when a bank is situated in New York or some other money center in which even the failure of a bank engaged in purely local business has more than a local effect upon public confidence. Unfortunately there seems to have been a distinct tendency in this direction in recent years, and there is an almost entire lack of definite public opinion opposed to the practice. The good nature and optimism characteristic of the country extends even to financial matters, regarding which there is a painful absence of thorough unflinching criticism in any financial journal The attitude of publicists is commonly weak and ineffective, and is well illustrated by the following comment upon the particular case of the Morse banks taken from an influential New York journal:

> A few capitalists of no great standing, actively engaged in speculative industrial schemes of their own, were gaining control of a group of banks through mere stock ownership on a margin * * * The possibility of danger had been known for six years past If it be asked why no one interfered, the answer is that no one outside of the banking department had a right to examine the soundness of these banks and challenge the manner of control, second, that the very hazards involved in existing conditions rendered open accusation extremely perilous [a]

Surely a money market in which urgently needed remedies are thus treated can hardly escape an occasional up-

[a] The Nation, October 24, 1907, p 384

heaval A healthy tradition should be cultivated which would lead depositors to desert a bank known to be controlled by one man, or closely identified with a single enterprise Even when honestly managed there is the obvious danger which arises from lack of a wide distribution of risks. The evidence in the Morse trial certainly suggested an absence of rigor on the part of the Comptroller of the Currency in suppressing abuses. An even more effective remedy might have been applied through clearing-house action, a promising means of improvement which is now being adopted in many cities

TRUST COMPANY DIFFICULTIES.

Returning to the narrative of events in New York, it may be noted once more that there had been nothing in the nature of a crisis during the week the clearing house was putting its affairs in order Crisis conditions developed the following week and were occasioned by the difficulties of a certain trust company. The Knickerbocker Trust Company was the third largest trust company in New York, having deposits of $62,000,000 The connection of its president with some of the Morse enterprises engendered distrust, which made itself felt in a succession of unfavorable clearing balances. On Monday, October 21, the National Bank of Commerce announced that it would discontinue clearing for the Knickerbocker on the following day. An unofficial committee representing a few trust companies and banks was not given an opportunity to examine its affairs until the last moment, so that it would have been difficult if not impossible to take definite action Nothing was done aside from the issue of a reassuring statement by the directors in which the resignation of its president was announced. On Tuesday, after a run of three hours, during which $8,000,000 were paid out, the company was forced to suspend. Whether the company could not have been assisted is not clear, but that, if possible, it would have been of advantage both to the banks and the other trust companies is certain The size of the company alone rendered assistance an undertaking of no little difficulty, but the condition of its assets at the time could not have been hopelessly unsatisfactory, as the company was able to resume business in the following March under a plan of reorganization agreed upon by its depositors and shareholders The plan of reorganization adopted, however, showed that the assets of the company were even then far from being in liquid condition, and in the absence of any association among the trust companies or of any feeling of responsibility on the part of the clearing-house banks, the suspension of the company was unavoidable.

Had the Knickerbocker Trust Company been a bank and a member of the clearing house, it is highly probable that it would have been assisted, following the precedent of 1884. Relative to the increasing magnitude of banking operations in New York, the Knickerbocker was not so large as the Metropolitan Bank in 1884. Apparently no proposal to assist the company was considered, and this is readily explicable Relations between the banks and the trust companies had been somewhat strained for a number of years. The banks complained of the unfairness of competition with institutions which were not required to hold a large cash reserve. In 1903 the clearing house had adopted a rule which required all trust companies clearing through members of the association to accumulate a reserve which, though smaller than that of the banks, was considerably larger than was held by most of the trust companies. Rather than submit to this requirement, nearly all of these gave up clearing-house privileges, the most important exception, curiously enough, being the Knickerbocker Trust Company.[a] It would therefore seem to have deserved peculiar consideration on the part of the clearing-house authorities. It may also be suggested that assistance might well have been granted from purely selfish motives. A group of banking institutions is very similar to a row of bricks, the fall of one endangering the stability of the rest. When all the circumstances are considered, however, the failure of the clearing-house authorities to take any action was doubtless the most natural course, and though unfortunate in its consequences, can hardly be regarded as blameworthy.

Equally mild judgment can not be passed upon the means which were adopted at the next stage of the crisis. On Wednesday, October 23, a run began on the Trust Company of America, the second of the trust companies in size, having deposits of $64,000,000. The president of the Knickerbocker was one of its directors, but the unfortunate disclosure that its affairs had been the

[a] The reserve of the Knickerbocker Trust Company on August 22, the date of the last return to the state superintendent of banks, was $4,745,000, a little more than that of any other trust company in the city and very much more than that of most of them.

subject of a conference on Tuesday was the chief influence in precipitating a panic among its depositors. The company withstood a run which continued for two weeks, during which it paid out some $34,000,000, on Wednesday and Thursday paying $12,000,000 and $9,000,000. The Trust Company of America and also the Lincoln Trust Company upon which a run began on Thursday were assisted, since their assets were apparently in a more satisfactory condition than those of the Knickerbocker, but still more because it was clear that the foundation of the entire credit structure was endangered The steps taken, however, were slow and the means adopted were not sufficiently clear in import to renew general confidence On Wednesday, October 23, a committee of five trust company presidents was formed to receive applications for assistance, make examinations, and report to meetings of all trust company presidents. Through this committee money was provided from day to day in large amounts, bonds contributed by various trust companies being turned over to national banks, which used them as security for additional government deposits Confidence was not restored until, on November 6, announcement was made that a majority of the shares of the Trust Company of America and of the Lincoln Trust Company had been placed under the control of a committee of trust company presidents and that the "necessary financial arrangements had been made to enable both companies to proceed with their business." The inference can not be escaped that the New York money market was not adequately organized to cope quickly and effectively with an emergency of this kind.

With the rapid growth of trust companies, an increasingly large part of the banking business of the city was entirely without organization The trust companies should either become members of the clearing-house association or at least form some organization of their own. They would then have the machinery ready for prompt action and some sense of common responsibility would be developed. It is indeed true that on account of their past the three companies were not deserving subjects for assistance. Their methods of attracting business, absurdly high interest on deposits, and the collection of out-of-town checks without charges, were generally regarded as unsafe and even piratical. But the unwillingness of some of the trust companies to join in measures of relief at all, or at least in proportion to their resources, can not be attributed to this cause alone But for the powerful influence of Mr. J P. Morgan it is probable that no united action whatever would have been taken. It is certainly an element of weakness in our central money market that influential credit institutions should have to be dragooned into doing what is after all in their own interest as well as to the general advantage.

This trust company episode suggests one conclusion of general application. Unless it is possible at the outset to take measures which are almost certain to restore confidence in threatened banking institutions, it is far better to leave them to their own devices, either liquidation or reorganization. The money furnished the two trust companies saved them from failure, but served no purpose of general importance. If it had been used to meet the demands of banks throughout the country, alarm might possibly have been delayed and general suspension avoided.

UNFORTUNATE DELAY OF THE CLEARING HOUSE.

During the three days of heavy runs upon the trust companies New York was threatened with a general panic, and a number of other trust companies experienced runs of varying degrees of severity A few small mismanaged banking institutions in the outskirts of the city were forced to suspend Depositors began to withdraw money from savings banks and they were obliged to exercise their right to require sixty days' notice. Loans could only be secured with extreme difficulty and the fall in stock exchange prices, while not so extreme as in March, was alarmingly violent and affected securities more generally The strenuous efforts that were made to relieve the situation were but partially successful, because they lacked the authority and backing of the Clearing House Association As in the case of the Trust Company of America, the relief afforded was of a piecemeal character without any certainty of its continuance On Thursday, in order to prevent complete collapse on the stock exchange, Mr J. P Morgan formed a money pool of $25,000,000, to which some of the leading banks and financiers subscribed On Friday, also, a similar pool was formed, though $10,000,000 proved adequate for the purpose In no crisis since the civil war have matters been allowed to drift along during so many days of acute panic.

Even though it would have been impossible to secure agreement among members of the clearing house to provide the trust companies with the assistance they required, the immediate issue of loan certificates should have been authorized to meet the general situation. The failure to issue certificates on Tuesday or Wednesday would be difficult to explain, if the reasons for delay had not been set forth by no less an authority than the president of the clearing house, who observed subsequently.

> Well, the panic occurred The institutions that had been weakened by unwise investments went down New York was the storm center. The paramount question was, Could the storm be stayed before its work of devastation and ruin should spread over the entire country? This was the problem confronting the clearing-house committee The committee knew that the issuance of clearing-house certificates would immediately bring about a restriction of cash payments throughout the country, causing widespread business inconvenience and embarrassment Hoping that the panicky condition might subside, the committee postponed from day to day the issuance of clearing-house certificates, honoring the drafts that were being made against our rapidly falling reserve until it showed a deficit of $53,000,000[a] [sic], and then concluded it would be folly to hesitate longer, and clearing-house certificates were issued

The failure to issue clearing-house loan certificates at least as early as Tuesday was the most serious error made during this crisis All experience in former crises went to show that the early issue of certificates had a calming effect upon the community, because they made it possible for the banks to extend relief more freely by granting accommodation to borrowers, and because they prevented in part the weakening of particular institutions through unfavorable clearing-house balances. Had clearing-house loan certificates been issued early in the week it would

[a] It was not until two weeks after the issue of loan certificates that the bank statement showed a deficit of $53,000,000

not have been necessary to resort to the cumbersome device of money pools. Liquidation on the stock exchange would have been somewhat less, and the alarm, to which the sudden fall in security prices contributed, would have been in part escaped

During the three days of heavy runs upon the trust companies the strain upon the clearing-house banks was very severe, as they had to furnish most of the money required by the trust companies, whose reserves were deposited with them At the same time they were shipping money to the interior banks, and they also suffered some loss from payments to their own frightened depositors. But at the close of the week there were many indications that the worst of the panic in New York was past Withdrawals of money by local depositors were diminishing, the savings banks were exercising their right to require sixty days' notice from depositors, and the trust companies had agreed to pay depositors so far as possible in certified checks upon clearing-house banks Had New York been a city with only local responsibilities it is probable that the disturbance would have gone no further; but, as in 1873 and in 1893, the disasters in New York had caused alarm to spread throughout the country. The country banker and his depositors were apparently unmoved by the Morse-Heinze troubles, but hard upon the news of the difficulties of the Knickerbocker Trust Company came telegraphic demands from all over the country, including the other central reserve cities, for the calling of loans and the shipment of currency. A number of adverse developments had also taken place in various parts of the country while New York was struggling with its own difficulties The Heinze troubles involved a bank in Butte, Mont., and in Goldfield, Nev , runs on the banks due to local causes forced them to suspend. In Providence, R I, a large trust company with deposits of $25,000,000 was obliged to close, and other smaller banks were subjected to runs. The various Westinghouse companies went into the hands of receivers on account of inability to secure the renewal of large floating indebtedness, and as a consequence the Pittsburg Stock Exchange was closed[a]—an exchange dealing almost exclusively with local securities.

These widely scattered troubles contributed to, but were not the principal cause of, the alarm which spread throughout the country, but which was mainly due to the panic in New York Everywhere the banks suddenly found themselves confronted with demands for money by frightened depositors, everywhere, also, banks manifested a lack of confidence in each other. Country banks drew money from city banks and all the banks throughout the country demanded the return of funds deposited or on loan in New York The evidence of lack of confidence in and between the banks is clear and it points to a serious difficulty in carrying on banking in this country. For a historical parallel in England we should need to go back to the first quarter of the last century. Explanation is simple, however, if the course of our previous crises is recalled. Seven times during the last century the banks

[a] The Pittsburg Exchange remained closed throughout November and December, as did also that of New Orleans

suspended payment in some measure at least, and there has been a currency premium, the last occasion having been so recent as 1893 There is a well-grounded belief among the people that it will be difficult to secure cash during periods of economic disturbance In all countries in times of crisis some depositors withdraw their money and hoard it from unreasoning fear. In the United States there are also withdrawals by prudent depositors who wish to be absolutely certain to have the money needed in their affairs, and by others who are influenced by the prospect of a handsome profit in a few weeks through the sale of money at a premium. Former suspensions have established a tradition which is an ever-present source of weakness and which can only be broken by successful endurance by the banks of the strain of a crisis The crisis of 1907 provided an exceptionally favorable opportunity, since general economic conditions were far less unsound than on many occasions when payment was suspended in the past. Unfortunately almost as soon as withdrawals began, and before the New York banks had suffered a serious loss in reserve, cash payments were restricted once more. Moreover, payments were restricted for the first time immediately upon the issue of clearing-house loan certificates

EXPLANATION OF THE SUSPENSION OF PAYMENTS BY THE NEW YORK BANKS

Before the beginning of the week ending November 2 a few banks elsewhere may have already suspended, but this is not a matter of importance, as it was restriction in

New York that inevitably precipitated more or less complete suspension throughout the entire country. This discreditable step was taken when the New York banks were much stronger than on other occasions and when prospects for securing additional funds were far more promising. The reasons for this action and the necessity for it are the most important questions to which the course of this crisis gives rise. In order to answer them it will be necessary to interrupt the narrative of the crisis in order to make a detailed analysis of the condition of the New York banks at the time clearing-house loan certificates were authorized.

The bank statement for the week ending October 26 must serve as the point of departure, though it is, of course, unsatisfactory, because, being based upon averages, it shows a better condition than was actually the case. The following table gives the principal items in the statement for October 26, with the changes from the previous week:

[Expressed in millions.]

	Oct. 26, 1907	Difference from previous week, increase (+) decrease (−)
Loans	$1,087.7	+$10.9
Net deposits	$1,023.8	− $1.9
Reserve held	$254.7	−$12.9
Reserve percentage	24.9	....
Surplus reserve (deficit)	$1.2	$12.4

A somewhat more accurate idea of the condition of the banks can be gathered from the following table, which shows the condition of the five banks which had been obliged to request assistance, and the condition of all the other clearing-house banks:

[Expressed in millions.]

	Five Morse-Heinze banks.		All other clearing-house banks	
	Oct 19	Oct 26	Oct 19	Oct. 26
Loans	$60.8	$52.3	$1,016.0	$1,035.6
Net deposits	$55.4	$39.9	$970.3	$982.9
Reserve held	$10.7	$4.5	$256.9	$250.2
Reserve percentage	19.3	10.8	26.5	25.5
Surplus reserve	----------	----------	$14.4	$4.5

The really solvent banks, it will be observed, had relieved the situation by an increase of nearly $20,000,000 in loans. Their cash loss was only $6,700,000, and they still held a surplus reserve of moderate proportions. But these changes do not adequately represent actual conditions. The statement for the following week shows an increase in loans of $60,000,000 and a loss in reserve of $30,000,000. Some part of this increase in loans, with its resulting increase in deposit liability, was certainly made during the previous week, and doubtless an even more considerable part of the loss in cash had been incurred since payments were restricted during the later week. If we may assume that half the loan and deposit increase was made as early as October 26 and that two-thirds of the cash loss had then been sustained, the statement would have been as follows:

Loans	$1,065 ($1,035+$30)
Net deposits	$992 ($982+$30—$20)
Reserve	$230 ($250—$20)
Reserve percentage	23.2

This table has an unreal appearance, but it is based upon an analysis of all the available data The bank statement for November 9 showed a very small loss in reserve, only $4,300,000, not very far from the amount of reported movements of money between the banks, the interior, and the subtreasury The statement for November 2, therefore, probably represented actual conditions very closely The reported movements of money between banks, the interior, and the subtreasury for the week ending November 2 showed a loss of $7,000,000, and since the banks must have lost some money locally it is safe to assume that at least $10,000,000 of the reported $30,000,000 decrease in reserve came during the week In the case of loans the figure given is hardly more than a guess, but as the banks made loans more freely after the issue of loan certificates, the assumed increase of $30,000,000 for the week ending October 26 is prabably too large rather than too small

The actual condition of the banks can hardly have been worse than the showing in the table, and was probably somewhat better The estimated loss in reserve of $36,000,000 is small after so eventful a week, and does not indicate the extent to which the banks supplied depositors with money. On Thursday, October 24, $25,000,000 was deposited with the New York banks by the Secretary of the Treasury, and between October 19 and October 31 $36,000,000 was secured in this way.[a] Just about half of the money which was paid out by the

[a]Response of the Secretary of the Treasury to Senate Resolution No 33 of December 12, 1907, pp 57-59 Senate Doc No 208, 60th Cong, 1st session.

banks during the two weeks ending November 2 was secured from the Government. Reported movements of money between banks and the interior accounted for a net loss of $33,344,000. As a result of subtreasury operations which included some transfers of money to banks in other cities having subtreasuries the New York banks gained $29,500,000 It will thus be seen that the Government supplied the banks with nearly all the money with which they responded to the demands of outside banks. The loss in reserve of the banks is, therefore, accounted for by payments made to meet the demands of local depositors, including the trust companies This statement may, of course, be reversed with equal truth—the Government supplying local needs, outside needs being supplied from the reserves of the banks. In any case it can not be said that the New York banks had experienced an exhausting depletion of their reserves Out of a total reserve of $256,900,000 on October 19, the solvent banks paid out only $36,000,000 from their reserves during the two weeks to November 2, and if we may assume some approach to the real condition of affairs in our estimate of the actual condition of the banks, they had only paid out $26,000,000 at the time payments were restricted

It may, however, be urged, and with truth, that the test of the ability of the banks to maintain payments is not the amount of the aggregate reserve unless it is distributed with some evenness among banks in proportion to their liabilities In earlier crises we have seen that the few banks holding bankers' deposits were subject to particularly severe strain and that when their reserves were depleted suspension was unavoidable in the absence of any pooling agreement. The condition of the individual banks was not disclosed during the crisis. October 26 is the last date for which such information is available. The following table shows the condition of the six banks holding the bulk of bankers' balances and that of the other clearing-house banks (not including the five already eliminated) on October 19 and October 26 1907

[Expressed in millions.]

	Six banks		Other clearing-house banks.	
	Oct 19	Oct 26	Oct 19	Oct 26
Loans	\$544 2	\$568 4	\$471 8	\$467 7
Net deposits	\$507 4	\$522 6	\$462 9	\$461 2
Reserve	\$139 7	\$132 2	\$117 2	\$118 0
Reserve percentage	27 2	25 3	25 3	25 6

No very striking differences between the two groups of banks are disclosed in the table. The tendencies indicated, however, are significant The six banks taken together had relieved the situation somewhat by a moderate increase in loans, while there had been a little contraction by the other banks The reserves of the six banks had fallen away by $7,500,000, and their reserve ratio was rather less satisfactory, although still above the legal requirement On the other hand, the reserves of the other banks had increased slightly, and also their reserve percentage There is no means of determining whether the actual condition of the six banks relative to the other banks was less favorable than that based on averages.

It is probable that the six banks made a large part of the loans not shown in the statement, and probably much of the estimated actual loss in reserve was due to payments made by them. On the other hand, between October 19 and October 31 the six banks secured additional government deposits to the amount of $30,700,000, while the other banks in the clearing house secured only $6,000,000. This distribution of the government money was entirely proper, as it corresponded, at least roughly, with the relatively greater strain which was imposed upon the six banks in consequence of the panic. But its complete justification depended upon whether the banks securing the lion's share of the government deposits fully lived up to their responsibilities. Finally, it may be observed that even if all of the $20,000,000, by which we have assumed the actual reserve was below the average reserve, had come from the six banks they would still have held $112,000,000 to meet further requirements, an amount equal to at least 20 per cent of their deposit liabilities. The suspension of payments by the banks can not, therefore, be attributed to the exhaustion of the reserve held by any particular group of banks in the clearing house.

If this analysis is carried one step further and attention is given to the condition of particular banks, the explanation of suspension while reserves in the aggregate were still large will be disclosed. It is with some hesitation that the writer singles out the particular banks whose reserves happen to have been depleted most seriously. It is proper to say that the differences disclosed between different banks do not in the slightest degree reflect upon the management, the credit, or the standing of the individual banks. None of the banks was subjected to any influences except those arising out of the general situation. And, furthermore, the banks which were apparently the greatest sufferers were so because they were doing, either absolutely or relatively, more for their customers and the community at large than their fellows.

The following tables show the condition of the six most important banks in the New York Clearing House on October 19 and 26, 1907:

[Expressed in millions.]

	Loans.		Deposits.	
	Oct. 19.	Oct. 26.	Oct. 19.	Oct. 26.
City	$148.2	$159.5	$126.8	$138.1
Commerce	130.1	129.0	104.0	138.1
First	91.6	102.7	84.5	88.1
Park	69.3	68.0	76.5	73.5
Hanover	53.3	56.6	61.6	64.7
Chase	50.7	52.4	53.9	54.7

	Reserve held.		Percentage.		Government deposits received between Oct. 19 and 31.
	Oct. 19.	Oct. 26.	Oct. 19.	Oct. 26.	
City	$35.2	$37.2	28.5	26.9	$9.5
Commerce	26.8	27.0	25.7	26.2	1.6
First	26.7	19.8	31.5	22.4	9.2
Park	19.7	18.2	25.7	24.6	1.0
Hanover	17.6	17.3	28.6	26.6	5.4
Chase	13.7	12.7	25.3	23.3	3.2

Examination of the table brings out some striking differences among the banks. All but two of the banks increased their loans, but only in the case of the First National and the National City was the increase at all considerable The other banks do not seem to have been rendering anything like that assistance which their resources would have permitted. The two largest banks (the City and the Bank of Commerce) increased their cash holdings and one of them its reserve ratio. Making every allowance for the effects of the average system, the conclusion can not be escaped that these two banks were not doing their utmost to relieve the situation. Changes in reserves and reserve ratios of the six banks were not very great, except in the case of the First National Bank. Although it received over $9,000,000 from the Government between October 19 and October 31, its reserve was reduced nearly $7,000,000 during the week ending October 26, and at the same time its reserve ratio had dropped from 31.5 per cent to 22.4 per cent. The loss of cash for the six banks taken together was only $7,500,000, but that of the First National alone was $6,900,000. When it is remembered that the actual situation of the banks was less satisfactory than the average showing of the bank statement, it can readily be realized that the reserves of particular banks may have been seriously depleted at this time, while those of others were, perhaps, still above legal requirements

The explanation of this seemingly unfavorable showing of the First National Bank is in every way creditable to its management, while at the same time it illustrates the way in which failure to issue clearing-house loan certificates at the beginning of a crisis may hasten general suspension. As we have already seen, demands for currency were made upon New York from all parts of the country, including the other central reserve cities, as soon as the troubles of the Knickerbocker Trust Company became known. To some extent outside banks directed shipments to be made against their balances with New York banks, but more largely the demand was for immediate liquidation of call loans and the shipment of the money received in payment therefor At the same time the New York trust companies were reducing loans upon a wholesale scale. This double liquidation of loans could not be carried very far unless additional loans were made by the New York banks. It would simply have forced borrowers into insolvency. The clearing-house banks did shoulder this burden, but on account of the delay in the issue of loan certificates it was not distributed among the banks with any regard to their available resources.

Banks with relatively large New York trust company deposits or numerous correspondents in the West and South were subject to the greatest demands for cash and for the liquidation of loans. When the outside banks and the trust companies called their loans, brokers, to whom call loans are principally made, immediately resorted to the banks carrying their regular accounts, and the banks felt under obligation to afford them accommodation so far at least as it could be shown to be absolutely necessary. It naturally followed that the particular banks which happened to have a relatively large number of such accounts were obliged to lend heavily and to provide the means for paying the loans that had been called. In some instances the loan called would have been made to a broker whose account was with the reserve agent of the interior bank which had ordered its liquidation. In that case the New York bank would be obliged to shoulder the loan itself and to ship the cash, taking it from its own reserve In other instances the loan may have been made for an outside bank by some other New York bank In that case, if the broker's account happened to be with the New York bank mentioned in the first instance, its loan to the broker would tend to create an unfavorable balance against it at the clearing house. The reserve agent calling the loan for the outside bank would thus secure the means of payment from that member of the clearing house which assumed the loan for the broker It might thus easily happen that while some banks were losing very little cash and making few new loans, others would be rapidly expanding loans and quite as rapidly paying out cash from their reserves. This seems to have been the situation on October 26. Now, if loan certificates had been issued earlier in the week it would have been possible for a bank in the position of the First National to escape the unpleasant necessity of strengthening other banks upon which demands both from correspondents and from brokers happened to be considerably less than those made upon itself. On account of the delay in issuing loan certificates there were, therefore, greater differences in the condition of the banks at the close of the week ending October 26 than would otherwise have been the case. Finally, if the issue of loan certificates had been still further delayed it is clear that suspension would not have been prevented Some of the banks whose reserves were being depleted would have been forced to contract loans in a wholesale fashion Disastrous failures would have occurred among borrowers, the solvency of the banks would have become doubtful, and runs would have forced on suspension just as was the case in 1857.

On October 26 clearing-house loan certificates were at length authorized, thus enabling the banks to meet the local situation, and to an even greater extent than in the past they served this purpose effectively For the week ending October 26 the bank statement showed a loan increase of only $10,800,000, but during the next week it was $60,700,000, and for the week ending November 9 $38,900,000, a total of over $110,000,000 for three weeks This great increase in loans was partly responsible for the large reserve deficit which on November 2 was $38,000,000, and on November 9, nearly $52,000,000 On both these dates the reserve deficit would not have been more than half what it was but for the increase in deposit liability through loan expansion. In adopting this policy with reference to loans the banks were pursuing a course which was eminently wise and proper and in accord with the requirements of the situation But, as has so often been observed in previous chapters, the responsibilities of the New York banks do not end with loans and the local situation. If the banks resort to arrangements which make it possible for them to extend credit to borrowers, they ought also at the same time to agree upon arrangements which may be expected to remove the necessity for suspension

Particularly is this true when, as in 1907, the banks have received enormous amounts of money from the Government

Even if the banks had resorted to the use of loan certificates at the outset of the crisis it is highly improbable that suspensions would have been escaped An important change had taken place in the attitude of the banks regarding the use of loan certificates. In 1890, it will be recalled, the Bank of Commerce passed resolutions urging the advisability of taking out certificates in order to grant needed accommodation to the business community. There was then apparently a widespread feeling among bankers that to resort to certificates was an indication of weakness Since that time the pendulum has swung to the opposite extreme The largest banks, including those in the strongest condition, hastened to take out certificates, and they became immediately almost the sole medium for the settlement of balances between banks One important bank met a large unfavorable balance with cash on Monday, October 28, but, finding that it stood alone, did not repeat the experiment. During the last five days of October 84 per cent of clearing-house balances were settled in certificates, and in November practically all payments (96 per cent) were settled in this way [a] Whether the same course would have been pursued if the certificates had been issued at the outset, is not certain, but if so, suspension would probably have followed. It was inevitable when banks which had seized the opportunity to strengthen themselves afforded by the delay in issuing the certificates fol-

[a] See Appendix, Note J, p 431.

lowed up this selfish action by their use in the settlement of balances. Experience with the certificates in 1907 again illustrates the ineffectiveness of this device when shorn of its essential and original complement, an arrangement for equalizing reserves. Recalling the course of events in 1873, it can not be questioned for a moment that suspension would not have occurred had similar action been taken in 1907, nor would agreement by all the clearing-house members have been necessary. The six large banks acting in concert could have sustained the local situation by making loans and at the same time could have supplied the demands of outside banks for money. Had that course been followed, alarm would have been speedily allayed in the country at large, as it was already being allayed in New York City before the discreditable step of restricting payments was taken.

Unfortunately there seems to be distinctly less unwillingness among bankers to resort to suspension than was the case twenty or thirty years ago. It may be attributed in part to the growing tendency since 1893 to look to changes in legislation alone as a remedy for financial ills. It seems also to be in part the result of a feeling common among New York bankers that they can not reasonably be expected to remit funds which are the proceeds of loans made in the New York money market by outside banks and liquidated in an emergency. Some bankers seem to have felt that it was entirely proper to refuse to ship currency in such cases, and it is in connection with these loans that they have taken the first step in restricting payments in successive crises. It should be remembered, however, that responsibilities are incurred in return for the advantages which accrue to the New York banks from their peculiar position. London holds its commanding position because it is known that money lent there can be instantly recalled Similarly, New York is not meeting the obligations of its position as our domestic money center, to say nothing of living up to future international possibilities, so long as it is unable or unwilling to respond to any demand, however unreasonable, that can lawfully be made upon it for cash

Finally, there can be little doubt that the seriousness of the general economic situation was greatly exaggerated by observers in New York For years the possible ill effects of government activities designed to regulate corporations had been magnified beyond all reason in financial circles, and the idea was quite honestly held that the people generally cherished similar views Mercantile and banking failures approaching in extent those of 1873 and 1893 were expected. The course of events, however, conclusively proved that general economic conditions were not unsound During the week ending November 2 there was but a single important banking failure, a San Francisco trust company, with deposits of $9,000,000, and, aside from the temporary closing of the National Bank of Commerce in Kansas City on December 5, there were no further important banking disasters during the last two months of the year, i e, to the end of this period of financial strain.[a] Notwithstanding the severe

[a] Early in November there were a number of additional banking failures in Oregon and California, and a month later came the failure of a national bank of medium size and an important banking firm in Pittsburg.

strain to which business generally was subjected in consequence of the restriction of payments by the banks, mercantile failures were not extraordinarily large in number or in amount of liabilities. During October according to Dunn's Reports the amount involved in commercial failures was $27,400,000, contrasted with $10,553,000 in October, 1906, and $18,387,000 in 1903. In November, 1907, liabilities were only $17,637,000, compared with $11,980,000 in the same month for 1906. Even more convincing evidence of the comparatively sound condition of general business is afforded by the small number of railroad receiverships and by the short duration of general business depression following the crisis of 1907, contrasted with either 1873 or 1893. In all these respects, as well as in the immediate cause of the outbreak, the crisis in 1907 seems to have paralleled most closely that of 1884, though some of the conditions, such as the greater number of railway receiverships in 1884, tend to the conclusion that the situation was fundamentally more healthy in 1907 than in the earlier year. The most striking difference is that in 1907 the banks restricted payments, thus involving all branches of business in severe strain, whereas in 1884 the banks united quickly upon a common policy, and, acting wisely and boldly, escaped that discreditable measure.

One of the unfortunate effects of suspension is the creation of seemingly conclusive evidence for its necessity. During the two months that elapsed before the restriction on cash payments was entirely removed an enormous amount of money was added to the amount in circulation, but none of it was secured by the banks. Through gold imports, government deposits, additional issues of bank notes, and payments of cash by the banks, something like $300,000,000 was added to the amount of money in every-day use or in hoards Furthermore, a vast amount of substitutes for money was set afloat in the community. It has been assumed that as much as this amount of money, perhaps more, would have been taken from the banks if they had not restricted payments. This view is, however, contrary to experience in every instance where banks have met the demands of depositors fearlessly in an emergency Suspension increases enormously the propensity to hoard money, it also makes more sluggish the movement of money which remains in actual use We can not be absolutely certain that the New York banks would have been able to maintain payments until calm was restored; but the amount of money which went out of sight after suspension is no indication whatever of the amount which would have been required to maintain cash payments.

Summarizing the results of this analysis of the influences which led to suspension in New York, it may be said that it came about primarily because no real effort was made to prevent it It was directly due to uneven distribution of the reserves held by the New York banks and to the use of clearing-house loan certificates as the sole medium of settlement of balances at the clearing house. It was not because the available reserves of the banks were exhausted, nor was it because there was no prospect of replacing, at least in part, the outgo which would have been incurred had an attempt been made to maintain payments The influences leading to suspension have been considered in much detail because a quite different view of its causes has been widely accepted An illuminating indication of the unsound principles upon which the policy of the banks was based appears in the address, already referred to, of the president of the New York clearing house, which is so significant that it may be quoted at some length.

The clearing-house committee knew by experience that the dissipation of the New York banking reserve, upon which practically the credit volume of the nation rests, would alarm the nation, intensify the panic, and greatly prolong the period of recuperation * * * New York bankers have been severely criticised because they did not more fully respond to the demands of country correspondents by shipping currency against balances To have fully honored the demands that were pouring in from all sections of the country would have dissipated our banking reserve in a fortnight How could it be replenished? Were the interior bankers sending currency to New York? What would have been the effect upon the country if the New York banking reserve had been entirely depleted? It would have so intensified the panicky feeling that widespread commercial disaster would have resulted * * * The $53,000,000 deficit in our banking reserve occurred in less than ten days after the failure of the Knickerbocker Trust Company, and was caused by the shipment to interior institutions of the larger portion of that amount in that short time We kept the door of our treasure house wide open until for the good of the whole country it became necessary to everywhere close it It never was fully closed, currency shipments continued in a restricted way throughout the panic, and a large number of our banks kept up their counter payments as usual [a]

RESUMPTION DELAYED UNNECESSARILY.

Additional money was secured and in large quantity, but it served no useful purpose, not even that of limiting the duration of suspension to a short interval. Cash payments were not completely resumed until the begin-

[a] Commercial and Financial Chronicle, Oct 10, 1908, Bankers' Convention Section, p 84

ning of January. For exactly two months, about twice as long as in 1873 or 1893, money was regularly bought and sold at a premium in New York For this prolongation of suspension there was not even a shadow or semblance of excuse After the loss of $30,000,000 during the week ending November 2 the New York banks held a reserve of $224,000,000; on November 23 it had been reduced by only $9,000,000, and thereafter it increased week by week and stood at $251,000,000 at the time the currency premium disappeared. It is significant that the much smaller banking reserve of the Bank of England was reduced during the first two weeks of this period from £24,000,000 to £17,000,000 without the remotest thought of suspension being entertained by anyone, either in London or elsewhere

It is not a little surprising that American financial opinion was far from unfavorable to the banks, the suspension of which seems generally to have been thought unavoidable This view is a natural and inevitable consequence of an entirely erroneous habit of thought in this country with reference to banking reserves Before the establishment of the national banking system in 1863 insufficient reserves were a constant source of weakness, though something had been accomplished after the crisis of 1857 through legislation and agreement among the banks The national banking law required a certain minimum of reserve from banks entering the system, the percentage varying with the location of the bank For a system composed of thousands of banks, large and small, this legislation was unquestionably wise, but under its influence undue importance has come to be attached to the maintenance at all times and at all costs of a certain minimum ratio between reserve and deposit liabilities. On November 2, when the New York banks had $224,000,000, there was a reserve deficit of $38,000,000, and two weeks later the deficit was $54,000,000 The following table shows the reserve and the reserve deficiency of the New York banks during the period of the currency premium, which lasted from October 31 to December 31, inclusive. The statement for January 4 being based upon rapidly rising reserve averages, probably shows very nearly the actual condition at the time of resumption

[Expressed in millions]

	Reserve held	Reserve deficiency
1907		
Oct 26	$254 7	$1 2
Nov 2	224 1	38 8
9	219 8	51 9
16	218 7	53 7
23	215 9	54 1
30	217 8	53 0
Dec. 7	222 5	46 2
14	226 6	40 1
21	233 1	31 8
28	242 6	20 2
1908		
Jan 4	250 6	[a] 5 4

[a] Surplus

This reserve deficiency was indeed far greater than ever before, but the reserve ratio was at no time below 20 per cent, contrasted with 12 8 per cent on October 18, 1873 [a]

[a] The available reserve was at that time less than 4½ per cent See p 55

The reserve deficit was apparently regarded by bankers and the public as a sufficient reason for partial suspension and as evidence that everything had been done to the full extent of the power of the banks to relieve the situation. Without exaggeration, this arithmetical ratio of reserve can only be adequately characterized as a sort of fetich to which every maxim of sound banking policy is blindly sacrificed. Even though the banks outside of New York manifested a still more slavish attention to reserve requirements, it remains true that the New York banks were primarily responsible because of their position as the central reserve banks of the country, and because they initiated the policy of restriction.

THE CURRENCY PREMIUM.

Aside from its longer duration, the currency premium in 1907 presents no peculiarities contrasted with 1873 or 1893 Its course is given for each day in the following table, which was compiled by Prof. A. P. Andrew from data procured from various New York newspapers: [a]

	Currency premium	
	High	Low
	Per cent	*Per cent*
Oct 31	3	2
Nov 1	3 ½	2
2	3	2
3	(b)	(b)
4	3 ½	3

[a] A P Andrew, "Hoarding in the Panic of 1907." Quarterly Journal of Economics, February, 1908 For similar tables for 1873 and 1893, see p 57 and p 187

[b] Sunday

	Currency premium	
	High	Low
	Per cent	*Per cent*
Nov 5	(a)	(a)
6	4	2
7	2 3/4	3
8	3	2
9	3	----------
10	(b)	(b)
11	3	2 3/4
12	4	3 1/2
13	4	3 1/2
14	3	2 1/2
15	2 1/2	2
16	2	----------
17	(b)	(b)
18	3	2 1/2
19	2 1/4	1 1/2
20	3	----------
21	3 1/2	2 1/2
22	2 3/4	1 1/2
23	1 1/4	----------
24	(b)	(b)
25	1 3/4	1
26	1 3/4	1
27	----------	3/4
28	(c)	(c)
29	----------	1/2
30	----------	----------
Dec 1	(b)	(b)
2	1 1/4	1
3	2	----------
4	1 3/4	3/4
5	1 1/2	3/4
6	1	3/4
7	1 1/8	5/8
8	(b)	(b)
9	----------	----------
10	----------	----------
11	1	----------
12	1	----------
13	1 1/2	3/4
14	----------	1/2
15	(b)	(b)
16	1 1/4	1 1/8
17	7/8	5/8

[a] Election Day [b] Sunday [c] Thanksgiving Day

	Currency premium	
	High	Low
	Per cent	*Per cent*
Dec 18	----------	----------
19	1¼	----------
20	⅞	¾
21	----------	----------
22	(a)	(a)
23	----------	----------
24	----------	----------
25	(b)	(b)
26	----------	----------
27	¼	----------
28	⅛	----------
29	(a)	(a)
30	----------	----------
31	(c)	(c)

a Sunday b Christmas c No premium

No estimate can be made of the amount of money which was brought into circulation from hoards [a] by the currency premium, and the reader is referred to the discussions of this subject in previous chapters for reasons tending to show that it would be likely to diminish rather than increase the available money supply [b]

FOREIGN EXCHANGE

The course of the foreign exchanges and the gold import movement were not unlike those in previous crises. During the week ending October 26 exchange rates had fallen rapidly owing to dear money and to the expectation of

[a] About $25,000,000 of domestic money was supposed to have been bought by brokers in New York, but the extent to which it came from hoards is uncertain See the Financial Panic in the United States by A D Noyes in The Forum for January, 1908, p 302

[b] See pp 68 and 195

increasing cotton exports, and on Friday, October 25,[a] exchange was at the gold import point. A blockade in exchange was threatened, but the example of an important New York bank in continuing and increasing its purchases of bills soon had the good effect of inducing purchases by other banks and exchange dealers. Gold engagements were announced at the beginning of the following week when sight exchange was quoted at \$4 82¼ to \$4 82½ During the week about \$25,000,000 was engaged, and although exchange rates advanced to \$4.87, far above the import point, indeed well above par, the gold engagements continued On Monday, November 4, exchange advanced to the highest point of the month, \$4.88¾, well above the gold export point in normal times, and still gold imports continued upon an enormous scale. As was explained at length in the chapter on the crisis of 1893, the currency premium was the cause of the high rates quoted for exchange, but not the principal cause of the gold movement.[b] It was primarily due to an enormous increase in merchandise exports and a considerable falling off in imports. The gold was not secured to any considerable extent by means of borrowing in the London market Contrasted with \$373,000,000 during the last two months of 1906, exports for the same period in 1907 were \$411,600,000, while imports were \$254,000,000 in 1906 and \$203,000,000 in 1907. The excess of merchandise exports in 1906 was only \$119,000,000, while in 1907 it was no less than

[a] Gold could have been engaged on Friday, October 25, if importers had been able to secure the necessary advances from the banks

[b] See p 192

$208,000,000. As there were practically no finance or anticipatory bills to be liquidated, this sudden increase in the excess of exports provided the means of payment for the gold which was imported The export movement of commodities was not checked, as shippers were able to dispose of bills drawn against commodities sold in foreign markets. In this one respect the situation was handled most satisfactorily in 1907.

The amount of gold received in New York during November was about $58,000,000 and in December $38,000,000 This total of $96,000,000 was far greater than the amount imported during any other crisis in our history and affords further evidence of the ability of this country to secure additional supplies of gold in an emergency. This power will remain so long as our foreign trade is made up principally of imported luxuries and exported necessities But, as we have already seen, no reliance was placed upon the prospective imports of gold, nor was the actual receipt of the gold made use of to cut short the period of suspension Payments were not resumed until the cash holdings of the New York banks began to increase rapidly through the return of money from circulation in consequence of general business depression; until, in other words, outside banks manifested more confidence in the New York banks than they had in themselves

Although we made no use of the gold which was imported, its departure occasioned great disturbance in foreign countries The Bank of England was obliged to advance its rate to 7 per cent, not to check gold exports, but in order to secure payment from other countries of money which was due by them to the United States. London being the central money market of the world, if its rates had not advanced other countries would have made payments to the United States by drawing down London balances or by creating credits in London by discounting bills. The advance in the Bank-of-England rate caused other countries to remit to London a large part of the money which was due from them to this country[a] in payment for our exports.

In New York much was made of the fact that large amounts of money continued to be shipped to interior banks throughout November and December. The following table prepared by the clearing-house authorities[b] shows that this was indeed the case:

Week ending—	Receipts from the interior.	Shipments to the interior.	Net loss.
Oct. 26	$4,544,500	$19,556,800	$15,012,300
Nov. 2	3,644,600	21,930,400	18,285,800
9	2,566,300	15,963,500	13,397,200
16	3,079,700	24,730,500	21,650,800
23	3,555,300	19,083,600	15,528,300
30	2,483,500	13,711,500	11,228,000
Dec. 7	4,169,900	15,989,200	11,819,300
Total	24,043,800	130,965,500	106,921,700

The significance of these large shipments requires some explanation. Those of the first two weeks were offset by government deposits in New York banks, and as for the

[a] For an illuminating account of the various influences at work in the London money market at this time, see Hartley Withers, The Meaning of Money, p. 292.

[b] Response of the Secretary of the Treasury to Senate resolution No. 33 of December 12, 1907, Senate Doc. 208, 60th Congress, 1st session, p. 215.

remainder they were simply the proceeds of commodities produced in the West and South which were exported to Europe. The gold which was imported did not belong to New York; New York was merely the channel through which bills of exchange went out and gold entered. If New York had attempted to retain this gold, the gold-import movement would have ceased entirely and at once

SUSPENSION THROUGHOUT THE COUNTRY

Restriction of cash payments by the New York banks was the signal for similar action elsewhere, and by the close of the week ending November 2, partial suspension was general throughout the country. The extent to which suspension was carried can not be accurately determined. It varied in the different sections of the country and with different banks in the same place, and also from day to day by the same bank. The governors of some of the western States declared a succession of legal holidays, though not in every case at the desire of the banks. This novel device was resorted to in Oklahoma, Nevada, Washington, Oregon, and California The following proclamation issued by the acting governor of Oklahoma on Monday, October 28, will serve as an example. [a]

Whereas, It appears to the undersigned acting governor of the Territory of Oklahoma that all of the leading cities of the United States, through their clearing-house associations, have entered into an argeement to protect themselves against conditions which they are apparently unable to control, and by such concerted action are refusing to ship currency to country banks which have deposits with them or to honor the bills of

[a] Commercial and Financial Chronicle, November 2, 1907, p. 1118

lading drawn upon the banks of such, or to pay checks of customers over the counters, and,

Whereas, Such action makes it impossible for the banks of Oklahoma to meet the immediate demands upon them for currency to pay for the cotton and other products of the Territory, and,

Whereas, Our banks appear to be in a solvent condition, therefore, be it

Ordained, That a legal holiday extending from October 28 six days to November 2 be proclaimed

(Signed) CHARLES FILSON,
Acting Governor

More generally, as in the past, the banks simply "discriminated" in making payments [a] In Chicago, a central reserve city, it was reported [b] on November 1 that "the banks stopped shipping currency, for two or three days, to their correspondents South and West, but for the past day or two have resumed such remittances on a moderate scale in cases where the demand seemed imperative" From various reserve cities came similar reports, e. g, "in Indianapolis and St. Paul the banks agreed to suspend temporarily the payment of money on checks, certificates of deposit, or drafts, except for small sums, and further for the present to furnish no money for bank correspondents" "In New Orleans the Associated Banks have limited currency payments to any one depositor for $50, except in cases where deviation from the rule seems necessary." Restriction was perhaps more complete in many cities than it was in New York,[c] but that does not relieve the banks of the metropolis of responsibility for

[a] For examples of the recommendation of the policy of suspension by the banking officials of some of the States, see Appendix, Note K, p 435

[b] Commercial and Financial Chronicle, November 2, p 1119

[c] For specific instances of the refusal of New York banks to cash checks drawn on them by other banks, see Senate Doc 435, 60th Congress, 1st session, pp 6, 12, 14, 15, and 27

having been the main cause of suspension. The reasons for this view, however, have been stated at length in previous chapters and need not be repeated.[a] As in 1873, in many places resolutions were adopted by the banks setting forth the reasons for restricting payments and the peculiar arrangements which were being set up. In every instance the refusal to ship currency by the banks of the money centers, and particularly by those of New York, was said, and with truth, to have made suspension necessary. The following resolutions adopted by the banks of Atlanta, Ga., and Portland, Oreg., are appended as typical examples The Atlanta Clearing House Association adopted the following resolutions on October 30.[b]

In view of the action taken by the New York Clearing House, and subsequently adopted by Chicago, St Louis, Philadelphia, Cincinnati, New Orleans, Nashville, Birmingham, Baltimore, Louisville, Memphis, Montgomery, Mobile, and many other principal cities throughout the country, restricting the shipment of currency, and the restriction of other business to its proper channel, the Clearing House, therefore, be it

Resolved by the Atlanta Clearing House Association—

1 That until further notice collections and bank balances be settled in exchange or clearing-house certificates

2 That checks drawn on the members of this association be paid through the Atlanta Clearing House, and correspondents and customers be requested to so stamp their checks

3 That payments against all accounts, including certificates of deposit, be limited to $50 in one day, or $100 in one week (Monday to Saturday).

4 That exception shall be made to the above in case of pay rolls, which shall be paid as follows All denominations of $5 and over in clearing-house certificates, and all denominations of under $5 to be paid in cash as desired

Resolved further, That the manager of the Atlanta Clearing House Association be instructed to give notice to the correspondents of the Atlanta Clearing-House banks that the above resolution is in effect on and after this date and until further notice

[a] See p. 126

[b] Commercial and Financial Chronicle, November 9, p 1182

The Portland (Oreg.) Clearing House Association adopted its resolutions on October 28 [a]

Whereas, The banks of Portland have received telegraphic advices that all the principal clearing-house associations in the United States have decided to refuse to ship coin or currency against the deposit balances of their correspondents, therefore, be it

Resolved, First, that the banks of the Clearing-House Association of Portland decline to ship coin or currency to their out-of-town correspondents

Second, that all checks, certificates of deposit or drafts of customers and out-of-town correspondents be paid only through the clearing house and in clearing-house funds

Third, that all items on out-of-town banks be taken only for collection, subject to payment in legal tender

Fourth, that the savings banks of the city of Portland be instructed to demand notice of withdrawal of funds

Fifth, that this action be and remain in force as long as the leading cities of the United States maintain a similar policy

The following resolution was also adopted:

For the purpose of enabling the banks, members of the Portland Clearing House, to afford proper assistance to the mercantile community, and also to facilitate the inter-bank settlements resulting from their daily exchanges, be it

Resolved, That any bank in the clearing house may at its option deposit with the loan committee of the clearing house an amount of bills receivable, bonds or other securities, to be approved by said committee, who shall be authorized to issue thereon to said depositing bank certificates of deposit, bearing interest at 7 per cent per annum, in denominations of $5,000, to an amount equal to 75 per cent of such deposits These certificates may be used in the settlements of balances at the clearing house for a period of thirty days from the date thereof, and they shall be received by creditor banks during that period, daily, in the same proportion as they bear to the aggregate amount of the debtor balances paid at the clearing house The interest which may accrue upon these certificates shall at the expiration of thirty days be apportioned among the banks which shall have held them during the time

The securities deposited with said committee as above named shall be held by them in trust as a special deposit, pledged for the redemption of the certificates issued thereupon

The committee shall be authorized to exchange any portion of said securities for an equal amount of others, to be approved by them at the

[a] Commercial and Financial Chronicle, November 9, p 1182

request of the depositing bank, and shall have power to demand additional security, either by an exchange or an increased amount, at their discretion

Clearing house loan certificates were issued in a far greater number of cities than in previous crises. Nearly 60 of the 106 clearing houses in the country made use of the device, and with the exception of Washington all cities of the first rank were in the number.[a] In more than twenty instances the use of certificates was not confined to payments between banks. They were issued in small denominations for payment to individual depositors. This policy was wise after payments had been restricted. They were perhaps the best possible substitute for money for local requirements. Certainly it is better to use loan certificates in this way than to refuse depositors any available means of payment In New York and elsewhere bankers have been inclined to take credit to themselves because they had confined the use of certificates to payments with each other But by this means the form and not the substance of cash payments is preserved It is little more than straining at the proverbial gnat at a time when depositors are not being paid cash on demand.

Upon the whole, pay roll difficulties do not seem to have been so serious as in 1893. In some parts of the country the banks seem to have supplied very generally the requirements of their depositors for this purpose. It may also be presumed that as a result of past experience the banks and the business community are becoming expert in devising quickly various substitutes for cash which will serve for local purposes.

[a] For a detailed account of the issue of loan certificates during this crisis, see Appendix, Note K, pp 438-452

THE DOMESTIC EXCHANGES.

The dislocation of the domestic exchanges can not, however, be prevented by the various substitutes for money which have only a local credit, and would seem to have been no less complete and disturbing in its effects than on other occasions The course of exchange was, however, subject to somewhat different influences, and quoted rates followed a course quite unlike that already considered in the case of the crisis of 1893 This may be readily seen if the following table is compared with the similar table for 1893 on page 204

Table showing the rates of New York exchange in the various parts of the country between October 26 and December 15, 1907

	Boston	Philadelphia
Oct 26	25 cents discount	Par
Nov 2	25 cents discount	
9	30 cents premium	$2 50 premium
16	$1 50 premium	$5 premium
23	$2 premium	$2 50 to $4 premium
30	Par	$2 to $3 premium
Dec 7	25 cents discount	$1 50 to $2 50 premium.
14	30 cents discount	$2 50 premium

	Chicago.	St Louis
Oct 26	50 cents discount	$1 discount
Nov 2	$1 to $1 25 discount	Par
9	Par to $1 25	$3.50 premium.
16	75 cents premium	$7 premium
23	$1 premium	$7 premium
30	$1 premium	$4 to $5 premium.
Dec 7	Par	$2 50 premium
14	Par	$4 50 premium.

	Cincinnati.	Kansas City.
Oct. 26	25 cents discount	25 cents premium.
Nov. 2	50 cents discount	25 cents premium.
9	Par to 25 cents discount	$1 premium.
16	Par to 60 cents discount	$1 premium.
23	Par to 60 cents discount	$1 premium.
30	$1 premium	$1 premium.
Dec. 7	30 to 50 cents discount	$1 premium.
14	50 cents discount	$1 premium.

	New Orleans.
Oct. 26	$1 discount.
Nov. 2	$1.50 discount.
9	$2.50 discount.
16	$3 discount.
23	Par.
30	Par.
Dec. 7	Par.
14	Par.

The rates in the table for October 26 may be taken as ruling within normal limits, as they were not very different from those of the weeks immediately preceding. Before the close of the week ending November 2, the banks of New York and other cities had issued clearing-house loan certificates and had also restricted payments, and the premium on currency had made its appearance. It will be observed that no great change took place immediately in exchange rates, and that it was not until the middle of November that rates in many cities reached an abnormal level. At no time did rates reach such extraordinarily abnormal points as the rate of $30 discount per $1,000 in Chicago in 1893. It should be noted also that exchange was very generally at a premium, whereas in 1893 it was below in quite as many instances as above par.

There is no part of our banking machinery which has received so little elucidation as that of the domestic exchanges. Even for normal times the subject is obscure, and the writer therefore ventures upon an explanation of its course during a period of crisis with hesitation, and he is by no means confident that important considerations may not have been overlooked.

As in the case of foreign exchange, domestic exchange rates fluctuate within limits fixed by the cost of shipping money, and also, in the case of cities distant from New York, by the loss of interest while currency is in transit. The quoted rates apply principally to business between banks, the rates being determined by demand and supply. A Boston bank, for example, receives from its customers New York drafts and also checks drawn on banks in New York and its vicinity. All these items will serve to build up its balances in that city. On the other hand, its depositors have been sending out checks, many of which will in the course of time reach New York and reduce its balances there The Boston bank will also have received from banks of New York and from banks elsewhere items for collection in its vicinity, and remittance in ordinary course will be made by it in New York funds Similarly it has sent away items for collection to banks in other cities upon which it expects a like remittance. As a result of all these various influences the balances of the Boston bank may either increase or decrease. If they increase it may be ready to sell exchange to other Boston banks whose balances are running low It may also happen that the bank is desirous of reducing its New York balances, and in that case it will also appear as a seller of exchange in the market

Now, if in the course of a crisis clearing-house loan certificates become the principal or sole medium of payment between banks, it may well happen that a bank will be unwilling to sell exchange unless it is unusually well supplied with New York funds. By the sale of exchange it can at best only secure a favorable clearing-house balance, which will be settled in loan certificates, and if this balance should be unfavorable it can meet it by taking out certificates on its own account. Each bank, therefore, to a greater extent than in normal times, is obliged to rely upon itself for means of payment in New York. The loan certificate does indeed yield a return or involve an expense of 6 or 7 per cent, while the return on New York balances is only 2 per cent. This advantage does not, however, seem to have induced the banks to sell exchange as freely as in normal times

This is, however, not the only disturbing influence. The Boston bank may have remitted to New York upon items collected by it for other banks—let us say those of Philadelphia—but it may happen that the Philadelphia banks delay or even discontinue remitting to New York upon items sent to them for collection by banks of Boston and other cities. The Boston bank can then no longer rely upon what would normally serve to build up its own New York balances It will be simply acquiring a mass of unavailable credits at scattered points throughout the country. The supply of New York exchange which it might have been willing to sell is consequently diminished, and the premium on exchange must rise to a point at which it will tempt some of the banks to sell exchange, even though it intrenches upon their balances with agents which are available for reserve

The premium would naturally be especially high in those cities where the banks were most unwilling to reduce their New York balances Philadelphia seems a case in point, as its deposits with reserve agents, which were $30,995,000 on August 22, were reduced to only $29,389,000 on December 3 At that time the premium on currency in Philadelphia ranged from $1.50 to $3 per $1,000 It is, therefore, a reasonable conclusion that the banks were strongly disinclined to make use of their New York balances In a few cities it is probable that the premium reached a high level because the banks had exhausted their New York balances St Louis may be mentioned as a probable example. Being a central reserve city, its banks would naturally have only such balances in New York as normal business requirements made necessary. The dislocation of exchange elsewhere or the course of payments between New York and St Louis may have combined to produce such a balance of payments as would have required currency shipments if the St. Louis banks had remitted promptly to New York

The extent to which banks in different cities delayed or refused to remit to New York on items collected by them for other banks can not be determined Banks in one city, very naturally and honestly, were inclined to lay the blame upon banks elsewhere The banks in other places, however, may not have been able to secure payment of the items sent to them for collection from other banks in their locality with the usual promptness. When every allowance has been made, however, there can be no question that banks in certain cities, in these as well as in other matters, adopted a policy wholly designed to strengthen themselves regardless of consequences

The general prevalence of the premium on New York exchange is, as we have seen, accounted for in part by the use of clearing-house loan certificates in settling balances between banks and by the delay in remitting in New York funds upon items collected for other banks. It seems probable, however, that, taking the country as a whole, the course of payments was favorable to the New York banks At the beginning of November withdrawals for crop-moving purposes have in recent years begun to diminish, except to the South, and movements of money from eastern centers are distinctly in favor of New York at that season of the year If this were indeed the case in 1907, it affords still another reason for thinking that the New York banks might have met the crisis successfully without restricting payments They would probably have been obliged to meet only withdrawals arising from lack of confidence and not real needs for crop-moving purposes, such as would have increased the difficulties of the situation had the crisis begun at the beginning of September

Finally, it should be noted that the restriction of cash payments to depositors and the currency premium seem to have increased the demand for New York exchange. Only in that city was it possible to buy any considerable quantity of money Many banks in various parts of the country purchased gold and currency at a premium in New York and, instead of drawing on their own balances, then entered their home market as purchasers of exchange which was remitted in payment.

In the few instances where exchange was below par the currency premium was a more direct influence, but exchange could not have dropped to the low figures recorded in 1893 in the case of Chicago, because the Chicago banks in 1907 did not maintain payments among themselves as they had done on previous occasions Exchange was at a discount only in those cities where the course of payments was so strongly against New York that practically all the banks found their balances in that city increasing Chicago might have been expected to belong to this group, but its banks made extensive use of bills derived from grain exports to secure gold which was shipped directly to them In general, exchange was at a discount, or at par only, in the Southern States, the banks of which, by means of cotton sales, are normally in position to draw money from the northeastern part of the country during the late autumn

In conclusion, it should perhaps be pointed out that the quoted rates of exchange were often without much significance The ordinary course of dealings was so completely disorganized in many places that the rates were purely nominal, representing little or no actual transactions

LOAN CONTRACTION

From this analysis it will be evident that rates of domestic exchange might have been somewhat less abnormal if the banks had been prepared to make more use of their balances with reserve agents in New York. The rates in themselves, however, were of comparatively slight general importance; they were simply symptomatic of disturbed conditions and did not measure the extent of the disturbance The dislocation of the domestic exchanges exercised an unfavorable effect upon business activities, because it increased the general lack of confidence, and, more directly, because of the delay which it both created and encouraged in remittances of all sorts between different parts of the country When items for which the banks would ordinarily give immediate credit are taken for collection only, and when these collections are delayed, it is obvious that a greater amount of accommodation in the form of loans will be required to carry on a given volume of business than is needed in normal times. The restriction of payments by the banks, with its consequent dislocation of the exchanges may, therefore, be regarded as partially responsible at least for the scarcity of loans to which the trade journals very generally attributed the depression in trade that marked the closing months of the year. Only on the supposition that the demand for loans had become greater can complaints of the business community of inability to secure loans be satisfactorily explained since the extent to which loans were reduced by the national banks at any rate was insignificant—far less than in 1893. Between August 22 and December 3 loans were reduced from $4,709,000,000 to $4,624,000,000—only $85,000,000—almost exactly 2 per cent. While the returns of the national banks provide a far less certain indication of banking operations than formerly, on account of the rapid growth of state credit institutions, this contraction was so much less than in 1893 that it seems fair to assume that positive loan contraction was a comparatively slight disturbing factor. There were, it is true, wide variations between different cities and sections of the country, but on the Pacific coast where contraction was most drastic loans were reduced only 7 per cent. In particular cities, especially those in which there were banking troubles, such as Kansas City and San Francisco, loans were reduced to an extent which must have been positively disturbing, but upon the whole in this respect the banks made a better showing than ever before. The following table shows the changes in loans in the various cities and sections of the country (not including the cities which appear separately) between August 22 and December 3, 1907

[Expressed in millions]

	Loans and discounts	
	Aug 22	Dec 3
Boston	$167 7	$169 0
New England States	229 0	260 5
New York City	712 1	775 1
Philadelphia	177 2	178 0
Pittsburg	147 7	139 8
Baltimore	56 5	57 0
Eastern States	693 2	679 9
Savannah	2 5	2 6
New Orleans	26 6	27 4
Southern States	527 9	496 5
Cincinnati	55 1	52 9
Cleveland	54 2	52 8
Indianapolis	25 3	21 2
Chicago	231 2	220 1

	Loans and discounts	
	Aug 22	Dec 3
Detroit	$23 7	$23 7
Milwaukee	33 1	32 0
Minneapolis	37 8	41 5
St Paul	22 4	23 6
Kansas City	45 6	26 5
St Louis	117 8	114 9
Middle Western States	704 4	676 6
Omaha	25 8	22 2
Denver	22 6	21 6
Western States	257 4	245 3
Seattle	17 2	17 0
Portland	13 4	9 7
San Francisco	54 8	46 9
Pacific States	154 7	149 4

Nowhere throughout the country was there any considerable increase in loans except in New York, where loans increased by $63,000,000—from $712,000,000 to $775,000,000. In every period of financial strain hitherto the New York banks had been able to contract loans somewhat. Explanation of the different result in 1907 is simple The trust-company situation compelled them to liquidate loans wherever possible, and the outside banks also followed the same course These two groups of lenders more than exhausted the possibilities of contraction in New York, and a part of their loans had to be taken over by the clearing-house banks to prevent a general disaster We have already seen that call loans were particularly favored both by trust companies and the outside banks Even in 1873 the clearing-house banks were able to reduce loans of that kind[a] relatively

[a] See p 84

little, and it might naturally be expected that still less contraction would have been feasible in 1907. The following table shows that such an expectation would be entirely in accord with the facts of the situation

[Expressed in millions]

	Aug 22, 1907	Dec 3 1907
On demand, paper with one or more individual or firm names	$16 2	$22 3
On demand, secured by stocks, bonds, and other personal securities	251 8	306 1
On time, paper with two or more individual or firm names	161 1	170 2
On time, single-name paper (one person or firm), without other security	130 5	119 4
On time, secured by stocks, bonds and other personal securities, or by real estate mortgages or other liens on realty	152 4	156 9
Total	712 0	774 9

Among the many lessons which may be drawn from a study of the experiences of the national banks during crises, the entire absence of liquidness in call loans, so far as the New York banks are concerned, is the most certain and by no means the least important Out of a total loan increase of $63,000,000, call loans account for $54,000,000; and, furthermore, time loans with collateral security, which are largely of stock-exchange origin, account for another $4,000,000 The only kind of loan which was reduced at all was one of the varieties of commercial loans—the time loan on "paper with a single individual or firm name" Commercial loans can be reduced somewhat in New York, because that market is resorted to by many outside borrowers, and they can be thrown back upon their local banks. Moreover, with any decline in business activity, the demand for commercial loans naturally falls off unless it is counteracted by the dislocation of the domestic exchanges Call loans, on the other hand, are local New York loans, and consequently the amount of them which must be made by New York banks increases whenever other lenders retire from the market The opinion may be ventured that a New York bank would be in a better position to meet an emergency if all its loans were upon commercial paper than it is under existing circumstances, though of course it would not then be in position to slide along just above the 25 per cent requirement in normal times

Another cause of disturbance in connection with loans, independent of their volume, is the vast amount of shifting of loans which takes place in consequence of the inability of note brokers to dispose of commercial paper during a crisis. It would probably be under rather than above the mark to assume that this business is reduced very much more than one-half in an emergency like that of 1893 or 1907 Borrowers are forced to resort almost entirely to their own banks, just as was the case with the stock brokers whose loans were liquidated by trust companies and outside banks in New York This shifting of loans involves much strain and uncertainty, and in many instances it is not possible to carry it out at all.[a]

It would seem, then, that business distress from lack of credit facilities was due to at least three influences: The restriction of cash payments by the banks increased the

[a] To this circumstance may perhaps be attributed the relatively numerous instances of failure or suspension among concerns of large size which was a notable feature of the crisis of 1907 See the analysis of failures in 1907 in Dun's Review for January 11, 1908.

requirements of borrowers, the supply of loans was reduced by a moderate amount of contraction, and the shifting of loans involved considerable uncertainty and inconvenience. From the two last-mentioned causes it is probable that no serious difficulty would have been experienced by borrowers aside from those whose requirements were ordinarily placed through note brokers One of the satisfactory features of our system of local independent banks is that they do not press hardly upon their regular customers in emergencies Those who place paper only through note brokers naturally suffer, because the banks take such paper either to employ temporarily idle funds or as a peculiarly liquid resource, a sort of quasi-reserve. For such borrowers the banks feel no responsibility; but with the inevitable increase of such borrowing, on account of the increasing size of the reproducing and distributing unit, there is coming to be a greater need somewhere in our banking system for a reserve of lending power for emergencies

THE CONDITION OF THE BANKS.

Following the method adopted in the investigation of previous crises, an analysis of the returns of the national banks to the Comptroller of the Currency just before and after the crisis of 1907 may be expected to throw light upon the course of events. Unfortunately, the statistical data is far from satisfactory. The first of the two returns was made on August 22—about two months before the crisis, and the second, on December 3, came after the worst of the panic was passed It was because the returns in 1873 were made at more significant dates that particular attention was given to this side of the subject in the treatment of the crisis of that year. For 1907 it is necessary to assume that no great change had taken place in the condition of the banks between the end of August and the middle of October, an assumption which, judging from the weekly bank statements in New York, Boston, and Philadelphia, is not far from the facts of the actual situation It would, however, be somewhat hazardous to draw conclusions if it were not that the same tendencies are disclosed which were so clearly manifest both in 1873 and in 1893

As in former periods of crisis the reserves of the banks, taken as a whole, were not made use of to any considerable extent. On August 22 the banks held $701,600,000, and on December 3, $660,800,000—a loss of only $40,800,000 If the holdings of the notes of other banks are included, this loss is reduced to only $31,400,000 This cash loss can be more than matched on many occasions when conditions were entirely normal, e g , between August 25 and November 9, 1905, when the reserves of the banks fell off more than $43,000,000 By means of loan contraction, the loss in cash, and the diminution in indebtedness between the banks, net deposits were reduced from $5,256,000,000 to $4,629,000,000, and there was a slight increase in the proportion of cash held, which advanced from 13 35 per cent to 13 45 per cent. This slight increase in the reserve ratio was entirely in accord with precedent, and its explanation is to be found in changes in the condition of the country banks, which are shown in the following table:

Country Banks

[Expressed in millions]

	Aug 22	Dec 3	Decrease
Loans	$2,401 0	$2,324 0	$77 0
Net deposits	$2,627 0	$2 485 0	$142 0
Cash reserve	$199 6	$246 0	[a] $47 6
Percentage of reserve	7 6	9 9	----------
Net deposits with reserve agents	$410 0	$356 0	$54 0

[a] Increase

The increase of $47,600,000 in reserves of this group of banks exceeded by $6,800,000 the total loss in reserves of the banks taken as a whole This increase, as well as that in reserve ratio, will cause no surprise to the reader of the previous chapters of this investigation At the time, however, it was apparently regarded by many as something unusual, and country banks were accused of hoarding and the blame for suspension was laid at their doors There is no reason to believe that country banks were endeavoring to hoard the money which they withdrew from their reserve agents at the beginning of the crisis They needed additional supplies of cash if they were to meet the demands of their own depositors But after the New York banks suspended and suspension became general they naturally held with a tight grip all the money which they had in their possession at the moment and also very naturally endeavored to extract more from their reserve agents. The withdrawal of money was entirely in accord with what the teachings of past experience ought to have led reserve agents to expect and to be in readiness to meet. In the future, as in the past, whatever the causes of financial strain, country banks will withdraw money in order to strengthen their reserves. These demands will be particularly large until the New York banks pass through a crisis triumphantly, meeting every demand for payment. The crisis of 1907 was the most favorable opportunity which the city banks have had since the establishment of the national banking system Outside of New York and a few other cities there were almost no failures either of national or of state banking institutions to cause alarm to spread and be renewed at intervals, as happened in 1893 The general business situation, moreover, was comparatively sound, and the means for securing additional supplies of money were not entirely lacking, as was the case in 1873 It requires no gift of prophecy to foresee a general scramble to get money from New York on the next occasion of financial strain unless it is fortunately deferred to another generation to whom the course of events in 1907 will be merely a vague tradition.

Some observers, particularly in other countries, have expressed the view that the banking troubles of 1907 were the result of deep-seated moral causes, assuming that, during the years immediately preceding, the many disclosures of corporate greed, mismanagement, and wild financiering had created distrust of the banks. In the case of the early runs upon New York banks and trust companies there is, perhaps, some ground for this opinion It does not, however, apply to the banks in general or to the withdrawal by country banks of their deposits with reserve agents. In the absence of branch banking, the banks in each place are, with few exceptions, owned as well as managed by local people The misdeeds, real or fancied, of trusts and railways can not be supposed to weaken the confidence of the people in those of their neighbors who happen to be engaged in banking. It might, however, be thought that the withdrawal of their deposits by country banks was due to the distrust of the large city banks were it not that the country banks in this matter were simply following the course which they had taken in previous crises and which their situation made necessary. Moreover, after the crisis money was returned to the city banks as in former years, though there had been no change in the management of these banks such as might have restored confidence had it been lost. The country banks may have been influenced in part by unreasoning fear, and to a greater extent by past experience of the difficulty of obtaining money from the reserve banks in times of crisis, but the principal reason was the inadequacy of their cash reserves to meet extraordinary requirements. The fact that the country banks held more cash in December than in August is no indication whatever of what their position would have been if the banks in New York had not inaugurated the policy of suspension Surely it can not be held that the country banks should not withdraw any money from their reserve agents in an emergency! And after suspension, the country banks in holding their reserves intact were following a course not unlike that of the city banks The New York banks themselves, as we have seen, held a larger reserve at the beginning of December than at the beginning of the previous month.

Country banks in all sections of the country increased their cash holdings, though the increase was comparatively slight in the North Atlantic States At the beginning of the crisis the withdrawals of money from reserve agents were naturally most considerable on the part of those banks which were at a distance from their agents, and by banks generally in the West and South, where there had been numerous failures in 1893, and where, consequently, confidence in the banks was weak. The following table shows changes in the cash holdings of the country banks in different sections of the country:

[Expressed in millions]

	Aug 22	Dec 3
New England States	$20 1	$22 1
Eastern States	55 9	63 1
Southern States	34 0	44 8
Middle Western States	54 6	66 1
Western States	21 5	31 0
Pacific States	13 1	18 7

Turning now to the reserve cities, we shall find a similar repetition of the course taken by this group of banks in previous crises:

[Expressed in millions]

	Aug 22	Dec 3	Decrease
Loans	$1 246 0	$1,187 0	$59 0
Net deposits	$1,423 0	$1,263 0	$160 0
Cash reserve	$190 3	$162 6	$27 7
Reserve percentage	13 4	12 9	
Net deposits with reserve agents	$166 5	$139 7	$26 8

As in 1873 and in 1893, the reserve city banks reduced loans somewhat, in fact relatively rather more than the country banks, and their cash reserve was also reduced, but from the decline in reserves with agents it is clear that they shifted as much of the burden as possible upon the banks of the central reserve cities. By means of a very considerable reduction in net deposit liability the ratio of cash reserve suffered no very appreciable decline. There were, of course, wide differences in the policy pursued by the banks of the forty reserve cities. In the East a relatively greater amount of cash was paid out than in the West and South. In general it may be said that reserve cities which were at the greatest distance from the eastern money centers exhibited the greatest unwillingness to make use of their cash holdings. As in the case of the country banks, the confidence of the people in the banks is somewhat less than in the East, and there were not so many absolutely real needs among depositors for money for pay-roll and similar purposes as in the manufacturing sections of the country.

On account of the importance of the central reserve cities the changes in their condition are presented separately.

[Expressed in millions.]

	Aug. 22	Dec. 3	Decrease
ST. LOUIS			
Loans	$117.9	$115.0	$2.9
Net deposits	$116.8	$107.1	$9.7
Cash reserve	$26.8	$21.0	$5.8
Reserve percentage	23.0	19.6	....
CHICAGO			
Loans	$231.3	$220.3	$11.0
Net deposits	$262.9	$226.3	$36.6
Cash reserve	$66.1	$54.0	$12.1
Reserve percentage	25.2	23.9	....

Neither Chicago nor St. Louis shows very striking differences from the reserve cities taken as a whole. It would indeed be possible to pick from among the reserve cities some in which the banks experienced as great or even greater loss in reserve and in which, moreover, there was no contraction of loans It is far more true to the facts of actual banking practice to include these cities among those of reserve-city rank, because, after all, the full force of any financial strain rests primarily upon the banks of New York and in a way quite unlike that upon the banks of any other city. The following table shows the changes in the condition of the New York banks between August 22 and December 3, 1907

[Expressed in millions]

	Aug 22	Dec 3	Increase (+) decrease (−)
Loans	$712 7	$776 9	+$64 2
Net deposits	$825 7	$824 4	− $1 3
Cash reserve	$218 8	$177 1	−$41 7
Reserve percentage	26 5	20 5	

The causes of the increase in loans of the New York banks have already been set forth As a consequence of that increase, net deposit liability remained almost unchanged, notwithstanding the loss of $41,700,000 in reserve Both the percentage of the total reserve which was used and the decline in ratio of reserves to deposits make a good showing for the New York banks in comparison with those elsewhere, though allowance must be made for the fact that the loss in cash came before the New York banks restricted payments and before any considerable withdrawals were made from banks elsewhere The showing is not particularly flattering when one considers that New York is the central money market of the country. Less than one-fifth of their reserves was used by the banks According to the statement for the beginning of December the banks were then a little above the lowest point in their reserves, but as the Morse-Heinze banks were included in that statement it may be safely assumed that at no time did the active solvent banks use more than about that portion of their cash holdings

On account of the concentration of bankers' deposits in a few banks it is desirable to carry the analysis one step further In New York the six large banks having the bulk of such deposits held a cash reserve of $139,700,000 on August 22, on October 26, according to the bank statement, they held $132,200,000, on December 3 these banks held $112,500,000, a loss of $27,200,000 since August, almost exactly the 20 per cent by which the reserves of all the banks were reduced. The utility in an emergency of that part of the reserves of the national banks which can be placed with reserve agents is indeed slight Emphasis is placed upon the case of the six banks because of their relative importance, but in this respect they were not appreciably better or worse than other banks in New York or elsewhere It is quite possible that some individual banks may have made great efforts to meet the requirements of their banking depositors, but upon the whole it seems probable that they gave far more attention to the needs of individual local depositors. No recognition of the peculiar responsibility incurred in accepting bankers' deposits, such as was expressed in the report of the special clearing-house committee in 1873, seems to have been felt by the banks which acted as reserve agents in 1907.

In order to show the ineffectiveness of the deposited portion of the reserves of the banks, the following table has been prepared. The banks in each of the central reserve cities holding any considerable amount of bankers' balances are arranged in the order of their importance. The various items of indebtedness between banks are given and also the amount of cash reserves for August 22 and December 3, 1907. The table includes in the case of New York seventeen of the thirty-eight banks and all but 7 per cent of net bankers' deposits. For Chicago, nine of the fourteen banks, and 98 per cent of deposits; and for St. Louis, five of the eight banks and 98 per cent of net bankers' deposits.

The table does not show the full extent to which reserve agents responded to the demands of their correspondents, since bankers' deposits were increased through inter-bank borrowing. Among the national banks alone there was an increase of $41,800,000 in rediscounts and bills payable. Making every allowance for this factor, however, the comparatively small reduction in the cash holdings of the banks of central reserve cities proves conclusively that balances with city banks were of slight utility. Our banking system would be strengthened by a very moderate increase in cash reserve, even if much of that portion of the reserve now deposited was no longer required, and owing to the concentration of said deposits the profits of a comparatively small number of banks would be seriously diminished.

Bankers' deposits and cash reserves of the important banks in the central reserve cities on August 22 and December 3, 1907

[Expressed in millions]

	August 22, 1907				December 3, 1907			
	Due from banks	Due to banks	Net liabilities to banks	Cash reserve	Due from banks	Due to banks	Net liabilities to banks	Cash reserve.
NEW YORK								
National City	$4.7	$68.5	$63.8	$40.2	$4.3	$64.0	$59.7	$33.7
National Bank of Commerce	7.6	75.9	68.3	27.7	1.5	64.9	63.4	24.5
First	1.2	41.0	39.8	19.3	.8	40.7	39.9	15.2
National Park Bank	3.7	50.2	46.5	21.1	5.8	41.3	35.5	14.2
Hanover	2.9	46.2	43.3	16.9	1.9	47.1	45.2	12.7
Chase	2.7	45.0	42.3	14.5	3.9	50.3	46.4	12.0
Seaboard	1.7	14.1	12.4	4.9	1.0	14.8	13.8	3.7
Importers and Traders	1.3	13.3	12.0	5.2	1.6	12.1	10.5	4.7
Fourth	2.1	14.0	11.9	3.9	2.3	14.8	12.5	5.6
Mechanics	1.5	9.9	8.4	4.9	1.6	11.6	10.0	3.6
Merchants	2.1	9.8	7.7	3.8	2.4	9.9	7.5	3.0
Bank of New York N B A	1.5	7.9	6.4	3.9	.9	8.7	7.8	3.4
American Exchange	3.8	9.4	5.6	4.9	2.9	10.9	8.0	4.9
Irving National Exchange	.9	6.4	5.5	3.8	1.4	5.4	4.0	2.5
Citizens Central	1.6	6.3	4.7	3.9	2.4	4.2	1.8	2.8
Liberty	.7	5.1	4.4	2.9	.8	5.8	5.0	1.5
Chemical	2.1	6.4	4.3	6.1	2.8	9.6	6.8	9.8
CHICAGO								
First	15.2	53.6	38.4	20.0	12.9	45.9	33.0	17.0
Continental	6.6	39.4	32.8	14.1	9.3	35.4	26.1	10.2
Corn Exchange	6.8	24.2	17.4	10.6	6.2	20.6	14.4	9.0
Commercial	4.9	21.8	16.9	7.4	5.8	18.1	12.3	6.3
Bankers	3.8	12.3	8.5	3.0	4.1	11.3	7.2	2.8
Bank of the Republic	3.0	9.7	6.7	3.2	4.5	9.0	4.5	2.8
Fort Dearborn	2.1	5.4	3.3	2.0	1.7	2.5	.8	1.2
Drovers Deposit	.7	3.8	3.1	1.2	.5	2.9	2.4	.7
National Live Stock	1.5	4.4	2.9	1.7	1.2	2.9	1.7	1.2
ST LOUIS								
National Bank of Commerce	8.5	32.3	23.8	10.3	8.2	26.0	17.8	7.8
Mechanics American	6.8	19.8	13.0	4.8	4.2	15.5	11.3	3.5
Third	7.8	17.9	10.1	5.5	7.7	14.9	7.2	3.6
Merchants Laclede	2.0	5.6	3.6	2.0	1.6	6.1	4.5	2.1
Central	1.4	4.2	2.8	1.1	1.5	4.2	2.7	.6

EXPANSION OF THE CIRCULATING MEDIUM.

The various substitutes for money used during the panic were made the subject of an elaborate investigation by Dr A P. Andrew, now Director of the Mint, and copious extracts from a paper by him are reproduced in the appendix to this report [a] A total of $238,000,000 of clearing-house loan certificates of large denominations solely for use between the banks was issued. An estimated amount of more than $250,000,000 was provided for everyday use in the form of small clearing-house loan certificates, clearing-house checks, cashiers' checks, pay checks, and other devices. By no means all of any of these various substitutes for money were in circulation at any one time. It has been estimated, for example, that of the $101,000,000 of loan certificates issued by the New York Clearing House not more than $74,000,000 was actually in use [b] Although the amount of these substitutes was greater absolutely, and probably relatively, than in previous crises, it does not follow that the banks restricted cash payments more completely As has already been observed, it seems likely that by means of these substitutes the local requirements of individual depositors were met more completely than in the past. It may also be mentioned that the issues of loan certificates for payments between the banks did not represent any addition to the circulating medium. They simply obviated the customary shifting of money between the banks in the settlement of daily balances, with the result that the money held by the

[a] Appendix, Note K, pp 434-459

[b] See the Commercial and Financial Chronicle, May 30, 1908, p 1315

banks remained just where it was at the time they were authorized.

An enormous increase in the money supply of the country was made between the end of August and the beginning of December The following table shows the estimated amount of money in circulation, including that in the banks at the close of each month from August to December, 1907:

[Expressed in millions]

	Amount	Increase
August	$2,789	
September	2,805	$16
October	2,876	71
November	3,008	132
December	3,078	70

The increase during September and October was almost wholly owing to deposits of additional government funds in the banks During November and December it was due chiefly to gold imports and issues of bank notes The increase of $219,000,000 during the first four months of the period, together with the loss of $41,000,000 by the banks, a total of $260,000,000, represents the amount of money which had gone into use or into hoards as a result of the crisis. During December money began to flow back into the banks to an extent it may be assumed at least equal to the increase in the money supply of the country during that month The composition of the $219,000,000 by which the money in circulation was increased between the end of August and the beginning of December was as follows the gold supply was increased

$90,000,000, of which $70,000,000 was due to imports; there was a slight addition of $5,000,000 to the amount of silver money, and an increase of $52,000,000 in bank notes, to this total of $146,000,000 must be added further government deposits with the banks to the amount of $73,000,000 This large increase in the available supply of money indicates the extent to which the banks were in a better position to cope with the crisis of 1907 than were the banks in 1873.

THE TREASURY AND THE PANIC.

One much discussed measure taken during the crisis would have been seen to be quite unnecessary had experiences in former crises been familiar On November 19, although the Treasury was amply supplied with funds, subscriptions were invited for the issue of $50,000,000 of 2 per cent Panama bonds and for $100,000,000 of 3 per cent certificates The object in view was to provide the banks with securities as a basis for additional issues of bank notes It was arranged that the banks should retain 90 per cent of the purchase price of the bonds as a deposit, and 75 per cent in the case of the certificates. A considerable percentage of the new securities would thus have been required as a security for the deposits created in purchasing them, but most of this requirement was met by the use of state and municipal bonds which were not available for circulation The offer of $150,000,000 of these new securities excited much opposition, and in fact bids were accepted to the amount of $24,631,000 of bonds, and $15,436,000 in the case of the certificates. The positive effect of these new issues in additional circulation was not experienced until December, during which there was an increase of $34,000,000, a large part of which would not have been made if these securities had not been issued In his able defense of his resort to this arrangement even the Secretary of the Treasury seems to have felt that the issue of notes at that time served no useful purpose Money was then flowing back to the banks because of trade depression, and continued to do so for many months thereafter He rested his case upon the moral effect of the relief offered, urging that—

> The most potent weapon at such times in bringing a crisis to an end is often as much one of moral effect as of the definite action taken It has been the history of many great crises in Europe, as well as in this country, that the knowledge that adequate resources existed to avoid disaster was often sufficient to obviate the necessity for employing such resources to their utmost limit An illustration in point is the action of the chancellor of the exchequer in Great Britain in the panic of 1866, when the announcement that he had authorized the Bank of England to disregard the bank act and to issue its notes to any necessary limit promptly arrested pressure upon the banks So prompt was the response of public feeling to this action in suspending the demand for discounts and the withdrawal of deposits that the bank did not find it necessary to avail itself of the authority to issue additional notes The fear that accommodation could not be obtained by solvent business men was completely allayed and the panic almost immediately subsided [a]

But the situation in the United States was quite unlike that in England The Bank of England had used its inadequate reserves, the national banks had not It was prepared to issue the notes secured by this special device, while the national banks, including those of New York, seem merely to have taken advantage of their issue to build up their reserves a little more rapidly and did not resume the ordinary course of payments. If the Secre-

[a] Response of the Secretary of the Treasury to Senate Resolution No 33 of December 12, 1907 Senate Doc, 60th Congress, 1st session, p 17

tary of the Treasury had offered to issue these securities during the week ending October 26 on condition that the New York banks enter into arrangements with each other which would have made possible further efforts to maintain payments, much could be said for the wisdom and courage of the policy But after suspension the condition of affairs was entirely changed A few millions more or less in the reserves of the banks or in the hands of the people could make little difference one way or another. The dislocation of the exchanges could only be overcome by resumption of payments by the banks, but they showed no willingness to resume until the people, manifesting more confidence in the banks than the banks manifested in the people, began to restore the money which had been withdrawn

CONCLUSION

We have already seen that restrictions upon cash payments were not removed until the beginning of January. Long before that time the banks in many parts of the country had intimated their readiness to resume if the New York banks would lead the way. Money was accumulating in banks both in New York and elsewhere, but the New York banks took no definite action, until at length in the last week of the year reported movements of money between the banks and the rest of the country showed a considerable balance in favor of the city The returns of the banks to the Comptroller of the Currency on February 15 showed, as usual after a crisis, an enormous increase in the cash reserves of the banks, an increase in this instance of no less than $124,000,000 A considerable part of this amount must have been received during December, and its beginning should have been marked by the immediate resumption of cash payments

It is impossible to escape the depressing conclusion that the banking situation in 1907 was handled less skillfully and boldly than in 1893, and far less so than in 1873 No new elements of weakness were disclosed, but no real effort was made to overcome difficulties which had been met with partial success at least on former occasions A situation which was certainly less serious than in 1873 or 1893 and probably less serious than in 1884 was allowed to drift into the most complete interruption of its banking facilities that the country has experienced since the civil war The fundamental cause of the trouble would seem to have been a lack of faith in the possibility of escaping suspension in an emergency under the existing banking system This feeling has been intensified as a result of the crisis of 1907 It is based upon vivid perceptions of the effects rather than an understanding of the causes of the breakdown of the country's credit machinery These effects are indeed most serious, but if this investigation may be made the basis for any conclusion, it is that though the causes of crises are extremely various, the method of handling them on the banking side is simple.

Somewhere in the banking system of a country there should be a reserve of lending power, and it should be found in its central money market. Ability in New York to increase loans and to meet the demands of depositors for money would have allayed every panic since the establishment of the national banking system. Provision for such reserve power may doubtless be made in a number of different ways This investigation will have served its purpose if in showing the causes and consequences of its absence in the past it brings home to the reader the need not only of this reserve power, but also of the readiness to use it in future emergencies

NOTE A [a]

EXTRACTS FROM THE ANNUAL REPORT OF THE SECRETARY OF THE TREASURY (WILLIAM A. RICHARDSON) RELATING TO THE CRISIS OF 1873. [a]

The prevailing practice, not only of national banks but of state banks and private bankers, of paying interest on deposits attracts currency from all parts of the country to the large cities, and especially to New York, the great financial center At seasons of the year when there is comparatively little use for currency elsewhere, immense balances accumulate in New York where, not being required by the demands of legitimate and ordinary business, they are loaned on call at a higher rate of interest than that paid to depositors, and are used in speculation.

Every year, at the season when the demand sets in from the West and South for currency to be used in payment for and transportation of their agricultural products, there occurs a stringency in the money market arising from the calling in of such loans to meet this demand.

Until this year, though annually creating some embarrassment, this demand has been met without serious difficulty

During the past summer, anticipating the usual autumn stringency, the Treasury Department sold gold while the market price was high, currency abundant, and bonds for sale in the market were scarce, and while there was a surplus of gold in the Treasury; and thereby accumulated about $14,000,000 of currency with the view of using the same, or such part thereof as might be necessary,

[a] Finance Report, 1873, pp xi–xviii

in the purchase of bonds for the sinking fund at times during the autumn and winter when they could be bought at a price not above par in gold, or in meeting demands upon the Treasury, as circumstances should require

This year there was a great demand for currency to pay for the heavy crops of a bountiful harvest, for which the European countries offered a ready market The suspension of certain large banking houses, the first of which occurred on the 18th day of September, alarmed the people as to the safety of banks and banking institutions in general Suddenly there began a rapid calling in of demand loans and a very general run on the banks for the withdrawal of deposits. Entire confidence was manifested in United States notes and even in national-bank notes, and they were drawn wherever they could be obtained, and were largely hoarded with as much avidity as coin was ever hoarded in times of financial distress when that was the circulating medium of the country The banks found themselves unable to meet the demands upon them, currency in circulation became exceedingly scarce, and the business of the country became greatly embarrassed.

In this condition of things great pressure was brought to bear upon the Treasury Department to afford relief by the issue of United States notes The first application came from a number of gentlemen in New York, suggesting that no measure of relief would be adequate that did not place at the service of the banks of that city $20,000,000 in United States notes, and asking that the assistant treasurer at New York should be authorized to issue to those banks that amount of notes as a loan upon a pledge of clearing-house certificates secured by ample collaterals, and for which certificates all the banks were to be jointly and severally responsible This proposition was declined, it being clearly not within the duty or the authority of the Treasury Department, under any provisions of law, thus to employ the public money.

Exchange on Europe having fallen to unusually low rates, and indeed having become almost unsalable in the market, to the embarrassment of our foreign and domestic trade, applications were made to the Secretary of the Treasury to use the money in the Treasury in the purchase of exchange The Treasury Department having no occasion to do this for its own use and no necessity for transferring funds to Europe, was compelled to decline this proposition, which if accepted would have put the department in the position of becoming a dealer in exchange, a position clearly inconsistent with its duties

Subsequently the New York Produce Exchange made a proposition to accomplish the same result in a different form, and also requested, as others had before, that the Secretary should pay at once the twenty-million loan of 1858, to which the following reply was made.

TREASURY DEPARTMENT,
Washington, September 30, 1873

SIR Your letter of the 29th instant, covering two resolutions of the New York Produce Exchange, has been received and the subject-matter fully considered

The resolutions are as follows

"Whereas the critical condition of the commercial interests of the country requires immediate relief by the removal of the block in negotiating foreign exchange, therefore be it

"*Resolved*, That we respectfully suggest to the Secretary of the Treasury the following plans for relief in this extraordinary emergency

"First. That currency be immediately issued to banks and bankers, upon satisfactory evidence that gold has been placed upon special deposit in the Bank of England, by their correspondents in London, to the credit of the United States, to be used solely in purchasing commercial bills of exchange

"Second That the President of the United States and the Secretary of the Treasury are respectfully requested to order the immediate prepayment of the outstanding loan of the United States due January 1, 1874 "

While the Government is desirous of doing all in its power to relieve the present unsettled condition in business affairs—as has already been announced by the President—it is constrained, in all its acts, to keep within the letter and spirit of the laws, which the officers of the Government are sworn to support, and they can not go beyond the authority which Congress has conferred upon them Your first resolution presents difficulties which can not be overcome It is not supposed that you desire to exchange coin in England for United States notes in New York at par If your proposition is for the Government to purchase gold in England, to be paid for in United States notes at the current market rate in New York, it would involve the Government in the business of importing and speculating in gold, since the Treasury has no use for coin beyond its ordinary receipts, and would be obliged to sell the coin so purchased at a price greater or less than was paid for it If your object is to induce the Treasury Department to loan United States notes to banks in New York upon the pledge and deposit in London of gold, it is asking the Secretary of the Treasury to loan the money of the United States upon collateral security for which there is no authority in law If the Secretary of the Treasury can loan notes upon a pledge of coin he can loan them upon a pledge of other property in his discretion, as he has recently been requested to do, which would be an extraordinary power as well as a most dangerous business to engage in, and which my judgment would deter me from undertaking, as the Secretary of the Treasury, even if by any stretch of construction I might not find it absolutely prohibited by law The objections already mentioned to your first resolution are so insuperable and conclusive that it is unnecessary for me to refer to the many practical difficulties which would arise if an attempt should be made to comply with your request Your second resolution calls for the payment at once of the loan of 1858, or the bonds commonly called "fives of 1874 " Upon a thorough investigation I am of opinion that Congress has not conferred upon the Secretary of the Treasury power to comply with your request in that particular, and in this opinion the law officers of the Government concur Under these circumstances you will perceive that, while I have great respect for the gentlemen comprising the New York Produce Exchange, I am compelled, by my views of the law and of my duty, to respectfully decline to adopt the measure which your resolutions propose

I have the honor to be, very respectfully,

WM. A RICHARDSON,
Secretary of the Treasury

The Chamber of Commerce of Charleston, S C, petitioned for the transfer of currency to that city, and the purchase with it at that point of exchange on New York, to aid those engaged in forwarding the cotton crop to the market The following letter was sent in answer to this petition.

TREASURY DEPARTMENT, *October 3, 1873*

SAMUEL Y TUPPER, Esq,

President Chamber of Commerce, Charleston, S C

I have the honor to acknowledge the receipt of the memorial of the Charleston (S C) Chamber of Commerce, addressed to the President of the United States, and referred to this department, which, after rectifying the present stringency in the money market and the difficulty of obtaining currency, requests "that the sum of $500,000 be placed and maintained on deposit with the assistant treasurer at Charleston, to be used by him in the purchase of New York exchange from the banks"

To comply with the request, it would be necessary for the Treasury Department to send currency by express to Charleston from time to time, and to buy with it exchange on New York in competition with private bankers

Should this request be granted, a hundred other places in the country might, with equal propriety, ask for the same relief, and if all such requests were impartially granted the department would find itself engaged in an extensive exchange business, fixing and regulating the rate of exchange between different places in the country, and the public money, raised by taxation only for the purpose of carrying on the Government, would be employed to a very large amount in a business which Congress has not given the Secretary of the Treasury any authority to engage in

With a due regard to the proper management of the Treasury Department, within the provisions of the law, I have felt it to be my duty to decline all similar propositions from other places, and your request must therefore receive the same response

I have the honor to be, very respectfully, yours,

WM A. RICHARDSON,
Secretary of the Treasury

The executive department of the Government was anxious to do everything in its power, under the law, and with due regard to the protection of the Treasury and the maintenance of public credit, to allay the panic and to prevent disaster to the legitimate commercial and industrial interests of the country, but it was found impossible to afford the relief in any of the many forms in which the relief was asked It was decided, therefore, to adopt the only practicable course which seemed to be open to it—the purchase of bonds for the sinking fund to such an extent as the condition of the Treasury would allow, and thus release a considerable amount of currency from its vaults. Purchases of bonds were commenced on the morning of the 20th of September and were continued until the 24th, when it became evident that the amount offering for purchase was increasing to an extent beyond the power of the Treasury to accept, and the purchasing was closed after bonds to the amount of about $13,000,000 had been bought, and without the use of any part of the $44,000,000 of United States notes generally known as the reserve

It should be stated that in the excitement there were many persons in the city of New York who insisted with great earnestness that it was the duty of the Executive to disregard any and all laws which stood in the way of affording the relief suggested by them—a proposition which indicates the state of feeling and the excitement under which applications were made to the Secretary of the Treasury to use the public money and which, it is scarcely necessary to add, could not be entertained by the officers of the Government to whom it was addressed

These facts are recited in order to lay before Congress and place on record in a concise form exactly what the Treasury Department was asked to do, and what it did, in the late financial crisis.

The currency paid out of the Treasury for bonds did much to strengthen many savings banks and to prevent a panic among their numerous depositors, who began to be alarmed, and had there developed an extended run upon those useful institutions it would inevitably have caused widespread disaster and distress. It also fortified other banks and checked the general alarm to some extent But the loss of confidence in the value of a great amount of corporate property which immediately followed the failure of banking houses connected with largely indebted corporations, the distrust of the solvency of many other institutions, the doubt as to the credit of firms and individuals whose business was supposed to be greatly extended, and the legitimate effect thereof in disturbing the business of the country could not be avoided by any amount of currency which might be added to the circulation already existing

Confidence was to be entirely restored only by the slow and cautious process of gaining a better knowledge of true values and making investments accordingly and by conducting business on a firmer basis, with less inflation and more regard to real soundness and intrinsic values

There can be no doubt that the practice of banks of allowing interest on deposits payable on demand is pernicious and fraught with danger and embarrassment to borrower and lender, as well as to the general business interests.

Deposits payable on demand should be limited to that surplus which individuals require over and above their investments, and no part of that from which they expect an income. Such deposits are comparatively stable in average amount, and constitute a healthy basis for banking purposes within proper limits, which prudent bankers know how to determine

But if deposit accounts are employed as temporary investments, the interest attracts a large amount of money to those cities where such interest is paid, and where speculation is most active, at seasons when as much profit thereon can not be secured elsewhere. With the first return of activity in legitimate business these temporary investments are called in and jeopardize in their sudden withdrawal the whole business of the banks, both affecting the legitimate depositors on the one hand by excitement and distrust, and on the other creating a condition of things in which the borrowers on call are also unable to respond. The banks have borrowed their money of depositors on call They have loaned it on call to speculators, who by its use have contributed to inflate the prices of the stocks or merchandise which have been the subject of their speculations The speculator wants it till he can dispose of them without a loss This he is unable to do in a stringent money market The banks, their depositors, and the borrowers all want it at the same time, and of course a stringency is developed which spreads distress throughout the country.

The system creates immense amount of debts payable on demand, all of which thus suddenly and unexpectedly mature at the first shock of financial or commercial embarrassment in the country and at the very time when most needed by debtors and when they are least able to respond.

There is no safety for corporations or individuals whose capital employed is wholly or mostly borrowed on call. Many savings banks were protected from ruin in the recent financial excitement by availing themselves of provisions in their rules requiring sixty days or other periods of notice before paying depositors, thus making all their deposits payable on time Every cautious and well-managed savings institution has such a rule among its by-laws

Without attributing the stringency in the money market which is experienced every autumn and occasionally at other seasons of the year solely to this practice of paying interest upon deposits in the large cities, it is evident that when money is less needed in legitimate business the practice encourages overtrading and speculation, always detrimental to the best interests of the country, and the bad effects of which upon those interests become more apparent and the disaster more widespread when the necessary contraction begins to be felt

I recommend that the national banks be prevented from paying interest on deposits, or that they be restricted and limited therein, either by direct prohibition, by discriminating taxation, or otherwise.

While legislation by Congress can not prevent state banks and private bankers from continuing the practice, it can prevent national banks from becoming involved in and instrumental in producing the embarrassments and difficulties to which it necessarily leads.

The national banks, organized by law of Congress and having relations with the Government in the issue of circulating notes, ought to be the most cautious and safe banking institutions of the country, and should be kept aloof from all hazardous business which it is not possible to prevent sanguine, venturesome, and speculative individuals from engaging in at the risk of their capital and their credit

With a fixed amount of circulation of bank notes and of United States legal-tender notes not redeemable in coin and with gold above par in currency, there must be each year times of redundancy and times of scarcity of currency, depending wholly on the demand, no method existing for increasing the supply.

With a circulating medium redeemable in coin, a redundancy is corrected by the export, and a scarcity by the import of specie from other countries.

There is a prevailing sentiment that more elasticity should be given to the volume of the currency, so that the amount in circulation might increase and diminish according to the necessities of the business of the country. But the difference of opinion on this subject is so great and the real difficulties attending its solution are so numerous that, without discussing any of the multitude of plans which have been presented to the public through the press and otherwise, I earnestly commend to the wisdom of Congress a careful and thorough consideration of this important subject, rendered more obviously important by the present embarrassed condition of large business interests which have suffered by the recent financial crisis, and that, in such inquiry, avoiding further inflation of the issue of irredeemable legal-tender notes, the most desirable of all financial results to be attained, namely, a permanent return to the sound basis of specie payments and a gold standard to which all our paper issues shall be made of equal value, shall be the aim

To allow national banks to use part of their reserves at seasons of the greatest pressure, under proper restrictions and regulations, would afford some flexibility.

Rigid statute laws applied to all banks at all seasons and in all places alike often prove an embarrassment and injury when they conflict with economic principles and the laws of trade and business, which are stronger than legislative enactments and can not be overthrown thereby. Associated banks at the several redemption cities named in the banking law, which are the great controlling centers of business, might do much to give steadiness and safety if they were authorized, through properly constituted boards or committees of their own officers, to exercise a large discretion in the use of their reserves in the rate of interest to be charged at different seasons and under different circumstances and in other matters within limits prescribed by law.

6158—10——22

NOTE B.

EXTRACTS FROM THE ANNUAL REPORT OF THE COMPTROLLER OF THE CURRENCY (JOHN JAY KNOX) RELATING TO THE CRISIS OF 1873.[a]

The crisis was caused in a great degree by the desire of the country banks to withdraw their balances from the city banks, first, because in the month of September the amount on deposit with the city banks was needed for the legitimate purposes of trade, and secondly, because the country banks, foreseeing and fearing the return of the experience of previous years, thought it safer to withdraw their balances at once When the reserves of the New York City banks became alarmingly reduced by the drafts of their country correspondents, the only resource left to the city banks was to convert their call loans, amounting to some $60,000,000; but these, if paid at all, were paid in checks upon the associated banks, and the latter found, the next morning, at the clearing house, that, although a portion of their liabilities had been reduced by the payment of call loans, they were in the aggregate no richer in currency than on the previous day. * * *

[[b] The reserves of the 1,900 national banks located elsewhere than in the city of New York are held to a great extent in that city For most of the time during the past year an amount equal to more than one-fifth of the capital of all these national banks has been held on deposit by the national banks of the city of New York to

[a] Finance Report, 1873, pp 86–96

[b] The three succeeding paragraghs which are enclosed in brackets are a part of an excerpt from the report of 1872

the credit of their correspondents In many cases these credits amount to twice the capital of the bank with which they are deposited, in other cases the amount of deposits is three, four, and even five times the capital, which amount has been attracted thither largely by the payment of interest on deposits. The failure of one of these New York City banks in a time of monetary stringency would embarrass, if not ruin, many banks in the redemption cities, and, in turn, the country correspondents of these banks would suffer from the imprudence of the New York bank, which would be responsible for wide-spread disaster * * *

In times of excessive stringency loans are not made by such associations to business men upon commercial paper, but to dealers in speculative securities, upon short time, at high rates of interest; and an increase of call loans beyond the proper limit is more likely to afford facilities for unwarrantable stock speculations than relief to legitimate business transactions * * *

The variations in the liabilities requiring reserve in the banks of the city of New York are very great. The banks outside of New York during the dull season send their surplus means to that city for deposit upon interest, to await the revival of business. The banks in the city of New York at such periods of the year have no legitimate outlet for these funds, and are, therefore, threatened with loss. The stock board takes advantage of this condition of affairs, speculation is stimulated by the cheapness of money, and a market is found for the idle funds upon doubtful collaterals, and the result is seen in the increased transactions at the clearing house, which during the past year exceeded $32,000,000,000, or an average of more than $100,000,000 daily—not one-half of which was the result of legitimate business, the total amount of transactions being greater than that of the bankers' clearing house of the city of London The evil arises largely from the payment by the banks of interest on deposits, an old and established custom which can not easily be changed by direct legislation. A considerable portion of these deposits would remain at home if they could be used at a low rate of interest, and made available at any time upon the return of the season of active business No sure investment of this kind is, however, open to the country banks, and the universal custom is to send forward the useless dollars from vaults comparatively insecure to their correspondents in the city, where they are supposed to be safer and at the same time earning dividends for shareholders]

* * * * *

The rule requiring a reserve was adopted by the voluntary action of the Clearing House Association of the city of New York previous to the passage of the national currency act At a meeting of bank officers, representing 42 of the 46 banks of the city of New York, held at the rooms of the Clearing House Association in March, 1858, it was agreed "to keep on hand at all times an amount of coin equivalent to not less than 20 per cent of our net deposits of every kind, which shall be made to include certified checks and other liabilities, except circulating notes, deducting the daily exchanges received from the clearing house." This resolution was adopted five years previous to the passage of the national currency act, and its phraseology is not unlike the provisions of that act in reference to reserves to be held by the national banks of New York City The resolution did not provide for a reserve on circulation for the reason that the circulation of the city banks was at that time redeemable at par in coin, so that no action was necessary in respect to the reserve to be held upon circulating notes From that time to the passage of the national currency act the resolution was generally observed, and since the passage of the act neither the New York Clearing House Association nor the clearing house association of any city has requested the repeal of such restrictions. On the contrary, the New York association has repeatedly refused to modify the rule by agreeing that national-bank notes, which by the law can be used in payment of debts to each other, may be so employed.

The national currency act requires that the national banks "shall at all times have on hand" the reserve required in lawful money, and the advocates of a repeal of the reserve laws insist that, under this provision, the national banks are absolutely prohibited from using these reserves at any time The provision requiring that a reserve shall be kept on hand at all times was intended to protect the depositor and to keep the bank in funds for the purpose of responding at all times to the demands of its creditors This is evident from the fact that the bank is required, when its reserves become deficient, to cease discounting and making dividends until the amount of the reserve shall be restored The word "reserve" is used, as has been suggested, in the same sense as it is used in an army, and "the fact that a military commander can not be definitely instructed when he may employ his reserve force is not regarded as a reason why that important portion of the army organization should be abandoned or be reduced in number of efficiency." To claim that a bank can not redeem its own notes upon presentation, and can not pay the checks of its depositors on demand if the payment of such debts shall intrench upon its reserves, is equivalent to declaring that the national currency act was intended to provide for the destruction of the very institutions it had created From the first organization of the system to the present time the uniform decisions have been that the object of the reserve is to enable the bank at all times to pay its debts In times of panic the depositors of a bank, and not its officers and directors, are its masters, and it is absurd to maintain that a bank, liable at such times to be called upon to pay its debts would, if there were no reserve laws, loan upon commercial paper, at the risk of almost certain failure and disgrace, the money which belongs to its creditors

While the Comptroller concedes that experience may hereafter justify a modification of the provisions of the act in this respect, he is clearly of the opinion, in view of the lessons to be derived from the late suspension in New York, that he would not be warranted in recommending any change at present.

* * * * *

THE PANIC OF 1873

The monetary crisis of 1873 may be said to have had its beginning in New York City on September 8 by the failure of the Warehouse Security Company and of two houses which had left their regular business to embark in enterprises foreign thereto, which were followed on the 13th by the failure of a large firm of stockbrokers On the 18th and 19th two of the largest banking houses in the city, well known throughout the country, and which were interested in the negotiations of large amounts of railroad securities, also failed, and on the 20th of the same month the failures of the Union Trust Company, the National Trust Company, the National Bank of the Commonwealth, and three other well-known banking houses were announced On the same day the New York Stock Exchange, for the first time in its existence, closed its doors, and they were not again opened for a period of ten days, during which period legal-tender notes commanded a premium over certified checks of from one-fourth of 1 per cent to 3 per cent. An active demand for deposits commenced on the 18th, and increased rapidly during the 19th and 20th, chiefly from the country correspondents of the banks, and their drafts continued to such an extent, "calling back their deposits in a medium never before received," that the reserves of the banks were alarmingly reduced

The "call loans," amounting to more than $60,000,000, upon which the banks relied to place themselves in funds in such an emergency, were entirely unavailable, because the means of the borrowers upon the realization of which they depended to repay their loans were, to a great extent, pledged with the banks These collaterals could in ordinary times have been sold, but at that moment no market could be found except at ruinous sacrifices Had there been a market, the payments would have been made in checks upon the associated banks, which would not have added to the general supply of cash A meeting of the clearing-house association was called, and on Saturday evening, September 20, the plan for facilitating the settlement of balances at the clearing house was unanimously adopted

* * * * *

The suspension of currency payments followed and was at first confined to the banks of New York City, but afterwards extended to other large cities, because the New York banks could not respond to the demands of their correspondents in those cities, and these, in turn, could not respond to the demands of their correspondents Exchange on New York, which would otherwise have commanded a slight premium, was at a discount, and to a considerable extent unavailable. The suspension of the banks in other leading cities, almost without exception, therefore followed, and their partial or entire suspension continued for forty days, until confidence was in a measure restored by the resumption of the New York City banks on the 1st day of November

Although predictions had been made of the approach of a financial crisis, there were no apprehensions of its immediate occurrence. On the contrary there were in almost every direction evidences of prosperity

The harvest was nearly or quite completed, and the bins and granaries were full to overflowing. The manufacturing and mining interests had also been prosperous during the year, and there was good promise that the fall trade, which had opened, would be as large as during previous years The value of the cereals, potatoes, tobacco, and hay for 1872 is estimated by the Department of Agriculture at $1,324,385,000. It is supposed that the value of these products for the present year, a large portion of which was at this time ready for sale and awaiting shipment to market, will not vary materially from the abovementioned estimate of last year. An estimate based upon the census returns of 1869 gives the probable aggregate value of the marketable products of industry for the year as $4,036,000,000, and a similar estimate upon the same basis and upon returns to the Agricultural Department gives an increase of $1,788,000,000 for 1873 over the amount for 1868.

It is not the province of the Comptroller to explain the causes which led to this suspension In order to enter upon such an explanation it would be necessary to obtain comparative data for a series of years in reference to the imports and exports, the products of industry, the issue of currency and other evidences of debt, and, in fact, a general discussion of the political economy of the country. The immediate cause of the crisis is, however, more apparent The money market had become overloaded with debt, the cost of railroad construction for five years past being estimated to have been $1,700,000,000, or about $340,000,000 annually, while debt based upon almost every species of property—state, city, town, manufacturing corporations, and mining companies—had been sold in the market Such bonds and stocks had been disposed of to a considerable extent in foreign markets, and so long as this continued the sale of similar securities was stimulated and additional amounts offered. When the sale of such securities could no longer be effected abroad, the bonds of railroads and other enterprises of like nature which were in process of construction were thus forced upon the home market, until their negotiation became almost impossible The bankers of the city of New York, who were burdened with the load, could not respond to the demands of their creditors, the numerous holders of similar securities became alarmed, and the panic soon extended throughout the country

The present financial crisis may in a great degree be attributed to the intimate relations of the banks of the city of New York with the transactions of the stock board, more than one-fourth, and in many instances nearly one-third, of the bills receivable of the banks, since the late civil war, having consisted of demand loans to brokers and members of the stock board, which transactions have a tendency to impede and unsettle, instead of facilitating, the legitimate business interests of the whole country Previous to the war the stock board is said to have consisted of only 150 members, and its organic principle was a strictly commission business, under a stringent and conservative constitution and by-laws. The close of the war found the membership of the stock board increased to 1,100, and composed of men from all parts of the country, many of whom had congregated in Wall street, adopting for their rule of business the apt motto of Horace.

Make money, make it honestly if you can, at all events, make money

*　　*　　*　　*　　*

The quotations of the stock board are known to be too frequently fictions of speculation, and yet these fictions control the commerce and business of a great country, and their influence is not confined to this country, but extends to other countries, and seriously impairs our credit with foreign nations. The fictitious debts of railroads and other corporations which they have bolstered up, and which have obtained quotations in London and other markets of the world, have now been reduced to a more proper valuation, or stricken from the list.

*　　*　　*　　*　　*

Many measures of reform are proposed in order that the lessons of the crisis may not be lost, and others be led hereafter to repeat similar errors. Unity of action among the leading banks of the great cities will do more to reform abuses than any congressional enactment; for, unless such corporations shall unite and insist upon legitimate methods of conducting business, the laws of Congress in reference thereto will be likely soon to become inoperative, such enactments being observed in their true spirit by the few, while the many evade them, and thus invite a repetition of similar disasters

If, however, the banks are disinclined to unite for such a purpose, the legislation required of Congress will be such as will induce associations outside of the city of New York to retain in their vaults such funds as are not needed at the commercial center for purposes of legitimate business

*   *   *   *   *

INTEREST ON DEPOSITS.

In my last annual report I referred briefly to the evils resulting from the payment of interest upon deposits, and my predecessors have frequently referred more at length to the same subject The difficulty has been that the proposed legislation by Congress upon the subject would apply only to the national banks The effect of such legislation would be to bring state banks and savings banks, organized by authority of the different States, in direct competition with the national banks in securing the accounts of correspondents and dealers, the national banks would be desirous of retaining their business, and the more unscrupulous would not hesitate to evade the law by offering to make collections throughout the country free of charge, to buy and sell stocks without commission, and to rediscount paper at low rates. The proposed action of the clearing house in the city of New York, if adopted by the clearing houses of the principal cities of the Union, would do more to prevent the payment of interest upon deposits than any congressional enactment, but the evils resulting from the payment of interest upon deposits are by no means confined to the city banks It may be safely said that this custom, which prevails in almost every city and village of the Union, has done more than any other to demoralize the business of banking State banks, private bankers, and associations under the guise of savings banks everywhere offer rates of interest upon deposits which can not safely be paid by those engaged in legitimate business National banks desirous of retaining the business of their dealers also make similar offers, and the result is not only the increase of the rates of interest paid to business men, but, as a consequence, investments in unsecured loans, bringing ultimate loss both upon the shareholders of the bank and the depositors The kind of legislation needed is that which shall apply to all banks and bankers alike, whether organized under the national-currency act or otherwise A law prohibiting the payment of interest on deposits by the national banks will have little effect unless followed by similar legislation under authority of the different States, and there is little hope that such legislation can be obtained. The national-currency act, which was passed during the war, provided for a tax of one-half of 1 per cent upon all deposits, and subsequently internal-revenue legislation extended this tax to all deposits made with state banks and individual bankers. If legislation prohibiting the payment of interest on deposits shall be proposed, I recommend that this law be so amended as to repeal this tax, so far as it applies to demand deposits, and that an increased rate of taxation be imposed uniformly upon all deposits which, either directly or indirectly, are placed with banks and bankers with the offer or expectation of receiving interest Such legislation if rigidly enforced would have the effect not only of reducing the rate of interest throughout the country, but at the same time preventing the illegitimate organization of savings banks, which organizations should be allowed only upon the condition that the savings of the people shall be carefully and prudently invested and the interest therefrom, after deducting reasonable expenses, distributed from time to time to the depositors and to no other persons whatsoever.

CERTIFICATION OF CHECKS.

The act of March 3, 1869, authorizes the appointment of a receiver "if any officer, clerk, or agent of any national bank shall certify any check drawn upon said bank unless the person or company drawing the said check shall have on deposit in said bank at the time said check is certified an amount of money equal to the amount specified in such check."

Receivers have been appointed during the past year for the National Bank of the Commonwealth of New York and the New Orleans National Banking Association for violations of this act, and it is the intention of the Comptroller to hereafter rigidly enforce this act whenever he is satisfied of such violation.

NOTE C

EXTRACTS FROM THE ANNUAL REPORT OF THE COMPTROLLER OF THE CURRENCY (H. W CANNON) RELATING TO THE PANIC OF 1884

CAUSES OF NEW YORK BANK FAILURES IN 1884.[a]

The most notable national-bank failure of the year in the United States was that of the Marine National Bank, of the city of New York, which closed its doors about 11 a. m. on the 6th of May. The bank examiners of the city of New York immediately took possession of the bank and found that it had been indebted to the clearing house that day in the sum of $555,000 The examiner also found the account of one firm overdrawn on the books of the bank to the amount of $766,570 14. Upon further examination it was found that this firm owed a total of about $2,430,500, being more than six times the capital of the bank. A portion of this indebtedness was in the names of other parties—clerks in their office and relations of one of the firm How far the officials of the bank are criminally responsible for these matters is a subject now under investigation in the courts The Comptroller finds, from the report of the examiner, that this firm had three different accounts with the bank—a private account of a member of the firm, a general account, and a special account It appears, from an examination of the transcript

[a] Report of the Comptroller of the Currency, 1884, pp. 41–43

of these accounts, that on May 5 their special account was overdrawn by certified checks $383,402 07 and that on the same day their general account was also overdrawn It is apparent, therefore, that the bank had violated the law in regard to certifications by permitting these overdrafts It is claimed, however, by the officers of the bank that these certifications were made against securities which were subsequently obtained from the bank by one of the firm upon his representations that he had obtained a loan upon them elsewhere and would make good his account A further examination of the various accounts of the firm shows that while the certification of their checks was carried on to an enormous extent, they also made very heavy deposits from day to day, and it will, perhaps, be very difficult to furnish evidence proving conclusively that the checks were certified before the deposits were made.

An examination of the minutes of the board of directors of the bank shows that on the 11th day of April, 1884, twenty-five days before the failure of the bank, the committee of examination appointed by the board of directors reported that they had examined the securities, counted the bills and specie, and examined the balances on the ledgers of the bank, and found the recorded statement of the 7th of April, 1884, to be correct The minutes further show that the directors were in session about an hour before the bank closed. They apparently had no suspicion of the state of its affairs, and voted to discount certain offerings of commercial paper, and within half an hour after the adjournment of this meeting the bank closed its doors. It would seem, therefore, that the board of directors were grossly deceived as to the true state of affairs

In this connection I desire to state that the records of the comptroller's office show that many of the transactions of the Marine National Bank of the city of New York have been looked upon with disfavor, and that the association has been frequently reprimanded for irregularities during the past few years. None of the reports of examinations of the bank made to this office, however, disclosed any violations of the law forbidding the overcertification of ckecks or gave the department any adequate idea of the dangerous character of its loans, and this is not surprising, the directors of the bank having been equally deceived in regard to the situation

After reviewing the information in his possession, it seems to the comptroller that the failure of the Marine National Bank is in consequence of the board of directors having chosen for their president a man who was willing to risk his own honor and the funds of the bank in speculation. He joined with himself another, who is now in Ludlow street jail under indictment, and who was also a member of the board of directors of the bank. While it is true that the final failure has shown that there were overcertifications on the last day, the comptroller judges, from the information which he has received, that the bank has been for a long time in the power of the firm to whom the certifications were granted, through the president's copartnership. This matter was carried to the extent of permitting one of the firm to have access to, and apparently free disposal of, the securities left as collateral to his loans, and, so far as actual results are concerned, he might as well have had the combinations of the cash vaults of the bank and helped himself to their contents

The Metropolitan National Bank suspended and closed its doors about noon on May 14, and opened again for business at 12 o'clock on the following day, the bank examiner remaining in charge of the bank during its suspension. He also remained at the bank during the first days of its resumption, and has frequently visited it since, and forwarded reports as to its liquidation of deposits. Before permitting the bank to resume business the comptroller received assurances from the examiner that the bank was solvent, and also received telegrams from the president and chairman on loans of the New York Clearing House, stating that in their opinion the bank was solvent and should be permitted to resume The bank is now closing its affairs, having arranged to pay its depositors in full and gone into voluntary liquidation under sections 5220 and 5221 of the United States Revised Statutes.

It is difficult to determine, in the case of this bank, what brought about its suspension. From the information which the comptroller has, however, it appears that the president of the Metropolitan National Bank had the credit at least of being a very large speculator. He was supposed to be a man of very large means and was interested in many enterprises which required the use of large sums of money The general liquidation in railroad and other securities which had been going on for the past two years had no doubt affected the properties in which the president was interested, and the public having become suspicious, and apparently believing that he was a large borrower from the bank, and had loaned money to parties who were interested with himself, all of whom were assumed to have lost largely by this depreciation of property, rumors were circulated which excited distrust and suspicion against his bank and caused the run upon it which resulted in its suspension Reports of examinations do not disclose any overcertification of checks, and I can not conclude that irregularities of this kind had anything to do with bringing about the suspension

The Metropolitan National Bank was examined on April 28, 1884 The examination disclosed certain irregularities, and a letter was promptly written to the bank, requiring the correction of the irregularities, and forbidding the declaration of any further dividends until this had been done. While this letter was acknowledged, the matter was pending at the time of the suspension of the bank.

The trouble at the Second National Bank of the city of New York grew out of a defalcation amounting to $3,185,000 by the president of the bank. The amount of this defalcation was immediately guaranteed and the money paid in by the directors Owing to this prompt assistance the bank did not suspend, and is going on with its business in a solvent condition. As far as this office is advised, the president used the money in speculations in Wall street, and was able to conceal the fact of his misappropriations of the funds of the bank on account of the securities being kept in a vault located at some distance from the regular banking rooms, which are at the corner of Twenty-third street and Fifth avenue It appears that the president had access to these securities without check or hindrance, and used them to obtain money for his own private speculations

In the matter of the failure of the Marine National Bank of New York, and the defalcation of the Second National Bank of New York, it appears from the information on file at this office that there have been not only irregularities, but violations of section 5209, United States Revised Statutes The United States district attorney at the city of New York is in communication with the national bank examiner and the receiver of the Marine National Bank in regard to these matters, and the facts, which have been submitted to this office, the Comptroller has formally transmitted to the Attorney-General of the United States through the Secretary of the Treasury

CLEARING-HOUSE LOAN CERTIFICATES IN 1884.[a]

As has been stated, a meeting of the members of the New York Clearing House Association was held on May 14, 1884, to consider what measures could be adopted to protect the reserves of the associated banks and to prevent suspension of gold and currency payments in New York.

Resolutions were there adopted, which are given elsewhere, authorizing the issuance by the loan committee of the Clearing House Association of what were termed

[a] Report of the Comptroller of the Currency, 1884, pp 36-38

clearing-house loan certificates, of which the following is a copy:

No —] [$10,000

LOAN COMMITTEE OF THE NEW YORK
CLEARING HOUSE ASSOCIATION
NEW YORK, *May 15, 1884*

This certifies that the ——— National Bank has deposited with the committee securities in accordance with the proceedings of a meeting of the association held May 14, 1884, upon which this certificate is issued This certificate will be received in payment of balances at the clearing house for the sum of ten thousand dollars from any member of the Clearing House Association On the surrender of the certificate by the depositing bank above named, the committee will indorse the amount as a payment on the obligation of said bank, held by them, and surrender a proportionate share of collateral securities held therefor

----

-------------------- *Committee*

These certificates were to be issued to banks who were members of the association upon their securities or bills receivable at the rate of 75 cents on the dollar By the cooperation of all the members of the Clearing House Association the certificates were accepted in payment of balances at the clearing house Similar resolutions were adopted and certificates issued during the panic of 1873, but this measure of relief was not taken until after the panic had assumed such proportions that their use and the consequent relief to the banks in settling their balances at the clearing house could not restore confidence There is little doubt but that the prompt action of the associated banks in May last in issuing loan certificates had a most excellent effect not only in the city of New York but throughout the country The greatest amount of these certificates outstanding on any one day was on May 24, 1884, when they amounted to $21,885,000 After that date they were issued in limited amounts only, and on June 7 their further issue was discontinued

Of the 82 banks, members of the Clearing House Association, only 20 took out these certificates, and several of the banks so taking them out did so simply as a precautionary measure and did not use them The total amount issued was $24,915,000, and about $7,000,000 of these were issued to the Metropolitan National Bank On and after June 10 balances at the clearing house were paid in lawful money. The principal security on which these certificates were issued consisted of mercantile paper

On July 1 all of the loan certificates, with the exception of a portion of those which had been issued by the loan committee to the Metropolitan National Bank, had been returned to the committee and canceled and the securities taken up This bank had been compelled, owing to its suspension and the lack of confidence which was caused thereby, to liquidate almost its entire deposit account, having reduced its deposits from $11,294,000 in May to $1,338,000 on September 30 Owing to this enormous liquidation of deposits the Metropolitan National Bank was unable to collect its loans and realize upon its securities with sufficient promptness to cancel its loan certificates by July 1, and as these certificates bear interest at 6 per cent and are secured by a deposit of ample collaterals, as heretofore stated, the associated banks were willing to carry them as loans, and on October 3, 1884, were still carrying $5,290,000 of the certificates issued to the Metropolitan National Bank Since that time this bank has gone into voluntary liquidation, and these certificates will be paid and canceled as rapidly as the collection of the securities upon which they are based can be made

The following table shows the aggregate issuance and cancellation of clearing-house certificates from day to day from May 15, 1884, to October 3, 1884

Date	Issued	Canceled	Outstanding
May 15	$3,820 000		$3,820,000
16	6,885,000		10 705,000
17	6 740,000		17,445,000
19	1,190,000	$200,000	18,435,000
20	1 950,000		20 385,000
21	580,000	800,000	20,165,000
22	1 560 000		21,725,000
23	140,000	160,000	21,865,000
24	180,000	415,000	21,885,000
26		460 000	21,470,000
27	640 000	450,000	21,650,000
28		400,000	21 200,000
28	700,000	1,100,000	21,500,000
29	335 000	90,000	20,735,000
June 2	70,000	1.030,000	20 715,000
3	40 000	120,000	19,725,000
4		1 050,000	19,605,000
5	85,000	9,070,000	18,640 000
6		2,850,000	9,570,000
June 6 to July 1		1 220,000	6,720,000
July 1 to Aug 1		210 000	5,500,000
Aug 1 to Sept 1			5,290 000
Sept 1 to Oct 3			
Total	24,915,000		

ILLEGAL CERTIFICATION OF CHECKS.[a]

In reference to the matter of illegal certification of checks by the national banks of the city of New York,

[a] Report of the Comptroller of the Currency, 1884, pp 44–50

the records of this office show that immediately upon the passage of the act of July 12, 1882, the bank examiner of New York City was directed to furnish information as to whether it was the custom and practice of the national banks of that city to certify checks in violation of section 13 of that act and section 5208, United States Revised Statutes Many of the banks in New York immediately took advice of their attorneys, and opinions were sent to this office which were deemed of importance in the matter. The main point of these opinions was that the certifications forbidden were a form of acceptance, and that the right to make a general acceptance was not interfered with, reference being made to the third clause of section 5136, United States Revised Statutes, which confers upon national banks the power to make contracts Many of the banks of New York, acting upon these opinions of their attorneys, changed the form of certifications, and the majority of the banks seem to have stamped their checks for the purpose of certification with the word "accepted," giving the date, and with the name of the teller written underneath.

On October 4, 1882, a letter was addressed to the Secretary of the Treasury asking him to refer certain questions which had arisen under the law to the Attorney-General for an opinion

On November 24 the Attorney-General returned his opinion. In reply to the first question, whether a national bank had the right to accept checks drawn upon it unless the drawer has the amount stated in the check actually on deposit in the bank, he replied in the negative. To construe otherwise he held would be to allow a device to evade the provisions of law

In reply to the second question, whether an acceptance under such circumstances would create a liability to the bank for money borrowed, and as such be subject to the limitation of section 5200 of the Revised Statutes, confining such liability to one-tenth of the capital stock of the bank, the Attorney-General replied in the negative, as the acceptance under such circumstances would not be a loan of money but of credit

To the third question, as to whether such acceptance to an extent greater than the capital of the bank would be a violation of section 5202 of the Revised Statutes, the Attorney-General replied in the affirmative

Immediately upon receipt of this opinion the banks were notified of the same, and warned that due regard must be had to the law as interpreted

On July 19, 1883, a circular letter was sent to the New York banks asking information as to the large amount of certified checks and acceptances appearing in their last previous quarterly report, to which answers were duly received.

By an examination of the Wall Street National Bank, made on September 4, 1883, what appeared to be a clear case of violation of law was discovered, and a letter was addressed by my predecessor to the Secretary of the Treasury, inclosing a copy of the report, and asking him to transmit it to the Departmentof Justice for action Although an endeavor was made by the district attorney to have all the officers of the bank indicted, yet the grand jury found an indictment only against the teller of the bank When brought up for trial he plead guilty, but presented an affidavit showing that he had acted under the direction of his superior officers The judge suspended sentence to admit of evidence of the implied charge against these officers. The district attorney was heard in this matter before a United States commissioner, and presented evidence against the officers, and a decision has been rendered holding all the officers for trial, as follows.

The teller, ——— ———, stands indicted for the offense with which the defendants here are charged, and I am informed that the court has suspended action pending proceedings to ascertain the relations of the principal officers of the bank to the transactions in question The bank examiner, during his examination, stated that this was the first case arising under the law in which proceedings had been instituted I feel the delicacy of my position in having to pass upon the questions involved in the absence of any adjudication It appears that the defendants, Evans and Timpson, had no knowledge of these transactions with reference to Cecil, Ward & Co, and it had been suggested in the course of this examination that they be regarded as practically out of the investigation The statute reads, "Any officer, clerk, or agent who shall," etc The clerks did not adopt the plan of accepting checks in lieu of certifying What part the cashier may have had in the adoption of it remains to be seen I do not regard him as necessarily the guilty party or the only offender simply because he carried out the instructions of the bank or its policy The device which constitutes this evasion need not to have originated on the day in question when it resulted in the violation of the law The cause, the device, may have originated long prior I shall surely hold those who caused the violation From the evidence before me I can not avoid the conviction that the model of accepting was resorted to purposely to avoid the law, in other words, that they might in this way give customers credit beyond the amount of their deposit, that is exactly what the law forbids by certified checks, and it forbids it also by resorting to a device to accomplish it otherwise That the law has been violated I have no doubt Whom of the defendants should be adjudged the guilty party, and whether one or more is for the court to determine and not for me to say. I have come to the conclusion to hold all the defendants, that all questions presented by this case may be fully heard and determined by the court.

The reports to Congress of my predecessor, the Hon. John Jay Knox, for the years 1882 and 1883, contained full information in regard to the certification of checks, legal and illegal, and enumerated the numerous ways there were of evading a technical violation of the law. At the same time a history of the growth of the practice of certifying checks was given. Certification was in use as a method of business for more than thirty years previous to the organization of the national banking system and at least twenty years previous to the establishment of the clearing house It is the province of the office of the Comptroller of the Currency to call the attention of the proper officers of the Government to evidence by which violations of law may be punished In regard to over-certification of checks, unless they result in loss, it is almost impossible to obtain evidence which will convict the offenders The examiner can not be in the bank at all times. He must depend for his knowledge of its business upon an examination of its books and accounts and the general conduct of its business while he is making his examination In any case of certification, where no loss is encountered, the books at the close of the day, as a rule, show deposits equal to or greater than the checks drawn In the case of the Wall Street National Bank a loss occurred by which the violation of the law was made apparent, and proceedings were commenced In the case of the Marine National Bank, the Comptroller judges from the information on file that there is good evidence of over-certification, and, as has been seen, action has already been taken by the United States district attorney. It has been stated to the Comptroller that on the day of the suspension of the Metropolitan National Bank many of the brokers engaged in business on Wall street, in New York, were very indignant at the national banks because they would not overcertify their checks and in this way lend their credit to afford the brokers relief in the emergency. It is the opinion of the Comptroller that since the passage of the act of July 12, 1882, the officers of the national banks of New York have given the matter of certification of checks their serious attention, and that they have endeavored to diminish the dangerous features of this method of doing business

After the passage of the act of July 12, 1882, my predecessor suggested the establishment of a stock clearing house to enable the brokers to make their settlements without calling upon the banks to certify their checks for the purpose of clearing their stocks. This matter has received careful consideration by the brokers and bankers of New York No plan has yet been suggested, however, which has seemed to meet the peculiar requirements of the stock-exchange business in New York The Comptroller hopes that the recent troubles growing out of Wall street speculations will force the bankers and brokers of New York, for their own protection, to agree upon a stock clearing-house system, and he believes that the present is an excellent time for the conservative bankers in the city of New York to make a move in this matter.

The Comptroller believes, however, that overcertification of checks, viz, the certification of checks as "good" when no funds are to the credit of the drawer of the checks, is not only practiced for the accommodation of the brokers who deal in stocks, but is also done for the accommodation of the dealers in produce These dealers often require large temporary accommodations of money to take up bills of lading for produce which has been shipped to them from the interior, and which they desire to take from cars and warehouses for shipment abroad, and some accommodation is necessary in the interim until the ocean bills of lading can be obtained and exchange drawn against the consignment While this practice is reprehensible and is not legitimate as a banking transaction, business has been and is carried on in this manner, and the fact that the national banks of the city of New York are endeavoring to comply with the law in regard to illegal certification of checks has caused many dealers in produce to withdraw their accounts from the national banking associations and has largely increased the business of certain of the state banks, which are under no restrictions of law in this matter This is particularly noticeable in the case of the bank which was organized under the auspices of the New York Produce Exchange

BANK EXAMINATIONS

The recent financial disturbances throughout the country, and the consequent failures of national and state banks, have called the attention of the public to the official examination of banks as conducted under the authority of the national-bank act, and under various state laws.

The national-bank act provides for the issue and regulation of a national currency secured by United States bonds, and provides, also, for a banking system, in order to facilitate the issue of this circulation. It contains provisions bestowing certain privileges upon the banks organized under it, and provides many safeguards for the public by imposing on these banks such restrictions as the history of banking throughout the world has seemed to indicate were of a character to create a safe and permanent banking system. This law has been amended and improved from time to time, but it is not supposed that the national banking system is absolutely perfect, nor that imprudent banking under it can be altogether prevented.

In order to enable him to ascertain if the provisions of the law are followed, section 5240, Revised Statutes, authorizes the Comptroller to appoint suitable persons to make an examination of the affairs of every national banking association It has been customary from the establishment of the system to have a regularly appointed examiner visit each national bank at least once a year, in many cases twice a year, and when deemed necessary, even more frequently. The examination of national banks is conducted by the examiners in accordance with instructions issued from this office, which instructions, both general and specific, have grown with the growth of the system The first general instructions to examiners were issued September 15, 1864, by the Hon Hugh McCulloch, then Comptroller of the Currency, and as the bank act has been amended and revised these instructions have been altered as circumstances seemed to warrant It has been the aim of the Comptroller to increase the efficiency of the examinations by carefully noting the causes that have in particular cases led to the suspension or failure of national banks, and calling the attention of the examiners to these causes, suggesting such methods of examination as seemed to be best calculated to prevent repetition of such disasters, and to expose violations of law which led to the same.

This official inquiry into the affairs of a national bank does not end with the mere inspection of the cash, bills receivable, books, and accounts of the association, but the examiners are instructed to closely scrutinize the business of the bank, to investigate the standing and fitness for their positions of the persons to whom the management of the affairs of the association are intrusted, and the manner in which the business is usually conducted, whether prudently or otherwise, to ascertain as far as possible the character of the loans and discounts of the bank and what losses, if any, have been or are likely to be sustained.

The examiner is also instructed to ascertain how frequently the board of directors meet together to consult in relation to the affairs of the bank, and to discover, if possible, any malfeasance in office or willful neglect of business on the part of the management, and is, moreover, particularly instructed to report to the Comptroller whether any excessive accommodations are granted in violation of section 5200, Revised Statutes, and to note if the officers of the bank are borrowing largely from the association, to ascertain the customary state of the lawful money reserve by examining the daily statements from some time previous to the examination, whether or not the bank borrows money to loan again, and in short, to discover and report to this office all violations of law of whatever character

Upon receipt of the report at this office all matters above mentioned, and such others as may be referred to therein, are carefully reviewed and considered, and the directors of the bank are immediately notified of all violations of the law, and they are required to have the same promptly corrected The attention of the directory is also specially called to the reform of such matters as are deemed detrimental to the safety and welfare of the association

The general public do not understand the amount of labor performed weekly, monthly, and yearly by the examiners of national banks, many of whom have for years rendered most excellent service It can hardly be expected, however, with the limited compensation allowed by law for making these examinations, that the Comptroller can in all cases retain the services of the most expert accountants, although by systematic division of the labor he has endeavored to obtain the best results possible under the circumstances [a]

For the purposes of bank examination the United States is apportioned into 25 districts, bank examiners being

[a] It is submitted that the compensation allowed national-bank examiners by section 5240, Revised Statutes, is often insufficient The assessments upon the banks, by which the law provides that the examiners' fees shall be paid, are based upon the capital of the national banks examined, and vary, according to capital, from $20 to $75 In many instances the capital is not the proper basis upon which to compute the compensation of national-bank examiners, as many banks with a comparatively small capital have large lines of deposits, and consequently do a much larger business and require more time and labor from the examiner than other associations with the same capital The Comptroller is of the opinion that the fees paid to national-bank examiners should be based upon the capital and average deposits of the national banking association

stationed in each district. Important reserve cities, such as New York and Boston, generally form a district of themselves, and the duties of the examiner stationed there are usually confined to that city and its immediate vicinity. Owing to the nature of the work, the position of a national-bank examiner is one of great responsibility Notwithstanding this vigilance, the most competent examiners are liable to be deceived, and sometimes find it impossible to discover and remedy in time even gross mismanagement of the affairs of national banks.

No laws or system of examinations will prevent dishonest men from keeping false accounts and rendering untrue statements, and by means of these and other devices they can conceal from the examiner the fact that they are using the money intrusted to their charge in private speculations until final disaster makes longer disguise impossible. It is thus exceedingly difficult to detect violations of law or misuse of the funds of a bank.

The surest preventive is to have an honest, active, and competent board of directors A rogue or a dishonest man who acquires the confidence of his associates to such an extent that he can appropriate the funds of a bank for his own use without their knowledge or that of the board of directors, can have but little trouble in deceiving the examiner and hiding his peculations from him

In times of financial disaster and of a stringent money market the acts of dishonest and corrupt officials in any bank or banking firm or private corporation are more liable to be discovered, and naturally during the past year the consequences of disastrous speculation, which

6158—10——24

had been for a long period carried on with impunity with the aid of misappropriated funds, have been brought to the surface. Men who were supposed to be worthy of the entire confidence of communities, whose character stood so high that they were intrusted not only with the management of corporations, but with the investment of private funds, have now been proven to have dishonestly betrayed their trust. Never were the instances of this kind more numerous than during the financial troubles of the present year

Such practices and the resulting disasters, however, do not prove that the national banking laws are inefficient, or that the national-bank examiners do not do their duty They rather indicate that the shareholders of joint-stock corporations of all kinds, and particularly those of banks, should be more careful to elect men as directors and trustees who are competent and who will exercise proper care and supervision over the management of the affairs intrusted to them, who will select competent and honest officers, provide suitable rules and regulations for the conduct of the bank, keeping its accounts, etc., and appoint regular committees of examination, whose duty it shall be not only to verify the accounts but to keep a watchful eye over the affairs of the association and the officers who immediately carry them on

The public frequently draw wrong deductions as to the responsibility of the Government and the bank examiners in particular cases For instance, in many cases where failures occur the principal cause is found in the character of the loans made, which are either excessive or made on improper security. There are 2,671 national banks in the country The loans and discounts of the banks at the close of business September 30 aggregated more than $1,240,000,000, and it is of course not the province of the bank examiners to supervise the making of these loans Section 5200, Revised Statutes, provides that no loans shall be made to any one individual, firm, or corporation in amount exceeding one-tenth of the paid-in capital of a bank, but there are many ways of evading this law, and it is a physical impossibility for the Government to maintain the constant espionage over the affairs of the national banks which alone would prevent the violation of this statute Any attempt to direct the making of loans and to dictate to the directors and managers of the national banks throughout the country as to what use they shall make of their funds would of course be impracticable

Many instances occur daily, which are not seen or known to the general public, where the banks are notified of violations of law, and where their condition is improved by action upon the reports of the examiner When, however, some unexpected failure occurs, brought about by injudicious banking, bad management, or adventurous speculation, or by dishonesty and fraud on the part of the officers or directors, who are the very men to whom the examiner must more or less look for information, the Government and the national banking laws are unjustly criticised. The fault is not with the law and not with the examiner, on whose reports the directors have very likely been notified and warned to exercise more care in the management of their affairs and to hold their officers in check.

A national bank being a joint stock association, its aggregation of capital having been brought together by bankers or other persons for the purpose of utilizing more effectually the resources of the locality in which it is doing business, it is not the intention of the bank act to interfere with the business of said association so long as it is conducted in accordance with the law. The exact line at which the Government shall interfere and the point at which government discipline shall commence is a matter of some delicacy to determine. It is exceedingly difficult to add materially to the restrictions of the national-bank act without such an interference with the business of the banks as would be practically prohibitory, for it is well known that banking can be carried on under the laws of most of the States of the Union with but very little interference and scarcely any espionage on the part of the officials of the state government. It is because the national banking system has raised the standard of banking, and because it is generally understood that money deposited with a national bank is as a rule much safer than in institutions not under similar restrictions, that bankers and capitalists avail themselves of the national-bank act in order to gain the confidence and thereby the deposits and business of the public

The act appears to contain ample provisions for the punishment of criminal offenders, and the Comptroller is of the opinion that it is not so much the lack of law as it is the difficulty of detection of offenders and of obtaining sufficient evidence to convict that has prevented the punishment of officers and others connected with the national banks who have violated the criminal sections of this act. In some cases the directors and shareholders of banks have apparently suppressed information and evidence, and in many instances it has been with great difficulty that the Comptroller was able to present the necessary facts to the Department of Justice to make a case. For obvious reasons the number of instances in which this office has endeavored to secure the arrest and conviction of offenders by reporting to the proper officers of the law facts that came to the knowledge of the Comptroller which seemed to indicate certain violations of law can not be presented, but it is believed that the records of the various State and United States courts show a larger number of indictments and of convictions for violations of the national-bank act than is generally known to the public

It is possible that the provisions of the act relating to the punishment of offenders in the matter of false oaths of officers of banks with intention of deceiving the Comptroller as to the correctness of reports might be profitably amended. The Comptroller is of the opinion that if the criminal provisions of the bank act are to be amended, the Department of Justice of the United States should be consulted for suggestions as to any weakness or defect in the existing law.

INTEREST ON DEPOSITS.[a]

The practice of paying interest on deposits by the national banks has been the subject of discussion for some time past It is the custom of the country banks to pay interest on current accounts and also to issue certificates

[a] Report of the Comptroller of the Currency, 1884, pp 57–59.

of deposit bearing interest, which latter usually state upon their face that no interest will be paid for three, six, nine, or twelve months, as the case may be.

Banks located in the cities where a portion of the lawful money reserve of the country banks may legally be kept have been for many years in the habit of paying interest upon the daily balances of the accounts of their country depositors Owing to the fact that the banks in the reserve cities other than New York keep large current accounts with their correspondents in that city, who in turn pay interest on the average daily balances of their correspondents, the result is that in times of easy money large sums accumulate in the city of New York subject to interest on current account It is believed that this accumulation of money in the New York banks occasioned by this custom has a tendency to encourage speculation in stocks, as these banks are compelled to find some use for the money deposited with them on which they are in turn compelled to pay interest, and as this money is liable to be called for at any time it is necessary to make loans payable on demand, and dealers in stocks called on the stock exchange, which theoretically can be readily sold at any time, are in consequence enabled to obtain money for speculation by pledging these securities as collateral and agreeing to repay the sum advanced on demand The panic of 1873 and the financial troubles of May, 1884, have shown that these so-called "demand" loans are of such a character that the banks are not always able to realize upon them in case of emergency. The members of the New York Clearing House Association after the panic of 1873 discussed the abolition of the payment of interest upon current accounts Again, upon the 4th of June, 1884, the association endeavored to have its members agree to discontinue the payment of interest on daily balances, but owing to the persistent dissent of a few members the association was unable to make the arrangement.

While the united action of the Clearing House Association in favor of the abolition of the payment of interest on deposits would doubtless have great effect, yet so long as it is the almost universal custom of banks, state and national, and of private bankers throughout the country, to pay such interest it is probable that if the associated banks shall discontinue the practice they would do so to their own great detriment and loss of business Many of the accounts of country banks and out-of-town correspondents would be transferred to the trust companies, state banks, and private bankers who are not members of the association and who would not be bound by its regulations, and for this and other reasons it seems very difficult to bring about an absolute cessation of the practice Until all the bankers in the principal cities of the country agree to discontinue the payment of interest it is probable that it will continue to be paid upon current accounts

It has been held by the courts that the conferring of special powers upon national banking associations prohibited them from the exercise of certain other powers not specifically conferred, and the decisions of the United States courts seem to indicate that it is unlawful for a national bank to borrow money to lend again, or to receive deposits payable at fixed future dates with interest thereon.

Notwithstanding the fact that it has been held that national banks could not receive deposits payable otherwise than on demand, it is possible that in view of the fact that the custom of purchasing deposits by the payment of interest is so universal the courts might hold that national banks would have the same rights as other bankers to receive deposits subject to repayment upon a notice of from five to thirty days, and if this should be the case it is submitted that they should pay interest only upon deposits of this character, for there can be no doubt that it is extremely injudicious to receive current accounts payable on demand subject to interest. It would appear that if this course was adopted two classes of accounts would have to be maintained with most of the country correspondents of national banks in reserve cities, as it would be impracticable for a national bank in the interior to have any portion of its reserve deposited in such a manner that it could not be drawn upon demand In view of the facts as stated, it is doubtful if any legislation upon this matter should be had which would discriminate against the national banks.

NOTE D

BANKING REFORM PROPOSALS IN NEW YORK IN 1884.

A.—ADDRESS OF GEORGE S. COE.[a]

At a meeting of the New York Clearing House Association, held on Wednesday, June 4, 1884, E. H. Perkins, Jr., Esq., chairman, presiding, the following resolution was unanimously adopted, viz.

Resolved, That the experience of the associated banks in the New York clearing house during the recent panic, having again shown that every member of the association, in a time of general and serious financial disturbance, is involuntarily compelled to make common cause with every other member in the risks attending any practical expedient for general relief, or of any effective combination for the public good, it is therefore proper and necessary to enquire whether the methods of business, as conducted by the several members of this association, are uniform and correct in their operation with the public, and equitable to all the banks which are thus bound together in the Clearing House Association.

Mr. George S. Coe, president of the American Exchange National Bank, in presenting this resolution, made substantially the following remarks, which were ordered to be printed for the use of the members.

MR. CHAIRMAN: In offering this resolution, I may at first warmly congratulate this association and the country at large, upon the great good which has been accomplished in the recent financial crisis by means of the organized power of this combination of banks.

After the failure of the Marine Bank, followed as it was so soon, by the announcement of the startling events connected with the Second National, the whole community was stirred to its depths with excitement and apprehension, fearing every form of financial disaster. The reputation before enjoyed by these institutions and the eminence of some of the men directly and indirectly involved in their failure were such that faith in human character was for the moment almost destroyed.

---

[a] Bankers' Magazine, July, 1884, pp. 44–51.

As bank officers, we were called here together suddenly by the promptness of our friend Mr Tappen, and unanimously decided to reestablish our clearing-house expedient for the issue of loan certificates, which had proved so effective in former great public exigencies, and we appointed a committee of safety to provide for any new event that might occur Immediately after that meeting the suspension of the Metropolitan National Bank was reported, which added still greater intensity to the already inflamed condition of the public feeling

Under these circumstances the clearing-house committee were summoned together at midnight to examine the condition of that institution and to decide what action should be taken respecting it A fearful responsibility was thus hastily thrown upon that committee It was impossible in a few short hours, and in the apprehension of further possible events, to reach a definite conclusion upon the value of the large and diversified assets of that bank When we examined its books, this most important fact at once appeared That it owed some eight to nine millions of deposits, a large proportion of which consisted of the reserves of interior banks, which could not be imperiled or locked up for another day without producing a further calamity of widespread dimensions throughout the country It was also evident that the consequent certain suspension of many banks in the interior cities would occur, and be followed by the suspension of business men depending upon them, and by heavy drafts upon those banks which held similar deposit reserves, and that the immediate danger to our city institutions was great, just in proportion to the extent of such liabilities and to the amount that each bank was expanded relatively to its immediate cash in hand That, should the threatened wild excitement pervade the country, a general suspension of banks, bankers, and merchants was inevitable, and in such case the magnitude of the loss to every institution would be incalculable

The committee therefore came to the unanimous conclusion that it was better to confront the risk of losing one or two millions, if need be, by taking possession of the total assets of that bank, and by paying off its depositors, rather than by waiting to incur the hazard of an indefinite and greater loss, by a general financial and commercial derangement throughout the country, and that it was their manifest duty to promptly accept this grave responsibility, confidently relying upon their associates for approval and support On behalf of the combined capital and surplus of the banks in this association, amounting to about a hundred millions, and also to protect the property and assets held by them together, of more than three hundred millions, your committee unhesitatingly acted, and thus saved the nation from immeasurable calamity The Metropolitan Bank was, obviously the key to the whole situation When this decision was announced the next morning, confidence was instantly restored and business resumed its even tenor Seven-eighths of the deposits of the Metropolitan Bank have already been paid off Its many shareholders have been saved from threatened personal responsibility, and time is gained in which its large property may be more deliberately converted into money The restoration of confidence was as sudden as was its loss, so sudden, indeed, that the immensity of the danger can now hardly be appreciated

I rapidly review these important events, Mr Chairman, because they have once more illustrated the power and importance of this voluntary association, and have also shown how the several members comprising it are mutually dependent upon it and upon each other in any great emergency for the safety and stability of their own banks

It must be borne in mind that the banks in New York, holding as they do the reserves of other institutions and of bankers in this city, and also of banks and bankers throughout the country, and standing between home and foreign commerce, are the last resort of this whole nation for cash reserves, and that a financial disturbance or distrust in any part of the land is sure to bring upon them a greater or less demand Acting singly and alone, what could each one of sixty or seventy independent institutions have done to stem the tide, which, in such an unnatural and simultaneous call for money from every quarter of an alarmed nation, must have swept over them? No time was allowed to any bank to gather in its loaned resources, and no power on earth could so suddenly respond to a demand that—not any natural commercial want, but—general demoralization and wild panic alone had so unexpectedly created It is perfectly apparent that without this combined support each bank would have been not only powerless in itself but the occasion of peril to others It was only because we were thus associated and had in hand the printed forms and instruments provided in past experience that we were able at the tap of the drum instantly to fall into line and present an unbroken front and a disciplined force to this formidable enemy Our numbers, now no longer a weakness, were thus converted into the greatest strength, and we were able easily to carry away this heavy and disabled member, and to relieve its creditors, shareholders, and friends from the danger of utter destruction, and also to arrest the panic so rapidly spreading I think the association may well feel proud of this achievement, which for promptness, efficiency, and breadth of influence has no superior in the annals of commerce

Now, the association being of such importance and the connection with it of each member being of this peculiar character, how can any honorable gentleman among our number claim the right to selfishly pursue his business in utter disregard of these delicate relations by which the association itself is sustained and the business of the nation is safely conducted? We are in a most important sense directly responsible for each other and can not avoid being disturbed by the ignorance, selfishness, or immoral conduct of our most remote members

Crises will arise in the future as in the past, and it is not only just but necessary that we adopt such safe and uniform methods of business as experience has approved, that we clearly understand what those methods are, and freely invite from each other the utmost scrutiny in their observance In the light of recent experience, it seems no longer credible or possible that an intelligent body of men, composing an association of such dignity and importance as this, can deliberately consent to remain responsible partners in times of peril with those who are eager competitors and antagonists in days of prosperity The burdens, responsibilities, and profits of this great trust ought to be shared together upon recognized and uniform conditions, with special reference to the public welfare, and the only basis of competition for such business should consist in superior character, fidelity, and intelligence in its management Thus can this association become one homogeneous body, composed of many members, like the Government under which we live, and capable of efficiently performing the highest duties, such as single financial institutions—conformably to their political constitution—in older countries, render to commerce, in being the safest custodians, and the ultimate resort of the money reserves of the people

The issue of loan certificates, although practically equivalent to a supplemental issue of currency, exclusively for local uses between the members of the association, are only, in fact, convenient instruments by which the bills receivable and negotiable securities belonging to one bank are readily transferred to another, in exchange and as a substitute for its ready money, thus covering the weaker by the stronger, and, in fact, by all the other banks in the association during a time of common peril For the time being, these certificates form a connecting medium between the banks, by which they all substantially become one in power, through the ebb and flow of the vital elements which compose them, and by which their total money in hand is made available at any special point of danger In one sense our action was outside of law In fact, the law could never anticipate such experience, nor establish a union so effective, and any legislation to enforce such generous and voluntary cooperation would only prevent it The occasion was sudden and momentous, and the banks proved equal to the occasion. It was the same after the panic of 1857, when, as state institutions, our similar organization first originated Also in 1861, after the battle of Bull Run, when with our colleagues in Boston and Philadelphia we united and furnished the Government from week to week in its greatest extremity a total of $150,000,000 in gold Likewise in 1873, when the country was again convulsed by financial trouble In all these great financial disturbances—each one like the present, but originating from a different cause—the beneficent influence and power of this association were fully illustrated, and some of us now present can bear testimony to the fact that several banks here represented owe their continued existence to the protection afforded them upon one or another of those important occasions

I appeal to you members of the association to give this subject the most serious consideration We are responsible not alone to our directors and stockholders Our responsibility takes a far wider range. Like the

Bank of England in the British financial system, the banks composing the New York Clearing House Association are the final reservoirs of the cash reserve of the nation and its refuge in commercial commotion Every one of the thousands of banks and bankers throughout the land has intimate financial relations with us, and all the multitudes who depend upon them are thus indirectly concerned in the stability and safety of our methods of daily business Every added facility of communication or of commerce only tends more closely to unite us to them and ourselves to each other The very conditions of modern life compel us to be more and more mutually dependent

There are three special abuses to which I desire for a moment to call your attention

First The payment of interest upon deposits of money payable on demand This subject has upon several occasions in years past been under consideration, and its total abolition has been almost unanimously agreed to among our banks by written contract Yet by the refusal of one or more members it has failed to become a binding obligation Like some other great reforms, this one does not admit of partial application or of compromise Any attempt to make exceptions to the prohibition among partners mutually dependent can only result in entirely releasing them all from any obligation respecting it Yet every banker will freely admit that the purchase of deposits payable on demand operates, in some degree, as an absolution of the obligation to be always in condition to meet the contract Both the giver and receiver of interest on such deposits, by the nature of the business, substantially, though not expressly, agree to such use of the money as may prevent its immediate return

What, Mr. Chairman, is the nature of bank deposits? Every responsible person in regulating his own affairs must withhold from permanent investment and keep in ready money enough for his current wants This is his reserve. When such sums, for greater safety, are placed in charge of another person, they do not lose their essential character, and when they become further aggregated and pass into the possession of a bank or banker they are still subject to the same immediate wants of every original owner for the very purpose for which he set them aside And when these rivulets of capital become streams, and streams gather into rivers and flow toward the ocean until they reach this city, where they come into financial relations with other men in other continents, the parties who here take them in charge assume new and accumulated responsibilities They are subject not only to the necessities of the people at home but also to the world-wide influences of commerce

Now, there is a constant and irrepressible conflict going on in the mind of every intelligent man or woman between the desire to invest their own capital so that it may earn them the utmost revenue and the necessity of retaining enough of it in ready cash to meet their current necessities. This question decided, each for himself, that portion of the total which is thus reserved becomes charged with peculiar functions It is the national reserve, and the chief cause of financial disturbances arises from trespassing upon it

Is it not evident, Mr Chairman, that when these reserves are attracted by banks and bankers who pay interest for them, they immediately lose their peculiar character and become, so far, at once changed from reserves into investments, and that their original purpose is greatly reversed? The people's ready cash by the very condition of receiving interest for it, necessarily passes through the banker into fixed forms never intended Reserve and investment! Idleness and work! They are adverse and irreconcilable conditions It is true that in the hands of sound commercial banks some of these deposit funds may be legitimately used for the best interests of society, in the negotiation of business notes representing articles of human want and subsistence, passing from production into consumption This is using the fund by promoting the very object for which each person originally provided it But such, we all know, is not the tendency nor the operation of the practice now in question Money payable on demand with interest is chiefly loaned here upon fixed property intended for permanent investment and upon bonds, stocks, and other obligations made for the construction of public enterprises and works of established purpose, whose large expenditures are not again resolvable into money They are in their nature fixed, and they demand, not their ready cash reserve, but the permanent savings of the people to construct them So that temporary loans of reserved capital upon such securities are certain to be called in when they are hardest to pay, because the ready-money reserves so injudiciously absorbed by them are called back by their owners in apprehension or for the supply of their own needs

We all know by experience that those deposits upon which interest is paid are the most fugitive and evanescent of all Those who placed them with us well understand their danger While they receive interest, they do so with doubt and suspicion of those who allow it, and with the consciousness that they themselves are partially compromising principle in placing them with those who are willing to pay the price

From the very start the vicious practice of paying interest for the custody of the people's cash reserves pursues such funds like an enemy from place to place and impairs their integrity at every point And when those deposits have at last concentrated in New York banks, the same evil overtakes them there, all tending to the reduction of tangible cash assets to the lowest point, and to the weakness and impoverishment of the whole country Arrest this practice here, at the termination of the line, and the reform will, of necessity, run back through every link of the chain in other cities, adding strength to the whole to the incalculable benefit of the nation Every institution that accepts the reserves of the community, agreeing to return them upon instant demand, gives a full equivalent in their faithful care It is in duty bound to retain so large proportion of such deposits, in actual cash, that no other compensation can be safely allowed Any such payment should be taken at once as a confession that the fund is to be used in some manner inconsistent with its real nature and is to be placed more or less in peril Deposits so unnaturally attracted are necessarily capricious and transitory They fly away at the first whisper of danger, to the detriment of the many who have touched them Those banks which so purchase them are objects of special dread to their colleagues in business, while at the same time they are continually held up as patterns of enterprise and as models for imitation Differing so widely from their associates in principle and in practice the two can not work harmoniously together, nor equally and honorably share the burdens of a national financial system, whose stability requires the New York banks voluntarily to stand firmly and compactly together as one united body.

Experience among ourselves has again and again proved that the interest-paying banks are the first to become embarrassed by any kind of financial disturbance, even if they themselves are not the means of producing it, and that they are then almost alone in being compelled to seek protection from the loan committee, by a pledge of their securities

Will a few members of this association, on the one hand, longer continue a practice that subjects them to this humiliation? And is it just, on the other, for a large majority to tacitly submit to having their business thus drawn away, and the community periodically disturbed by associates whom, in the hour of peril, they are compelled for their own protection to support?

There is no necessity whatever, as there is certainly no profit, for the banks in the New York Clearing House, to continue this practice Public safety, business convenience, and social needs all absolutely require the service which these banks perform The commanding position of this metropolis will constantly bring to it all the capital that healthful commerce and trade can safely employ and any fictitious attractions only tend to false estimates of wealth, and betray the community into unprofitable and dangerous enterprises

If the banks composing this body should unanimously agree to totally abolish this practice, the business of each would not seriously diminish, because no dealer could secure better terms by changing from one member to another, and even if, in the course of time, the disparity between the banks in deposits should consequently not continue as great as now, the loss by any one in volume would be more than compensated by a gain in terms, and by diminished risk, labor, and expenses

Taken as a whole, whatever the banks composing this association pay to their dealers and correspondents as interest is a totally unnecessary and gratuitous payment It is worse than money thrown away, so far as, and because, it tends to divert the current of capital of the country from its natural flow If it be expedient for one member to practice it, it is expedient for all, and then the special and selfish advantage to any single one is lost If it should be continued after our recent experience, it must be distinctly recognized as a defect in our financial system, and a standing cause of contention and of sharper competition among banks in their pursuit of public favor, which must separate the two classes of institutions into known and irreconcilable divisions

In the business indirectly done through the New York Clearing House there enters another element which it is also proper for us to consider as affecting the stability of the whole system The trust companies and other depositories of funds, very much of which are payable on demand and bear interest, are receiving the full benefit of this association through the medium of one or another of our members, and so they successfully compete with us all They thus secure every facility of exchanging their checks with all the banks, and are by that means enabled to divert to themselves a large proportion of the current deposits of the city and country, which have always been regarded as a special function of banking institutions. Instead of being trust companies in the real meaning of the term, many of them are banks of deposit, paying interest This large volume of deposits is not only in much greater ratio to capital than are the deposits in banks, but it is supported by no special cash reserve of its own whatever The only ready means it has consist in keeping current balances at credit in banks like other dealers It thus leans upon the same reserve as do the banks themselves If such institutions are to enjoy the privileges of the clearing house, they should certainly at least bear the same burdens which rest upon its members, and also contribute their full share of the reserve funds in cash, by which the stability of the business is maintained By a strange generosity on the part of the Clearing House Association, it enables these lively competitors to do their business with the public upon better terms than they can do their own, while they do not contribute to the public safety

Second Another abuse to which I invite your attention is that of receiving and crediting to dealers, as cash in hand, checks drawn upon banks out of the city The aggregate amount of such checks in progress of collection by all the members of this body is not less than ten millions, and may average fifteen or twenty millions

These checks can not be converted into cash here in less time than one week, and for that period they remain as dead assets to the banks How did this absurd practice arise? Simply by the eagerness of one bank to draw to itself the business of others by superior inducements, an advantage which, in the nature of the case, could be but temporary Others, in self-defense, were necessarily compelled to follow the pernicious example, until the practice became general But for this practice this large sum would naturally lie as deposits in New York banks from their correspondents throughout the country, held here for the purposes of exchange They are not expelled from their natural commercial resting place, and their true position is actually reversed

Third There is still another subject of solicitude with which we are all daily familiar I allude to the reception of checks of large amounts, drawn upon banks which particularly deal with brokers and operators in bonds and stocks The sums represented in such transactions by the nature of the business are of great magnitude The custom has become established of pivoting the operations of the brokers' board through the banks by expressing and accounting for their money value in detail, thus making it necessary to draw upon banks the immense total that is passed from hand to hand They give rise to checks in sums greatly disproportioned to the capital of banks which keep such accounts, and are the occasion of constant embarrassment to bank officers, who desire to treat their associates in the clearing house and their own dealers with generous confidence, and mean at the same time to avoid extraordinary risks. The effort has been partially made to conduct this business by a clearing house arrangement where shares, not money or checks, and only balances resulting from them are thus paid, and it is the earnest desire of bank officers that this effort should be accomplished I believe that the experiment, if seriously attempted, can be made successful to the satisfaction of brokers, the relief and safety of the banks, and the good of the community.

The present mode of conducting the transactions of the stock exchange adds enormously, and I believe unnecessarily, to the daily volume of business in the clearing house, increases the risks of the exchanges between banks, and expresses a false idea of the commerce of the country

These, Mr Chairman, are three most important reforms Their adoption will remove all cause of alienation and distrust between the banks and members of our fraternity, will unite us together for greater efficiency and mutual protection in doing the public business, and will make the Clearing House Association a power for good and a tower of strength in the nation

Our country needs a reliable, ultimate financial resource in time of trouble, such as every other commercial nation in the world enjoys Here it may be secured, without the danger which is always apprehended from any single colossal institution Each one acting independently, yet all restrained by honorable agreement, the 60 or 70 banks composing this association already possess the power to supply, if they will, this long-felt defect in the American commercial system, and that, too, not by any deliberately formed legal or corporate organization, more complete than we now possess, but by the simple voluntary adherence to sound and self-evident principles of business, using our freedom to do right These considerations must appeal to every man of common justice and common sense I present them to you now in the belief that the peculiar circumstances which have called us together will secure for them the most serious attention and cordial assent

After further discussion, the resolution offered by Mr Coe was unanimously adopted and referred to a committee of five members to consider and report to the association

The chairman subsequently appointed the following as that committee, viz: George S. Coe, president American Exchange National Bank, George H. Potts, president National Park Bank; O. D. Baldwin, president Fourth National Bank; John J. Knox, president National Bank of the Republic; R. L. Edwards, president Bank State of New York.

B—Report of the Committee of the New York Clearing House Association [a]

The committee appointed by the New York Clearing House Association on June 4 "to recommend such reforms in the practices of the associated banks as would render their business safer to the public and more equitable to each other," having made report, was increased at a subsequent meeting of the association by three new members and requested to consider further the whole subject.

At a meeting of the association held on July 29 the following report was presented

That while they substantially concur in the recommendations of the committee in its previous report, they have endeavored to remove some of the objections made during the discussion, so as to secure what they consider very desirable—a cordial and unanimous adoption of these reforms by the whole association

The most important and, in fact, the special reform which is essential to the efficient and harmonious union and cooperation of the banks in one association is the total abolition of the payment of interest upon current deposits

This reform has been urged upon the banks from time to time for more than twenty-five years and it has always received the most favorable consideration Upon two special occasions after violent financial revulsions throughout the country, like the present, it was adopted by almost unanimous agreement, and in each instance it failed of becoming a binding obligation only by the dissent of two or three members whose active opposition was unfortunately permitted to defeat the wishes of the very large majority

Your committee believe that the careful custody of money held in such a manner as to be always responsive to call is itself sufficient compensation

[a] Bankers' Magazine, August, 1884, pp 129–33

to its owners and depositors, and that banks which carry their full proportion of the reserve cash of the nation and at the same time preserve their assets in legitimate commercial securities render a just equivalent and furnish a perfect guarantee for the trust committed to their care; and that any further consideration or compensation than this must be given either at the expense of the needful reserve or of the safety of the investments The proportion of cash to deposits, which from long experience conservative institutions in national commercial centers find it expedient to hold, is at least from one-quarter to one-third the amount. It must be evident that at the average rate of interest this ratio can not be maintained by any bank where compensation is given for its deposits.

The responsible duty of holding and maintaining the ultimate cash reserve of this great nation is especially imposed upon the associated banks in New York, and from doing its full part of this imperative duty no one can honorably escape They are all so inextricably bound together by the daily transfer of portions of the nation's deposits from one bank to another, by the difficulty of recovering checks upon defaulting members after they pass through the clearing house, by the universal distrust which one failing institution casts upon its associates, and by the urgent demand made upon the stronger in time of trouble to combine their resources for the protection of the weaker to avert public disaster, that an identity of interest is created by the very existence and necessities of this association This organization can therefore no longer be regarded as a simple place of meeting of bank officers, without responsibility for and utterly independent of and indifferent to each other's welfare and habits of business These banks, as custodians of an interchangeable public trust, have practically and within certain limits become a federative community, with mutual responsibilities and obligations, and it is no less the privilege than the duty of the members to conduct their own business and to scrutinize the practices of others with a view to the stability of this association and the welfare of the nation

This view of the mutual relation of members was fully recognized in the recent action of the association, when they took possession of one of the largest institutions and discharged its liabilities to the public of some eight millions of dollars, and when they further agreed to participate in any loss by the issue of loan certificates to that and to other banks, and also when they so changed the constitution as to permit official visitation and examination into the condition of members, and gave power to demand security for their exchanges

Powers so great and so important as these, which have been exercised and concurred in by every member, are sufficient to show that this association no longer regards itself as a simple meeting place for the exchange of papers, without further responsibility, but that it has become an institution of national significance and value, competent to consider any question vital to its own interests

If the association can thus promptly meet the necessities of a great financial crisis, it may certainly venture to urge upon its members the importance of such reform in their modes of business as they believe will tend to prevent such a crisis, and will enable them the better to meet one if it come

Although this has been the practical experience of the New York Clearing House Association, and although in every great emergency since its organization it has proved itself possessed of vast capacity to benefit the country and protect its own members, yet it must ever be kept in mind that this is simply a voluntary association, subject to dissolution by a vote of the majority, and subject also to the withdrawal of members at their own pleasure From the nature of the business, no bank, however prosperous, is so independent of all circumstances that it may not on some special occasion find it convenient to seek the aid or the consideration of its colleagues A solemn obligation, therefore, rests upon everyone to concede something to the common good. If the measure now proposed should, upon trial, prove erroneous, it may be revoked as readily as it is adopted

With the rapid growth of this nation it is more and more important that this commercial depository be always kept specially strong in cash reserves, and be prepared to meet any sudden exigency that may arise within our vast domain When the intention to do this is distinctly declared by the associated banks, by their abolishing the payment of interest upon deposits and by thus removing a great cause of weakness and of alienation among them, your committee believe that capital will be attracted to this city and to this associated body as a place of special security Thus it has proved with those members who have tried it If a small proportion of the deposits hitherto secured by purchase be consequently drawn away to other institutions within this city, or to other places without it, that which remains will be more permanent and reliable, and will be sufficient to make our business safer and more profitable than before

If it result in the retention of a larger cash reserve by interior banks, or in the withdrawal of those funds which are particularly subject to alarm and which betray the depositaries into questionable temporary loans, it can be no cause of regret to the banks nor to the nation

The present occasion seems to your committee most opportune for this reform The subject has been ripening in this association for more than a quarter of the century The business of the nation requires the financial support which this united and compact body can give it, and the experiment, if it be an experiment, ought now to be fairly and honorably tried

To their special and important recommendation of ceasing to pay interests upon deposits your committee have added but one more, viz

That of confining the use of the clearing house exclusively to its own members

Hitherto the practice of permitting exchanges through members of the association of checks drawn upon parties not members has freely given every facility enjoyed by those who carry the burthens of the banking business to those who do not, and who neither fairly participate it its expense nor in its responsibilities Such parties, therefore, possess advantages superior even to banks who created and who sustain the institution

In order effectually to secure the object of strengthening the association as proposed in the first recommendation of your committee it is manifestly necessary to withhold gratuitous facilities from active outside competitors, who would otherwise use our own appointed instrument to subvert the object we have in view If desired every legitimate depository possessed of the needed requisites and responsibility may find entrance into the clearing house subject to the same conditions and restrictions as are imposed upon existing members More than this can not be justly required, and less will not afford adequate protection

In respect to the subject of receiving upon deposit as cash checks drawn upon places out of the city, your committee have thought it inexpedient now to make special recommendation, but they suggest that a separate and special committee be appointed to investigate this question, and also to advise whether an arrangement could not be made through the clearing house to secure some safe and prompt clearing of such checks, which will accrue to the benefit of all banks in the association

Finally, your committee can not disregard the just complaint of the banks respecting the large volume of checks which arise from transactions in the stock exchange, and which embarrass them in their dealings with each other and greatly increase the risks of the clearing house The committee, however, content themselves by the simple expression of the wish generally entertained among the banks that some arrangement may be made by the parties interested to establish a special clearing house for stocks, so that these large checks may be abated

With these general remarks your committee present the following summary:

First That no member of the New York Clearing House Association shall pay interest upon or allow compensation for deposits after the 1st January, 1885.

Second That to secure uniformity in the business of the banks no checks shall pass through the clearing house except those drawn upon members of the association

Third That any infraction of the above rules shall be regarded as a forfeiture of membership of the association, subject on complaint of any member to investigation by the clearing-house committee, in the manner provided in the constitution

Fourth That the association recommend that some mode of settlement of transactions at the New York Stock Exchange be adopted, whereby the large volume of checks which now pass through the clearing house from that business may be diminished or avoided

Fifth If these measures be adopted by the association, that the committee recommend the same to clearing houses in Boston, Philadelphia, Chicago, and other cities

All of which is respectfully submitted by the committee

GEO S COE,
President American Exchange National Bank.
GEO H POTTS,
President National Park Bank
JOHN JAY KNOX,
President National Bank of the Republic
R L EDWARDS,
President National Bank of the State of New York
JAMES T WOODWARD,
President Hanover National Bank
F A PALMER,
President National Broadway Bank
WM L JENKINS,
President Bank of America

A minority report, dissenting from the above, was as follows·

The undersigned member of the committee appointed June 4, 1884, and continued on July 8 with three members added "to inquire if the methods of business (in respect especially as to payment of interest on deposits and the receiving of checks on out-of-town places as cash) as conducted by the several members of this association are uniform, etc ," begs leave to report as the result of his individual inquiry

First That the vital principle of the business of banks of deposit and discount lies in the gathering together of temporarily idle funds into a center where they can be made useful for the common good, that the payment of interest and negotiation of exchange, drafts, checks, etc , have been among the means employed for this purpose from time almost immemorial by all commercial nations and communities, and that the methods of business as conducted by the members of this association in this respect are substantially uniform, 69 out of 72 banks in this city paying interest and all receiving checks on out-of-town places as cash for deposit

Second That the infinite multiplicity and variety of the combinations and complications which arise in the transactions of the business of a great commercial country and a great commercial city, between banks and their correspondents, the intimate confidential personal relations between banks and their individual customers, make it absolutely necessary that there should be the utmost possible freedom of action between them, that a faithful compliance with our national and state laws will secure perfect safety for all

Third That the total abolition of the payment of interest upon or allowance of any compensation or consideration in any form, directly or indirectly, for deposits, as also the receiving of checks or drafts on other cities as cash by an agreement of this association, would be productive of great and lasting injury to the city of New York, endangering and retarding its commercial prosperity and also to the United States, that such an agreement is impracticable, and if made would be found impossible of enforcement by the association or execution by its individual members

It is therefore respectfully recommended that the further consideration by this association of these matters be indefinitely postponed

Respectfully submitted

O. D BALDWIN,
President Fourth National Bank

NOTE E.

CLEARING-HOUSE LOAN CERTIFICATES IN 1890.[a]

The effect of a general monetary stringency is felt first and most seriously by banks located in the larger of the reserve cities Whenever financial affairs are in a normal condition the surplus funds of the local banks find their way to the vaults of their correspondent banks located in the great centers of business activity. This is undoubtedly due in part to the fact that these deposits may be made available for lawful money reserve and that a small rate of interest is, as a rule, paid upon bank balances by associations in the larger cities, and to the further fact that the maintenance of a good balance with their city correspondents strengthens the claim of the interior banks upon the former for rediscounts when the temporary condition of redundancy passes away and the increased demand for money is greater than the interior banks from their resources can conveniently supply

Thus it results that the wants of a continent in case of general depression are at last brought through various channels of business activity, by way of withdrawals or loans, to the bankers of the great metropolitan cities for relief, and they are presented in such a form, in many cases, as to preclude the possibility of refusal, if general bankruptcy is to be avoided.

During the period of the stringency above discussed the cities of New York, Philadelphia, and Boston were subjected to the most pressing demands, and after very care-

[a] Report of the Comptroller of the Currency, 1891, pp 12–15

ful consideration it was decided by the associated banks that the exigency made necessary a resort to the issuing of clearing-house loan certificates for the purpose of settling clearing-house balances This expedient had been successfully resorted to during the panics of 1873 and 1884.

At a meeting of the New York Clearing House Association on the 11th day of November, 1890, the following resolution was unanimously adopted:

Resolved, That a committee of five be appointed by the chair, of which the chairman shall be one, to receive from banks members of the association bills receivable and other securities, to be approved by said committee, who shall be authorized to issue therefor, to such depositing banks, loan certificates bearing interest at 6 per cent per annum, and in addition thereto a commission of one-quarter of 1 cent for every thirty days such certificates shall remain unpaid, and such loan certificates shall not be in excess of 75 per cent of the market value of the securities or bills receivable so deposited, and such certificates shall be received and paid in settlement of balances at the clearing house

Under this resolution a committee of five was appointed, and they proceeded, upon deposit of proper securities, to issue to applying banks loan certificates in the following form.

No —] [$20,000

LOAN COMMITTEE OF THE
NEW YORK CLEARING HOUSE ASSOCIATION,
New York, , *1890*

This certifies that the has deposited with this committee securities in accordance with the proceedings of a meeting of the association held November 11, 1890, upon which this certificate is issued This certificate will be received in payment of balances at the clearing house for the sum of twenty thousand dollars from any member of the Clearing House Association

On the surrender of this certificate by the depositing bank above named the committee will indorse the amount as a payment on the obligation of said bank held by them and surrender a proportionate share of the collateral securities held therefor

($20,000)

——— ———,
——— ———,
Committee

These certificates were, by unanimous agreement upon the part of the clearing-house banks, accepted in lieu of money in the settlement of clearing-house balances.

In order to provide for the retirement of these securities in case the collaterals pledged were found insufficient, the several boards of directors of the associated banks were requested to, and did, pass a resolution in the following form

Resolved, That any loss resulting from the issue of loan certificates shall be borne by the banks comprising the Clearing House Association pro rata of capital and surplus, and this resolution shall be ratified by the boards of the respective banks members of the association, and a certified copy of such consent delivered to the chairman of the loan committee

This committee, acting under the authority granted by the above resolution, issued to the associated banks loan certificates aggregating $16,645,000. The first issue was made November 12, 1890, and the entire issue was retired on February 7, 1891. The largest amount outstanding at any one time was $15,205,000, on the 13th of December, 1890

On the 17th of November, 1890, similar proceedings were had by the Boston Clearing House Association. On that day, at a meeting of the association, the following resolution was unanimously adopted.

Resolved, That a committee of five be appointed by the chair, of which committee the chairman shall also be a member, to receive from banks members of the association bills receivable and other securities, to be approved by said committee, who shall be authorized to issue therefor, to such depositing banks, loan certificates bearing interest at 7 3 per cent per annum, and such loan certificates shall not be in excess of 75 per cent of the market value of the securities or bills receivable so deposited, and such certificates shall be received and paid in settlement of balances at the clearing house

It is observed also that the ultimate payment of the certificates, in case the pledged collaterals proved to be insufficient, was provided for through the ratification, by the boards of directors of the respective banks, of the following resolution passed by the Boston Clearing House Association at the meeting above noted:

Resolved, That any loss arising from the issue of loan certificates shall be borne by the banks comprising the Clearing House Association pro rata, according to the average daily amount which each bank shall have sent to the clearing house during the preceding year It was also voted that this resolution shall be ratified by the boards of directors of the respective banks members of the association, and a certified copy of such consent delivered to the chairman of the loan committee

When a bank applied for and received loan certificates it was required to deposit the necessary securities and to also execute and deliver an obligation, of which the following is a copy.

The ---------------- Bank has this day received of --------, loan committee of the Boston Clearing House Association, loan certificates issued by said committee in pursuance of a vote of said association, passed November 17, 1890, to the amount of ------ thousand dollars, and has deposited with said committee the securities a statement whereof is hereto annexed, and said ------------ -- Bank receives said loan certificates on the terms set forth in said vote, and agrees to pay the amount of said certificates, with interest thereon, as provided in said vote

Under the operation of the resolution of authority granted by the clearing-house committee, as above noted, loan certificates were first issued on November 19, 1890, and the last were issued on December 6, 1890 On the latter date the issue reached its maximum of $5,065,000. The last of the issue was retired on January 6, 1891.

The Clearing House Association of Philadelphia took action on November 18, 1890, at which time, at a meeting of the Clearing House Association, the following resolution was adopted.

Resolved, That, in accordance with resolution of September 24, 1873, as amended October 18, 1873, the clearing-house committee will issue loan certificates to banks applying, and receive them in payment of balances

The resolution of September 24, 1873, as amended October 18, 1873, reads as follows.

For the purpose of enabling the banks, members of the Philadelphia Clearing House Association, to afford proper assistance to the mercantile and manufacturing community, and also to facilitate the interbank settlements resulting from their daily exchanges, we, the undersigned, do bind ourselves by the following agreement on the part of our respective banks, viz

First That the clearing-house committee be, and they are hereby, authorized to issue to any bank member of the association loan certificates bearing 6 per cent interest on the deposits of bills receivable and other securities to such an amount and to such percentage thereof as may in their judgment be advisable

These certificates may be used in settlement of balances at the clearing house, and they shall be received by creditor banks in the same proportion as they bear to the aggregate amount of the debtor balances paid at the clearing house The interest that may accrue upon these certificates shall be apportioned monthly among the banks which shall have held them during that time

Second The securities deposited with the said committee shall be held by them as a special deposit, pledged for the redemption of the certificates issued thereupon, the same being accepted by the committee as collateral security, with the express condition that neither the Clearing House Association, the clearing-house committee, nor any member thereof shall be responsible for any loss on said collaterals arising from failure to make demand and protest, or from any other neglect or omission, other than the refusal to take some reasonable step which the said depositing bank may have previously required in writing

Third On the surrender of such certificates, or any of them, by the depositing bank, the committee will indorse the amount as a payment on the obligation of said bank held by them, and will surrender a proportionate amount of securities, except in case of default of the bank, in any of its transactions through the clearing house, in which case the securities will be applied by the committee, first, to the payment of outstanding certificates, with interest, next, to the liquidation of any indebtedness of such bank to the other banks, members of the Clearing House Association

Fourth The committee shall be authorized to exchange any portion of said securities for others, to be approved by them, and shall have power to demand additional security, at their own discretion

Fifth That the clearing-house committee be authorized to carry into full effect this agreement, with power to establish such rules and regulations for the practical working thereof as they may deem necessary, and any loss caused by the nonpayment of loan certificates shall be assessed by the committee upon all the banks in the ratio of capital

Sixth The expenses incurred in carrying out this agreement shall be assessed upon the banks in equal proportion to their respective capital

Seventh That the clearing-house committee be, and they are hereby, authorized to terminate this agreement upon giving thirty days' notice thereof at any stated meeting of the Clearing House Association

PHILADELPHIA, *November 18, 1890*

At a meeting of the clearing-house committee, held this day, it was, on motion—

Resolved, That in accordance with resolutions of September 24, 1873, as amended October 18, 1873, the clearing-house committee will issue loan certificates to banks applying, and receive them in payment of balances

It will be observed that the original agreement under which the committee proceeded in this case was adopted during the panic of 1873, and after that subsided no further action was had under it until November, 1890, but the machinery was kept standing during the whole intervening period, ready for immediate use whenever required.

The clearing-house committee having, by the agreement aforesaid, been authorized to issue loan certificates, resolved, on November 5, 1890, to exercise this power, whereupon the banks desiring to take out loan certificates were required to adopt a resolution empowering the hypothecation of securities, under which the issue of loan certificates, signed by not less than three members of the committee, was commenced on November 19, 1890, and ceased on May 22, 1891, the total issue being $9,655,000. The maximum issue, $8,870,000, was reached on January 9. The certificates have all been retired excepting $170,000 issued to the Keystone and Spring Garden national banks.

Note F

The Treasury and the Money Market in 1890 [a]

During this period [the fiscal year 1890] the Secretary was able to purchase United States bonds at constantly decreasing prices, so that at the end of the fiscal year 1890 the Government was paying for 4 per cent bonds 7 per cent less than at the beginning of that period, and for 4½ per cent bonds 4½ per cent less, but the diminished supply of bonds held for sale, together with the lower prices being paid, had been gradually curtailing the government purchases, and soon after the beginning of the present fiscal year the growing surplus and the prospective needs of the country made it advisable that steps be taken to obtain more free offerings of bonds to the Government

Accordingly, on July 19, 1890, a circular was published rescinding that under which purchases had been made since April 17, 1888, and inviting new proposals, to be considered July 24, for the sale of the two classes of bonds before mentioned Under this circular there were offered on the day prescribed $6,408,350 4 per cents and $594,550 4½ per cents, at prices varying from 121.763 to 128 263 for fours, and from 103¼ to 104 40 for four and one-halfs, of which there were purchased all the 4 per cents offered at 124, or less, amounting to $6,381,350, and all the four and one-halfs offered at 103¾, or less, amounting to $584,550 As the amount obtained on this day was less

[a] Report of the Secretary of the Treasury, 1890 Pages XXVIII to XXXII

than the Government desired to purchase, the provisions of the circular were extended, with the result that further purchases were made, amounting in the aggregate to $9,652,500 fours and $706,450 4½ per cents.

It was soon apparent that these purchases were inadequate to meet existing conditions; therefore, on August 19, the department gave notice that 4½ per cent bonds would be redeemed with interest to and including May 31, 1891, and two days later the circular of August 21 was published, inviting the surrender for redemption of 20,000,000 of those bonds upon condition of the prepayment after September 1, 1890, of all the interest to and including August 31, 1891, on the bonds so surrendered. Under this circular there were redeemed $20,060,700 4½ per cents.

Notwithstanding the disbursements resulting from purchases and redemptions of bonds under the circulars of July 19 and August 21, the industrial and commercial interests of the country required that large additional amounts should be at once returned to the channels of trade. Accordingly, a circular was published August 30, 1890, inviting the surrender of an additional $20,000,000 of 4½ per cents upon the same terms as before. This was followed by another, dated September 6, inviting holders of the 4 per cent bonds to accept prepayment of interest on those bonds to July 1, 1891, a privilege which was subsequently extended to the holders of currency sixes. Under this circular of August 30 there were redeemed $18,678,100 4½ per cent bonds, and under that of September 6 there was prepaid on the 4 per cent bonds and currency sixes interest amounting to $12,009,951.50.

These prepayments of interest are expressly authorized by section 3699 of the Revised Statutes. They were deemed expedient because of the disposition of the holders of bonds to demand exorbitant prices for them

The amount of public money set free within seventy-five days by these several disbursements was nearly $76,660,000, and the net gain to circulation was not less than $45,000,000, yet the financial conditions made further prompt disbursements imperatively necessary. A circular was therefore published September 13, 1890, inviting proposals, to be considered on the 17th, for the sale to the Government of $16,000,000 of 4 per cent bonds The offerings under this circular amounted to $35,514,900, of which $17,071,150 were offered at 126¾, or less, and were accepted

The total disbursements since June 30, 1890, by the means above set forth, are recapitulated as follows

	Bonds redeemed	Disbursement
Under circular of—		
April 17, 1888	$2,133 350 00	$2,358 884 00
July 19, 1890	17,324,850 00	21,225,989 46
August 19, 1890	560,050 00	581,138 12
August 21, 1890	20,060 700 00	20 964 868 42
August 30, 1890	18,678 100 00	19 518,176 83
September 6, 1890	(a)	12 009,951 50
September 13 1890	17,071,150 00	21,617,673 77
Total	75,828,200 00	98,276,682 10

[a] Prepayment of interest

Another circular inviting the surrender of 4½ per cent bonds for redemption, with interest to and including August 31, 1891, was published October 9, 1890. The amount surrendered under that circular during the month of October was $3,203,100.

The total amount of 4 and 4½ per cent bonds purchased and redeemed since March 4, is $211,832,450, and the amount expended therefor is $246,620,741 72. The reduction in the annual interest charge by reason of these transactions is $8,967,609 75, and the total saving of interest is $51,576,706 01.

It will be seen from the above statement that during the three and one-third months, from July 19 to November 1, 1890, over $99,000,000 were disbursed in payment for bonds and interest

There are many grave objections to the accumulation of a large surplus in the Treasury, and especially to the power which the control of such surplus gives to the Secretary I am sure these objections appeal to no one with so much force as to the head of the Department, upon whom rests the difficult and delicate responsibility of its administration

In my judgment, the gravest defect in our present financial system is its lack of elasticity The national banking system supplied this defect to some extent by the authority which the banks have to increase their circulation in times of stringency and to reduce when money becomes redundant, but, by reason of the high price of bonds, this authority has ceased to be of much practical value.

The demand for money in this country is so irregular that an amount of circulation which will be ample during ten months of the year will frequently prove so deficient during the other two months as to cause stringency and commercial disaster. Such stringency may occur without any speculative manipulations of money, though, unfortunately, it is often intensified by such manipulations. The crops of the country have reached proportions so immense that their movement to market in August and September annually causes a dangerous absorption of money. The lack of a sufficient supply to meet the increased demand during those months may entail heavy losses upon the agricultural as well as upon other business interests. Though financial stringency may occur at any time, and from many causes, yet nearly all of the great commercial crises in our history have occurred during the months named, and unless some provision be made to meet such contingencies in the future, like disasters may be confidently expected.

I am aware that the theory obtains in the minds of many people that if there were no surplus in the Treasury a sufficient amount of money would be in circulation, and hence no stringency would occur The fact is, however, that such stringency has seldom been produced by Treasury absorption, but generally by some sudden or unusual demand for money entirely independent of Treasury conditions and operations. The financial pressure in September last, which at one time assumed a threatening character, illustrates the truth of this statement. There was at that time no accumulation of money in the Treasury from customs or internal-revenue taxes, nor from any other source that could have affected the money market. On the contrary, the total disbursements for all purposes, including bond purchases and interest prepayments, during the last preceding fifty-three days had been about $29,000,000 in excess of the receipts from all sources.

The total apparent surplus on September 10, when the money stringency culminated, was $99,509,220.53. Of this amount $24,216,804.96 was on deposit in the banks, and presumably in circulation among the people, and $21,709,379.77 was fractional silver, which had been in the Treasury vaults for several years, and was not available for any considerable disbursements. Deducting the sums of these two items, viz, $45,926,184.73, left an actual available surplus of only $53,583,035.80. The amount of the bank-note redemption fund then in the Treasury, which had been transferred to the available funds by the act of July 14, 1890, was $54,000,000, being substantially the amount of the available surplus on September 10, 1890. This bank-note fund had been in the Treasury in varying amounts for many years. In August, 1887, it was $105,873,095 60, which had been gradually reduced by disbursements to the amount above named. It is apparent, therefore, that the financial stringency under discussion was not produced by the absorption of money by the Treasury, but by causes wholly outside of Treasury operations. At the time when the financial pressure in September reached its climax the extraordinary disbursements for bond purchases had substantially exhausted the entire ordinary Treasury accumulations, and but for the fact that Congress had wisely transferred the bank-note redemption fund to the available cash there would have been no money at command in the Treasury by which the strained financial conditions could have been relieved and threatened panic and disaster averted. Had this fund been in the banks instead of the Treasury the business of the country would have been adjusted to the increased supply, and when the strain came it would have been impossible for the banks to meet it The Government could not have withdrawn it from the banks without compelling a contraction of their loans and thus diminishing their ability to give relief to their customers.

The more recent financial stringency in November, immediately after the disbursement of over $100,000,000 for the purchase and redemption of bonds within the preceding four months, furnishes another forcible illustration that such stringencies are due to other causes than Treasury operations.

NOTE G.

BANK FAILURES AND SUSPENSIONS IN 1893.[a]

It does not seem essential, nor would it be possible, to enter into a minute statement of all the circumstances attendant upon the closing of the banks during the past year. It is sufficient to say that the cause which brought about the large proportion of such suspensions was the action of depositors who, becoming doubtful of the solvency of the banking institutions of the country, withdrew their deposits The result was that many banks, after paying out on the one hand all the money in their vaults and failing to collect their loans on the other, suspended and passed into the hands of the Comptroller. With a full knowledge of the general solvency of these institutions and the cause which brought about their suspension, the policy was inagurated of giving all banks, which, under ordinary circumstances would not have closed and whose management had been honest, an opportunity to resume business. This policy was one which seemed to commend itself to the Comptroller as proper to pursue under the circumstances, and it is believed the results have justified the experiment of its adoption

In no instance has any bank been permitted to resume on money borrowed or for which as an association it has become liable Whenever those active in the management of the banks resuming, either as executive officers or directors, have been debtors to such banks, their indebtedness has been paid or secured, and whenever impairment

[a] Report of the Comptroller of the Currency, 1893, p 10–12

of capital stock has been found, such impairment has been made good, either by voluntary or enforced assessment on the shareholders. In a number of instances changes have been made in the directory and official corps of resuming banks. The criticism to be made on the management of these banks was the improper distribution of their loans, a circumstance which greatly retarded the conversion of such loans into money at a time when it was needed to avoid suspension

Of the banks which failed to resume many had long been under the continual criticism of this Bureau for violations of law and imprudent methods of banking, and the closing of them was only hastened by the general condition of financial affairs. Some failed because of criminal acts on the part of the officials in charge and others because of a lack of proper appreciation of the purposes of a bank.

An analysis of the suspensions and failures which occurred showed that during the year 158 banking associations, as heretofore stated, were compelled to suspend business, being 4 09 per cent of the number of existing associations. Their capital stock aggregated $30,350,000, or approximately 4 3 per cent of the paid-in capital stock of all the banks in the system.

Of the banks which suspended 65, or 41.14 per cent, with a total capital stock of $10,935,000, were insolvent, and required the appointment of receivers, 86, or 54 43 per cent, with a capital stock aggregating $18,205,000, were able to resume business, and 7, or 4 43 per cent, with a capital stock of $1,210,000, were placed in charge of examiners in the expectation of resumption. Of the suspended banks 2 were located in the New England States, both in New Hampshire, with a total capital stock of $250,000, for each of which a receiver was appointed.

In the Middle States there were 3 suspensions—2 in New York, with a total capital stock of $500,000, and 1 in Pennsylvania, with a capital stock of $50,000. Those in New York were placed in the hands of receivers, and the 1 in Pennsylvania in charge of an examiner pending proposed resumption.

There were 38 suspensions in the Southern States, the capital stock involved aggregating $8,815,000 Of these 19, with a total capital stock of $5,630,000, resumed business, and the same number, with a total capital stock of $3,185,000, failed In this geographical division Texas furnished the greatest number of suspensions, namely, 12, with a total capital stock of $1,480,000, of which 6, with a total capital stock of $430,000, resumed business, and the remainder, capitalized to the amount of $1,050,000, failed. There were 6 suspensions in Kentucky and the same number in Tennessee The total capital stock of those in Kentucky was $2,300,000 and of those in Tennessee $2,750,000. In Kentucky all the banks that suspended, except one, with a capital stock of $50,000, were permitted to resume business Two of the banks in Tennessee, with a total capital stock of $2,000,000, resumed business and 4 were placed in the hands of receivers. Four banks in Georgia suspended and the same number in Alabama, with a total capital stock of $675,000 and $550,000, respectively. Of these, 1 bank in Georgia, with a capital stock of $250,000, and

3 in Alabama, with a total capital stock of $400,000, resumed business. Two banks in North Carolina suspended, with a total capital stock of $300,000, both of which were able to resume business, but the 2 which suspended in Florida, with a total capital stock of $200,000, required the appointment of receivers, as did also the 1 in Mississippi, which had a capital stock of $60,000, and the one in Arkansas, with a capital stock of $500,000

The Western States furnished 49 suspensions, with an aggregate capital stock of $10,250,000. Of these, 31 resumed business, 17 failed, and 1 was placed in charge of an examiner pending resumption or the appointment of a receiver The capital stock of the banks which resumed aggregated $6,275,000, and of those which failed $3,750,000. The greatest number of suspensions which occurred in this section was in Kansas, namely, 8, although the capital stock involved—$880,000—was less than that of the banks in four other States. Four of the banks in Kansas, with a total capital stock of $480,000, resumed, and 3, with a capital stock of $300,000, failed. Of the 7 banks in Indiana which suspended, 4, with a total capital stock of $450,000, resumed, and 3, with a total capital stock of $550,000, were placed in the hands of receivers. In Iowa 6 banks suspended, with a total capital stock of $575,000, of which number but 1 failed, with a capital stock of $50,000 The same number of banks in Nebraska suspended, 3 of which, with a total capital stock of $350,000, resumed business, and receivers were appointed for the remaining 3, the total capital stock of which was $450,000 Five banks suspended in Wisconsin, with a total capital stock of $625,000, all of which resumed business, while in Illinois there were 4 suspensions, with a capital stock aggregating $2,150,000 All of these were placed in the hands of receivers In Missouri 3 banks suspended, with a total capital stock of $1,300,000, all of which resumed In Michigan there were the same number of suspensions as in Missouri, but the capital stock involved aggregated only $215,000. But 1 of these banks resumed, the capital stock of which was $65,000. The fewest suspensions which occurred in any State in this division was in Ohio, there being but 2, the aggregate capital stock of which was $180,000. One of these banks, with a capital stock of $80,000, resumed business, and the other failed.

Sixty-six banks suspended in the Pacific States and Territories, being nearly 42 per cent of the total suspensions which occurred and represent capital stock amounting to 35 per cent of the total capital involved Of these, 36 banks, with a capital of $6,300,000, were solvent and resumed business; 25, with a capital of $3,250,000, were placed in the hands of receivers, and 5, with a total capital of $1,060,000, in charge of examiners pending resumption The greatest number of suspensions was in Colorado, involving the largest amount of capital stock of suspended banks of any State in the Union, the number being 16 and the capital $3,600,000 All of these banks resumed except 2, the capital stock of which was $300,000. The second greatest number of suspensions occurred in the State of Washington, 14 banks, with an aggregate capital stock of $1,735,000 Of this number, 4, with a capital stock of $425,000, resumed, 3, with a capital stock of $510,000, were placed in charge of examiners pending resumption, and 7 failed The suspensions in Montana numbered 10, and their capital stock amounted to $1,875,000 Of these, 2, with a capital stock of $300,000, resumed, and 7, with a capital stock of $1,075,000, were placed in charge of receivers Six suspensions occurred in Oregon, and the same number in California, the aggregate capital stock represented being $800,000 and $1,200,000, respectively There was but one failure in each State, the capital stock in the case of the Oregon bank being $100,000 and that of the California bank being $250,000 There were 3 suspensions in Utah, 3 in North Dakota, and 3 in South Dakota. The 3 banks in Utah, with a capital stock aggregating $250,000, resumed business, while the 3 in North Dakota, with a total capital stock of $400,000, failed Two of the banks in South Dakota, with a total capital stock of $100,000, were placed in the hands of receivers, and 1, with a capital stock of $125,000, resumed Two suspensions occurred in Wyoming, and the same number in New Mexico One bank in Wyoming, with a capital stock of $200,000, resumed, and 1, the capital stock of which was $50,000, failed Of the banks in New Mexico, 1, with a capital stock of $175,000, failed, and the other, with a capital stock of $50,000, was placed in the hands of an examiner pending resumption on the appointment of a receiver The only other suspension in this geographical division occurred in Oklahoma, being that of a bank with a capital stock of $50,000, which, being solvent, resumed.

Note H

A.—Clearing House Loan Certificates in 1893 [a]

The unprecedented condition of the money market from June to September called for extraordinary remedies, not only to avert general disaster to the banks, but to prevent commercial ruin. This remedy was the issuing of clearing house loan certificates, which were brought into use, as in 1873, 1884, 1890 to 1891, by the associated banks of New York, Boston, Philadelphia, Baltimore, and other cities where needed The service rendered by them was invaluable, and to their timely issuance by the associated banks of the cities named is due the fact that the year's records of suspensions and failures is not greatly augmented

The form of these certificates, with the conditions under which they were issued in 1890–91 (the form and conditions being the same during the late issuance of them as then), is described at length in the Comptroller's Annual Report for 1891 [b] The subject is alluded to again only because it constitutes a very important part of the year's banking history, and for the additional reason that here and there are to be found those who entertain an entirely erroneous idea of the purpose for which these certificates were issued and what was accomplished by their issuance Briefly stated, they were temporary loans made by the banks associated together as clearing-house associations, to the members of such association, and were available to

---

[a] Report of the Comptroller of the Currency, 1893, pp 15–16

[b] See Appendix, Note E, p 388.

such banks only for the purpose of settling balances due from and to each other, these balances under normal conditions of business being always settled in coin or currency. Each clearing-house association selected a committee charged with the issuing of the certificates to each bank desiring the same, such bank being required before receiving them to deposit with the committee its bills receivable, or other securities, as collateral for the loan The amount of certificates issued to each bank was limited to 75 per cent of the value of the securities deposited. They bore interest at rates varying from 6 to 7.3 per cent. Immediately upon their surrender to the committee they were canceled and the securities held as collateral were returned to the bank depositing the same

At a time when vast sums of coin and currency were being withdrawn from the banks to be hoarded these loan certificates, by performing the functions of the currency or coin customarily required for settling daily balances at the clearing house, released so much currency or coin to legitimate and current demands of business and unquestionably placed it within the power of the banks in the cities named to extend to outside banks the aid needed on the one hand and liberally granted on the other. In no instance were these certificates designed to, nor did they, circulate as money They were due bills, and their sole function consisted in discharging the single obligation at the clearing house An attempt on the part of a bank in any of the associations issuing these certificates to use them otherwise would have incurred a fine and other penalties provided in the rules governing such associations Their issuance at so early a date in the financial derangement of the country was most opportune in not only preventing an acute panic but intending to restore public confidence, such action demonstrating that by mutual agreement of all, the weak banks of the association would be, so far as depositors and other creditors were concerned, as strong as the strongest.

In inaugurating the issuing of certificates so promptly and issuing them to so large an amount the clearing-house association of New York in particular rendered the country great service, and the associated banks of that city are entitled to the credit which the public generally accords them

The following figures, showing the movement and amount of the issue of loan certificates in 1893 in the cities named, will indicate the measure of relief afforded by them

	Date of issue of first certificate	Date of largest amount outstanding	Largest amount outstanding	Amount outstanding October 31
New York	June 21	Aug 29 to Sept 6	$38 280 000	
Philadelphia	June 16	Aug 15	10,965,000	$3,835,000
Boston	June 27	Aug, 23 to Sept 1	11,445,000	
Baltimore	do.	Aug 24 to Sept 9	1,475 000	845,000
Pittsburg	Aug 11	Sept 15	987,000	332 000
Total			63,152,000	

B.—Report of the New York Clearing-House Loan Committee

New York, *October 31, 1893*

To the New York Clearing House Association

The loan committee of 1893 respectfully present the following report

Early in June of this year, at an informal meeting of several banking officers, the subject of the financial outlook was discussed, and those present thought the situation was sufficiently grave to call for some action by the Clearing House Association

On the 14th of June a meeting of the clearing-house committee was called, at which all the members were present After a protracted discussion it was moved that the following be adopted as the opinion of the committee

> The clearing-house committee think it advisable to call a meeting of the Clearing House Association for Thursday, the 15th instant, at 12 o'clock The committee will recommend at that meeting an issue of loan certificates

This was unanimously adopted, and in accordance with this action a meeting of the Clearing House Association was held Thursday, June 15, at 12 o'clock, 58 banks being being represented thereat.

The President, Mr. Williams, stated that the meeting had been called in order that the recommendation of the clearing-house committee having reference to the disturbed financial condition of the country might be presented for action by the association.

Mr. E. H. Perkins, jr., chairman of the clearing-house committee, presented the views of that committee, as above expressed.

After a protracted discussion, in which several members of the association participated, the following resolution was adopted.

Resolved, That a committee of five be appointed, with the President, to receive from banks, members of the association, bills receivable and other securities to be approved by said committee, who shall be authorized to issue therefor to such depositing banks loan certificates bearing interest at the rate of 6 per cent per annum, and such loan certificates shall not be in excess of 75 per cent of the market value of the securities or bills receivable so deposited, and such certificates shall be received and paid in settlement of balances at the clearing house, and all the rules and regulations heretofore adopted in the issue of loan certificates shall be in force in the present issue

The president, Mr. Williams, appointed the following gentlemen as the loan committee Mr. F. D. Tappen, Mr E. H. Perkins, jr., Mr J. Edwards Simmons, Mr. Henry W Cannon, Mr. William A Nash, and Mr. George G Williams, president ex officio.

The loan committee met immediately after the adjournment of the association, June 15, and organized by the selection of Mr Tappen as chairman, and Mr. Nash as acting chairman in the absence of Mr. Tappen. The form of certificate to be used and the necessary blanks were adopted, and the manager was requested to have the same prepared for use. The first issue of certificates under the above resolution, $2,550,000, was made on June 17 The first cancellation of certificates, to the amount of $100,000, took place on the 6th day of July The committee have met daily up to the present time, and have held 105 meetings The aggregate amount of certificates issued was

$41,490,000 The greatest amount outstanding was $38,280,000, on August 29, and continued at that amount until September 6 The amount of collateral received by the committee, in a round sum, was $56,000,000, 72 per cent, or $40,000,000, being in bills receivable, 28 per cent, or $16,000,000, being in stocks and bonds. The total number of pieces deposited with and examined by the committee was 11,029 Four thousand and forty-nine pieces were also examined as substitutions

It has been frequently stated and feared by some that the amount of certificates issued during the present crisis was in excess of the amount issued, in proportion to the deposits held by the banks, during any previous panic On examination of the figures, however, we find that this has not been the case, as in 1873 the deposits were $152,640,000 and loan certificates $22,410,000, being 14.7 per cent; in 1884, on deposits of $296,575,300, certificates were issued to the amount of $21,885,000, being 7.3 per cent; in 1890, on deposits of $376,746,500, $15,205,000 certificates were issued, being 4 per cent, in 1893, $374,010,100 deposits, certificates $38,280,000, being 10.2 per cent. The greatest amount of certificates in proportion to deposits was issued in 1873 Had the same proportion of loan certificates been issued in 1893 as was issued in 1873 the amount would have reached the sum of $55,000,000

The percentages of loan certificates used in the payment of balance have been as follows. In June, 9 per cent; in July, 78 per cent, in August, 95 per cent, in September, 30 per cent, in October, nil, being a total of

6158—10——27

certificates used in the payment of balance $299,273,000. The amount of interest paid on certificates has been $535,513 33 The expenses of the committee for stationery, clerk hire, etc., $562 27 All of this work has been accomplished without loss to the association

The committee takes this occasion to express their thanks for the courtesy shown by the Chase National Bank and the First National Bank in allowing the committee to use the vaults in their banks to deposit the securities held by the committee, there being no suitable accomodations connected with the clearing house for this purpose

Full and complete statistics of the transactions had with each bank by the loan committee will be filed with this report

Respectfully submitted.

F. D. TAPPEN, *Chairman*,
E. H PERKINS, Jr.,
J. EDWARD SIMMONS,
HENRY W CANNON,
WILLIAM A NASH,
GEO. G. WILLIAMS, *Ex-officio*

WILLIAM SHERER, *Secretary*.

Note I.

The Banks and the Panic of 1893.[a] By A. D. Noyes.

* * * * * *

It was on the western banks that the shock of panic fell in 1893 with greatest violence The records of no previous panic show in this regard such impressive sectional contrasts The list of national and state bank failures for 1893 shows for the New England and Middle Atlantic States 17 suspensions, with total estimated liabilities of $13,138,073 This list includes such financial centers as New York, Boston, and Philadelphia. On the other hand, the failure of similar institutions in the five States of Ohio, Indiana, Illinois, Michigan, and Wisconsin numbered 49, with aggregate liabilities of $23,163,537. In the 11 granger and Rocky Mountain States, still farther to the west, the state and national bank failures reached the yet more disproportionate number of 147, and reported liabilities footed up no less than $24,781,181 [b] Taking the country as a whole, the record shows that out of 360 national and state banks suspended during 1893, with liabilities of $109,547,556, no less than 343 failures, with liabilities of $96,409,483, occurred in sections of the Union west or south of Pennsylvania. The failures of private banks and savings institutions were distributed in almost exactly the same proportion.[c]

---

[a] This note contains rather more than half of an article by Mr Noyes which appeared in the Political Science Quarterly, March, 1894

[b] Figures compiled and published by Dun's Mercantile Agency

[c] Total failures of such institutions in 1893 were 250, liabilities, $41,895,346. Outside of the New England and Middle Atlantic States failures were 224; liabilities, $35,543,801

For this remarkable disparity there were several reasons Rapid development on other than local capital had been the chief feature of the West's recent career, and this was a double element of weakness. The collapse of the "land booms" in 1899 and 1890 had served as a wholesome check to speculation, but the two enormous grain harvests of 1891 and 1892 had again revived it The warnings of 1890 and of the brief succeeding period fell in that section on deaf ears The evils of a vicious currency took root for this reason far more extensively west of the Ohio "Bad loans" made up a startlingly large proportion of the assets of bankrupt institutions The East, on the other hand, where foreign capital was concentrated, felt much more severely the shock and the significance of the London crash of 1890. When, in 1891, the expulsion of gold by our accumulated paper currency began, it was the eastern banks from whose vaults the gold was first withdrawn to meet such export requirements It was through these banks that the "run" began, with 1893, on the Government's gold reserve for the redemption of legal-tender notes. It was on the eastern stock exchanges that foreign investors poured for two years continuously their holdings of American securities These multiplied signs of coming trouble were not ignored The eastern institutions were indeed subjected to the same demoralizing pressure from currency overissues, and they furnished their share of reckless ventures and dishonest speculation But the weeding out of such concerns was very thorough in 1890 and in the ensuing year or two, and, as a rule, the policy of the Eastern city banks on the eve of the general breakdown was sound and conservative [a]

But all this relative conservatism in the eastern banks failed to offset the results of a thoroughly dangerous practice embodied in our banking system This is the carrying and loaning out, in city banks, of interior banks' legal reserves. This account, which Prof Amasa Walker aptly described as the most "explosive" element in American banking, arises from the larger opportunity offered in great financial centers for the steady use of capital At nearly all times western banks are glad to get the 2 per cent allowed for use of their deposits by eastern institutions. The national-bank law, moreover, permits the so-called "country banks" to deposit with other banks in certain specified cities three-fifths of their 15 per cent cash reserve. Since the country banks can at no time legally lend out this last-named fund, it is kept, as might be supposed, perpetually on deposit with the reserve city institutions. In recent years this trust fund has reached phenomenal proportions At the close of 1892 the national banks reported "due from approved reserve agents" the sum of $204,948,159 The total amount due from other banks was more than double this. In May of 1892 the New York City banks alone held $293,078,195 subject to call from other institutions. Let it be noted not only that this fund was money belonging

[a] The truth of this was illustrated when New York's bubble of speculation in the "industrial stocks" broke in May This group of stocks fell on the average 25 points within a week, and some of them 40 or 50, but no bank suffered This was, moreover, before the issue of loan certificates As a matter of fact, the banks had long been notoriously shy of these securities

to private depositors in other banks, and subject to their instant call, but that a large proportion of it was the very money prescribed by law to be held for the purpose of meeting "runs" by the western banks' own creditors This will explain the violence of the strain on city banks when the country institutions all at once took fright.

Nor were the bad results of the system by any means confined to cities whence interior deposits were withdrawn. The city depositories kept on hand by law a cash reserve of 25 per cent. The country banks held in their vaults only the insignificant reserve of 6 per cent. Grant, what was generally true, that the city banks were conservative in their use of deposited interior reserves and invested them as a rule in demand loans on stock or bond collateral A bank in Iowa or Colorado, with its three-fifths reserve deposited in New York City, may easily enough, when panic threatens, telegraph an immediate call for the return of such deposits But actual money, even if ready for delivery, can not be shipped from New York to Denver in a day, and forty-eight hours' delay may easily settle the fate of the western institution. This is the reason why so many banks throughout the West suspended in last summer's crisis, when they were perfectly solvent on their books, and indeed resumed payments in a few days' time—as soon, in fact, as the money shipped from their reserve depository reached them.[a] The whole practice, in a

[a] The comptroller reports that out of the total of 158 national bank failures, with a capital stock of $30,350,000, 86, with a capital of $18,205,000 resumed business within a short time None of the 5 banks which suspended in the New England and Middle States resumed payment Of

country of such vast distances as ours, is full of continual possibilities of mischief. Whether or not a serviceable reserve-deposit plan with better safeguards could be devised, I shall not here discuss But it is worth our while to note that the Bank of England, the most conspicuous of all depositories of tributary bank funds, carries in its entire deposit liabilities a less amount than our eastern banks hold from deposits of interior reserves alone. In England delay in transferring currency against withdrawals by interior banks reaches a minimum Yet the Bank of England habitually holds against its total deposits a cash reserve of 40 to 45 per cent, and even now Mr Walter Bagehot's argument is being repeated by a score of excited London critics, that the bank, as depository for other institutions, is in the nature of a public trustee, whose directors must content themselves wholly with ultra-conservative investments and with profits below the average

The facts undoubtedly make it hard to say exactly how far the banks as a whole were culpable in this inflation process, or how far they were themselves victims of outside circumstances. Both conclusions will be found in many cases correct. When we discuss, however, the conduct and policy of the banks after the panic of 1893 had actually begun, we stand on firmer ground. Every banking institution has its own peculiar responsibility placed upon it in time of panic, but the

the 6 national banks which suspended in Iowa, all but 1 subsequently resumed. Sixteen national banks suspended in Colorado, of which all but 2 resumed, and 6, respectively, in Oregon and California, of which in each case all but 2 resumed gravest responsibility by far rests on the great city depositories * * *

* * * The reserve cities furnished throughout the crisis a memorable exposition of the principles of sound panic banking. The time-honored rule, established by the "Bullion report" to Parliament in 1810, that in time of panics banks should discount freely and fearlessly for all solvent customers, was observed in a remarkable degree. In New York City in ordinary times the loan account often falls far below the deposit total,[a] it rarely exceeds it. Between June 4, 1893, the week when panic may be said fairly to have begun, and August 5, which may be called the height of actual panic, deposits in the 64 New York clearing-house banks decreased $58,466,000, and actual specie and legal-tender holdings $49,621,800. This was a terribly sudden and violent impairment of reserves, the actual money decrease being 38 per cent. Yet in the face of it, outstanding loans were contracted only $7,972,700. This remarkable maintenance of bank accommodation to borrowers, in the face of monetary crisis, was made possible by two distinct and wise measures of policy. The first was a firm and continuous curtailment of outstanding loans before the panic's actual outbreak.[b] This was to strengthen cash resources and reduce pressing liabilities. The second measure was the

[a] In the first week of 1893 New York clearing-house bank loans were $441,283,700, deposits, $455,367,800. In the last week of 1893 loans were $417,606,900, deposits, $506,437,800.

[b] Between the first week of April and the first week of June loans were reduced in New York $16,834,300, although in the same time the total cash reserve increased $8,304,700, and the surplus reserve over the required 25 percent of net deposits, $10,374,125.

adoption, when once real panic had begun, of a policy almost exactly opposite.[a] This was the issue of clearing-house certificates in order to maintain the loan account

I shall not enter into a lengthy discussion of this financial contrivance It is enough to say that the loan certificates are a purely American invention, and that their safe and satisfactory operation in financial crises[b] has won for the system the approval of practically all competent judges They are, as is generally known, a species of currency issued by a clearing-house committee to all banks in the association applying for such accommodation and furnishing approved and sufficient collateral These certificates are by agreement accepted in payment of balances between banks of the clearing house They can not, of course, circulate outside the limits of this clearing house, and an annual interest rate of 6 per cent charged up daily against the bank in whose name such certificates are outstanding insures their early redemption when the money market is restored to equilibrium

[a] The banks followed another thoroughly sound principle in lending only at high rates, the sufficient reason being that a high rate is a matter of no concern to a borrower in real extremity, while a low rate is a temptation to unscrupulous borrowers to engage the money and then relend it at a rate fixed by the needs of others The banks were therefore entirely right in lending at one-eighth per cent and interest, or 51 per cent yearly, the $5,000,000 later obtained through loan certificates and released in preparation for gold imports An effort then to "break" the money market by offers at a low rate would have had extremely bad results So in the ensuing week the action of the New York banks in raising the rate for interior rediscounts to 12 per cent was fully justified Both actions have ample precedent in the skillful financiering of the Bank of England during the Baring crisis of November, 1890

[b] The real origin of the plan was in the action of the New York clearing house in 1857, when certificates of credit were issued through the Metropolitan Bank to state banks which could not redeem their notes, the notes being deposited as security against the certificates

Through the use of this ingenious emergency device last summer solvent borrowers were protected by the courageous advance of banking credits at the very worst hour of panic. Nor were the system's benefits extended to individual borrowers alone. Not only did the interior banks, at the panic outbreak, call in from city institutions a great part of their own deposited reserves, but they were clamorous for "rediscounts;" in other words, for the purchase from them for cash of paper already discounted for their own customers. To this demand, too, which came with no impropriety from heavy depositors, the larger banks responded The total of notes and bills rediscounted for other institutions rose from $14,021,596 in March to $18,953,306 in May, and to $29,940,438 in July, the height of the summer's panic. In 1873, during a corresponding panic period, the account increased only from $5,403,043 to $5,987,512

The clearing houses of four other cities followed New York's example in the issue of loan certificates. Chicago, however, where a strong local prejudice exists against the plan, refused to follow. In the worst of the August panic a resolution authorizing such issues was indeed adopted by the Chicago clearing house, but no bank availed itself of the opportunity The result was exactly what might have been foreseen. In the eastern cities the use of loan certificates so far offset the violent shrinkage in reserves that between May 4 and July 12 the loan account of the New York national banks actually increased; the loans of Philadelphia were cut down only 2 per cent, and those of Boston only 4 per cent. But Chicago, lacking the emergency provision of the eastern clearing houses, was forced to reduce its loans no less than 15 per cent[a] In a city where local enterprises were already inflated by speculation incident to the World's Fair, the result of this contraction was a collapse more violent than that of any other large commercial center. * * *

* * * There was no bank suspension in the reserve cities during 1893, except where the strain of panic forced public insolvency This statement needs, however, one important qualification, involving discussion of a very delicate and unpleasant question It will be remembered by those who watched the course of panic financiering that accusations were freely made, as early as July, that banks were refusing cash payments to large depositors. At first the country banks were charged with refusing to remit their cash collections.[b] Banks in some larger cities were next accused of withholding similar remittances At length it was alleged, in the daily press and on the floor of the United States Senate,[c] that New

[a] The contraction of loans in Chicago was far more violent in July and in August, dates not covered by the national reports The Chicago banks themselves publish no statements except when called for by government authorities

[b] Some novel and curious incidents arose in this connection The express companies did a very large business during the panic in presenting out-of-town checks at the banks on which they were drawn and bringing the money to the city bank whence the check was remitted The out-of-town banks frequently resisted this by paying in silver dollars or fractional coin Domestic exchange between two great eastern cities was at one time fixed by the express charges for transporting silver dollars On August 30 Chicago exchange on New York sold at $3 premium per $1,000

[c] In the debate on Senator Peffer's resolution of August 22, instructing the Comptroller of the Currency to inform the Senate whether certain New York banks were or were not violating the national-bank act by refusing cash to depositors and by charging exorbitant discount rates. The resolution was advocated by Senator Hill and opposed by Senators Hoar, Gorman, Hawley, and others

York City banks were refusing to redeem checks of their own depositors in legal-tender money This accusation was made with bitterness, and it was not denied. The popular sentiment was, however, strongly against the proposed Senatorial investigation No bank depositor to whom cash payment was refused ever gave public utterance to complaint No legal process was invoked. The newspaper critics soon found their attack on the banks impolitic. The Senate resolution for an inquiry was referred to the Finance Committee, where it was smothered, as it ought to have been and everyone knew it would be, and there can be no doubt that its advocates paid the penalty of their aggressiveness in a considerable loss of popularity. Thus far, then, it might be argued that public opinion sustained the action of the banks in question.

From an economic standpoint, however, this by no means ends the matter That some of the New York clearing-house banks did thus suspend cash payments is a matter of public knowledge. No formal or concerted action, indeed, was taken by the banks, the clearing house ignored the whole performance, the majority of New York institutions continued to pay cash on demand to all depositors, and those which did refuse cash payments not only offered to such depositors checks on other banks,[a] but cashed small checks without inquiry, and larger checks when the need was shown to be imperative. Nevertheless it was suspension, its effect on business and

[a] Most of these banks sent to their customers rubber stamps marked "payable through the clearing house " This was to be stamped on checks when drawn, by way of a polite and euphemistic hint to receivers of the checks that the bank declined to pay cash

credit was mischievous in the extreme, and it can be justified only on the plea of absolute necessity.

This plea, in my opinion and in the judgment, I believe, of the soundest clearing-house authorities, is quite untenable. The issue of loan certificates was a recourse still open to every solvent bank, and the banks which did shut down on cash payment to depositors included several of the soundest institutions in the city. July's shipments of currency, to meet deposit withdrawals of interior banks and other institutions, were indeed extremely heavy, but on August 5 there was still left in the New York clearing-house bank reserves $79,218,500 specie and legal tenders. Moreover, at the very time when banks resorted to such partial suspension, importation of gold from Europe had begun Any bank with securities on which to take out loan certificates was able, within seven days, to replace such certificates in American gold coin.

But the plea of necessity was not the bankers' only plea. It was openly argued that the restriction on cash payments had positively good results, in that it stopped withdrawals by money hoarders Let us observe what were the actual results of this restriction It was followed by a market phenomenon unfamiliar to the present generation Currency, as the phrase was, went to a premium. Two or three active Wall street money brokers at once inserted newspaper advertisements offering a premium for gold or silver coin, or for paper legal tender currency This premium was at first 1½ and 2 per cent, it rose once to 4 per cent. In quick response to these advertisements, the hoarded money of New York and its vicinity poured into the Wall street offices. The brokers paid for this currency, in turn, by certified checks on their own bankers. They sold the currency at an average advance of one-half of 1 per cent Two classes of buyers chiefly furnished the demand. First, and most naturally, there were employers of labor with large weekly or monthly pay rolls, whose deposits lay in banks which flatly refused to pay them cash for checks Second, and more numerous than might have been supposed, there were banks which were unwilling to refuse cash payments, but which were not averse to paying a premium to replenish their cash reserves.

The first of these transactions makes the operation easy of analysis Currency, it is said in common phrase, was bought with checks. But this statement involves an absurdity, for nothing had happened to alter the value of the currency The actual transaction was a sale of bank checks for money Something had very obviously happened to make the checks less valuable than they had been before. At the bank on which they were drawn these checks were now worthless for the one purpose for which their makers drew them—conversion into coin and bills of small denomination. They were sold in Wall street, therefore, for what they would bring in cash. Like irredeemable paper currency, their percentage of depreciation—in other words, the premium on the kind of money needed—was measured by the ratio of supply and demand, and by the probability of their ultimate cash redemption The supply of such checks offered last year in exchange for currency was large. But, on the other hand, early resumption of full cash payment by the banks was universally expected, and the checks themselves, still being good for all banking transactions and exchanges through the New York clearing house, were as good as cash for the most of ordinary purposes. Therefore the "premium" on currency never rose exorbitantly high

But did this operation check individual hoarding of money? Obviously not. Withdrawal of funds from banks which refused cash payments ceased of course, but withdrawals from other banks were doubled The logic of the bank restriction, therefore, pointed, if sound, to nothing short of general suspension. Nor was this all. A large part of the regular and individual bank depositors of money were driven away at once The chances that a man with $100 currency will deposit it in bank, when the bank announces that it will not return the money on demand, and when the currency may be "sold" for $102 in Wall street, are certainly small The argument that the banks were forced to refuse cash payment, *because* of the premium in Wall street, utterly confuses cause and effect Of course, after the premium was offered, there was a chance that a depositor would withdraw his $100, sell it for $102 in Wall street checks, withdraw the $102 against this check, sell it again, and so on *ad infinitum* But this ignores the fact that the bank restrictions caused the currency premium Had the banks all continued to pay cash, no premium would have been possible. It is astonishing that anyone should question this What Wall street broker in his sober senses would pay a $102 check for $100 currency when he could get $102 money by presenting the same check at bank?

Hoarding was certainly increased by the bank restrictions Deposits of cash in banks almost wholly ceased, and domestic exchange was completely blocked. The experience of August proved beyond dispute the effect of the Wall street premium This premium undoubtedly brought to sight great quantities of previously hoarded currency[a] But no sooner had this money been exchanged and again disbursed than it vanished once more from sight No one who passed that month in New York City will dispute this So completely, under the bank restrictions, did paper money disappear that by the middle of August business of every kind was being done with specie, and people who in years had never touched a gold piece for their common uses were making daily payments in eagles and double eagles This money came not from the "purchases" from currency hoarders, but from the European gold importations By the end of August practically all the banks had resumed full pay-

[a] For obvious reasons it is very hard to arrive at any trustworthy estimate of the amount of money thus brought into the market The Wall street firm which did the largest proportion of the business estimates the amount of money which changed hands during the currency premium at $15,000,000, but this, though based on personal experience, is largely guesswork Some uptown retail stores sold their daily receipts of currency, a fact pretty publicly proved by the vigor with which other retail houses, in their advertisements at the time, boasted that they had regularly deposited their cash receipts in bank There were, moreover, many sales of large blocks of currency, chiefly gold certificates, in lots as high as $100,000, which had evidently been locked up in safe deposit vaults It was a striking incident that on the death, several months before the panic, of a well-known New Yorker, a man of wealth and financial reputation and a bank director, his executors found in his safe several hundred thousand dollars in gold certificates The hoarding in New York was largely, and perhaps chiefly, speculative, in the interior, where it had far more serious effects, it was a natural result of the deposit and savings bank failures

ment to depositors. But for a long time hardly any paper currency was paid; and how little the Wall street purchases contributed to the recovery the bank exhibits show. From August 5 to September 2, a period covering the existence of the currency premium, the specie holdings of the New York City banks increased by $10,930,700[a] But holdings of legal tenders increased only $1,785,800, and deposits only $1,064,900

[a] The net gold import during July was $5,776,401; during August, $40,622,529 Much of this gold was, however, ordered by Chicago and Boston capitalists and shipped direct to them Still more was imported by Wall street exchange bankers and sold by them at a premium to savings banks, corporations, and business houses The restriction on bank payments to depositors was the reason why no gold, except that ordered personally by bank officers, was deposited in the banks

Note J

REPORT OF THE NEW YORK CLEARING-HOUSE COMMITTEE, ACTING AS A LOAN COMMITTEE IN 1907

At a meeting of the Clearing House Association, held October 26, 1907, to consider the disturbed state of financial affairs and to take such remedial action as might be possible, the undersigned clearing-house committee, with the president of the association, were appointed to act as a loan committee with power to associate with them such other bank officers as they judged necessary.

It had been hoped that the crisis imminent for a week previous might be successfully met without the necessity for the issuance of clearing-house loan certificates, in spite of the urgent application for assistance from several banks, members of the association. Such assistance had been given through joint action of many of the banks who advanced cash to the applying banks, receiving participating receipts for their several payments and the clearing-house committee holding the collateral security at the clearing house

Public apprehension grew so rapidly, however, and the drain upon all the banks so severe that it was soon evident that no inferior expedient would suffice to make effective the aid which it was apparent must shortly be solicited by other members of the association, and the committee then determined to recommend the appointment of a loan committee

The committee was unanimously appointed at noon, October 26, 1907, and forthwith proceeded to issue loan certificates, blank certificates and proper stationery having been stored at the clearing house for such an emergency.

Under the terms of the resolution creating the committee, the following bank officers were appointed as associates of the committee. Messrs. James G. Cannon, vice-president Fourth National Bank, Henry P. Davison, vice-president First National Bank, Walter E. Frew, vice-president Corn Exchange Bank, Gates W. McGarrah, president Mechanics National Bank, Albert H. Wiggin, vice-president Chase National Bank.

To these gentlemen was assigned the duty of passing upon the collateral offered for loans, and certifying to its sufficiency before the issuance of certificates.

The assistance rendered by the members of the associate committee materially lightened the labors of the loan committee, and the systematic methods employed in handling the mass of collateral pledged for certificates insured the transaction of the business of the committee without delay or complication

Eleven million two hundred and thirty-five thousand dollars in certificates were issued to take up the participating receipts given for loans advanced from October 19 to October 26, and the interest due for such advances was included in the first distribution of interest on the 15th of the following month

Until near the retirement of all but a small portion of certificates issued, your committee met on the morning of every business day and frequently after noon, at least three members always being present and generally all of the committee.

The date of the first issue was October 26, 1907.

The date of the first cancellation was November 14, 1907.

The date of the final issue was January 30, 1908.

The date of the final cancellation was March 28, 1908.

Gross issue, $101,060,000.

Maximum amount outstanding was $88,420,000, December 16, 1907.

During this period there passed through the hands of the committee, including original deposits of securities, substitutions of securities (both withdrawals and deposits) collateral aggregating in amount $453,000,000, of which $330,000,000, or 72 92 per cent, consisted of commercial paper and $123,000,000, or 27 08 per cent, was made up of stocks, bonds, and short-time railroad and other similar notes

Of the 52 banks constituting membership in the association 32 took out loan certificates, from whom was received in interest $1,116,245.83, which amount, of course, was paid to banks holding said certificates

Three thousand five hundred and forty-eight loan certificates were issued, as follows

412 at $100,000 each	$41, 200, 000
522 at $50,000 each	26, 100, 000
1,005 at $20,000 each	20, 100, 000
1,123 at $10,000 each	11, 230, 000
486 at $5,000 each	2, 430, 000

The greatest amount of certificates issued to any one bank was $17,000,000 and the smallest $250,000, the latter amount in two cases.

The time elapsed from the first issue, October 28, 1907, to the final cancellation, March 28, 1908, was twenty-two weeks, or one hundred and fifty-four days, as compared with nineteen weeks, or one hundred and thirty-three days, in 1893

Respectfully submitted

JAS T. WOODWARD, *Chairman.*
W A. NASH,
DUMONT CLARKE,
A B. HEPBURN,
EDWARD TOWNSEND,
A GILBERT,
Clearing House Committee.

NEW YORK, *April 7, 1908.*

Additional data relating to loan certificates

RESOLUTION APPOINTING COMMITTEE

(Adopted October 26, 1907.)

Resolved, That the clearing-house committee, with the president of the association, be authorized to receive from banks, members of the association, bills receivable and other securities to be approved by said committee, who shall be authorized to issue therefor to such depositing banks loan certificates bearing interest at 6 per cent per annum, and such loan certificates shall not be in excess of 75 per cent of the market value of the securities or bills receivable so deposited, and such certificates shall be received and paid in settlement of balances at the clearing house, and all rules and regulations heretofore adopted in the issue of such certificates shall be in force in the present issue. Said committee shall have power to associate with it such other bank officers as they may judge necessary.

The percentage of maximum amount of certificates outstanding December 16, 1907 ($88,420,000), to total net deposits of clearing-house banks ($1,066,865,900) was 8.28.

The percentage of aggregate amount of certificates issued ($101,060,000) to deposits as above was 9.38.

Table showing use of loan certificates in paying balances at the clearing house

	Total balances	Loan certificates paid in	Per cent
1907			
October [a]	$64,648,593	$54,460,000	84
November	218,702,635	211,475,000	96
December	203,340,855	198,200,000	97
1908			
January	337,895,293	64,575,000	19
Total	824,587,376	528,710,000	64

[a] Five days.

Loan certificates of the New York Clearing House

Loan comm of	Date of first issue	Date of last issue	Date of first cancellation	Date of final cancellation	Aggregate issue	Maximum amount outstanding	Date	Rate of interest	Nature of collateral
								P ct	
1860	Nov 23 1860	Feb 27, 1861	Dec 12, 1860	Mar 9, 1861	$7 375 000	$6, 860 000	Dec. 22 1860	7	United States stock Treasury notes stocks of State of New York
1861	Sept 19, 1861	Feb 17 1862	Oct 7, 1861	Apr 28, 1862	22, 585, 000	21, 960, 000	Feb 7, 1862	6	Temporary receipts of United States for purchase of government bonds
1863	Nov 6, 1863	Jan 9, 1864	--------------	Feb 1, 1864	11, 471 000	9, 608, 000	Nov 27 to Dec 1 1863	6	United States or New York State stocks, bonds, etc or temporary receipts, as in 1861
1864	Mar 7, 1864	Apr 25, 1864	Apr 20 1864	June 13 1864	17, 728, 000	16, 418 000	Apr 20, 1864	6	Same as in 1863, comm of that year continued
1873	Sept 22, 1873	Nov 20, 1873	Oct 3, 1873	Jan 14, 1874	26, 565, 000	22, 410 000	Oct 3 1873	7	Bills receivable stocks, bonds, and other securities
a1884	May 15 1884	June 6 1884	May 19, 1884	Sept 23, 1886	24, 915, 000	21, 885, 000	May 24, 1884	6	Do
1890	Nov 12, 1890	Dec 22, 1890	Nov 28, 1890	Feb 7, 1891	16, 645 000	15, 205, 000	Dec 12, 1890	6	Do

1893	June 21, 1893	Sept 6 1893	July 6, 1893	Nov 1, 1893	41,490,000	38,280,000	Aug 20 to Sept 6 1893	6	Do
1907	Oct 26, 1907	Jan 30 1908	Nov 14, 1907	Mar 28, 1908	101,060,000	88 420,000	Dec 16 1907	6	Do

[a] The certificates of all the banks, except part of those issued to the Metropolitan National Bank, were canceled by September 1, 1884, and these were gradually retired as the bills receivable became due and were paid

Note K

Substitutes for Cash in the Panic of 1907.[a]

By A Piatt Andrew

The autumn of 1907 witnessed what was probably the most extensive and prolonged breakdown of the country's credit mechanism which has occurred since the establishment of the national banking system Upon no previous occasion have the banks of so many cities resorted to clearing-house loan certificates for the settlement of their mutual obligations, never before have they issued them in such large amounts, nor for such long periods of time, and never have these certificates been so extensively issued in small denominations to meet ordinary bank obligations in lieu of cash. Even during the critical periods of 1873 and 1893 it is unlikely that as many banks limited the payment of their obligations in cash, although the proportion of existing banks which so restricted payments may have been as large. In the pages that follow will be found some record of these phenomena, of the several ways in which banks and other firms limited their cash payments, of the issue of loan certificates in the clearing houses of the country, and of the ingenious invention of multifarious other substitutes for legal currency during the weeks of hoarding and suspension.

Of official encouragement to suspension, singular and striking examples occurred in several States The most extreme instances were the legal holidays declared by

[a] The Quarterly Journal of Economics, August, 1908.

some of the Western governors, which were intended to authorize banks, as well as other firms and individuals, to decline payment when unduly pressed or wherever they saw fit The governor of Nevada was the first to resort to this measure Beginning on October 24, he declared legal holidays continuously up to and including November 4 On October 28 the governor of Oregon also began declaring such holidays, and he continued to declare them by subsequent proclamations until December 14 In California such holidays were proclaimed without interruption for a still longer period, from October 31 to December 21, thus suspending all debts for more than seven weeks This method of relieving business involved great inconvenience in unexpected ways. The whole judicial system was thereby brought to a standstill, the courts being even restrained from trying criminal cases The governor of California very soon felt obliged to call a special session of the state legislature, and so secured authority to declare "special holidays" during which only civil actions based upon expressed or implied contracts for the payment of money would be precluded.

Scarcely less radical was the action of the officials who supervise banking in several Middle Western States In Indiana the attorney-general, who had been invited to the meeting of the State Bankers' Association at which it was decided to suspend payments, advanced the opinion that no state law was violated in limiting payments on deposits, when demanded, if it was proposed to make a small payment in each case At the same time the auditor of the State addressed the following hastily composed letter to all banks and trust companies within his jurisdiction, virtually advising them to suspend and giving assurance that the question of their solvency would not be officially raised:

INDIANAPOLIS, *October 28, 1907*

To the Indiana Banks and Trust Companies

GENTLEMEN Your bank being solvent, should it adopt the same rule that has been adopted by the banks of Indianapolis and refuse to pay to any depositor or holder of a check only a limited amount of money in cash and settle the balance due by issuing certified checks, or drafts on correspondents, such act, in this emergency, will not be considered an act of insolvency by this department

The same rule will apply to trust companies

JOHN C BILLHEIMER,
Auditor of State

P S —The question of your solvency is to be determined by yourselves upon an examination of your present condition

Similarly, in South Dakota, the public examiner and superintendent of banks wrote to the state banks throughout that State, calling their attention to the action of the banks of Sioux Falls and Madison in limiting the size of cash withdrawals to $10, and in issuing cashier's checks to take the place of currency. He recommended that they do likewise, as indicated in the following excerpt

I would suggest and recommend that where there is more than one bank in a town they get together and agree along similar lines, for the protection of themselves as well as the public, and where there is only one bank that such bank take the matter up single-handed or confer with banks in the towns near by

I would also suggest that you get the business men of your town together and explain to them the situation and the proposed plan, and in this way secure their approval and support

This method will of course be trying and unpleasant as well as inconvenient not only to the banks but to their depositors, but when the people understand they will gladly cooperate for the mutual good Conditions will improve rapidly and the situation will soon become normal

Respectfully,

JOHN L JONES,
Public Examiner.

So, too, in Iowa, the auditor, B F Carroll, at the outbreak of the panic, wrote a circular letter of similar import to the bankers of that State containing this advice·

I therefore suggest that you call your board of directors together at once, canvass the situation, take such precautionary steps as may be necessary in order to protect your interests and the interests of your depositors The department will temporarily permit such latitude as to reserve and other legal restrictions as circumstances may demand You should take the depositors into the confidence of the bank, fully explain to them the situation and ask them to cooperate to the extent of accepting checks, drafts, and other forms of credit where the same can be used current and to withdraw just as small amounts of cash as is possible for them to use in the transactions of their business It may be necessary for your bank to limit the amount of cash payments to depositors

In Oklahoma, at a meeting of the State Bankers' Association, "the bank commissioner when asked to make a statement regarding the plan upon which the bankers had agreed, and which, in brief, was to make only limited cash payments, stated that while he could not officially agree to the plan, that no banks would be closed because they followed the plan."

In the majority of States, however, it is only just to say that the bank commissioners and superintendents, though tacitly tolerating the restriction of payments, very much as did the Federal Comptroller of the Currency in the case of the national banks, nevertheless gave no explicit assent, much less recommendation to the practice.

The record presented in the accompanying table endeavors to exhibit as concisely as possible the extent to which the banks in the larger cities of the country limited their payments of cash and created substitutes therefor during the panic It is the result of inquiries addressed to banks in all cities of 25,000 or more inhabitants. According to the census of 1900 there were approximately 147 such cities which were independent of each other We exclude by the use of the word "independent" those cities which are really suburbs or parts of larger neighboring cities, and which directly or indirectly "bank" through their institutions. In the neighborhood of Boston, for instance, we exclude from separate reckoning such separate municipalities as Cambridge, Malden, Newton, Somerville, and Chelsea, the banks of which practically "clear" through the Boston clearing house, and consequently follow its policy. In the case of New York we omit environing and related cities like Hoboken, Jersey City, Newark, Passaic, and Elizabeth; in the case of Pittsburg, Allegheny City, in the case of St. Louis, East St Louis; in the case of Omaha, South Omaha, etc. No sharp line can be drawn, however, between the "independent" and the "affiliated" cities, and several of the inclusions as well as some of the exclusions will doubtless appear arbitrary

Reports from the 145[a] largest independent cities show that during the disturbances of 1907, in at least 71, or nearly half, resort was made by the banks to clearing-house loan certificates, clearing-house checks, cashiers' checks payable only through the clearing house, or other substitutes for legal money; in 20 others the larger customers of the banks were asked to mark their checks "payable only through the clearing house," and in at

[a] From two cities of more than 25,000 inhabitants, Pueblo, Colo , and Lawrence, Mass , repeated letters of inquiry have elicited no response

least one other, where these practices were not pursued, the size of checks that would be cashed was restricted Roughly speaking, in two-thirds of the cities of more than 25,000 inhabitants the banks suspended cash payments to a greater or less degree

From the last column of Table I it will be seen that in 36 of the larger cities, where an emergency currency was issued, the banks for a time limited by agreement the cash which any customer could withdraw to a stipulated amount This limitation varied all the way from $10 to $300. In the other cases, marked "discretionary," customers were asked, and generally obliged, to limit their withdrawals of cash, and were asked to stamp their checks "payable only through the clearing house," but no mathematical limit was placed upon the amount that could be withdrawn.

TABLE I.—*Cash restrictions and currency substitutes in cities of more than 25,000 inhabitants*

City	Kind of device	Total amount issued	Date of first issue	Date of retirement	Largest amount outstanding	Date of same	Restrictions upon cash withdrawals
Atlanta, Ga.	B	$1,500,000	Oct 31 1907	Jan 16, 1908	$996,409	Dec 5 1907	$50 per day, $100 per week
Augusta, Ga.	B	320,000	Nov 4, 1907	Jan 15, 1908	320 000	Jan 15, 1908	Do
Baltimore, Md.	A	3,094,000	Oct 28, 1907	Feb 6, 1908	2,786,000	Dec 16, 1907	Discretionary
Bayonne, N. J.	D	Amount not obtainable		----	----	----	Do
Birmingham, Ala.	A	300 000	Oct 28 1907	Nov 20 1907	----	----	$25 per day, later $25 per week
	D	550,000	Nov 20, 1907	----	----	----	
	E	1,000,000	Ave amt outstanding Nov and Dec		Circ 1,000,000	----	
Boston, Mass.	A	12 595,000	Oct 28, 1907	Jan 24 1908	12,595 000	Dec 3–10, 1907	Discretionary
Buffalo, N. Y.	A	915,000	Nov 1, 1907	Jan 25, 1908	550 000	Nov 16, 1907	Do
Canton, Ohio	D	810,000	Nov 10, 1907	----	----	----	Scale proportionate to depositor's balance
Cedar Rapids, Iowa	A	154,000	Nov 6, 1907	Jan 17, 1908	154 000	----	$25 per day
Charleston, S. C.	B	100 000	Nov 15, 1907	Mar 1 1908	70 000	Nov 15, 1907	
Chicago, Ill.	A	32 160,000	Oct 28, 1907	Jan 27 1908	16 140,000	Nov 29, 1907	Discretionary
	C	7,080,000	----	----	7,080,000	----	
Cincinnati, Ohio	D	2 200,000	Nov 5, 1907	Feb 7 1908	2 200,000	Nov 5, 1907	$300 with discretion
Cleveland, Ohio	C	3,220,000	Dec 3, 1907	Jan 29 1908	3,220,000	Jan 6 1908	$50 with discretion
Columbus, Ohio	A	1,220 500	Oct 28 1907	Feb 1, 1908	803 500	Dec 17 1907	Discretionary
Council Bluffs, Iowa	A	75,000	Nov 10 1907	Dec 1 1907	----	----	$10 per customer
	D	15,000	----	----	----	----	
Dallas, Tex.	A	90,000	Nov 15, 1907	Feb 29 1908	90 000	Nov 25 1907	
Davenport, Iowa	A	201,199	Oct 29 1907	Jan 10 1908	----	----	$25 per customer
	C	78 248	Nov 5, 1907	do	----	----	
Denver, Colo.	D	750,000	do	Feb 3, 1908	500,000	----	Discretionary

Des Moines, Iowa	A	880 000	Oct 28, 1907	Jan 28 1908	503,000	Nov 21 1908	$25 per day
	B	170,000			119,700		
Detroit, Mich	A	2,145,000	Oct 30, 1907	Jan 4, 1908	2,030,000	Nov 26, 1908	Discretionary
Duluth, Minn	D	117 000	Oct 28 1907	Jan 10 1908	117,000	Dec 20 1907	Do
	C	Amount not obtainable					
Easton, Pa	A B	136 375	Nov 20 1907	Jan 24, 1908			Interest bearing accounts restricted
Fort Wayne, Ind	A	345 000	Oct 31 1907	Jan 30, 1908	335,000	Dec 28 1907	
(Plates prepared in small denominations, but not issued)							
Harrisburg, Pa	B	357 000	Nov 12 1907	Feb 1, 1908			Discretionary
Houston, Tex	D	Amount not obtainable					$25 per day
Indianapolis Ind	A	1,650 000	Nov 4 1907	Jan 17 1908	835,000	Nov 19 1907	$100 per day
Joliet Ill	D	225,000	Nov 10, 1907	Jan 5, 1908			
Joplin, Mo	B	76 400	Nov 6 1907	Feb 7, 1908			Discretionary
Kansas City, Mo	A	7,256 601	Oct 30 1907	Jan 10 1908	5,956,601	Dec 4–6, 1907	Savings accounts $20
	B	745,000					Open accounts $100
Knoxville, Tenn	B	282 500	Nov 7 1907	Jan 14, 1908	183,000	Nov 23, 1907	Discretionary
Lexington, Ky	A	20 000	Nov 13, 1907	Feb 7 1908	20 000	Nov 27, 1907	No restriction
Lincoln, Nebr	A	198 000	Nov 1, 1907	Dec 16, 1907	136,000	Nov 6, 1907	$100 on accounts over $1 000
	D	Amount not obtainable					$50 on accounts under $1 000
Little Rock, Ark	A	183,000	Oct 31, 1907	Feb 8 1908	148 600	Nov 26, 1907	$50 per customer
Los Angeles, Cal	A	2,022,000	Oct 30 1907	Feb 15, 1908			$100 to $200
	B	3 563 500	Nov 25, 1907	Apr 1 1908			
Louisville, Ky	A	2 490,000	Oct 30 1907	Jan 28 1908	940,000		Discretionary
Lynn, Mass	D	Amount not obtainable					
Memphis, Tenn	D	Circ. 300,000					$100 per day later per week
Milwaukee, Wis	A	1 948,000	Oct 28, 1907	Feb 18, 1908	3,548,000		$50 to $100 per day
	C	1 600 000					
Minneapolis, Minn	A	1 730,000	Nov 1, 1907	Jan 14, 1908	1,060 000	Nov 10 1907	$200 with discretion
Montgomery, Ala	B	Amount not obtainable		Denominations as low as 25 cents			$25 per day
Nashville Tenn	B	417,000	Nov 5, 1907	Jan 30, 1908	417 000	Dec 1 1907	$50 per day

TABLE I — *Cash restrictions and currency substitutes in cities of more than 25,000 inhabitants* — Continued

City	Kind of device	Total amount issued	Date of first issue	Date of retirement	Largest amount outstanding	Date of same	Restrictions upon cash withdrawals
New Orleans, La	A	$5,226,000	Oct 29, 1907	Mar 27, 1908	$3,287,000		$50 per day
	D	Amount not obtainable					
New York, N Y	A	101,060,000	Oct 26, 1907	Mar 30, 1908	88,420,000	Dec 16, 1907	Discretionary
	G	Amount not obtainable					
Oakland, Cal	D	1,250,000	Nov 8, 1907	Jan 21, 1908	590,000		Do
Omaha, Nebr	A	2,007,000	Oct 29, 1907	Jan 10, 1908	1,544,000		$100 or 20 per cent of accounts under $500
	D	Amount not obtainable					
Peoria, Ill	B	227,000	Nov 1, 1907	Jan 1, 1908			$200 per customer
Philadelphia, Pa	A	13,695,000	Oct 26, 1907	Feb 8, 1908	13,495,000	Dec 16, 1907	Discretionary
	G	Amount not obtainable					
Pittsburg, Pa	A	7,445,000			7,445,000	Dec 14, 1907	Do
	G	47,000,000					
Portland, Oreg	A	1,000,000	Oct 30, 1907	Jan 15, 1908	2,200,000	Dec 1, 1907	$300 per customer
	B	1,422,750	Nov 6, 1907	Feb 1, 1908			
Providence, R I	D	Amount not obtainable					Discretionary
Racine, Wis	D	10,000					$25 per day
Sacramento, Cal	B	250,000	Oct 29, 1907	Jan 14, 1908			Discretionary
St Joseph, Mo	A	515,000	Oct 28, 1907	Jan 23, 1908	360,000	Nov 9, 1907	$200 per week
	B	180,000	Dec 12, 1907	Jan 20, 1908	Circ 100,000	Dec 19, 1907	
St Louis, Mo	A	15,965,000	Oct 28, 1907	Feb 5, 1908	10,578,000	Jan 3, 1908	Discretionary
	D circ	5,000,000					
St Paul, Minn	A	1,900,000	Oct 30, 1907	Jan 14, 1908	1,525,000	Oct 30–Dec 2, 1907	$200 per customer
Salt Lake City, Utah	A	802,000	do	Feb 17, 1908	802,000		$200 per week
	B	453,650			Circ 270,000		

San Antonio, Tex	A	344,000	Nov. 1, 1907	Jan. 15, 1908	321,000	Dec. 1, 1907	$50 per day.
	D	251 500			172,963	Nov. 20, 1907	
San Francisco, Cal	A	12 339,000	Oct. 29, 1907	Mar. 1, 1908	12,339,000	Dec. 24, 1907	Discretionary.
	B	7,390,000	Nov. 4, 1907		7,390,000	Dec. 16, 1907	
Savannah, Ga	B	265,000	do	Jan. 10, 1908	265,000	Nov. 15, 1907	$100 per customer.
Seattle, Wash	A	1,700,000	do				$100 with discretion.
	B	1,150,000	Nov. 8, 1907	Jan. 13, 1908			
Sioux City, Iowa	A	245,000	Oct. 28, 1907	do	245,000	Nov. 20, 1907	
	D	Amount not obtainable.					
South Bend, Ind	B	120,000	Nov. 10, 1907	Jan. 10, 1908	120,000		Only savings accounts.
Spokane, Wash	A	669,000	Nov. 1, 1907	Jan. 7, 1908	2,076,000	Nov. 1, 1907	$25 to Dec. 10, then $50.
	B	1 407,000					
Superior, Wis	D	Amount not obtainable.					
Tacoma, Wash	A, B	500,000	Nov. 7, 1907	Jan. 1, 1908	490,000	Nov. 22–Dec. 11, 1907.	$100 per customer.
Taunton, Mass	D	Amount not obtainable.					Do.
Topeka, Kans	B	40,000	Nov. 14, 1907	Dec. 31, 1908	22,500		Do.
Wheeling, W. Va	A	195,000	Nov. 8, 1907	Jan. 3, 1908	45,000	Nov. 29, 1907	Discretionary.
Wichita, Kans	A	173,000	do	Jan. 21, 1908	211,000	Nov. 28, 1907	$50 per customer.
	B	43,000					
Wilmington, Del	D	Amount not obtainable.					Discretionary.
Youngstown, Ohio	A	264,500	Nov. 20, 1907	Jan. 23, 1908	538,000	Dec. 12, 1907	Only savings accounts, $25.
	B	276,500					
Total		330,066,223					

A =Clearing-house loan certificates in large denominations for the settlement of bank balances
B. =Clearing-house loan certificates in small denominations for general circulation
C. =Clearing-house checks in convenient denominations for general circulation
D. =Cashiers' checks in convenient denominations payable only through the clearing house, and usually secured by the deposit of collateral with the clearing house.
E =New York exchange in convenient denominations for general circulation
F =Certificates of deposit in convenient denominations
G. =Pay checks in convenient denominations payable to bearer, and only through the clearing house.

In addition to the places named in the table the banks of the following cities of 25,000 or more inhabitants also restricted payments to the extent of asking their larger customers to mark their checks "payable only through the clearing house"

Allentown, Pa	Mobile, Ala
Bay City, Mich	New Haven, Conn
Binghamton, N Y [a]	Oshkosh, Wis
Dayton, Ohio (one trust company)	Pawtucket, R. I
Erie, Pa	Reading, Pa
Evansville, Ind [a]	Saginaw, Mich
Fall River, Mass.[a]	Springfield, Mass
Gloucester, Mass	Syracuse, N Y [a]
Hartford, Conn	Woonsocket, R I
McKeesport, Pa	York, Pa

In at least one other city, Grand Rapids, Mich., where neither clearing-house currency nor other emergency substitutes was issued, and where depositors were not asked to so mark their checks, the size of checks which would be cashed was nevertheless limited.

The cities rated by the census of 1900 as having more than 25,000 inhabitants, in which, if the replies of my correspondents are to be trusted, depositors were subjected to no restriction of payments, and no resort was made to emergency devices, numbered 53. In some of these, to be sure, as, for instance, Chattanooga, Tenn , Richmond, Va., and Galveston, Tex , cash payments were limited to the extent that clearing-house balances were settled during the panic in exchange on a reserve city instead of in currency, but this practice is frequently followed even in

[a] In these cities, customers sending checks out of town were asked to make their checks payable only through the clearing house in order to prevent their collection by express

quite normal times. The list of cities which, with this possible exception, remained upon a cash basis follows:

City	Population (census of 1900)	City	Population (census of 1900)
Akron, Ohio	42,000	New Britain, Conn	25,000
Albany, N Y	94,000	New Castle Pa	28,000
Altoona, Pa	38,000	Newport, Ky	28,000
Atlantic City, N J	27,000	Norfolk Va	46,000
Auburn, N Y	30,000	Paterson, N J	105,000
Brockton, Mass	40,000	Portland Me	50,000
Bridgeport, Conn	70,000	Quincy, Ill	36,000
Butte, Mont	30,000	Richmond Va	85,000
Camden, N J	75 000	Rochester N Y	162,000
Chattanooga Tenn	30 000	Rockford, Ill	31,000
Chester, Pa	33 000	Salem, Mass	35,000
Covington, Ky	42,000	Schenectady, N Y	31,000
Dubuque Iowa	36,000	Scranton, Pa	102,000
Elmira, N Y	35 000	Springfield, Ill	34,000
Fitchburg Mass	31,000	Springfield, Ohio	38 000
Fort Worth, Tex	26,000	Terre Haute, Ind	36,000
Galveston, Tex	37,789	Toledo, Ohio	131,000
Haverhill, Mass	37,000	Trenton, N J	73,000
Holyoke, Mass	45,000	Troy N Y	60,000
Jackson Mich	25,000	Utica, N Y	56,000
Jacksonville, Fla	28 000	Washington, D C	278,000
Johnstown, Pa	35,000	Waterbury, Conn	45,000
La Crosse, Wis	28,000	Wilkes-Barre, Pa	51,000
Lancaster, Pa	41 000	Williamsport, Pa	28,000
Lowell, Mass	94 000	Worcester, Mass	118 000
Manchester, N H	56,000	Yonkers, N Y	47,000
New Bedford, Mass	62 000		

The roll of honor among the cities, if one were to arrange them in the order of their magnitude, would begin as follows: Washington, Rochester, Toledo, Worcester, Paterson, Scranton. It includes 8 cities in Massachusetts, 8 in New York, and 8 in Pennsylvania, 4 in New Jersey, 3 in Ohio, 3 in Connecticut, 3 in Illinois, 2 in Kentucky, 2 in Virginia, 2 in Texas, and 1 each in Florida, Indiana, Iowa, Maine, Michigan, Montana, New Hampshire, Tennessee, Wisconsin, and the District of Columbia. In the remaining 26 States there was apparently no city with a population of 25,000 in which the banks did not partially restrict their payments during the panic.

The universality with which the panic of 1907 ranged over the United States is also well attested by the fact that there are only 6 States from which I have no record of restriction of payments and issue of substitutes for cash on the part of the banks, namely, Maine, Vermont, South Dakota, Montana, Idaho, and Wyoming Several of these States, it may be added, contained no city of 25,000 inhabitants, and from them no information was received at all. Their banks may also have limited payments and issued emergency currency without its appearing in the record here presented.

Financial excitement in 1907 was by no means confined to the larger cities Limitation of payments and the creation of emergency currency occurred in towns of every degree of smallness all over the country Our record (Table II) of such issues is of necessity fragmentary Names of a number of towns are included where emergency currency was known to have been issued, but from which repeated letters of inquiry failed to elicit any reply as to the amount Unquestionably, the names of scores of towns in which such currency was employed have not chanced to reach the writer's attention. The table here given presents an explicitly avowed issue of nearly $4,500,000 in the case of 33 towns and cities, but it doubtless includes only a small fraction of what actually existed in the smaller localities of the country during the panic.

TABLE II.—*Currency substitutes in cities of less than 25,000 inhabitants*

Cities	Kind of device	Total Amount issued	Date of first issue	Date of retirement.
Atchison, Kans	D	$40,000	Nov 1, 1907	Jan 1, 1908
Bainbridge Ga	B	125 000	Nov 6, 1907	Mar 1, 1908
Berlin, N H	D	Amount not obtainable		
Berkeley Cal	F	34,000	Nov 5 1907	Jan 10, 1908
Bishop Ga	B	Amount not obtainable		
Blakely Ga	B	Amount not obtainable		
Brunswick, Ga	B	109,000	Nov 6 1907	Mar 28 1908
Columbia, S C	B	250 000	Oct 24, 1907	Mar 1, 1908
Columbus Ga	B	320 000	Nov 1, 1907	Jan 22, 1908
Danville, Va	B	617, 200	Oct 30, 1907	Jan 9 1908
Dawson, Ga	B	45 000		
Douglas Ga	B	50,000	Nov 1, 1907	Mar 1, 1908
Fargo, N. Dak	B	33 500	Oct 29 1907	Jan 18 1908
Gadsden, Ala	B	8 000	Nov 15 1907	Jan 1 1908
Gaffney, S C	B	20 000	Nov 11, 1907	Jan 1 1908
Greensboro, N C	B	39, 100	Nov 4 1907	Jan 25 1908
Greenwood, S C	B	Amount not obtainable		
Guthrie, Okla	F	Amount not obtainable		
Hastings, Nebr	B	7,713	Oct 28 1907	Dec 20 1907
	F	Amount not obtainable		
Hattiesburg, Miss	D	40 000	Oct 1, 1907	Dec 15, 1907
Henderson, Ky	C	82 000	Oct 30, 1907	Jan 9 1908
Iron River, Mich	D	24 000	Nov 12, 1907	Dec 24 1907
Jackson, Ga	B	Amount not obtainable		
Key West, Fla	B	Amount not obtainable		
Kalamazoo, Mich	-------	Customers asked to make checks payable in exchange		
Las Vegas, N Mex	B	30 000	Nov 1, 1907	Dec 31 1907
Lynchburg, Va	B	381,000	Nov 18, 1907	Jan 13 1908
Macon, Ga	B	325,000	Nov 4 1907	Jan 31 1908
Milledgeville, Ga	B	Amount not obtainable		
Muskogee, Okla	D	Amount not obtainable		
Newnan Ga	B	Amount not obtainable		
New Carlisle, Ind	D	Amount not obtainable		
Oklahoma, Okla	A, B	200 000	Nov 1 1907	Jan 1 1908
Ogden, Utah	D	circ 275 000	Nov 1, 1907	Dec 31 1907
Rome, Ga	B	120 000	Nov 1, 1907	Jan 10, 1908
Sedalia, Mo	D	100 000	Nov 15 1907	Jan 15 1908
South Boston, Va	B	100 000	Nov 5, 1907	
Sylvester, Ga	B	Amount not obtainable		
Tampa, Fla	B	125 000	Nov 22 1907	Feb 1 1908
Thomaston, Ga	B	10 000	Oct 28 1907	May 1 1908
Thomasville, Ga	B	40,000	Nov 1, 1907	Jan 1, 1908
Tifton, Ga	B	50,000	Nov 6, 1907	Feb 15 1908
Valdosta, Ga	B	100,000	Nov 1, 1907	Feb 1, 1908 circ

TABLE II.—*Currency substitutes in cities of less than 25,000 inhabitants*—Continued.

Cities	Kind of device	Total Amount issued	Date of first issue	Date of retirement
Vicksburg, Miss.	B	$170,000	Nov 23 1907	Apr 25, 1908
Virginia, Minn.	D	200,000	Nov 10, 1907	Dec. 20, 1907
Waycross, Ga.	B	Amount not obtainable		
Willacoochee, Ga.	B	Amount not obtainable		
Winston-Salem N C.	F	350 000	Nov 1, 1907	Jan 1, 1908 circ
Total.		4 420 513		

A=clearing house loan certificates in large denominations for the settlement of bank balances

B=clearing-house loan certificates in small denominations for general circulation.

C=clearing-house checks in convenient denominations for general circulation

D=cashiers' checks in convenient denominations payable only through the clearing house, and usually secured by the deposit of collateral with the clearing house.

F=certificates of deposit in convenient denominations

An attempt has been made in the second column of Tables I and II to classify the various kinds of substitutes for cash, and to indicate which kind was employed in each city Seven different sorts have been distinguished, but some of them closely resemble each other, and the multiple variations among individual devices renders such a grouping at times uncertain

(*a*) The familiar expedient of issuing clearing-house loan certificates in denominations ranging from $500 to $20,000 for use in settling interbank balances has never been resorted to upon such a scale as in 1907. During the panic of 1893 eight cities were reported to have employed them, but during the disturbances of 1907 they were used by no less than 42 In 1893 their issue was confined mainly to the Northeast, New Orleans being the only southern, and Detroit the most western example,[a]

[a] See John De Witt Warner, The Currency Famine of 1893, in Sound Currency, vol ii, No 6, A D Noyes, The Banks and the Panic of 1893, Political Science Quarterly, vol 9

but in 1907 their use knew no geographic limitations They were issued in several cities of California, Washington, and Oregon, in cities of Texas, Alabama, Louisiana, and Arkansas, and in almost every sizable city of the Middle West, the most salient exceptions being Cleveland and Cincinnati, in which, however, the banks by agreement made no demand upon each other for currency in payment of balances during the panic

A comparison of the amounts issued in the same cities in the course of the two emergencies is of significance In New York City the issues of 1907 totaled a sum two and a half times the largest issues that had ever been made before, in Pittsburg they amounted to more than seven times those of the earlier date, in New Orleans, to five times; Detroit, to four times, in Baltimore, to twice the issues of 1893, but in Boston, Philadelphia, and Buffalo the amounts ran about the same in both crises. The aggregate issue of regular clearing-house certificates in the entire country during the panic of 1907 was 238 millions, or nearly three and a half times the total of 1893.

	1893	1907
New York	$41,490 000	$101,060,000
Boston	11,645 000	12,595 000
Philadelphia	11,000,000	13,695,000
Baltimore	1 475 000	3,094 000
New Orleans	1,029,000	5 226,000
Pittsburg	987 000	7 445 000
Buffalo	985 000	915,000
Detroit	500,000	2 145 000
Other cities		91,878,175
Total	69,111 000	238,053,175

(*b*) The original purpose of clearing-house certificates, as set forth by their authors and exponents and as they were employed down to 1893, was for use in settling balances between the banks During the panic of 1893, for the first time, clearing-house associations issued certificates in currency denominations to be used by the banks in paying their customers. Their issue, however, was practically confined to the Southeastern States [a] In the panic of 1907 Georgia was again, as in 1893, the center for emergency circulation of this sort, what were called "clearing-house certificates" being issued in at least 21 Georgia towns; but devices of that name were also put in circulation in many other parts of the country, and not infrequently even by banks of small towns, where no clearing house had ever existed. In such cases they were issued under the auspices of temporary committees of the local banks, which accepted and held the collateral offered to guarantee their redemption In Douglas, Ga., for instance, a town with an estimated population of 2,500, $50,000 in these so-called "clearing-house certificates". were issued, in Tifton, Ga , with less than 3,000 inhabitants, $50,000 in certificates were also issued; in South Boston, Va , with less than 4,000 inhabitants, an issue of as much as $100,000 in certificates was made; even in Bishop, Ga , with only 400 inhabitants, a limited amount was issued.

These small certificates, like the large ones, were secured by collateral deposited with the clearing-house committee, and were practically guaranteed by all of the

[a] See Warner, op cit , p 6.

associated banks, in that these banks agreed to accept them at par for the sum named. The description of collateral in most cases was a general affirmation that "this certificate is secured by the deposit of approved securities" But sometimes there was more detail, as in Portland, Oreg, where it was asserted that the banks have deposited 'notes, bills of exchange, and other negotiable instruments secured by wheat, grain, canned fish, lumber actually sold, and other marketable products, and bonds approved by the committee," etc., or in the case of Charleston, S C, where there were said to be deposited "securities of double the value of this certificate, or bonds of the United States or of the State of South Carolina, or of the city of Charleston, or of the city of Columbia, 10 per cent in excess thereof;" or in Danville, Va, where the payment of the certificate was "secured by the combined capital of these banks, also by collateral worth one-third more than all of the certificates issued." Sometimes redemption was promised on demand "in exchange" (Topeka, Kans.) or "in clearing-house funds" (Spokane, Wash.). Sometimes the certificates were made payable "on or before three months from date" (Des Moines, Iowa), or on or before some special date, like April 1, 1908 (Seattle, Wash.), or July 1, 1908 (Knoxville, Tenn.). The certificates issued by the clearing house in Las Vegas, N. Mex. (sample No. 7), were frankly to be paid only "when deemed advisable by the board of directors" Those of the associated banks of Howard county, Ind, announced that "due notice of redemption will be given through the daily papers" Many of the certificates were elaborately engraved (note reverse of San Francisco certificate), and were shaped and colored so as to resemble ordinary bank or government notes In denomination they usually ranged from $1 to $20, but in some cases, as in Montgomery, Ala , they were issued for convenient sums all the way from 25 cents to $50

The compilation here presented, though very incomplete, records an issue of $23,831,813 of such devices in the course of the panic of 1907.

(*c*) Identical with these certificates in character and function, though differing in form, were the clearing-house checks issued in a number of cities. Like the certificates, they were issued by the associations to member banks upon the deposit of approved securities. Like them, they were accepted for deposit in any of the banks, but were payable only through the clearing house They were also in currency denominations, and were often quite as elaborately engraved, so as to resemble currency. The one peculiarity which distinguished them from certificates was that, instead of merely certifying indebtedness on the part of the clearing-house association, they took the form of checks drawn upon particular banks, and signed by the manager of the clearing house. In Chicago a bank desiring such checks deposited with the clearing house a corresponding amount of the ordinary loan certificates of large denominations, and received the checks in currency denominations in exchange They were also issued in Cleveland, Milwaukee, Youngstown, South Bend, and some smaller cities. Our record includes $12,060,248 of such issues.

(*d*) In spite of the provision of the National Bank Act, that no national banking association shall issue "any other notes to circulate as money than such as are authorized by the provisions of this title," a large number of national banks issued what were practically circulating notes in the form of cashier's checks in convenient denominations. In spite also of the 10 per cent tax upon any notes issued by state banks, similar devices were issued freely and without hindrance by some of those institutions as well (e. g., in Superior, Wis.). These checks usually purported to be "payable to bearer," but they were "payable only through the clearing house," or "in exchange," or, as the phrase sometimes went, "in clearing-house funds." Occasionally, an apparent effort was made to circumvent their illegality by making them payable to a supposed person. In St. Louis, Mo., and in Muskogee, Okla., they were made payable to "John Smith, or bearer," and in Memphis, Tenn., to "Richard Roe, or bearer." While in the Southeastern States it was common for the banks in the small towns to issue conjointly what they called "clearing-house certificates," in small towns of the Middle West the "cashier's checks" of individual banks were much more common. Sometimes these cashier's checks, like clearing-house certificates and clearing-house checks, were secured by the deposit of approved collateral with a committee of the clearing house, as, for example, in Denver, Colo., Omaha, Nebr., and Birmingham, Ala. In Richmond, Va., cashier's checks of a peculiar sort, called "bank money orders," were prepared and printed by one institution, the American National Bank, but were never actually issued They optimistically declared upon their face that they were "good anywhere at any time, transferable as many times as desired," and "payable anywhere in the United States"

(*e*) Another variety of currency issued during the panic were the New York drafts in denominations of $1 and upward, issued by the banks of Birmingham, Ala., and which were used for pay rolls and general circulation in that locality. They were really cashiers' checks drawn on New York, but were drawn against actual balances held by particular New York correspondents. They were payable through the New York clearing house, and were not otherwise secured, yet they appear to have circulated in and about Birmingham to the extent of millions of dollars without difficulty The use of drafts upon reserve banks as currency appears to have been peculiar to Birmingham, although the cashiers' checks "payable in exchange," issued in many places, were not substantially unlike

(*f*) In a few instances the currency issued by the banks took the form of negotiable certificates of deposit in convenient denominations. Sometimes these certificates asserted that a particular person or company had made the deposit, as in the case of the bank of Winston-Salem, N. C Sometimes the assertion was altogether general, as in the example from Berkeley, Cal In some cases they bore interest, and were payable after the expiration of a certain period, in others they were immediately acceptable by the issuing bank through the clearing house, and in such cases they bore no interest

Of the issues of currency made by individual banks (*d*, *e*, *f*) I have only been able to obtain figures from a few cities. They reach a total of $13,541,500, but issues of that sort in the entire country would unquestionably build an aggregate several times this amount

(*g*) Last of all among the emergency devices were the pay checks payable to bearer drawn by bank customers upon their banks in currency denominations and used in all parts of the country in payment of wages and in settlement of other commercial obligations These checks were generally "payable only through the clearing house," but they differed from those which have as yet been considered, in that they were not a liability of the clearing-house association or of the bank on which they were drawn, but of the firm or corporation for whose benefit they were issued.

The pay-check system reached its largest development in Pittsburg, where during the panic some $47,000,000 were issued, much of which was in denominations of $1 and $2. Their issue involved much more labor to the clearing house, to the banks, and to corporations using them than the issue of clearing-house checks would have caused, for most of them were rushed back to the bank within a week or ten days, and new checks had to be issued in their stead [a] It was claimed that a fifth as many certificates for continuous circulation would have answered the same purposes, and would have saved much labor.

[a] It is believed that about $10,000,000 in clearing-house checks for continuous circulation would have answered all purposes, and would have saved much labor When the pay-check clearances were at their height many extra clerks were added to the regular forces of the clearing-house

Pay checks were also issued by railroads, mining companies, manufacturers, and storekeepers in a large number of other cities Shops and stores and places of amusement in the neighborhood of their issue generally accepted them, and it is indeed surprising, considering their variety, their liability to counterfeit, and their general lack of security, how little real difficulty was experienced in getting them to circulate in lieu of cash Of these issues, whose total doubtless ran into the hundred millions, we have no statistical data whatever except for the estimate in the case of Pittsburg

The banks of New York City determined upon the issue of their clearing-house loan certificates on Saturday, October 26, and on the following Monday, October 28, the associated banks of many other cities in all parts of the country followed their example. In several places, however, conditions hung fire for a couple of weeks, and substitutes for cash were not instituted until the week beginning November 11 This was the case in such widely

banks, and working until 10 o'clock at night was not infrequent on Tuesdays, Wednesdays, and Thursdays, when the pay checks came in by the basketfuls

During the height of the pay-check distribution some of the larger banks would receive from $500,000 to $700,000 worth of checks a day, including the amounts drawn on them and from the banks for which they clear A few of the banks had from twelve to fifteen men sorting the pay checks, and separate quarters had to be provided for the work The number of checks was very materially increased when the clearing house decided to issue the $1 and $2 checks, but after the third or fourth week the number of checks showed a marked falling off The offices of large corporations were also very busy places before pay days, as all the checks had to be signed Some clerks could sign 400 to 500 checks in eight hours, and the amount of men required and the labor involved in issuing from 30,000 to 40,000 checks twice a month can be appreciated —*Special Correspondence from Pittsburg to the Evening Post, New York, January 16, 1908* separated cities as Charleston, S. C.; Dallas, Tex ; Canton, Ohio, Council Bluffs, Iowa; Joliet, Ill., Lexington, Ky ; Harrisburg and Easton, Pa., and Topeka, Kans. In Cleveland, Ohio, cash substitutes were not resorted to until more than a month after the outbreak of the panic, not in fact until December 3, but this was altogether exceptional.

The date of retirement given in the tables is neither exact nor uniform. In cities where banks to which loan certificates were issued failed during the panic, such certificates may have remained uncanceled long after the certificates of solvent banks had been taken up and retired. In cities also where the cer.ificates and checks entered the general circulation and became scattered over wide territory, some may have remained outstanding for a considerable time after the notice of retirement was published. In fact, small amounts, lost or destroyed or taken by collectors, may never be presented for redemption. Some of the replies here tabulated indicate the date when the banks ceased paying out the devices or gave notice of their retirement, others represent the time when substantially all of the certificates and checks of solvent banks had been retired, only in a few cases do they record the time when the entire amount had been redeemed

It is perhaps worthy of record in this connection that in New York the time elapsing between the first issue and the date of final cancellation of the certificates was twenty-two weeks, or three weeks longer than in the crisis of 1893 In Pittsburg, Los Angeles, and New Orleans the emergency currency was outstanding also for about five months, but such duration was clearly exceptional In most places the notes and certificates were rapidly retired soon after the beginning of the new year, i. e., within eight or ten weeks after the date of their first issue

Surveying the record as a whole, we have here definite figures for $334,000,000 of emergency currency issued during the panic of 1907, classified as follows:

Clearing-house certificates (large)	$238,000,000
Clearing-house certificates (small)	23,000,000
Clearing-house checks	12,000,000
Cashiers' checks	14,000,000
Manufacturers' pay checks	47,000,000
Total	334,000,000

Making a very moderate allowance for the cashiers' checks and pay checks issued in cities from which their amounts have not been reported, including many of the largest cities like New York and Philadelphia, we may safely place an estimate of the total issue of substitutes for cash above $500,000,000. For two months or more these devices furnished the principal means of payment for the greater part of the country, passing almost as freely as greenbacks or bank notes from hand to hand and from one locality to another The San Francisco certificates, for instances, circulated not only in California, but in Nevada and in southeastern Oregon, some reaching as far east as Philadelphia, some as far west as the Hawaiian Islands. The banks of Pittsburg, on the other hand, reported remittances of certificates and checks in denominations ranging from $1 up from as scattered localities as Cleveland, Cincinnati, St. Louis, Chicago, Milwaukee, Duluth, Philadelphia, Danville, Va., and Spokane. Most of this currency was illegal, but no one thought of prosecuting or interfering with its issuers. Much of it was subject to a 10 per cent tax, but no one thought of collecting the tax As practically all of it bore the words "payable only through the clearing house," its holders could not demand payment for it in cash. In plain language, it was an inconvertible paper money issued without the sanction of law, an anachronism in our time, yet necessitated by conditions for which our banking laws did not provide. During the period of apprehension, when banks were being run upon and legal money had disappeared in hoards, in default of any legal means of relief it worked effectively and doubtless prevented multitudes of bankruptcies which otherwise would have occurred

6158—10——30

INDEX.

A

B

Index

Index

Index

G

J

K

L

Index

M

N

Index

CPSIA information can be obtained
at www.ICGtesting.com
Printed in the USA
BVHW042017120120
569318BV00003B/17/P

9 781376 112139